CRAZY RHYTHM

*My Journey from Brooklyn, Jazz, and
Wall Street to Nixon's White House, Watergate,
and Beyond . . .*

LEONARD GARMENT

DA CAPO PRESS

Grateful acknowledgement is made to Farrar, Straus &
Giroux, Inc., and Faber and Faber Limited for permission
to reprint "Long Sight in Age," from *Collected Poems* by
Philip Larkin. Copyright © 1988, 1989 by the Estate of
Philip Larkin. Rights throughout the United States are
controlled by Farrar, Straus & Giroux, Inc., and Faber
and Faber Limited.

Designed by M. Kristen Bearse

Cataloging-in-Publication data for this book is available
from the Library of Congress.

First Da Capo Press edition 2001
Reprinted by arrangement with the author
ISBN 0–306–81082–4

Published by Da Capo Press
A Member of the Perseus Books Group
http://www.dacapopress.com

Da Capo Press books are available at special discounts
for bulk purchases in the U.S. by corporations, institutions, and other organizations. For more information,
please contact the Special Markets Department at the
Perseus Books Group, 11 Cambridge Center, Cambridge,
MA 02142, or call (617) 252-5298.

1 2 3 4 5 6 7 8 9—05 04 03 02 01

Crazy Rhythm

To the memory of my friend John Osborne, a lucid and scrupulous reporter of the Nixon years for *The New Republic*, who insisted that sooner or later I must tell my own story

And for my wife, Suzanne, a similarly scrupulous journalist, who made it possible for me to present a coherent account of a sometimes incoherent life

Only he who says "in spite of all"
has the calling of politics.

—MAX WEBER, *Politics as a Vocation*

CONTENTS

INTRODUCTION

This book is in part about Richard Nixon and Watergate and the White House years, but it is mainly about me. After all, that's the story I know best.

A question frequently put to me over the years, in one form or another, has been: How could you, a birthright Democrat and lifelong liberal, become and remain not only a close professional colleague of Richard Nixon, but his friend? Could it be anything more than opportunism, with a touch of adventurism thrown in? The quintessential expression of this question came in a 1973 issue of the steadfastly progressive *New Leader* magazine, where a cover article titled "Letter to Lenny" asked me to resign from the administration. The piece professed not just disdain but real perplexity over the idea that I would use the remnants of my reputation as a liberal to clothe Nixon with decency. My answer to this criticism then and later was a shrug. I had not thought very hard about Nixon and me. Now, though, I have a somewhat more serious answer to offer.

What I have written is by no means a seamless account. It is three separate but intersecting stories—of my personal life, of my involvement in Nixon's political career, and of the post-Nixon combination of law and politics to which the White House years led me. But there is a unifying element: Everything is shadowed by Richard Nixon, even my memories of what occurred before we met.

Since the best way to tell *why* something happened is to tell *what* happened, I have concentrated here on the "what." In doing so, I have been mindful of the speed with which facts, even those closely and directly observed, change under the pressures of self-interest and uncertain memory, turning first into a mixture of fact and fiction, then into myth, and finally—if we're lucky—into a residual truth that may say something more than what originally passed for reality. That is why the telling of tales has always been an important part of what it means to be human. I have tried to be true to the texture of events. Given life's confusion, to claim any more certainty than this would be at best pretentious and possibly fraudulent. The reader will encounter a number of tilted staircases and cockeyed corners in the architecture of this memoir, but the journey, I believe, leads to daylight.

This book is not another retelling of the endlessly retold tale of Nixon's life, self-immolation in Watergate, and postresignation struggle to restore his reputation. Nor is it even a full telling of my own life. It is mainly about the accidental connections between two social immigrants, on the margins of polite society, with very mixed, archetypal feelings about coming to terms with the world around them. Our ways—Nixon's and mine—of adapting inner need to outer circumstance had enough resonance to bring us together in a relationship that was provisional but permanent.

Without me, there would, of course, still be a big Nixon story. Without Nixon, there would have been no Garment story—at least not the one told in this book.

Crazy Rhythm

❧ 1 ❧

THE GARMENTS GO WEST

There's always an Arthur.

When my mother told the story of her courtship with my father, she would always let us know that before my father there was Arthur, my mother's one true love, who "went away." On the rebound, she wanted to get married ("to someone," she said defiantly). My father was clean, neat, nice-looking, ambitious. He had good manners and a job. What more could she ask for? Romantic love was rarely part of the immigrant marriage contract; it was enough to find someone who looked like a suitable companion on the long road to assimilation.

My parents' story was one instance of the fact that the unhappy immigrant Jewish families of my youth in Brooklyn were all unhappy in the same way. That unhappiness was testimony to the ineradicable costs of being uprooted; like so many immigrants and their children, I set out to escape it.

One sign of the distance my family traveled to America is that our history, like that of many late-nineteenth-century immigrants, is riddled with blank pages. But my mother, Jennie Eckert, wove for herself and for us a vivid tale. In 1903, just thirteen years old, she was sent to America from her family's small farm near the Polish city of Przmezyl to escape the escalating dangers in Europe. Under the sponsorship of the Hebrew Immigration Assistance Society she traveled in a crowded wagon across Poland to a train that crossed Austria and Germany and deposited her on a packed steamer departing Hamburg for America. Her father, my grandfather—the one photograph I have of him displays a neatly bearded Sigmund Freud lookalike—was already in this country, the family advance man. He worked as a teacher of languages (he is said to have been fluent in English, Polish, German, Yiddish, and Russian) and saved patiently to pay for his family's passage to safety. One by one, the Eckert children—Jennie, David, Sasha, Bessie—came to America and grew up to be the gentler side of my inheritance. My mother's mother, along with the other Eckert children and myriad relatives, decided to stay in what they thought was their homeland. All of them perished during World War II.

Loneliness, fear, and physical misery were the elements of an ocean crossing in steerage, but my mother seemed to remember little about this. Instead, she offered to her children—and doubtless to herself—a sentimentalized version of the experience. She told us about Vienna, where she and her fellow refugees had paused on their way to Hamburg. Misty-eyed, she rhapsodized about the beauty of the grounds surrounding one of the Hapsburg palaces.

After Ellis Island, my mother's father took her to the Lower East Side. From there she embarked on the immigrant rites of passage, moving from one job and one crowded family apartment to another, polishing her English at night school. A friend introduced her to my father, whose father had brought him to this country from Poltava, in Lithuania, and who was following the same assimilationist path. After a short engagement, they were married on March 16, 1917. They began raising a family in Brownsville, an area on the undeveloped edge of the East New York section of Brooklyn, between the older part of the borough and adjoining Queens.

In the early part of this century, Brownsville, adjacent to still-unsettled farmland, was the American counterpart of a semirural European shtetl. The streets were packed with hastily thrown together three-story wood tenements and converted farm buildings, a jumble of ugly structures that looked like a Jewish Klondike. Yet the inhabitants milled around with pioneering excitement and energy that lent an agitated beauty to the chaos. Grocery stores, candy shops, fish and meat markets, delicatessens, horse barns, pool halls, pawnshops, social clubs, and synagogues spilled helter-skelter all over the place. The clamor of sounds and smells afflicted and delighted the senses—the steady hum of swarms of peddlers and shoppers, excited shouts from the children milling about underfoot, mouth-watering food odors mingling with the rancid air of a pushing, shoving, sweating market.

All of this buried itself deep in my memory but sometimes came into focus later on when a sound or smell or fragment of a dream suddenly evoked the old scene. One voice I can still hear is the wandering street peddler crying, "I cash clothes" (in Yiddish, "alte Zachen," or "old things").

I was born into this community on May 11, 1924, on a kitchen table in a three-room tenement apartment on Pennsylvania Avenue, next door to the horse barn of the Sheffield Milk Company. (The father of Norman Podhoretz, a close friend fifty years later, drove a horse-drawn wagon for the dairy at the time.) My birth was supervised by the Garment family's all-purpose aunt, family counselor, and midwife, my father's large, handsome sister, Sonia Swetlow.

Two brothers had preceded me: Charles, a redhead like my mother and the smartest of the Garment boys, and Martin, who was dark, small-featured, and handsome like my father. Marty was the "sickly" child in the family, born with dislocated hips and other congenital ailments that required him to spend the early months of his life encased in cement. When he was four, the year I was born, my mother was still nursing him, massaging him, and wheeling him around to doctors and physical therapists. Around 1927 we moved from Pennsylvania Avenue to nearby Stone Avenue, where we shared the upstairs half of a small frame house with a doctor named Rosenfeld. Dr. Rosenfeld was nominally in general practice, but he devoted most of his time to "female problems"—particularly abortion, then the conventional method of birth control among the poor. My mother worked as Dr. Rosenfeld's part-time receptionist.

I am told I was a good, quiet boy, given to hanging around the doctor's office and browsing through the photographs in his medical books. I also must have encountered, in the procession of unhappily pregnant ladies, the first whispered and unanswered mysteries of sex and marriage. In later years, my mother told me about her own multiple abortions at the hands of Aunt Sonia, and was not without sadness despite all the time that had passed. The number, I remember, was staggering, with the decision on whether or not to abort determined by a thumbs-up or thumbs-down from my father. I was spared but proved a bitter disappointment, because after two boys my parents had yearned for a girl. The most medically significant incident of my own youth occurred when I, age five, jumped off a high stoop on the dare of an older woman (maybe eight years old) and broke my nose. I lay in bed, happily accepting the day-and-night ministrations of my mother and learning, unfortunately, that illness has its rewards.

Both my parents were small, good-looking people. My mother was striking, with her red-gold hair, blue eyes, a farm girl's creamy white skin, a sweet, musing mouth, and a dimpled chin. Before me as I write is my parents' sepia-tinted wedding picture. They do not look like typical European Jews. They are dressed impeccably. My mother is bustily beautiful, my father darkly handsome. They appear confident and poised, a Typical American Couple.

In fact, my parents' "American" looks and accent-free facility with English played a large part in the family's relatively orderly adaptation to American surroundings. These same features caused my brothers and me considerable cultural confusion: Should we think of ourselves as Jews first or Americans first? Why can't we be *both* first?

My father was obsessively fastidious about appearances, first of all his physical appearance. Even when he was a beginner in the dress-manufacturing business, his hair was always neatly cut and combed, his expensive shoes shined each day, his fingernails manicured. He wore a long-sleeved shirt and a tie at work and at home on weekends, gartering the shirt to keep his sleeves at precisely the right length. He bought better clothes than he could afford, including stylish hats (straws in summertime). When he began to earn more money, he spent a great deal of it on expensive restaurant food and popular entertainment. He became an aggressive check grabber and a big tipper—fancying himself, and in time becoming, an authentic American-style "good-time Johnny."

But if appearance was the emblem of my father's life, the real core of that life was work, his personal pledge of allegiance to the land of opportunity. He rose before dawn six days a week to travel to his contracting factory in Ozone Park, Queens, where he assembled cheap ready-to-wear dresses for the New York "jobbers" (manufacturers). He returned home after dark, striding heavily into our apartment with his evening paper, the *World Telegram*, tucked under his arm for a quick scan (I never saw him read a book) before a simple straight whiskey and dinner. It was boiled beef on Monday, "dairy" on Tuesday, delicatessen-bought cold cuts on Saturday. (Sunday was ad lib, perhaps stuffed cabbage or the packaged leftovers of a restaurant meal.) Talk at the table might be about some factory problem, maybe a piece of gossip about neighbors or relatives—but no Joe Kennedy civics lessons, no Judge Hardy morality lectures, no talk about the great issues of the day. In point of fact, there was never much talk at all.

All three of us brothers were drafted to work in our father's factory in our free time. I hated the place passionately, most of all the mindless drudgery of my basic chores—cleaning threads from the hems of endless racks of dresses, hustling packages of trimmings and repaired dresses by bus and subway between the factory in Queens and the manufacturers on Seventh Avenue. I buttoned up thousands of dresses, frequently drifting into fantasies of unbuttoning them.

Yet weekend and vacation-time work at the Garment Manufacturing Co. did give me a chance to observe my father's impressive skill at inspiring his factory crew of some eighty Italian men and women to work not only quickly but carefully, in order to avoid the dreaded return of dresses for reworking. Giving equal and concentrated attention to what seemed like every task in the factory, he moved around the floor nonstop, repairing a botched garment, recutting a package of defectively prepared material, fixing a broken shuttle on a sewing machine, rethreading a needle for one of the older operators. Through the years, he had worked at every dressmaking specialty—sewing machine operator, presser, pattern maker, designer, plant foreman—and now could perform every one of these jobs expertly. He worked alongside his employees, coaxing the maximum effort from them by setting an example, working harder than anyone else, and practicing lip-biting diplomacy. He reserved his angry outbursts for broken machines (and for his family at the dinner table). I never saw him lose his temper at his employees. This was my father's domain. Here he was "Mr. Boss," respected by everyone, including me.

At lunchtime, we took a fifteen-minute break and went next door to Miller's, an old German delicatessen. It was usually a fresh ham sandwich, coffee, and silence for both of us, and, for my father, his corrosive Murad cigarettes. He sometimes had a pad of paper on which he scribbled production notes, piecework rates, and reminders (of payoffs, for example, that he had to make to police and fire inspectors). Then it was back to the dress racks, the dust and noise, the claustrophobic atmosphere, the crushing boredom.

I have one happy memory of the factory. I was four or five years old, not yet impressed into weekend work at the place, and one of those annoying kids who are precocious public performers. To my mother's delight, my father's indulgence, and my brothers' horror, I had memorized some popular songs of the day, which I sang and mugged my way through at the slightest hint of audience susceptibility. On a Saturday visit to the factory, I was presented with my first large audience. Jimmy the presser and I.L.G.W.U. representative, a handsome, black-haired man with powerful, hairy arms, lifted me onto one of the work tables, where I sang with the confidence of Shirley Temple for Old Josie, Young Josie, Little Tessie, Millie, Connie, and a crowd of other workers who had known me since I was born. With this audience of Italian mothers, I was, naturally, a huge hit. The song I sang was a popular piece of Tin Pan Alley philosophy about prudence, "Tiptoe Through the Tulips," which became a kind of personal anthem for the rest of my life.

When I was older, I swore I would get away from this brain-deadening work as soon as I could and never return to anything like it. At the age of twelve I escaped to my first outside job, a summer of work at a nighttime golf driving range managed by one of my cousins in the Sheepshead Bay area of Brooklyn, where, enclosed in a protective cage, I picked up several hundred thousand golf balls. I reveled in my freedom from the factory. I was alone, out in the fresh air, free to smoke Chesterfield cigarettes bought loose for a penny each (none of my father's Murads for me). I was also free from my father's most impressively unpleasant trait, a ferocious temper that generated premonitory waves of menace and anxiety even before it exploded into the open. When I was a youngster, my main thought about my father's temper was simply to stay out of its way. Beyond this, I vaguely associated his fits of anger with hard work, business worries, and a nasty disposition.

It was years, well after his death, before I came to something like an understanding of those titanic rages. The choleric Jewish father, denouncing his sons as "bums" and storming the neighborhood heath like Lear, is a cartoon staple of ethnic literature. Yet there was reason for the anger. Many immigrant men were, like my father, smothered by obligations, undertaken voluntarily or forced on them. They worked incredibly hard to keep up; it was still harder for them to edge ahead. They raised their children to succeed as Americans, and their reward was to watch helplessly as their own old-fashioned ideas of respect, loyalty, discipline, and otherwise correct behavior were defied or treated with condescension. They had little time for fun, while their sons never seemed to stop partying. They did not have the authority to coerce or time to persuade, so they resorted to shouts of rage. These circumstances made the estrangement of fathers and sons almost inevitable. Need pushed fathers one way while the culture pulled their sons in the opposite direction.

More than anything else, I think it was this psychological isolation from his family and the erosion of his energy by age, anxiety, and illness that progressively embittered my father. He had very little social time to spend with us—maybe a rare movie, a dinner out, or a major family occasion like a trip by subway to catch the ocean breezes at Coney Island on a sweltering summer Sunday. That was about it.

Writing this account, I found I could not summon up the recollection of a single serious conversation with my father. I thought there must be a psychological explanation for the hole in my memory, so I asked my brothers—who said he barely spoke to them either. My brother Charlie recalled my father saying he had realized, too late, that he should not have had children: He was not meant to be a father and did not have the patience for it.

Bad memories are not the whole story, of course. Looking at a snapshot of the Garment family, I see my father, smiling, his arm draped fondly around my shoulders. The photo reminds me of a cab ride I took with him. We were coming home from a nasty piece of nasal surgery I had just undergone. The Eastern Parkway potholes aggravated the postoperative bleeding, and blood soaked through the gauze packing. I remember my father holding me and carefully mopping the blood from my face. I know there were more such moments, but only a few small morsels of affectionate memory have survived his years of isolation and anger and the resentments and amnesia they bred.

One result of the immigrant father's enraged explosions was to drive immigrant mothers even closer to their children. These women were a complicated bunch. My mother, for example, was an angel of love and patience with her sons, working every day at her sacred mission of motivating us to excel in everything we did. She was a warmly devoted guardian, hemstitching our clothes and character by hand, ruling our lives by being indispensable. When I got into an occasional spot of trouble in school, my solution was a visit to the teacher by my charmingly manipulative mother (how could the son of such a lovely woman be a problem?). Yet my mother was something quite different to her husband. She gave him wifely measure, to be sure, rising in the dark to feed him and launch his day, caring for his needs, working at the factory in emergencies. But when met by his tantrums of anger, she defended her maternal positions like a lioness, raining on his head the virtuoso abuse that has been a survival skill of Jewish wives and mothers for hundreds of years.

My brothers and I were not immune from the lash of her tongue. But the really bitter battles were between my father and mother, and the sound of their exchanges, half heard through thin apartment walls, was the most familiar nighttime sound of my childhood.

The Garment family feuds were not unceasing. When we faced the outside world we banded together despite our intramural angers. Each of us had something of which the others were proud: my mother's strawberry-blond, blue-eyed beauty; my father's ambition, energy, and gutsy New York manner; the brilliance of my brother Charlie, who skipped grades and graduated from high school at fifteen; Marty's silky-smooth good looks and, after his years of treatment, his athletic prowess; my popularity.

Also, the family's battle lines were in some ways as complex and fluid as the coalitions at the Congress of Vienna. My mother sometimes defended my father in his battles with his sons—battles that she herself on occasion subtly initiated. I idolized Charlie and Marty but resented their excluding me from their games, so I informed on them to my father, spilling the beans about their basement hangout (the infamous Club Kent) and the card playing, crapshooting, and other forbidden activities that took place there.

They punished me with fists and other blunt instruments, but he punished them only with words—for despite my father's rages, he never raised a hand to any of us. My mother, on the other hand, frazzled by arguments with my father or the malfeasance of her sons, would administer inexplicable beatings to me, her favorite, with a clothes hanger. Her anger was usually occasioned by my absentminded loss of some costly piece of clothing, as when I left a new winter coat at the Utica Theatre and walked home in a snowstorm to dinner and bed, the coat gone forever.

There were other instances of forcible maternal instruction. When I was four years old, my mother took me to Abraham & Straus, the big downtown Brooklyn department store. It was hot, hectic, noisy, and packed with jostling housewives. I grew restless and wandered off to look around, assuming that my mother had me on her magic radar screen; I was lost and didn't know it. Some time must have passed, because when I next saw my mother, she was accompanied by the store police and a crowd of volunteer fellow mothers. She began running, screaming my name—"Lenny, Lenny" —but then I noticed that she was having trouble moving her feet. In her excitement she had broken the waistband of her old-style pink bloomers, and they were trapped around her ankles. In the following short order, she first pulled off the bloomers and stuffed them in her shopping bag; ran to me, lifted me to her bosom, and covered my face with tears and wet kisses; then put me down and gave me a terrific slam in the head with her black handbag. I don't remember which was worse, the embarrassment or the headache.

For years my mother would not let my father come close to her in any sense, emotional or physical. My brothers, telling me this when I was "of age," thought he was entitled to find (or buy) companionship and warmth where he could. But the result was that my father was driven still further from his wife, sons, and home, the only things that might have offered him some measure of comfort in his hard final years. Working like a horse, he was weighed down by a heart attack, painful intestinal problems, and a run of other illnesses, particularly an attack of Bell's palsy from which he only partly recovered. For a man who prized his appearance so highly, the slackened face that the strokelike palsy produces had to be a special horror. There was also his set of pink-and-white dentures soaking overnight in a bubble-flecked glass of water on his night table— a symbol, I now know, of prolonged physical misery and chronic embarrassment.

I saw the epic size of my father's frustration as he lay dying at the Long Island College Hospital in Brooklyn in 1951 of an intensely painful abdominal cancer that had spread through his stomach, liver, and pancreas. In his hospital room, I mistakenly tried to lighten the atmosphere by doing a Catskill-type shtick for the other visitors. My father did not think it was funny. Perhaps he felt I was making fun of his suffering or didn't care whether he lived or died. Maybe he was simply seething, as his life faded, at being surrounded by the cold, commonplace jokes of the living. That day he descended into his final fury toward me. He refused to see me again, until he died a few months later.

So my last memory of my father is of his familiar anger. I've always been sorry that I couldn't tell him I regretted my thoughtlessness, even though his wrath was really about something that could not be eased by apologies for a haphazard blunder. In his old and speechless bitterness, I stood as a surrogate for many things, especially his longing for commonplaces like love and fun that had been permanently denied to him. He had made the best of a bad bargain. A proud man, he gave his wife the security she wanted; a responsible man, he gave his sons the chance to study and succeed. Though semi-estranged from his family, he worked unceasingly to keep the immigrant parent's promise of a better life for his children. I know this now, but it's too late to tell him.

My father's day was not wholly circumscribed by the factory and the family table. After dinner he would make a speedy departure to the Parkway Democratic Club on Eastern Parkway and Utica Avenue for a couple of hours of pinochle with the regulars, including the Brooklyn Democratic leader, Irwin Steingut, and the local Democratic captain, Abe Beame.

Forty years after these games, in the winter of 1974, when Beame was mayor of New York, I came upon him in the Roosevelt Room at the White House, where he was sitting, alone and tense, waiting to meet with President Nixon to plead for federal assistance to his financially battered city. I introduced myself, and he instantly remembered my father: "How could I forget Johnny Garment? He was almost as small as me. Also a wonderful pinochle player." When Beame was finally summoned into the Oval Office, he mentioned this coincidence to Nixon—who, always uncomfortable with strangers, called me in to join the meeting. When it ended, Nixon appointed me coordinator of emergency aid to New York. It was satisfying to become instant financial angel for my hometown.

Those pleasant card games became, over time, only a minor form of my father's heavy gambling. His real excitement came from betting the horses, at local racetracks or through bookies, and playing in big-money crap games. At a Catskills hotel where I was working in the summer of 1942, I watched my father take a bunch of small-shot gamblers to the cleaners. He forced the action and dominated the betting all night long, like a real professional. Perversely proud of anything done well, I got one of my biggest family thrills out of his performance.

I don't know whether he won or lost more over the years. But in the last year of his life, terminally ill and determined to have the last word, he took his savings (around seventy thousand dollars, real money in those days), went alone to Miami Beach, and lost it all in a final two-week fling at the tracks and craps tables. After he died, we spent years fighting the Internal Revenue Service to a draw, insisting that John Garment's money had not gone into a safe deposit box.

My father also introduced me to America in better ways. In 1934, after a couple of successful years in business, he took the family for a two-week vacation at the Waldemere, a fancy Catskill hotel in Livingston Manor, New York.

I was ten years old. Until then I had experienced very little outside of family, school, and the Crown Heights neighborhood. I was the well-protected, well-behaved baby of the family. Diligent in my studies, I produced no skyrocketing displays of scholarship but did well enough. I played all the street games of a Brooklyn kid—stickball, stoopball, softball, skating through the basement, and a primitive version of football in which a single runner was pitted, seriatim, against everyone else. The idea was to run, kick, bite, punch, and gouge your way as far as possible through the whole lineup. I was large and heavy for my age, so this became my favorite game.

But the trip to the Waldemere was the first time I saw a piece of America outside my gray and brown Brooklyn. Here were great green lawns crawling up gently sloping hillsides; lakes, pools, tennis courts, softball fields, dressed-up vacationers and their pretty young daughters, bands and entertainers and comic tummlers, and, most startling, incredible quantities of delicious food served unendingly.

The Waldemere was a thoroughly assimilated Jewish resort. There was a gloss of weekend rabbis and kosher food, but this was essentially window dressing. My brothers quickly became the hotel's softball and basketball stars, and I was their cheerleader. My father placed his bets, enjoyed a strong winning streak, and presided cheerfully over the family table for the first and only time I can remember. Amid all these American pleasures, a soul-deep humming began in me that never ended. I decided I really liked the Waldemere world.

The next summer, my father provided for us again: This time my brothers and I were sent off to the Berkshires, to a coed camp called Camp Kee-Wah—Camp Kee-Wah-Wee for boys and Camp Kee-Wah-Kee for girls. Like the Waldemere, the camp was nominally Jewish, but it couldn't have been lower on the theology scale. It was run by two high school teachers named "Uncle" Iz Mones and "Uncle" Dave Geiger. The counselors were pre-med, pre-dental, and pre-law students, a collection of Philip Rothniks and Marjorie Morningstars. Kee-Wah was the summer camp of choice for upwardly mobile Brooklyn parents. It had most of the amenities of the Waldemere, except that the comics were homegrown and the food was awful (the midafternoon eucharist, a Fudgsicle, was the only exception).

Camp Kee-Wah was located on Lake Ellis, near Wingdale, New York. Hard by the camp was an interracial resort called Camp Unity, catering to mid-1930s friends of Marxism and the Soviet Union. They proclaimed the death of capitalism by day and feasted on its riches at night. But they were much friendlier to curious kids from Kee-Wah than the more elite resorts along the lake, which barred us altogether from their grounds. Camp Unity featured the best jazz music within a hundred miles, supplied by the trumpeter Frankie Newton and his band, so the counselors and senior campers, including my older brothers, would regularly go AWOL and return from Camp Unity with salacious lies to inflame their little wards back at Kee-Wah.

There was in fact much talk but little action between males and females at Kee-Wah (except for various forms of rubbing). The clumsy embarrassment of the young kept the sexes apart like an electric dog fence. But the summer at Kee-Wah was one of those defining times that set lives in motion, not necessarily in a specific direction but by illuminating what we enjoy doing and what we do best. I liked and was good at acting and nature studies. By contrast, I failed at every athletic activity on the two-month agenda. I did so, however, with so much energy and good cheer, even panache, that when the laughter died down there remained some residual respect. My nickname, "Tubby," summarized my appearance and my handicap. I ran hard but slow. I couldn't get over the barriers in the obstacle races, but my fingers bled from trying. I was prepared to fail cheerfully at anything. Swimming tests, for instance, were held at the beginning of the summer. Though I couldn't swim, I lined up with the self-identified swimmers, jumped in when the whistle blew, and sank like a stone, rising and plummeting two or three times before the counselors, choked with laughter, pulled me ashore.

In the big summer show I was cast as an overweight Fred Astaire on crutches singing "I Won't Dance" (I couldn't). In the season's climactic color war, I was made captain of the Red Team and led my troops to overwhelming defeat (having learned to swim, I appointed myself anchor in the swim relay; handed a full-lap lead, I splashed wildly in place and brought my stunned teammates in last). But I became popular by making people laugh and feel good about themselves. I was everyone's pal and used my excess weight to defend the runts against the rats; I enjoyed my popularity *almost* as much as victory. At the midyear camp reunion, when awards for outstanding performance were handed out, virtue triumphed over competence. To general astonishment, including mine, I was named All-Around Sophomore, the first and sweetest award of my life. The turtle had again beaten the rabbit.

My father went bankrupt that winter: Soon after becoming a full-fledged clothing manufacturer, he was victimized by a predatory partner. So 1935 was the first and last season at camp for the Garment boys. But I had learned many things about myself, and it took no additional camping to reinforce the lessons. Maybe the quick end of my camping career was a stroke of luck: If I had kept going back, I might have gotten thin and fast, turned into a rabbit, and married Marjorie Morningstar.

Thus fate decreed that my further dreams and fantasies would take place back in Brooklyn. Every Saturday afternoon, I, part of the new movie-head generation, would take my place at the Utica movie house, a block from our apartment. Sitting in the darkened theatre, a secret watcher, I made the movie stories my own. I became H. G. Wells's invisible man, with Superman's X-ray vision; I had the wisdom and longevity of the High Lama of Shangri-La *(Lost Horizon)*.

Sometimes the images were not so wholesome. One foul day at Winthrop Junior High School when I was eleven or twelve, I was caught red-handed with a bunch of "dirty" cartoon books that circulated among me and my fellows. They featured familiar Sunday morning cartoon characters—Popeye, Olive Oyl, the Katzenjammer Kids—in unfamiliar and exotic poses. The teacher summoned me, showed me the contraband now sitting in the desk drawer, and notified me that my mother would be told and actually shown the stuff. I was deeply shamed and terrified: This was the end of my Golden Boy world. I figuratively fell to my knees and pleaded tearfully for mercy. Luck was with me: Pontius shrugged and, so to speak, delivered me into my own hands. Ever after I was warier about the exposure of personal secrets.

Around this time I was discovering not just pleasures of the flesh and the ego but adventures of the spirit. My life's first serious passion, starting when I was age eleven, was religion—not the usual variety but an exotic offshoot of the conventional Hebrew school that I attended.

The Hebrew school—the cheder—was located about a block from our building, at the corner of Crown Street and Utica Avenue, in the small apartment of one Rabbi Cohen. It was a distinctly ad hoc operation; so, I fear, were the rabbi's qualifications. The apartment was old and shabby and smelled like mold, as did the rabbi himself. His living room served as our classroom, and from the adjacent kitchen poured the heavy, weird, sweet and sour smells of Eastern European cooking. Around us, side by side with the Hebrew lessons, the noisy (shrieking, actually) life of the Cohen family proceeded, while the rabbi commanded our attention by raining blows on our backs whenever we confused the alefs and the bets.

In that apartment I met a young Hebrew teacher who gave me my first feeling for the spiritual side of life. His name was David Minkowitz, and he was painfully thin, handsome, with pale blue eyes vaguely focused somewhere in the middle distance. He was a naturally mysterious man, a kind of Jewish Jack Kerouac who had been "on the road" for years all over America, preaching a self-invented brand of evangelical Judaism. David went beyond the numbing rituals of Hebrew school memorization. He had us read and discuss Old Testament passages in English and led us in a program of improvised English prayer and preaching—in the Cohen apartment and in public places like parks, courthouse steps, street corners, and subways.

Eight or nine young boys took part in this activity for a year and a half. We called ourselves "the Seed of Abraham, Isaac and Jacob." Our prayers and preaching, in English, were intensely personal, filled with exhortations to act charitably and ethically. We proselytized aggressively, contrary to Jewish tradition.

Deeply affected by our young leader and the way he opened the door to inexpressible things by leading us into the fallen world to preach righteousness, I stayed with David and our little band of preadolescent acolytes despite public abuse and embarrassment, the scoffing of my brothers, and the acute irritation of my father, who thought my sudden Jewish fervor was totally crazy. Even my mother, though loving and indulgent, was visibly upset when I confided to her my tentative plan to go to yeshiva and become a rabbi. This was not exactly her idea of the American Dream.

She need not have worried. Shortly before I turned thirteen, my religious activities suddenly stopped. David Minkowitz, who had mesmerized me with his otherworldliness, committed the quintessentially worldly act of marrying Miriam, the rabbi's lonely (and only) daughter. He moved into the rabbi's apartment and came under the sway of his autocratic father-in-law. The evangelical mission ended. Puberty struck. Our little group fell apart.

Years later, when I was practicing law on Wall Street in the mid-1960s and my name was beginning to appear in the press as one of presidential candidate Richard Nixon's advisers, David Minkowitz telephoned me and came to my office. He was still ethereally pale, thin, and sweet-mannered, but his zeal had been replaced by a look of faded disappointment. His new line of work, he said, was selling penny stocks for a small brokerage house in Manhattan. Was I interested? No. We were both embarrassed. The meeting ended quickly, with salutations to the old days.

Yet the real reason my faith did not survive its early abandonment by David Minkowitz had less to do with the young man himself than with the thinness of the Garment family's attachment to Jewish religious practice. My father openly disliked the trappings of the faith—the long Sabbath and holiday ceremonies, the severe and complicated rules of diet and daily conduct. More important, traditional religious observance offended his assimilationist impulses. Had he dragged himself from Poltava to Brownsville and spent fourteen-hour days working like a dray horse only to wind up in a shabby shul, wrapped in an old tallis, mouthing words he didn't understand?

My mother was no counterweight. She later blamed my father for the fact that none of her sons was Bar Mitzvahed. But my father was not wholly obstructionist in these matters: He did not object to my mother's lighting Sabbath candles or keeping a more or less kosher home or having big Passover family seders or sending the children to Hebrew school. If she had wanted Bar Mitzvahs for us, she could have had them. But she didn't press the point and her sons didn't much care—including me.

This is not to say my father hid or abandoned his Jewishness, though he could easily have done so, endowed as he was with an

American name, courtesy of Ellis Island, a translation of the family name Pergament, meaning "scribe." He also spoke plain American speech and had the face and manner of an Irishman. He was, however, quick to a fault to spot and condemn anything that smelled even slightly of anti-Semitism. He was aggressively proud of the achievements of Jews, especially American Jews and most especially American Jews who excelled in "non-Jewish" areas like prize-fighting and baseball—Abe Attell, Al Rosen, and Sid Luckman rather than Albert Einstein or Theodor Herzl. My father was prepared to ride with the Cossacks, but not under false colors. He wanted to get as far as he could from the shtetl, but success for himself and his sons meant not only to succeed on American terms but to be recognized as Jews who had succeeded.

In fact, my father had contempt for Jews who retained no Jewish identity at all. He called them "goys" or favor-currying "nebbishes." When he was in a relaxed mood, he would speak Yiddish with my mother and some of our older relatives. I enjoyed hearing the language. It, and the Jewish identity it bespoke, adhered to me like a faded but indelible birthmark that would later become more visible in the peculiar light of presidential politics.

As part of his combination of Americanism and ethnic pride, my father held the law in high regard and was scornfully furious with the local Jewish mobsters. This was not just an academic issue around our house. I went to junior high school with the daughter of the infamous "Gurrah" Shapiro of Murder, Incorporated. She was deposited at school each morning and picked up each afternoon by a long black limousine attended by two large men in black coats. (They didn't have to waste time changing for funerals.) "Extortionists, murderers, animals. They should be shot on sight" was John Garment's incautious judgment on Jacob "Gurrah" Shapiro, Louis "Lepke" Buchalter, and other such Brownsville neighbors of ours.

Though the God of Israel and I had parted at least temporary company, I missed the moments of exaltation and the friends with whom I could share it. Having tasted transcendence, I was no longer satisfied by stoopball and stamp collecting. It was not surprising that I soon found people and activities to take up the spiritual slack.

Music came first—in 1937, to be exact, when I was thirteen.

The instrument of salvation was a clarinet, a fine and expensive Buffet, which my mother bought for me at Wurlitzer's, a chain store selling musical instruments and lessons. She paid for it over a period of years in monthly installments saved from her household allowance. (There was also a ukulele for a couple of months, but that doesn't count.) In a year or so, I added a Martin tenor saxophone.

My brothers, hugely relieved that I had passed out of my weird religious phase, supported my music project energetically and even paid attention to me other than by hitting me periodically. They were early and passionate collectors of 78 r.p.m. jazz records, from New Orleans small-group jazz to Kansas City and Chicago styles and the big bands that were causing great excitement in the 1930s. They transmitted their enthusiasm to me, and I took to jazz quickly. I actually remember the first jazz record I ever heard—the tune was "Upstairs," with Stuff Smith and his band. My early idols were founding artists like Louis Armstrong, Earl "Fatha" Hines, Sidney Bechet, Henry "Red" Allen, Duke Ellington, Art Tatum, Jack Teagarden, Pee Wee Russell, et al., along with singers like Bessie Smith, Jimmy Rushing, and Billie Holiday. Soon it was Benny Goodman and Artie Shaw, the two great swing clarinetists of the late 1930s. I was one of the mob of kids who played hooky from school in March 1937 to hear and see the Benny Goodman Orchestra at the New York Paramount Theatre. My brothers were in the balcony at Benny Goodman's historic 1938 Carnegie Hall concert.

My mother had her own reason for supporting my interest in the clarinet. One of her first jobs when she came to America was at the Wallenstein and Gershwin Restaurant on the Lower East Side, where she worked as a cashier and served as occasional babysitter for the Gershwin family's young son, George. The remembered closeness of her relationship with George Gershwin kept pace with the growth of his reputation, and she felt sentimentally connected to him, his music, and especially his most popular work, "Rhapsody in Blue," which opens with that famous long, showy clarinet glissando. I soon learned how to play this passage, and into my mother's old age it never failed to delight her and summon up all her old Gershwin memories, real and apocryphal.

As for my father, he first viewed my interest in music with a wary neutrality—after all, I started to make money on club dates—

until it, like religion, became something more than a sideline. Then he came to loathe it as another proof of my modernist contempt for his conventional values. Before I was fifteen, I was on my way to achieving the status in his eyes of a certified bum.

Meanwhile, conscientiously practicing scales and exercises, I lived Benny, dreamed Benny, and memorized note for note those Goodman solos that were technically accessible to me. He was my hero, the first great mythic figure of my life.

Some forty years after this initial infatuation—in 1976, when I had returned to New York from Washington to practice law—I spoke to him for the first time. "There's a Benny Goodman on the phone for you," my secretary blankly announced. He invited me to lunch at the Century Association so we could discuss my helping him with what he said was an interesting legal matter. "Right up your alley," he put it, with a characteristic Goodman growl. "You may not remember," he said (I did), "but I was at the Duke Ellington birthday party you put on at the White House back in 1969. What I want you to do for me now is simple. You're a lawyer, and after your time with Nixon you must know all there is to know about tapes, like what happens if you don't get rid of that kind of garbage. Columbia Records has a bunch of my masters"—his raw recordings, that is—"that are really lousy, and I don't want them ever released. I want you to arrange for their destruction." I asked, "Are you serious? Columbia will never agree to destroy any Goodman tapes they own."

"Well, will you try?"

Naturally, I tried. Naturally, Columbia replied, in effect, "Are you crazy?" The company's counsel graciously allowed me to listen to parts of the Goodman inventory, which were wonderful. Some were actually released not long afterward with Benny's pleased consent. I've speculated that the tapes ploy may have been lonely Benny's typically curious way of doing things, in this case adding another name to his Rolodex of reliable helpers. Next came a request for advice on prenuptial arrangements for his daughter, Rachel; then other small personal projects; and, finally, a friendship for me and my family that lasted until his death in 1986.

Back in 1937, despite my enthusiasm, I was no great musical talent; I was never to become one. My training was the best that

Wurlitzer's could provide, which was not very good. My ear was less than first-rate, and I had zero education in music theory. But I had mimetic skills, a good sound, a strong sense of time, and lots of musical energy. Through a kind of aesthetic chutzpah, the whole of my playing was better than its parts, and at times I achieved a form of inspired mediocrity. What I loved most about the clarinet was its incantatory voice, whether playing jazz blues or Jewish klezmer, another sort of blues. In time, I came to prefer the warmer, more sensual sound of the tenor saxophone.

I loved everything about the jazz culture—practicing, listening, searching for the perfect reed, walking Brooklyn streets with musician friends singing the recorded jazz solos we knew by heart. Most of all, of course, I loved playing jazz. The feelings stirred by even my clumsy beginnings at improvisation were of the type that accompany the discovery of secret powers—that old gnostic magic in a modern musical form, a way of expressing ideas and emotions beyond words.

The other part of my "spiritual" life between 1937 and 1941 was my discovery of politics. By 1937 my family had moved to Crown Heights, enjoying the luxury of a five-room apartment in a building that boasted the ultimate symbol of rising middle-class status, an elevator. I divided my time among school, clarinet, and a new friendship, my first really enduring one, with a skinny, shy, hugely intelligent schoolmate named Frank Press, who became and remained my best friend until our graduation in 1942. Frank's origins were much like mine. He was the youngest of three sons of immigrant parents —in Frank's case a struggling but warmhearted father and a mother who, like mine, dominated and sustained the home. We were drawn to each other in part because we spoke the language of similar childhood experiences.

Kids like us didn't belong to real gangs; we were too serious for that. We hung out in twos and threes within the boundaries of our Jewish neighborhood, knowing—having been incessantly warned— that Out There were all the dangers of the hostile non-Jewish world. Yet even as we stuck to our own turf and with our own kind, Frank and I shared the experience of discovering a world of people and ideas that lay far beyond Crown Heights. The school where Frank and I met, Samuel J. Tilden High School in East Flatbush, was filled with hundreds of first-generation Jews, bright, ambitious, intensely competitive kids who were reminded each morning over breakfast of their obligation to justify the sacrifices of their parents. Along with the cornflakes came the constant assurance that the world was ours to conquer; wide-eyed with excitement, we set out to do just that.

Frank and I ran ahead of the pack. Weighing a future in science, history, or journalism, he led his classes in all three. My major, no surprise, was popularity. I was a good student, but my ambition—to run things—took me into school politics. I ran for and was elected president of everything. After graduation, I had decided, I would study law and proceed to save or at least change the world.

In 1942, after graduating from Tilden, Frank and I went separate ways. Frank headed straight as an arrow into science and soon distinguished himself as a world-class geophysicist. Except for one or two brief encounters, we did not see each other for thirty-two years. Then, in 1974, we met accidentally in the White House staff dining room. I was counsel to President Nixon; Frank was on a presidential science and education committee. He later became science adviser to President Jimmy Carter and, after that, president of the National Academy of Sciences. Friends again in Washington, we found that time had dimmed our hopes and enthusiasms, but not by much, and our friendship not at all.

When we finished high school in 1942, however, my life moved in a very different direction from Frank's. I left Tilden a seventeen-year-old model of Chamber of Commerce success: president of the student government and the senior class, member of the honor society Arista, and winner of a New York State Regents Scholarship, the American Legion Citizenship Essay Award, and graduation medals for this and that. But I was already drifting toward a full-time career as a jazz musician.

Apart from loving the music, I found jazz was great social fun. The musicians I knew were comic, inventive improvisers of language as well as of instrumental solos. The opportunities for casual sex were rumored to be numerous. The door was open to new experiences with different sorts of people—like playing with black musicians at clubs in Bedford-Stuyvesant that were normally off limits to white kids. The jazz life was all the street experiences, basement clubs, rooftop parties, pool halls, gangs, card games, and assorted nasty things that my brothers had boasted about and from which I had been excluded.

My first real musical jobs came during three summers in the Catskills. In 1939 I worked in a four-piece band at the Branlip Hotel, a converted farm, where we slept in a below-ground meat storage room and where the warmish milk came straight from the cows (it tasted awful). Still, it was thrilling. Courtesy of the war, which had taken more mature musicians out of the running, I had gone from no-time to small-time. I had a job, a bed, and a salary: seven dollars a week.

At the Branlip, I met my first semi-serious girlfriend, Audrey, a sinuous, shaking, shimmying lindy hopper who drove me to distraction. She once persuaded me to give her a hundred dollars for an abortion, even though (as I later figured out), on the basis of what we had done, pregnancy was impossible. I soon learned that she hadn't been pregnant; she just had to do some shopping.

The next year, 1940, I was at Stier's Hotel, where our band featured my neighborhood pal Terry Gibbs (né Julius Gubenko), drummer and xylophonist extraordinaire, who bet the horses on the basis of tips from Arty the headwaiter. Arty worked for some New York mobsters who fixed, or tried to fix, horse races; they scattered their action to various locations outside New York City to avoid obvious concentrations of bets that would arouse suspicion or affect the offtrack odds. Terry won enough money that summer to buy an expensive, top-of-the-line vibraphone, with which he eventually achieved world fame as a jazz peer of Lionel Hampton. In exchange, Terry, along with all us nervous and envious nonbettors in the band, had to play "My Heart Belongs to Daddy" endless times on demand for the affably menacing Arty.

My last Catskills job was billed as "Lenny Garment and His Orchestra," nine pieces, at Harry Dinnerstein's posh Stevensville Lake Hotel, which was actually located on Swan Lake, whose bottom, word had it, was paved with the bodies of rivals of Murder,

Incorporated. Terry Gibbs was by then in the service, playing his drums and vibes, but the headwaiter was the very same Arty. Remembering Terry's success, most of us finally started betting. Unfortunately, Arty was embroiled that summer in a nasty jurisdictional dispute between two gambling rings. He was in deep trouble, and, after a while, so were we. We fell haplessly into a cycle of betting, losing, playing "My Heart Belongs to Daddy," being forced by no-longer-affable Arty to keep on betting and playing his song, losing our summer earnings and more, until, panicked by thoughts of kneecapping or worse, I wired my brother Charlie at his army training base, pleading for help. Back came the funds plus a fraternal note: "Stick to bingo, fathead."

Matters did not end there. Such things never do. A decade or so later, after my bar exam, I was traveling around to former employers for the usually automatic certifications of character necessary to be admitted to the bar. But my former Catskills employer Harry Dinnerstein sounded like John Garment: "You a lawyer? Hah. You're a total bum, a gambler, a trombanik, a useless fool." I had to stay overnight at a nearby motel and spend hours the next day in passionate pleading to persuade Dinnerstein to give me his reluctant sign-off.

Music also offered an opportunity to get out of the house, which was becoming bleaker. I had stopped going to my father's factory on weekends, which angered him. I started making a little money and giving some to my mother, which pleased her and made him even angrier. One night, in a taste of worse to come, my father wouldn't let me leave the apartment with my saxophone for a club date. In a fury for some forgotten reason, he said he owned the instrument because it was bought with money he had given my mother for household expenses. My mother and brothers intervened, and I finally escaped with my horn, but the signals were all red. I knew I had to leave, and I could—if I could make a living at music.

So during my last year of high school at Tilden and my first year at Brooklyn College, I methodically shifted gears from law to music. Mornings, it was school, but not much; at night it was playing—anywhere. Afternoons I spent at Local 802's cavernous hiring hall and at Nola's Studios in mid-Manhattan, where the big bands rehearsed and auditioned new players. First playing occasional club dates around the city, I moved on to full-time jobs in second-rate clubs on Fifty-second Street, the kind of places where the girls drank watered champagne with the customers and sang "Blue Moon." I worked an occasional substitute job with better jazz groups, including a bracing two weeks with Bill Stegmeyer's Chicago Jazz Band at the Famous Door. The band was accompanying Billie Holiday, who appeared in the flesh, more or less on schedule, with her dog, gardenia, bad habits, and gorgeous voice. I worked with jazz virtuosos like drummer Stan Levey and pianists George Wallington and Al Haig. I was introduced, bug-eyed, to the work of new jazz figures like alto player Charlie Parker and trumpeter Dizzy Gillespie, who were playing in Harlem at Minton's Playhouse and with Jay McShann's band.

One afternoon at Nola's, I auditioned for Henry Jerome's sixteen-piece dance band and was hired to play the jazz saxophone chair for a long run at the Pelham Heath Inn in the distant Bronx. So in mid-1943, when I was nineteen, my double life of college by day and music by night ended, and I dropped out of school.

My Brooklyn College transcript records the evolution of my career. In 1941–42, I managed a B average; in 1942–43, a C average. In the first semester of the 1944 school year I got all F's, including failures in Hygiene (whatever that was) and, mystifyingly, in Music. The record generously notes, "Honorable dismissal granted."

These were the war years; and while I did not become draft-eligible until it was half over, from the start the war drew a line of uncertainty through the lives of my generation. We could drift, indulge ourselves, and suspend the making of serious plans and the doing of serious work. We could simply let events take charge. But it was not the war that made me quit school. The pressures of home life and the attractions of music combined to destroy my ability to concentrate on anything that required consecutive thought or disciplined effort. It was a relief to be finished with the ambitions of the square world.

Part of the pleasure was the thrill of acceptance into the glamorous world of the big bands. I received my "own" yellow band jacket —much used and ill fitting, but a badge of professional standing. At first I even liked the road trips, but that delight soon diminished amid scenes of grim, exhausting journeys to what always seemed like the same place, on what the author Elizabeth Hardwick has described as the Via Dolorosa of show business. Worst was the constant, desperate effort to get some sleep—on dressing-room tables or bus station benches steeped in the sour smells of smoke and stale food.

Still, by late 1943 I began getting some small recognition as a jazz player, mainly because the older, seasoned musicians had been drafted into military service bands. While working at Jimmy Brink's Lookout House in Covington, Kentucky, I sat in at an after-hours session with some members of Woody Herman's band, the first "Herd." The bassist and booker for the band, Chubby Jackson, liked my playing; it was largely imitative of the great saxophonist Ben Webster, who had recently recorded with Woody's band. When there was a temporary opening in 1944, between the departure of Vido Musso and the arrival of Joe "Flip" Phillips, I was invited to join the band. There I was, suddenly sitting in the middle of that immense jazz sound, between the alto saxophonist Ernie Caceres and the star guitarist Billy Bauer. It sounds like a dream come true. In fact, it was a nightmare, my first clear intimation of musical mortality. The saxophone leaked, my playing style (now an imitation of Lester Young) was not what Woody wanted, and the Providence audience was furious to find that Musso, their hometown-hero saxophonist, had been replaced by an unknown, pasty-faced kid from nowhere. Still, many years later, in the 1970s, when the political commentator and jazz writer Nat Hentoff doubted in print that a Nixon stalwart like me could have played with Woody Herman's band, William Safire was able to launch a successful defense in his column, accusing Hentoff of Stalinizing me out of my small place in musical history.

Shortly before the death of a debt-ridden Woody Herman in 1987, the bandleader Les Brown asked me to help challenge the sale by the Internal Revenue Service of Woody's last and best-loved home. We kept Woody and his daughter in the house, and I had the satisfaction of repaying him in part for all the mileage I made out of my brief appearance with his band in 1944.

My next stop that year was New Orleans, in the Hotel Roosevelt's Blue Room, where I rejoined a new Henry Jerome band that featured a platoon of trombones and me playing subtone tenor saxophone solos. I played "I'll Be Seeing You" maybe five thousand times and had to recuperate every night by sitting in after hours at French Quarter jazz clubs, smoking a respectable amount of marijuana, sleeping on the beach at Lake Pontchartrain, and breakfasting on chicory coffee and beignets.

I was starting to behave strangely during those days. There were fits of euphoria, sometimes Benzedrine-induced. There were also prolonged and paralyzing episodes of phantom "stomach trouble" that felt as if a long line of subway trains lay jackknifed inside me from neck to navel. There was manic behavior, along with various oddities of lifestyle associated with the jazz culture. Once, the band arrived after days of logistical screw-ups in the town of Dothan, Alabama, temperature 110 degrees, to play at the Napier Air Base graduation. I personally celebrated by drinking myself three-quarters blotto and diving fully dressed into the swimming pool between sets. Henry Jerome was, justifiably, furious. He began the next set by calling out "Body and Soul," which featured me from start to finish on the tenor saxophone. I manfully stood and played, soaked, sloshing noisily in my shoes, my precious yellow jacket stained an indelible blue by ink that the pool water had liberated from my fountain pen.

Nevertheless I was convinced that I was having a huge amount of fun—especially when, out of nowhere, I was befriended by John Hammond, Benny Goodman's brother-in-law and a perpetual talent scout, who was in the service somewhere in the area. Having no one else to discover, Hammond discovered me. He persuaded the bandleader Teddy Powell to hire me to fill the band's heavily featured tenor sax chair, left vacant by the drafting of the jazz star Charlie Ventura. I was scheduled to join the band at the Raymor Ballroom in Kansas City.

This was my big musical break. Before leaving for Kansas City, I stopped in New York for a routine draft board reexamination. I thought my congenital lower-spine cyst would once again produce a rejection. But in the summer of 1944, the rising momentum of the war in Europe, the casualties in the Pacific theatre, and the final island-to-island push that was under way created large manpower demands. Medical standards were eased, and instead of the Raymor Ballroom, I was soon ensconced in the Infantry Replacement Train-

ing Center at Camp Joseph T. Robinson in Little Rock, Arkansas. I
learned recently from a *New Yorker* profile that the musician who
took my place with Powell's band in Kansas City was the great alto
(then tenor) saxophonist Lee Konitz. By opening the way for him, I
can claim that my brief wartime service had some lasting value.

From the moment I got off the train in Little Rock, I was oppressed
by feelings of desolation and doom. This was not irrational, since
death was the subject that our combat-hardened squad leader talked
about incessantly. He warned us about the extraordinarily high ca-
sualty rates in the combat areas to which we would soon be dispatched and said we should be grateful for the hellish training we
would undergo for seventeen weeks before shipping out to one of
the bloody Pacific islands.

Added to this reasonable anxiety was the isolation I felt in a
barracks of men who were as strange to me—a New York Jew—as I
was to them. The Deep South and the Southwest were the main
places of origin of the group, in whose unfriendly company I did not
want to shave, shower, and shit, much less die. So the army and I
more than disliked each other. But this was true of probably the
great majority of draftees, who, out of necessity, gradually adjusted
to their circumstances. It is possible that I, too, would have done so;
but I was never to know.

Fate, in the form of a blistering hot Sunday and a softball game,
intervened. The southern noncom in charge of our company, a
frankly hostile fellow who particularly disliked New York "smart-
asses," decreed that we were to play by the hour, not the inning,
and assigned the pitching spot to me. After what seemed like a
hundred innings, with most of my vital fluids drained away, I fell to
the ground in convulsions, the literally unconscious beneficiary of
acute sunstroke. I woke up in the cool whiteness of a hospital ward.
I recovered pretty quickly from the sunstroke, but just as quickly
my chronic stomach spasms struck. As in the past, the condition
came and went mysteriously. As in the past, it was diagnosed
vaguely and variously as an "incipient" ulcer or "spastic" colitis or
"possible" diverticulosis.

But the internist in charge of my case decided it was unlikely, manpower shortages notwithstanding, that I would ever be in shape to storm Guadalcanal or Iwo Jima. After tests and interviews, a three-man board presented me with a medical discharge, my second "honorable dismissal" in two years. They also recommended that I explore more extensive psychotherapy than a combat training facility in Little Rock could offer.

In my last couple of weeks in the army, I made my first friend there. He was seemingly the only other ethnic within miles, a large ex–prize fighter from Newark named Tony Perna who shared my urban ways and protected me from the local knotheads. Tony was about to be mustered out of the service and was in the hospital for some patch-up work on his Pacific combat wounds. His enthusiasm for my early discharge was like a father's joy at his son's summa cum laude. My brother Charlie, serving in the Eighth Air Force Medical Corps in England, offered the same grunt's-eye view of the war, writing me Catch-22-style letters that urgently counseled me not to leave my hospital bed without a medical discharge clutched firmly in hand.

So after some seven weeks in the army, I rode the train back to New York with protector Perna. My Camp Robinson platoon sailed directly into combat in a series of campaigns to retake a group of small Pacific islands that had been overrun by the Japanese early in the war. The American casualties were, as our squad leader had predicted, extremely high—made up of soldiers who were not lucky like me, who went to fight and were killed or maimed not because of abstractions about freedom or patriotism but just because that's where chance and pride took them. I should have been saluting them, but I was too relieved to be ashamed of my good fortune.

I returned to Brooklyn to be met with bad news about my mother: She was suffering incoherence and hallucinations and was slipping rapidly into a schizophrenic psychosis. My brother Marty, now newly married, told me that before her collapse she had been asking constant, bewildered, frantic questions about the stories emerging from Europe concerning the slaughter of European Jews. There had been nothing but confirming silence from all her family members who had remained in Poland. Later I learned that in 1941 the Germans had occupied Przmezyl and its surrounding shtetls, including the one in which my mother's family lived. Mail to the United States was terminated. The area was declared "Judenfrei"—free of Jews—in 1943. Some Jews fled to adjoining Russian territory, but they, too, were liquidated when the German army moved in.

My down-to-earth sister-in-law Sylvia thought my mother's symptoms might be something more mundane, like the stress of menopause and the absence of all her sons, whose departure from home had left Jennie alone with John Garment. My father had no theories. He was simply devastated, finally forced to confront the depth of his dependence on her.

We never really knew why her illness began. She was institutionalized for three years and treated unsuccessfully with chemicals and electric devices. After we took my mother to the first of her psychiatric havens, the Hartford Retreat, I returned to the family's Brooklyn apartment and, out of financial necessity, lived there in a state of silent half truce with my father. I shopped and kept the place clean. My father took me to dinner most nights at a restaurant on Flatbush Avenue a block from our building.

Nothing had changed. My father's *World Telegram* shared our table. We must have said something to each other during those scores of meals, but I don't remember a word. Our train trips to Hartford and then to Katonah, the site of my mother's last sanitarium, were silent as well. My father's strategy was simply to hang on and wait out my mother's withdrawal from his life.

Then, almost overnight, her illness ended. As my mother began to emerge from her long psychotic holiday, the doctors said she needed more time and treatment before going home. Otherwise she was likely to relapse. My father angrily rejected this advice; he wanted her out immediately. My brothers and Sylvia argued with him while I stayed out of the way. But one evening, when I was alone with him in the apartment, he announced to no one in particular that, "goddamn it," he was bringing Mom home next Sunday morning, and to hell with his sons and the doctors. Words must have passed between us, but what I remember is that suddenly I was on top of him, throttling him, banging his head on the floor. I stopped in time to avoid a manslaughter charge but kept at it long enough to convince him that I was very serious. I remember muttering apologies; he didn't say a word. He was more startled, I think, than hurt.

My mother finally came home a few months later. She lived on, quite sane, totally in control of my father until his death. Then she became a working partner with my brother Charlie in the dress factory, until he wearied of pinking shears and ambient dust and went into radio writing. He eventually became editor of NBC's *Monitor* radio show. My mother moved in with him and his wife, Alice, and settled into a retirement of reading, TV watching, and creative complaining. At this last she was a true champion. Once Alice had a nasty gardening accident and came running into the house dripping blood. "What are you people doing to me?" my mother demanded in an accusing voice.

She could always be counted on to express her opinion incisively. Once I wore an expensive new blue coat to a dinner party at Charlie's house. Some people liked it, some (okay, most) didn't. Finally we called on my mother to settle the question. She took a long look and delivered her judgment: "It's a blue coat, Lenny. Wear it and forget about it."

She lived until the age of ninety-three, her last year spent dozing and dreaming at the Hebrew Home for the Aged in Riverdale, New York. She had lasted long enough to see her sons achieve her ambitions for them. When I came to visit, we mostly talked about the past or sat quietly; there wasn't that much to say anymore. Just before my mother's death, Suzi and I packed infant Annie in a baby bag and flew her to New York so she could meet her grandmother. Neither one of them seemed more than vaguely interested in the occasion. But my mother's smile was still the same, still sweet and young.

2

GROWING UP STRANGE

Shortly after my mother went over the edge, I followed. Back from Camp Robinson, I drifted for a while—practicing my instruments, sleeping a lot, hanging out with a few holdout 4-F friends, and trying to regain the momentum of my predraft enthusiasm. But just weeks after my mother was hospitalized, a collection of phobias and panic states began making it nearly impossible for me to function. Subways, trolley cars, elevators, and crowds became places of terror. Sleep was a problem. Waking was a problem. The stomach was a particular problem. Everything was a problem. The Camp Robinson medical board had been right: I really did need psychiatric attention. To figure out how and where to get it, I turned to my cousin, Aunt Sonia's son George Swetlow.

George had been a kind of surrogate father-uncle-brother to me from the time I was old enough to travel alone from our apartment in Crown Heights to his house on Eastern Parkway, near the Brooklyn Museum. There he had everything you would expect from a polymath like George, including a gymnasium, where he gave me lessons in boxing, wrestling, and philosophy.

George was a physician, both a neurologist and a psychiatrist. He was also a trial lawyer, professor of medical jurisprudence, skilled amateur cellist, singer, rancher, farmer, wood turner, and author. Of medium height and bull-chested, he looked like a blue-eyed Albert Einstein, with close-cropped white hair and a shaggy white mustache decorating a lined, craggy, deeply tanned face. George Swetlow in a crisp white shirt and navy suit, wearing one of his standard navy-and-white polka-dot bow ties, was, I thought, utterly dashing.

I thought so even into adulthood. When George died suddenly in his mid-sixties, the news reached me at an isolated fishing camp in Maine, sounding all the chords of family memory. I found myself awash in a flood of tears such as I had never before shed over any death and have shed only once in all the years since.

The death certificate said "coronary aneurysm"; it might better have said "broken heart." For if George was attractive, he was also enduringly miserable. In addition to his other achievements, George was an Olympic-gold-medal neurotic who had been psychoanalyzed by the cream of New York psychiatry—from Sara Bonnett, chairman of the New York Psychoanalytic Institute, to the famed Gregory Zilborg. He was one of a new tribe of brilliant, successful, psychologically peripatetic American Jews who never seem able to get their lives together.

I think George's agonies came in good part from his inability to make up his mind about assimilation. Should he go the whole way? Or should he cling to vestigial ties from his prehistory? Once, when he was in a "roots" phase, he conceived of a plan to bring the entire family back together in a traditional conclave, a circle that would meet, eat, and share history and problems on a regular basis. He went through weeks of preparation. Finally, the whole colorful, confused collection assembled in a large synagogue meeting room in Boro Park. Handsome George, the family celebrity, generously and carelessly allowed himself to be elected chairman of the founding meeting of the Dashe-Novak Family Circle (named after various tribal branches). At which point the ingathered relatives—mostly Russians and Poles, some deeply religious, some not at all, with their partially or wholly assimilated children, suspicious from the start about the purpose of George's mysterious intervention—spiraled into verbal, near-physical violence.

It had something arcane to do with the Brooklyn branch of the family once again lording it over the Bronx branch, or the Russians over the Poles, or the Galicianers over the Litvaks, and before the night was over every ancient slight and hurt had been dragged noisily into the open. The Balkans in Bensonhurst. Amid the furies, George's effort to discover his spiritual past came to an end.

My father did not like George, partly because of what happened to my older brother Charlie. Charlie wanted to be a doctor and had the brilliant school record that would have guaranteed his medical career—except for the quota system, then in force in all major American medical schools, which limited the number of Jewish admissions. But George, the family influential, was a trustee of the Long Island College Medical School and assured my parents he could push Charlie in. Everyone counted on it, especially my father, whose greatest wish was to see Charlie a doctor. But at the crucial moment, George got into a disastrous fight with one of his fellow trustees and resigned from the board. Charlie didn't get in. My father —reasonably enough, I now see—thought George had behaved self-indulgently and thereafter rarely spoke about George Swetlow without the sarcastic Yiddish appellation the "grosse knocker" (big shot).

At the time, I thought my father's hostility to George unfair; it made me closer to George, a grown-up who valued and openly sought my affection. My father bore up under the loss of my allegiance, shrugged, and kept on doing his hard job of supporting us.

George's perpetual ambivalence was not helped by his perpetual psychoanalysis. A half century ago it was believed that a daily dose of self-scrutiny, administered indefinitely on the analyst's couch, was the best way to deal with modern problems like the loss of faith in God, community, and family. (We have since learned to make more modest claims for psychoanalysis—such as, for example, that it provides useful insights into the transactions of daily life, art, and politics and is no more harmful than a midday nap.) When I hit bottom in the fall of 1944, George naturally arranged for me to be the first kid on my block to undergo a formal Freudian psychoanalysis, three years of fifty-minute hours, five days a week, made possible by a generously low rate from the eminent Dr. Bonnett, who viewed me as an interesting research subject, a kind of ethnic white rat.

Dr. Bonnett, an orthodox Freudian, was a counselor of adaptation. She thought her objective for a symptom-ridden, rough-edged, reasonably bright Jewish boy of twenty was to help him become more of a gentleman—to civilize him and transfer his feelings from a storm-tossed immigrant family to the maternal serenity of her richly elegant apartment and office at 895 Park Avenue. Reduction of anxiety through assimilation was high on the analytic agenda; but with me, as with George and most Jews undergoing this process, resistance to this kind of transformation was fierce, stoked by centuries of struggle to maintain a Jewish identity. The outcome could never be more than a workable compromise.

Still, for those days before reliable antidepressants, the idea of analysis was physically brilliant. You were not merely permitted but ordered to break away from the world at regular intervals, stretch out for an hour on a comfortable couch, and say any damn thing that came to mind, however foul, incoherent, mean, angry, stupid, weird, or loathsome. It was worthwhile simply as an exercise in spleen venting; if you got some insights along the way to help you soldier through a nasty world, so much the better. For me there were no stunning revelations or therapeutic miracles. But Dr. Bonnett's sympathetic intelligence and the education of the analytic process helped restore me to the ranks of the walking wounded. I became, once again, your average neurotic New Yorker.

The phobic symptoms were gone in fairly short order, and each day on the couch at 895 Park Avenue I slowly went about unraveling my past and deciding my future. Meanwhile, the only way I knew how to make money was to play the saxophone and clarinet, and this is what I resumed doing. My friend and former employer Henry Jerome was himself in a dark funk of layoff depression. I urged him to rouse himself (I desperately needed the work), he did, and I organized yet another new band for him. He arranged a booking at Child's Paramount Restaurant, a monstrous plaster and marble bomb shelter of a place, capacity fifteen hundred, directly below the Paramount Theatre on Times Square.

Largely because of my passion for new ideas, what had been a conventional 1940s dance band playing friendly pop tunes in a friendly way soon became an innovative and aggressive jazz ensemble, one of the first to use the Charlie Parker–Dizzy Gillespie bop style as the basis for a "new" big-band sound. The change attracted musicians but not paying customers. Jerome was later quoted in Ira Gitler's oral history *Swing to Bop:*

Lenny Garment, who later became Nixon's attorney, who had been with me since 1943, kept banging on my head. He was really responsible for this progressive band. He kept selling me and selling me and, "Look what's happening, Henry," and "This is what's going to be the thing of the future. . . ." Lenny Garment, Al Cohn, Bill Vitale—they were the big spokesmen. . . . And so [the radio announcer] would say, "Here he is, Henry Jerome and his orchestra," and they'd go, "Pow!!! Bomp-ba-da-da, beelya, deelyop!" Well, the first time we went on the air we . . . blew the limiter and the transmitter . . . altogether. And I used to play Loew's State every year, and Jesse Kaye, the booker, came down and said, "My God, what's that, Henry?" and he canceled us. The public was not ready for it. But the musicians, any musicians you speak to, say it was the start of it all.

Thus my first contribution to cultural history threatened the livelihood of fourteen musicians (at $55 a week) and the sanity of Henry Jerome. But somehow the band played on and hung on, gradually attracting a following of jazz fans who kept us from being fired. A statistically significant number of young stars in that band became part of jazz history, like Norman "Tiny" Kahn, an East New York neighborhood pal of mine since childhood, three hundred pounds of self-taught drummer and composer, killed early by genes, candy bars, and amphetamines; seventeen-year-old Johnny Mandel, a shy trumpet player turned trombonist and arranger, in later years composer of songs like "The Shadow of Your Smile" and the score for M*A*S*H and winner of multiple Academy Awards and Grammys; Gerry Mulligan, master of the baritone sax; and Stan Levey, a young drummer I came upon while playing at a jam session at the Downbeat Club in Philadelphia and brought to New York. Levey went on to play with Charlie Parker on the famous Dial recordings, picked up Bird's worst habits, and narrowly escaped with his life by leaving music for commercial photography.

There were others who made their public mark outside music, like Larry Rivers, who became a major force in contemporary painting; the trumpet player Jackie Eagle, who became a touring comic until he struck it rich as the little monk in the Xerox television commercials ("It's a Miracle!"), and the saxophonist-flautist Alan Greenspan, who helped with the band's payroll (yes, the books balanced) and spent intermissions reading Ayn Rand and general economics. Twenty years later Greenspan and I, not having seen each other since band days, bumped into each other on Broad Street in downtown Manhattan and I ended up introducing him to my law partner, the presidential aspirant Richard Nixon.

Then there was Al Cohn. If I had needed any further convincing that I would never be a first-rate musician, listening to Al Cohn and alternating jazz solos with him night after night at Child's Paramount would have done the trick. In a typical bit of musical muscle flexing, Cohn would take a standard tune like "All the Things You Are," set a tempo, and play six or seven choruses, each a half step higher, managing the clusters of accidentals and altered chord progressions without the slightest hitch in his improvisatory ease.

It was depressing, of course. But unlike Somerset Maugham's concert pianist, who took a bad review too seriously, I was not about to shoot myself. There were other options in life; soon, without abandoning music, I would begin to explore them. As for Al Cohn, his place as one of the great contributors to modern jazz was secure long before he died in 1988. He and I discovered one night that we had both been at Camp Kee-Wah in 1935—Cohn, who loathed camping, mostly in the infirmary, where he worked on beginner studies in scoring, while I prowled the wooded precincts for votes. I recently found an old photograph of our camp class—and there he was, right in back of me, both of us ten years old, staring quizzically at the camera and the future.

In important ways, jazz back then had very little to do with race. For example, it had nothing to do with civil rights or racial justice or anything remotely connected with social issues, at least as we have come to think and talk about these things. This was ten years before *Brown v. Board of Education*. Schools and neighborhoods were still segregated, while "the Negro problem," at least in the middle-class Jewish homes I knew about, was mostly table talk about abstractions, stick figures, cleaning women or entertainers. With few exceptions, both blacks and black-and-white political issues were invisible to Northern whites, including me.

The music business in the 1940s, like everything else in institutional America, was comprehensively segregated. White musicians also looked on black musicians as a race apart—but for vastly different reasons from those of most whites. We did not condescend to blacks as "political equals"; instead we thought them superior in the only sense that was important to us, which was not politics but musical invention. White musicians made large contributions to jazz in its formative and flourishing years, but the great jazz styles were created by the likes of Jelly Roll Morton, Louis Armstrong, Bessie Smith, Billie Holiday, Coleman Hawkins, Lester Young, Ben Webster, and Duke Ellington. Legions of white musicians in the 1920s and 1930s, including my idol, Benny Goodman, derived their style of playing from black models. Goodman also depended on Fletcher Henderson's arrangements to give his thirties band its special sound and swing.

These were the giants of my world. Louis Armstrong and Charlie Parker were black Mozarts, and we, their acolytes, were agape at their genius. We imitated not only black playing but the whole jazz aesthetic—the language, the "cool" style, the hipness and humor, as if being able to play the music of blacks required us to live their lives.

So interracial progress in jazz produced a situation of even more than the usual ambivalence. This peculiar bind was manifest in a ritualized form of hostility, the "cutting" session, in which a black jazzman, wielding a metaphorical knife, invited the hip white musician into the tent and then literally blew him away. (Something like this also happened in black-versus-black playing, but when it did, the exercise was an aesthetic competition, not a racial putdown.)

Consequently, what white musicians could learn about blacks and black life from jazz was limited. It was nonetheless important —the lesson that the great black jazz improvisers were the cultural equivalent not of athletes but of mathematicians. They were highly disciplined in their training, capable of imagining and almost simultaneously playing perfectly organized musical compositions of immense intricacy and beauty. Stanley Crouch's formulation is precisely correct: "Jazzmen supplied a new perspective on time, a sense of how freedom and discipline could co-exist within the demands of ensemble improvisation . . . the well-picked note on a moment's notice."

For a couple of decades, mainstream jazz was drowned out by

the pneumatic-drill noises of jazz screechers and rock-and-rollers. Classic forms, however, have a way of surviving. Jazz is now returning to its proper place in popular music, with assists by personalities from saxophonist Bill Clinton and jazz-classical trumpeter Wynton Marsalis to little Lisa, the saxophone-playing kid in the Simpson family cartoon.

The fly in the happy ointment is the current outcropping of argument over who, blacks or whites, should get credit for creating the jazz form. Such debate, the product of modern multicultural politics and its polemicists, is almost indescribably inappropriate as a way to understand jazz history and performance. Though race and segregation have played significant roles in the jazz story, the primary exclusionary standards applied by jazz musicians themselves have always involved time and timbre, not color.

These notions of race, work, and creativity stayed with me long after I abandoned the idea of a full-time career in music. Jazz instructed me in discipline and standards and gave me at least some ease of access to people and places that might otherwise have remained abstract or alarming. Perhaps the largest contribution of jazz to my education, though, was to enable me to improvise—to deliver that "well-picked note on a moment's notice," at least occasionally.

I also learned something from the jazz musician's perennial dilemma: This is an intensely individualistic art form, yet jazz players are usually chained by the mechanics of their enterprise to the talents of others in their group, including the least able. A weak drummer, for instance, will thoroughly demoralize his fellow players. Most organizations, in or out of music, face this problem to some degree. I was trained early to recognize it.

In 1945 my head began to clear and Dr. Bonnett achieved her primary objective: I returned to Brooklyn College. Though I required no great convincing to go back, the college did. After all, there was that solid string of F's with which I had celebrated my departure from college life just three years before. My status as a disabled veteran—one undergoing treatment, no less—mollified the admissions office, and I was reinstated as a part-time student. I was on probation, and the prognosis was not optimistic. But I became energetic and confident again, once more the beloved all-conquering boy. My college transcript became a scorecard of progress; the straight F's of 1942–43 became straight A's in 1945–46. (I continued to have some trouble with Hygiene.)

Still, there was no clear signal to tell me where my future lay and where I was to make my brilliant career. Finally the transforming event occurred: my random selection of a political science course, an introduction to constitutional law, taught by a Brooklyn College professor named Samuel I. Konefsky, who had just published a well-received biography of the former Supreme Court chief justice Harlan Fiske Stone.

With his gentle sweetness and powerful academic intelligence, Konefsky would have been an inspirational teacher under any circumstances. But Konefsky was also blind, which added a dimension of drama to his academic aura and to the classroom atmosphere. Conventional visual displays of personality counted for nothing with him; performance was everything.

Konefsky's principal assignment to us was to write a paper on the Interstate Commerce Clause in the form of an opinion by the Supreme Court on a hypothetical statement of facts. While not profoundly fascinated with the Commerce Clause, I sensed that whatever talent I had for the law would now be put to the test: Here was a scholar who would know me only by what I wrote and the way I defended it. So I gave it my lifetime-best shot. Day and night I plowed through huge amounts of stupefying stuff relating to the Commerce Clause, focusing particularly on the Court's recent opinions. For a very short time I was the world's Commerce Clause whiz kid. I also studied the writing styles of the sitting justices in order to mimic them; though my ear was not good enough to allow me to reproduce the sound of Charlie Parker, I could manage a pretty good imitation of judicial prose.

Soon after I turned in the paper, Professor Konefsky asked me to visit him. Upon assuring himself that I had had no outside help, he told me that I must become a lawyer. I should leave Brooklyn College, finish my undergraduate work at an Ivy League school, and go on to one of the major law schools. It was mother's love all over again. My course was set. I would become a great lawyer. On to the Ivy League. On to Harvard Law. On to the Supreme Court.

Well, not quite. I had to apprise Konefsky of my early Brooklyn College transcript, which suggested an eccentric rather than a scholarly turn of mind. He thought a bit, then decided to concentrate his efforts on Harry Carman, dean of Columbia College, where Konefsky had academic ties. Carman, a famed teacher, was also known as an administrator of broad-minded and generous impulses.

Off to Dean Carman went Konefsky's letter: Take this boy, Harry, warts and all. He will do Columbia proud. It was an altogether terrific piece of persuasion and resulted in my being summoned to St. Luke's Hospital, where Dean Carman was recovering from a fracture. The distinguished and benevolent gentleman sat up in bed—and guided me through a highly euphemistic letdown. Columbia has limited room and many applicants, he said. We are a national school, and we must, well, diversify the composition of the student body. Your transcript is also a bit of a problem. We are not free to follow our intuitions.

He was very kind, but it was a definite "no go." And while I can not claim an exact recollection of the particular words he used, I do have a photo-memory of the book that lay open on his lap that day. It was a best-selling novel by the playwright Arthur Miller, *Focus*, the story of a non-Jew who happens to look like a Jew and thereby learns some bitter lessons about anti-Semitism. I had read Miller's book and did not miss the irony of its juxtaposition in this hospital room with Columbia's historic quota system for Jews, which Carman was explaining to me sotto voce.

If I had had my wits about me, I would have said, "But, Dean Carman, I don't *look* Jewish." This wouldn't have gotten me into Columbia, but Harry Carman would never have forgotten our meeting.

Back I went to Brooklyn College. With Konefsky's encouragement and George Swetlow's help, I plotted an alternative career strategy. I would go to Brooklyn Law School, where George was an adjunct professor, and eventually join him in the practice of law. The dean of Brooklyn Law School, Jerome Prince, shepherded me into the school on a law-qualifying certificate, a shortcut that allowed veterans to enter New York law schools after two years of undergraduate work. Without further Ivy League ado, and sans college degree, I began law school in 1946.

Seating in the law school was by alphabet, which put me next to Glasser, Leo, the smartest and most egregiously obsessive worrier I was ever to meet. An observant Jew and an almost painfully serious young man, Leo Glasser called to mind David Minkowitz, Frank Press, and the days of my childhood. Leo was editor of the *Brooklyn Law Review* and academic class leader; I made my way through law school on his heels, studying, eating, debating, and double-dating with him. Leo elected to accelerate, finishing one term ahead of me, then joined the law school faculty and wound up teaching me Conflicts of Law in my final year.

Leo later became dean of Brooklyn Law School and is now a federal judge, as obsessive a worrier now as he was then. His last major case as a judge, before he took the semiretirement of senior status, was presiding over the successful prosecution of the mobster John Gotti. I had coffee with Leo in chambers the morning summations began, then watched some of the proceedings. Gotti looked terrific. Leo looked as if he were about to be led along death row to a gas chamber.

At Brooklyn Law School I worked nonstop, became editor of the *Law Review*, graduated first in my class in 1949, and terminated my first round of psychoanalysis. ("You haven't finished," Dr. Bonnett said, "but for now it's time to get educated.") Looking back, I count myelf lucky that Dean Carman turned me away. Konefsky's praise of me had put me into a high orbit, and I felt I had to justify his great expectations. At Columbia and then at a top law school, this might have been problematic, since the competition would have been tougher. But at Brooklyn Law School, my high trajectory could maintain itself through the years of my legal education and beyond.

The law school years widened the network of friends whose lives would circle around mine for decades to come. There was Gloria Hellman, a smashing green-eyed redhead, who dated first Leo, then me. Gloria's brother Jerry Hellman became a client, close friend, and major American filmmaker; among his productions were *Midnight Cowboy, Coming Home, The Mosquito Coast,* and *The Day of the Locust.*

A particular *Law Review* pal of mine was Beverly Lourd, bright, attractive, and very middle-class, whom I chased around the office furniture into a long-running, sporadic love affair. Under my "left-wing" influence, Beverly departed conventional politics and joined William Kunstler's law firm, then settled in San Francisco, where she became a lifelong lawyer for Black Panther–type defendants and a large assortment of radical groups. She delivered Eldridge Cleaver from prison and his manuscripts to East Coast publishers. Cleaver's famous racial polemic *Soul on Ice* was dedicated to her.

Another *Law Review* editor and quondam pal was Norman Dreyfuss, a superior mind and conscience. Decades later I found myself working with his son, the actor Richard Dreyfuss, on a television series, *The Class of the Twentieth Century*. I mention these names to illustrate a fact about the world and culture in which I became entangled over the years. People and events curled around each other and me like a double helix—touching, separating, and occasionally touching again, frequently in ways that had real consequences. It was like the genetic processes of life itself, with accident almost always the crucial solvent.

In my last year of law school, I was selected to lead a team of three students representing Brooklyn Law School in the first national moot court competition, sponsored by the Bar Association of the City of New York. Columbia, Yale, and other prestigious law schools were also entered in the round-robin contest.

The hypothetical case involved a First Amendment issue. The rules stipulated that two members of each team could participate in oral argument. I concluded that the rules also allowed one person to argue the case, and I gave myself that assignment. This was egotism but not purely so, because it gave me a tactical advantage: All the other teams split their arguments like proper gentlemen, thereby forcing each speaker to defer certain questions from the Court to his more knowledgeable partner. I was freed from this forensic clumsiness and won the competition for underdog Brooklyn Law School against Yale.

The *Columbia News* printed the results and a photo of me. I sent it to Dean Carman with a note. I reminded him of what he had told me—that being kept out of the Ivy League did not bar my chances for a rewarding legal career—and thanked him for his perspicacious advice. But the Bar Association, citing the creative way I had interpreted the rules, refused to engrave the name of pushy Brooklyn Law School on its permanent trophy as the first winner of the competition. This verdict stood until 1987, when the association revisited the issue *sua sponte* and put Brooklyn's name where it should have been all along.

Some people in the moot court audience were more comfortable with our victory. Among them was Joseph V. Kline, senior recruiting partner of Mudge, Stern, Williams, and Tucker, a prestigious law firm. Kline had come to hear two members of the Yale team in the final round. The next day, he called and asked me to visit his office to talk about possible employment. After a series of interviews I was offered a job at sixty dollars a week and accepted on the spot. My life in the genteel, Gentile world of a famous old New York law firm would begin in a few months.

I had finished my long run from East New York and sprinted the last quarter mile across the Brooklyn Bridge to Wall Street, the pay dirt of the *goldeneh medina*, the heartland of milk and honey, the place my parents long ago held me high on their shoulders to see and conquer. I thought I had made their dreams come true, but, oddly, nothing seemed to change. To my father, angrier than ever with the world, I was still a bum, albeit a bum with a summa cum laude law degree. To my mother I was still a lovable airhead who had to be warned away from the edge of subway platforms. Stubbornly, uncontrollably, perversely, they could not give up their versions of original sin. Unhappiness lingered with the Garments like a phantom limb. So finally, in 1950, I moved out—sad, guilty, torn, relieved. Hugging my law degree, saxophone, clarinet, and ambivalence, I settled into a tiny apartment at 110 MacDougal Street in Greenwich Village, whose dubious comforts I shared with a longtime family friend, Martin "Red" Werner. It was a fifth-floor walkup that was far below the standard of the Garment family's tenement apartment in Brownsville. My new place had a sink-and-hotplate "kitchen," a bathroom at the end of the hall, and a communal telephone five floors down.

But the view was a whole lot better. The street below was lined with restaurants, coffee shops, and the little theatres and night clubs of the New York avant-garde. One block north sat the historic Provincetown Playhouse. A half block south were the bars of Bleecker Street. At all hours, the sparkling bohemian life—and the pretty girls, denizens of the Village and New York University—were a few steps away, congregating in Washington Square Park. I was living in the middle of America's Left Bank.

The arrangement seemed perfect. Downtown I had my Wall Street base, the solid, disciplined, and protected world of an establishment law firm (not to mention the steady income). Meanwhile, on MacDougal Street I had a round-the-clock arcade of creativity, jokes, and jazz right below my window. I was finished with Brooklyn.

Or so I thought. The fact was that I could leave Brooklyn but Brooklyn wouldn't leave me. I found that wherever I moved, I still thought of myself as a citizen of what Brooklynites regarded as the "center of the world." Later on I made my permanent home there. I would sometimes get into the car with my children and trace the Garment family's moves from Pennsylvania Avenue to Stone Avenue to Eastern Parkway to Crown Street to Fenimore Street, visiting the special places in between—the schools, shuls, pool halls, restaurants; the Loew's Pitkin, the Utica Theatre a block from the Crown Street apartment. I took the children to Coney Island, the most important place in my childhood, where our family had found occasional relief from the sweltering summer days of the 1920s and early 1930s. The best moment of that trip, the one I always anticipated eagerly, came when the BMT subway train broke out of the underground dark and heat and entered the open-air zone of cool salt breezes and the vast sunlit expanse of ocean and multicolored amusement parks. The old Steeplechase with its roller coasters and park-circling iron horses, the immense, undulating sliding pond, the Fun House and the Hall of Mirrors were the stuff of my early nighttime dreams and daytime fantasies.

On Wall Street in 1950 I found myself cast in the role of ethnic icebreaker. I was one of a handful of Jews in my generation who squeezed through the keyhole of the tightly closed Gentile fraternity of Wall Street lawyers. Numerous other Jewish lawyers followed—for instance, Joe Flom, later the founder of one of the world's largest law firms, Skadden Arps Slate Meagher & Flom, and an adviser to the country's corporate moguls, who actually worked as my assistant in the 1960s, defending against a takeover of the Studebaker-Worthington Corporation. Flom would scribble brilliant "idea" memos to me during the day and come with me at night to a Romanian restaurant where each table was furnished with a pitcher filled with pure chicken fat.

But Flom was still in my future as I began with Mudge, Stern. Henry Root Stern, the head of the firm, was the elegant Episcopalian grandson of the elegant Jew, Simon Stern, who had founded the firm in 1869. The younger Stern, it later turned out, was a fellow member of the psychoanalyzed elite and actually made a due diligence call about me to Dr. Bonnett. When we first met, he subtly cautioned me that as a Jew and a Brooklyn Law School graduate, I carried special burdens and responsibilities—not unlike Jackie Robinson's. I must take care not to slide into second base with my spikes high.

My first assignment was to help Stern prepare a defense of the directors of the BMT subway system in a stockholders' derivative suit. The case was actually tried by Harold G. Pickering, the firm's chief litigator, who would soon succeed Stern as head of the firm. Pickering was a grizzled, white-haired, scarlet-faced lawyer who was so much of the old school that he actually wore double-breasted vests and a pince-nez.

The case was being tried at a Westchester County courthouse near his country estate, so Pickering sent his wife to San Francisco for the duration and we lived alone at his place for six weeks. Each morning, dressed in boots and mackinaws, we ran Pickering's hunting dogs, Punch and Judy, for a couple of heart-stopping miles. Then, after breakfast (prepared by me) and a day at court, we stopped at a liquor store and picked up a bottle of Jack Daniels, which we finished each night with soup and crackers around Pickering's bar, becoming increasingly incoherent as we prepared for the next day's hearing. On the one day I took off each week, I slept for twenty hours, recovering from my initiation into life among the WASPs. (It got worse; later came trout fishing in freezing streams.)

Somehow we won the case, and I was off to the races, professionally speaking. Given Pickering's somewhat advanced age and all that running around with Punch and Judy, he needed a physical mainstay, and in performing that function I got assignments that were in fact over my head. But I stayed afloat and learned, sooner than most young Wall Street lawyers, how to prepare and try complex lawsuits.

The most valuable education I got from Pickering was in the discipline of brief writing. He would sit me down in his office for hours at a time during his dictation and re-dictation of briefs, all the while chain-smoking, coughing, staring out the window, clearing his throat, and compressing arguments down to their microscopic core while his secretary, Fran Jones, and I sat in a zenlike daze, waiting—sometimes for fifteen minutes—until he squeezed out the next word or phrase.

It was an excruciating experience, but an essential corrective for a verbal manic-digressive like me. Under Pickering's whip I became an acceptable artisan in a profession that paid large rewards for precision, hard work, and personal agility and did not demand great originality or perfect pitch.

Weekends, on MacDougal Street, I remained part of the culture that sustained me—the world of Jews, jokes, and jazz. Reginald Rose, later the author of television's *Twelve Angry Men*, was the host of our crowd's hysterics. But "Doc" Simon, now known by his formal name, Neil, was the real comic group leader during weekends in New York and summers on Fire Island. He and his brother Danny gathered with other friendly Jewish fugitives—kids like Mel Brooks, Woody Allen, Carl Reiner, and Mel Tolkin—around Sid Caesar's *Your Show of Shows* writers' table at NBC, where they exorcised their particular demons with parodies, puns, and crazed caricatures, like Chasidic rabbis dancing on tables at a Williamsburg wedding. They made the comic archetypes of Jewish history into a modern art form.

In the summer of 1950 I hung out with this crowd on Fire Island. I shared a house with my friend Jerry Leitner, whom I had met in the early 1940s when he was president of the Brooklyn College Jazz Club. Jerry's girlfriend was there; so was Grace Albert, to whom Gloria Hellman had introduced me and who would soon become my first wife. Simon, Reiner, and Brooks were nearby, along with Everett Greenbaum, writer of *Mr. Peepers*, and Mr. Peepers himself, Wally Cox.

One of our big weekend diversions, in which I occasionally played a supporting role, was to tape-record interviews of bizarre people in strange situations, prototypes for Brooks and Reiner's famous "Two-Thousand-Year-Old Man." I remember a few: a golfer supplying the whispered narration of himself putting the last hole of a big tournament (Simon), a journalist conducting an in-depth interview of the man with the smallest private parts in the world, an interview with a drug-dazed jazz musician (me) whose vocabulary consists largely, then entirely, of the word "like." An interview with Doc Simon, as the tenant of a mechanical madhouse where everything works backward, is gathering dust in my brother Charlie's attic.

Grace Albert was the daughter of two lawyers, Helen Hicks Barnes of Boston (Hicks Street in Brooklyn Heights was named after a forebear) and Irving Albert, whose forebears were out of Minsk. Irving was a sweet, sad-eyed man, in all things—appearance, manner, speech—a product of New York's immigrant world. Helen's Christian Science family, by almost bizarre contrast, dated back to the sect's founder, Mary Baker Eddy, and Central Casting would have made her the librarian of a New England Christian Science reading room. She was a small, fine-featured, quiet, thoughtfully intelligent, generous, devout, truly Christian lady. She and Irving met at New York University Law School. Irving decided to marry not just Helen but her church; he chose full conversion rather than a compromise. This was his answer to his personal "Jewish problem."

Grace and her sister, Marianna, were raised in strict adherence to Christian Science beliefs, which literally rejected the reality of all material things—flesh, bone, blood, food, sleep, and especially disease and death. Readings, prayers, and consultations with Christian Science practitioners were prescribed to correct or mitigate the symptoms of these "errors," eliminate illness, and obviate the need for medical treatment. Mrs. Eddy did allow for insufficiently developed individual belief by permitting optional use of medical interventions like eyeglasses and professional bone setting, but it was clear that this latitude was only a concession to hundreds of centuries of ingrained human ignorance.

The denial of all universally observable phenomena is difficult to reconcile with the pursuit of ordinary life with its ordinary pleasures. The Albert home in Astoria, Queens, was a modest frame house, awesomely colorless and unornamented, a temple of silence and fundamentalist plainness. Grace once described it as "a coffin with a kitchenette." Marianna, when grown, walked with a limp, the result of a childhood fracture left untreated.

Both girls tried to break away when they went to college, Marianna to Vassar to study journalism and Grace to Northwestern as a speech and drama major. Marianna eventually became a Time Inc. staff writer. Grace, after a miserable freshman year, dropped out of Northwestern and joined a wartime U.S.O. troupe singing and acting around the country.

By the time I met Grace, her father had sustained a number of small strokes, which had gone undiagnosed and untreated because of Mrs. Eddy's strictures. He stumbled around in speech and gait, barely able to attend to his vanishing law practice. His daughters could not persuade him to see a doctor. For treatment he went to a neighborhood Christian Science practitioner to flush out the spiritual shortcomings that clogged his cerebral arteries.

It fell to me to ask him to make a small exception for the sake of his children. We had lunch downtown and afterward sat and talked in the Trinity Church graveyard. He was neither offended nor persuaded by my arguments, only grateful for his daughters' concern and my friendly solicitude. Smiling, his eyes shimmering with tears, he gently explained that I simply could not understand. This had been his choice, his life, his faith. It had sustained him, and he would stay with it to the end—which came soon enough and mercifully, from a cerebral hemorrhage. Some years later Grace's mother died, apparently though not provably (no postmortems permitted) from a massive abdominal cancer. She spent her last months in a Christian Science nursing home, with only the comforts of her faith to ease her way.

But untreated disease, by shortening life, also shortens pain; and the ministrations of a practitioner, like hypnosis or autosuggestion, can have anesthetic effects. At the time, I thought that Irving and Helen's behavior was crazy. Now, having seen so many people for whom the terror of death is worse than physical pain, I'm no longer so sure.

When I met Grace, she was working as a secretary at the Benton & Bowles advertising agency and looking around for something better to do. Her boss, a sunny, funny fellow named Tom McDermott, was in charge of a Procter & Gamble–sponsored soap opera called *Love of Life*. Grace became the show's production assistant, responsible for things like script distribution, rehearsal schedules, props, and coffee. At night she supplemented her salary and slaked her ambition by singing in a seedy Greenwich Village joint called Club Samoa, the same kind of tacky nightclub I had first worked in as a jazz musician.

She was not a roaring success. She could sing well enough—she had been winner of one of those early Arthur Godfrey talent shows —but she hated liquor, so the part of her work that involved drinking with the customers required nonstop dissimulation (via fake drinks or a practice called "spitting back"). Still, she liked this world. From her drinking companions she elicited sad monologues and acquired material for her desire to write soap opera scripts. This, though, was a tough guild to crack: The work was regular, the money good, and the shows ran forever.

It is hard to describe, through the blur of time, what made Grace, in her better moments, seem so vividly alive. Everyone who knew her during those years recalls her sense of humor. There are lots of good-looking and intelligent people—Grace had both qualities in abundance—but few with the real gift of wit, and those who have it are memorable. It was this quality, the ability to withhold judgment of most people and things so as to extract the comedy, that drew me to her and held us together through thin and thin. It was not just that she said funny things; she also had that much rarer kind of humor that produces laughter and understanding through unexpected sideswipes at the foolishness that surrounds us.

On a bright, hot day in June 1951 at the Unity Club, a massive old Victorian-style political clubhouse in the Park Slope section of

Brooklyn, Grace and I were married. If it had been left to the two of us, we would have legalized our live-in relationship very simply. But of course it wasn't. For the sake of my mother and Grace's aunt, a large, domineering, party-loving lady, we agreed to a traditional Jewish wedding, with a rabbi, a chuppah, a horde of relatives, and vast quantities of chopped liver, the whole affair preserved forever in three-dimensional photographs.

Grace and I got to select the entertainment, an all-star jazz rhythm section including the guitarist Chuck Wayne, drummer Ed Shaughnessy and bassist Eddie O'Brien from Stan Kenton's band, and the bop pianist Al Haig from Fifty-second Street. Haig arrived just before the wedding, sprinting up to the clubhouse, thoroughly stoned. He mumbled to Grace and me, as he passed us standing anxiously in the foyer, "Sweet Jesus, I can't remember the bridge to the Wedding March." To which Grace replied, "Fake it." After cutting the cake, I shed my groom's role and played the tenor saxophone.

We sank every penny of our wedding gifts and savings into a wandering, six-week honeymoon tour all over the Caribbean. The old photographs of the trip are all smiles, the memories mostly of disappointments. We returned home so broke that we had to sleep in our sporty new Hillman convertible at the side of a country road in upstate New York on our way to George Swetlow's farm, where a combined family reunion and final honeymoon blowout was scheduled.

So began my marriage, consecrated by religion, jazz, and jokes, to this handsome, preternaturally intelligent, gifted woman. Opposites, in our case, did not really attract. We were more siblings than spouses, temperamental clones glued to each other by similarities. We made our way through twenty-five hectic years on the edge holding hands like riders on a roller coaster. Friends said we were made for each other, but this, as most people know early on, is no guarantee of a happy marriage. It was our destiny to learn the hard way.

The source of Grace's wit, I soon found, and of her empathy for barflies and other marginal types, was that she was one of them. Where her own maladies were concerned, no one—not me, not the kids, not all the doctors—could give her more than occasional relief. There seemed no way for her out of her box of loneliness and depression. Only God knows why some people emerge from shell-shocked childhoods in irremediably bad shape while others, from even worse environments, come up smiling and strong. Grace and I explored all the routes of amelioration then available to try to break her free of her depressions: work, travel, children, psychotherapy, house decorating, medication—everything, I suppose, except religion, which our early forays into organized worship had discouraged. The pattern was established early and never changed: Suffering together, sometimes in tandem, she much more than I, we limped along searching for the magic formula that would cure us. We had good times, ran around and laughed a lot, played charades for fun and for real, but at the end of the day, so to speak, we always returned to find the same gloomy houseguests waiting for us.

We settled into a small rent-controlled apartment on Bank Street in Greenwich Village that I inherited from my brother Marty. Within weeks Grace sank into her first postmarital depression and went back into psychiatric treatment. I sank in my own way—into a frenetic work routine, putting in long hours for six or seven days a week. Things went well for me: I was made partner in record time. Occasionally I emerged to suggest projects that might distract Grace, like writing freelance television scripts. This she did successfully for a time, selling three scripts in a few months, two for a Jack and Cynthia Lemmon sitcom and one fictionalization of an arson-murder case that was produced by *Kraft Theatre* under the title "Make Me a Fire." But a package of scripts she wrote for the Wally Cox comedy show *Mr. Peepers* was rejected, and she abruptly abandoned writing, deciding to "rest up" for a while. She would concentrate on conventional activities like keeping house, cooking, sewing, movies, and adopting a cat.

The fifties passed this way. I tried cases, traveled on business, rose in the firm, and made more money. Anxiously carefree, we spent all of it. We lived a yuppie life long before the term was coined, moving from Bank Street to a spacious Central Park West apartment with a high, glorious view of the Ninetieth Street reservoir. Apart from peering out the windows to check the change of seasons, we kept the blinds drawn. The light was too bright. We next moved to Brooklyn Heights, where we rented two floors of a classic Victorian town house on Monroe Place and, with professional help, decorated ourselves into near bankruptcy. Purple flocked wallpaper, glittering brass chandeliers, a warehouse of period furniture and bric-a-brac— it was appropriate for the apartment but awful for us. Our reaction to this mistake was to build our own uncluttered contemporary house in Brooklyn, designed by a couple of young architects, Joe and Mary Merz.

Grace and I had two children, Sara and Paul, of whom more later. Sara, as a baby, had ghastly tantrums and was precociously verbal, so the sachems of child psychiatry concluded that she had an infantile neurosis (!) and recommended analytic treatment, which started when she was three and never really stopped. Only recently did we learn that she has, and may have been born with, temporal-lobe epilepsy, which would account for the early tantrums.

We enrolled Paul in a private school, which turned out to have a decidedly unpleasant atmosphere. He hid in the closet, declined to learn to read or write, began to stutter, and soon followed Sara into psychotherapy with an analyst who conducted most of their treatment sessions with slices of pizza in order to create an atmosphere of "nurture."

We tended our two kids lovingly but distractedly, surrounding them with Caribbean nannies and other household help. We had a large circle of bright, funny, successful friends and a thousand things to do—weekends in the country, jazz in the Berkshires, fly fishing in Maine and Canada, summering with the gang at Fire Island, weekend charade parties at Reggie Rose's place. We were rising economically and falling psychologically.

Such was our general state of affairs when Richard Nixon appeared on the scene in 1963 and, like the deus ex machina he would later prove to be in world affairs, transformed our lives.

ⳡ 3 ⳣ

NIXON GOES EAST

Richard Nixon's early history has been told a thousand times. Frequently overwhelmed by the detail, though, are a handful of events that I think played a central part in shaping his career and personality. How much, no one can say exactly, but to one who watched him closely over his last thirty political years, some things stick out.

To begin with, there were Nixon's parents: his mother, Hannah, dedicated to family and church, a Quaker pacifist, reserved, even distant, more a moral force than a nurturing parent; and his father, Frank, a Methodist convert of convenience to his wife's Quaker faith, intelligent, opinionated, a collector of resentments, a chronic shouter, a self-described "populist" but actually, according to Frank's cousin the author Jessamyn West, a closet socialist. Despite the contrasts, Hannah and Frank were united in their tenacious struggle against the hard circumstances of pioneer life in Yorba Linda, at the raw edge of the last great American migration. They worked from dawn to dark, and from large failures to smaller ones, to make a decent life for their family. Work was the central ethic of the Nixon family. As a teenager, Richard Nixon began his day in the dark at four A.M., driving to Los Angeles to select the day's produce for the family store, and ended it late at night when his chores and homework were done. (I don't know where he found the energy to stay awake listening to those "train whistles in the night.")

Richard was the third of five sons. Harold and Donald preceded him; he was followed by Arthur and, much later, Ed. Arthur, a beautiful and sweet-natured boy, died suddenly of meningitis at the age of four, when Richard was nine. Harold died of tuberculosis at the age of twenty-three, when Richard was twenty. Richard loved young Arthur and idolized the spirited and handsome Harold, who was often described by Frank Nixon as the best and brightest of the family.

The deaths were an incalculably numbing experience for the surviving brothers, whose sibling love was the most powerful emotion of their young lives. Even before Harold died, his years of illness were devastating. A special atmosphere of disease and death surrounded young Richard during the summer months, when he stayed with his mother and Harold in Prescott, Arizona. She partially paid their way by nursing not only Harold but three other young tuberculars, boiling their bloody laundry, cleaning their sputum cups, and attending to their other nursing needs.

During these years of family separation, Richard's summers in Arizona found him working at odd jobs, from stoop laborer in the Prescott bean fields to barker at a local "saloon," returning at night to the grim, claustrophobic atmosphere of his mother's small community of gasping consumptives.

It is said by friends and family members that when each of his brothers died, Richard sank into a "deep impenetrable silence." In the case of Harold's death, the grief was accompanied by Richard's fatalistic acceptance that he, too, would probably contract tuberculosis and die prematurely and awfully. Instead, Nixon went on to prepare himself with grim intensity for whatever worldly opportunities came his way.

Acting was his first career love, law his first serious career choice. He passed up a Harvard scholarship opportunity because his family could not afford the additional expense of school in the East; then he proceeded to work like the proverbial horse at Whittier College and Duke University Law School, graduating near the top of the class at both institutions and choosing New York's Wall Street as the venue for his first job. It was not to be. Lesser lights in his class made the grade, but Nixon didn't; there was already something off-putting about him. Then came World War II, a stint at the Office of Price Administration in Washington, marriage to Pat, a navy enlistment and Pacific tour, and Nixon's return to Whittier, with a sackful of poker winnings, to practice law.

At this point two crucial events occurred: First, Nixon was selected by a group of conservative Republican California businessmen who were looking for a young veteran to run against congressman Jerry Voorhis, a liberal Democrat. Second, Nixon met his Machiavelli, the political tactician Murray Chotiner, a hardheaded exponent of the campaign philosophy that politics is war.

Chotiner's influence on Nixon should not be exaggerated. The disparity between the romanticized versions of social conditions that Nixon had read and dreamed about and the real thing he encountered was grist enough for disillusionment. During the early part of this century, many young men like Nixon avidly consumed the inspirational writings of those years—the Horatio Alger books, religious pamphlets, novels of social protest by heroic authors like Jack London, uplifting stories and articles in magazines like the *Saturday Evening Post*. In addition, Nixon was raised on talk about heroism and political principle; Frank Nixon railed at Teapot Dome and other instances of public corruption, and young Nixon vowed to become an honest lawyer who would expose and punish political sinners. But it was not long before Nixon discovered that success in politics usually required values quite different from those represented in his adolescent readings and the idealism of his father. Nixon's contempt for these highminded ideas and their proponents followed. Murray Chotiner merely reinforced the lesson.

Then began the history of Richard Nixon that most Americans over fifty know well: Nixon as anti-Communist rhetorician and gut fighter during the 1940s and 1950s, eviscerating campaign rivals Jerry Voorhis and Helen Gahagan Douglas; the Hiss case; the Checkers speech; the vice presidency under Eisenhower; the stoning in Caracas; the Khrushchev confrontation. Nixon was on his way to the main part of his career and his apotheosis as the permanent great unknown of American politics.

. . .

Nixon's eastward migration in 1963 was the result of circumstances that are also familiar. Defeated by a hair in his 1960 campaign for the presidency against the incandescent John F. Kennedy, Nixon returned to California for a brief interlude with the law firm of Adams, Duque, and Hazeltine. He was persuaded that he could position himself for another presidential run if he became governor of California, so he went up against the incumbent, Edmund G. "Pat" Brown, in 1962 and was decisively beaten.

Various factors worked against Nixon. Brown was a popular and skillful politician, and the state's Republican organization had been weakened by intraparty strife, especially in the primary race that Nixon had to run against Joe Shell, a Birchite candidate with strong Orange County ties. National issues also broke the wrong way, particularly the Cuban missile crisis, which occurred virtually on election eve, distracting attention from Nixon's stretch run.

These factors aside, Nixon's years in Washington had diluted his California identity and made him a distant and ambiguous figure back home. In contrast, there was nothing fuzzy about Pat Brown, who was pure California and able to marshal all the elements of traditional Democratic support plus Nixon's independent and Republican enemies.

In the aftermath of the California defeat, Nixon took stock of his California prospects and his longer-term strategic situation. He departed for an extended vacation in the Florida Keys, then and later his favorite place for stock taking, took his solitary walks on the beach, and moved around the pieces of his career puzzle. To nearly universal surprise, he chose to go to New York City.

At the time Nixon made his move east in the spring of 1963, it was generally believed that he had been persuaded by Elmer Bobst, his friend and chairman of the Warner-Lambert Pharmaceutical Company, to leave California, abandon politics, and establish a new career in the law. Bobst, friend and adviser to the Nixon family since 1960 and an important client of Mudge Rose, did urge Nixon to make the move and acted as matchmaker between Nixon and the law firm. But it was clear to me from the time of my first conversations with Nixon in 1963 that he had not the slightest intention of abandoning the profession of politics for the practice of law in any decisive way. He had important business friends in New York and was prepared to give the law time and attention, but his heart and head would remain in politics.

Nixon decided to move from California to the exotic precincts of New York City precisely to make a fresh political start in a new location. He knew he was an old face in California but would be interesting and newsworthy in New York. He also saw no near-term future in national politics for a Republican candidate running against John Kennedy. New York, Nelson Rockefeller's territory, was a safe harbor against any party pressures to run in 1964—which would be a premature reentry for Nixon, an almost certain losing effort, and a death blow to his lingering hopes for national office.

The move to New York also had a quality of surprise about it, a bold entry into the enemy camp. As we all came to know, Richard Nixon loved to do the unexpected, not only for its tactical value but for the discomfort of the enemies who dismissed him as banal, provincial, and predictable.

Finally, Nixon was drawn to the big-time dazzle and energy of New York, the "fast track" where the best arc tested by the best. It was exactly the kind of place Nixon had daydreamed about as a youngster lying in bed listening to those train whistles in small, provincial places like Yorba Linda and Whittier.

While Nixon was rationally choosing Mudge Rose as the answer to his career question, Mudge Rose was much less rationally coming to see its need for someone like Richard Nixon. Thus it happened that in 1968 Nixon made his successful run for the presidency from a peculiarly appropriate base: a Wall Street law firm whose history foreshadowed Nixon's own Lazarus-like rise from the graveyard of great ambitions.

After its founding in 1869, the firm grew and prospered with the expanding city until it achieved eminence in 1930 as Rushmore, Bisbee & Stern, one of the three or four largest New York law firms. A fixture of the New York legal establishment, the firm served as counsel to a number of large companies, including major New York institutions—the Chase National Bank, its affiliate Chase Securities, The Bank of the Manhattan Company, the BMT subway system. On the side, the name partner Charles Rushmore wheeled and dealed in South Dakota mining properties, so enriching the community out there that it renamed the local mountain Mount Rushmore.

Then came the financial disaster of 1929 and a tumultuous Senate investigation by the Pecora Committee into Wall Street's financial institutions, particularly the Chase Bank. The fortunes of the law firm, tied as they were to Chase, plummeted. One of the firm's senior partners, Alfred E. Mudge, contributed to the firm's crisis when, in a moment of temper, he told Winthrop Aldrich, the head of Chase, to take the Chase legal business that remained with Rushmore, Bisbee and shove it (or whatever language a gentleman used to express this sentiment in 1940).

By 1949, when I graduated from law school, the firm—now Mudge, Stern, Williams & Tucker—was still alive but no longer a front-running institution. It was in a mood to take chances with outlanders like me.

From 1950 until 1963, when Nixon came to New York, the firm's fortunes underwent a gradual resurgence, thanks to a core of young partners led by an extraordinary South Carolinian, Randolph Hobson "Bob" Guthrie, who took control of the semicomatose partnership in 1954. Guthrie's most conspicuous feature was his round, dimpled, cherubic face. His eyes, edged with premature crow's-feet, were constantly active, crinkling expressively whenever he spoke and contributing to an aura of restlessness that hung over him even when he was doing something like thumbing through routine legal papers or a newsmagazine. Guthrie had a shrewd legal mind and endless commercial cunning. His manner was good-old-boy small-town southern insurance executive, not *Harvard Law Review* editor, as was the fact.

Early in Guthrie's career at the firm, he transferred from litigation to the corporate section—because that, as Willie Sutton said of banks, was where the money was. His professional passions were pursuing clients, charging large fees, and rebuilding the firm into a leading national institution. A hunter of men and opportunities, he set out to create a professional life that matched the size of his appetites. "Boy" was his customary greeting to everyone—partners and clerks, whites and blacks, men and women, as in "Boy, we're going to be the biggest and best goddamn law firm in America, make the most goddamn money, drink the most goddamn martinis, have the most goddamn fun. . . ."

It was my good luck that Guthrie noticed me early and chose me as his ward at the Mudge firm. He was impressed, he later told me, because I came from a working-class background, had knocked around a lot, was a "smart Jewish boy"—there was a Jew at Harvard he admired hugely—and displayed a near-freakish capacity to work long hours and roll up massive quantities of billable time.

Guthrie's hungers and energies pushed him toward the big, but his gut attraction was to the best. His blunt, idiomatic way of talking about politics and people would have him in perpetual trouble today, but he was not anti-black or anti-Semitic or anti-anything except mediocrity and bureaucratic jawing. He was an ardent advocate of intermarriage, Brazilian-style, to solve America's racial problem. He thought fixing the country's social ills was a "fine enterprise," but not for him: His business was mining for treasure. After coming to know Guthrie, Richard Nixon described him to me as the only man he had ever met who was more like Lyndon Johnson than Lyndon Johnson.

Between the time when Guthrie took over in 1954 and the early 1960s, the firm expanded through good lawyering and shrewd smallish mergers. It rose from its marginal status to a prosperous perch just below the level of the leading New York law firms. Over a hundred lawyers occupied five floors of the New York Stock Exchange Building at 20 Broad Street, with all the usual status trappings—internal elevator, numerous conference rooms, period furniture, collector-quality ship prints, a look of purposeful busyness, and a huge library displayed to clients through floor-to-ceiling glass walls. The firm could now count on growing revenues from corporate clients like Warner-Lambert, PepsiCo, General Cigar, Stone and Webster Engineering Corporation, Studebaker-Worthington, Continental Baking, and El Paso Natural Gas.

Despite the air of success, however, the firm seemed stuck. It had good clients, good lawyers, and interesting business, but not quite enough of each. It was rarely engaged in the supercases—the highly publicized litigation or other corporate dealings that are the emblem of the professional excitement to be found in the handful of frontline New York law firms. Something, or someone, seemed to be lacking.

This is where Richard Nixon entered the story. Acquiring him was almost accidental on the part of the Mudge firm, but in answering Nixon's need for a temporary career the firm got what it needed —a public partner, someone with a political or legal name well enough known to raise his or her firm above the legal mass. This tradition is especially well established in New York; examples are John W. Davis, Democratic candidate for president in 1924, at Davis Polk & Wardwell; Wendell Willkie, who ran for the presidency against Franklin D. Roosevelt in 1940, at Willkie Farr & Gallagher; and Thomas E. Dewey at Dewey Ballantine. This was the club that Richard Nixon joined when he arrived at the firm—now Mudge Rose Guthrie & Alexander—in 1963.

The firm changed its name to reflect this and other realities about its future: It became Nixon Mudge Rose Guthrie & Alexander. My contribution to this change was to lobby successfully for the retention of the Dickensian name of the long-dead Mudge as a symbol of continuity. The order of the names other than Nixon's was decided by drawing them from a hat. In 1966 the firm added John Mitchell's name when he merged his municipal bond firm with ours. The name then became Nixon Mudge Guthrie Alexander & Mitchell until Messrs Nixon and Mitchell went to Washington in 1969, one as president and the other as attorney general.

When the news arrived early in 1963 that Richard Nixon was moving to New York to join my firm, I was delighted. This might seem an odd reaction: Insofar as I was interested in politics, which was not very, I was a reflexive Nixon denigrator. But Nixon's answer to his career impasse seemed to offer an answer to the personal crisis in my own life.

I had had a great run as a litigator. I tried large, conventional cases, shareholder suits, takeover contests; I represented clients before regulatory commissions. My own *Jarndyce and Jarndyce* was an interminable, interconnected series of criminal and civil cases in which I defended a Midwestern grain company against charges that it had mishandled and misappropriated Commodity Credit Corporation grain. First, in the criminal cases, we argued successfully that we owned the grain and therefore could not steal it. Then, in the civil cases, we argued that our obligations in handling the grain were limited because it was government property. Improbably, we contended that the inconsistent criminal evidence should be kept out of the civil trials because of the different burdens of proof in the two types of cases. I will never forget the look on the face of the government's attorney when the judge agreed with us. Ah, the majesty of the law.

Almost as long, for different reasons, was a case involving a claim of mammoth construction fraud. The two adversaries, high-toned executives from the same social set, were especially indignant at having their honor impugned. Each ordered his counsel to "get at the truth"—that is, not to object to any question during discovery proceedings. As a result, pretrial proceedings went on relentlessly for years, in the course of which I suffered a medium-sized breakdown from exhaustion, and my adversary, a distinguished, tough old Wilmington trial lawyer, had a sudden stroke and died. We finally settled. Miraculously, we kept the client.

Sometimes the cases were memorable not for their legal interest but for the local color. Once I brought an antitrust suit to enjoin the acquisition of a manufacturer of Titan missile parts. I needed a security clearance. An F.B.I. agent interviewed me under a naked lightbulb in a dingy loft on Fourteenth Street. How did I explain, he asked, my subscription to the Communist magazine *New Masses?* I couldn't. My mind was blank. But that night I awoke and sat straight up in bed like a cartoon character. I had a jolt of memory: I had once sublet my Greenwich Village apartment to a college chum of militantly left-wing politics, a subscriber to *New Masses* and everything else that would alert a member of the Hoover-era F.B.I. Pacing the room anxiously until dawn, so I could call the F.B.I. at the earliest possible moment—or at least before they called me—I narrowly avoided a federal perjury investigation but never got my security clearance. Later, when I entered the White House, the president had to clear me personally.

Sometimes the stuff was just funny. In an otherwise dull Commodities Exchange case I ran up against a Doberman of an assistant

U.S. attorney named Bernie Nussbaum, who one day pummeled a witness of mine relentlessly until the lunch break. When we returned, Bernie got ready to do it all over again, and his first question was "Are you the same Joe Blow who was here this morning?" "Of course not!" I exclaimed, getting into the spirit of the thing. When Whitewater erupted, it seemed to me the most natural thing in the world that Bernie, by then counsel to the president, had given the F.B.I. a specially hard time.

Two friends of mine owned *Cue* magazine, a New York publication that offered a seal of approval to advertisers who ran allegedly gourmet restaurants. They learned that Colgate was going to give the name "Cue" to a new toothpaste that would prevent bad breath and other unappetizing conditions. We sued to enjoin Colgate under an obscure New York statute, the only one in the nation, that permits infringement-of-trademark suits not just when similar names cause confusion between two products but when someone else's use of a name "dilutes" the impact of your trademark.

Colgate's multimillion-dollar ad campaign was stopped in its tracks. The trial involved solemn expert testimony about trademark dilution through "cognitive dissonance," said to occur when a name is taken from one product and put on another, inappropriately different, product—e.g., Château Neuf du Pape Foot Bath, Gucci Scouring Pads, Steinway Toilet Seats. We were doing well enough until I called Colgate's president, David Mahoney, to the stand. Witty, street-smart, and informed, Mahoney explained with murderous skill how the prospect of the feared dilution was wildly, comically remote. I knew we were dead when the judge, at the end of both sides' presentations, arose and cheerily bade us all, "Happy motoring."

Mahoney made his own personal trophy of the occasion—a transcript of his testimony bound in leather and distributed to admiring friends, which, years later, included me.

By and large it was great fun. The scorecard of wins, losses, and intangibles eventually resulted in my becoming chief of litigation for Mudge Rose, where I could exercise my special skill and pleasure in recruiting gifted young litigators, supporting them, and building a strong department.

But after years of Wall Street law practice, I had run out of steam. Most of my small-scale ambitions had been achieved, and I had that bleak midlife feeling that I was doing what I would be doing for the rest of my life. No more changes, great goals, surprises. Trapped.

I couldn't have cared less that Richard Nixon was the political Antichrist of eastern liberalism. He was also an opening to a different life and the possibility of salvation. Besides, I had no strong feelings about political issues, except a general sympathy for the underdog. My real politics consisted of (a) a fervent belief in hard, focused work, and (b) a conviction that there were no solutions, only useful compromises. Nixon did violence to neither of these precepts. So personal ideology, what there was of it, took a backseat.

I first met Nixon at a fall 1963 cocktail party given for him and Mrs. Nixon by my partner John Alexander. The Nixons had recently returned from a long overseas holiday trip and were settling into their new home on Fifth Avenue (Governor Nelson Rockefeller was now their neighbor). Nixon was completing the residency requirements for admission to the New York bar, and the old Mudge Stern was being rechristened to mark his new role as head of the sort of prestigious Wall Street law firm that had rejected him after he graduated near the top of his Duke University Law School class.

The party, at the Alexanders' Sutton Place apartment, was a typically crowded New York bash. My memory of the evening is a noisy blur of smiles, handshakes, and that extra decibel of excitement that marks the presence of a name or face made famous by the media. One distinct impression I retain from that first viewing is that Nixon was bigger than I had pictured him—taller and bigger, more of a physical presence. He had a very large head and a sunny smile that lit up his face, smoothed out his jowls, and transformed him, momentarily, into the antithesis of Herblock's scowling, stubble-faced caricature. As for the Nixon nose, well, it was there, the famous ski slope, but it seemed to harmonize with the rest of his head and was, in any event, a physical trademark without which Nixon would not have been Nixon.

For all the half doubts and mumbled disagreements that some partners had voiced about the Nixon deal, they were all present at the party, most of them pleased, the others not-so-unhappily resigned. The enthusiasts varied in their motives—some were ardent

Republicans, others saw golden business possibilities—but for them as for me, the media-battered Richard Nixon was still a man who might open the door to a break from the predictable pace of our lives. So whatever our politics, we all became members of Nixon's extended professional family, our fortunes tied to his.

The first opportunity I had to talk alone with Nixon came after a weekly partnership lunch in the late fall of 1963, catered by Schrafft's in our conference room at a long, candlelit table dressed in linen for a formal meal. The partners sat down to a small self-administered treat, a crisp new twenty-dollar bill passed to each diner as a reward for showing up and attending to his professional well-being. I remember Nixon's surprised reaction to this weird little custom of the inscrutable East. The discussion, as usual, was Wall Street talk—major litigation developments, rivalries among the associates, client news, formal reports on the firm's financial status, and heavy-handed jokes.

Nixon's office was a few steps down the hall from the conference room. After lunch I asked his secretary, Rose Mary Woods, if I could have a chat with him. She told me to knock and go right in. It was as if both of them were waiting for me.

The office looked right for Nixon. Its size was spacious but not excessive. The furniture was comfortable but formal enough to discourage lounging around. Most striking was the careful collection of political curios. Lined up on the long table behind Nixon's desk were elegantly framed, warmly inscribed photographs of Queen Elizabeth, Jawaharlal Nehru, Albert Schweitzer, and other world figures. Scattered around the room were a golf scorecard documenting a Nixon hole-in-one, his cabinet room chair from the Eisenhower White House, objets d'art from places like Thailand and Vietnam, and pictures of the family, including his father, Frank, and mother, Hannah, on a separate table. It was all conventional, but in each case was something drawn from Nixon's life. And it was all very useful to break the ice with a visitor who didn't know Nixon. It was easy to picture him conducting properly impressed guests, as he did with me, around the personal museum of his public and private life.

During this first visit there were several phone-call interruptions that gave me my first view of Nixon's special skills. While lawyers, politicians, and even normal folk often shift and slide among different telephone personae, modifying their manner according to their relationship to the caller, Nixon's telephone skills were of another order of virtuosity. The phone, I started to learn, was his favorite instrument of persuasion. It separated him from the disturbing emanations of another person's physical presence, enabling him to concentrate on his words without having to compose his eyes and coordinate his hands to harmonize with them. He adjusted his conversational style to his audience and objective. The rambling start-and-stop and the hem-and-hawing spiked with profanity in the Watergate tape transcripts that provoked so much horror were always part of Nixon's conversational technique. They were his improvisational method of feeling his way through an uncertain conversation, probing, testing, targeting, gauging what the other fellow really had in mind (or what Nixon himself had in mind).

At our first meeting he waved away my repeated offer to duck out during his phone conversations. Hoisting his polished black shoes to the desktop, he settled into the appropriate voice and manner for "Ray" or "Bob" or "Tom," lining up a sequence of calls through Rose Mary Woods. It was mesmerizing. It was also clear that he was putting on a little show for me: Here's how I work, Len. See how many "languages" I can speak with ease, even if I'm not very good at all that Wall Street jargon around the luncheon table.

Even after we knew each other well, Nixon would from time to time favor me with one of these demonstrations. One day in 1964, the phone rang; it was my old friend Jerry Hellman calling from Hollywood. After years of working as an agent, he had managed to set up his own film company and had produced his first film, *The World of Henry Orient*, with Peter Sellers. It was a modest success. For his second, crucial, film, Jerry picked *A Fine Madness*. Sean Connery had agreed to star. Jerry was the quintessential old-style independent producer—always working against the establishment grain, uncompromisingly determined to have his artistic way, a young Walter Reuther at the throat of Hollywood's Henry Fords. He and the film's director, Irvin Kershner, were now fighting with Warner Bros., the producing studio. On the day Jerry called, his voice was tight with anxiety: "Jack Warner has taken *A Fine Madness* away from me, Len. I need help." The film was in postproduction, the editing and fine-tuning stage in which a movie is made or destroyed and the time when the big fights take place. "Colonel" Warner, as Jack Warner liked to be called, had just seen the first rough cut and realized that he was financing a black comedy, not a James Bond thriller. Hellman and Kershner were discharged, barred from the lot, and told—maybe hyperbolically, maybe not—that the guards had instructions to shoot on sight. Jerry remembered seeing Richard Nixon's photograph prominently displayed in Jack Warner's inner sanctum, affectionately dedicated to "Colonel Warner." My friend pleaded with me to ask Nixon to intervene, which I did.

Nixon told me to bring Hellman to the office; Jerry took the red-eye from Los Angeles that night. By noon the next day we were sitting with Nixon at 20 Broad Street, and Nixon was on the phone to Colonel Warner, making the case for reinstatement of "my brilliant young friend, Jerry Hellman"—who, said Nixon, "I expect will have a large place in my political future." Warner, startled and totally nonplussed, said the whole thing was a "terrible, terrible misunderstanding"; the "rotten apple" was not Hellman but director Kershner. Hellman should hasten home to Hollywood and finish the movie. Warner himself would welcome him back "with open arms."

It was a striking display of Nixon's still-formidable political power and a nice, cost-free favor to me. *A Fine Madness* turned out to be a fine movie—not as good as it would have been if left untouched by the studio, but considerably better than it would have been without Nixon's cameo intervention. Jerry later told me that when he made his third film, *Midnight Cowboy*, which won an Oscar for Best Film, prominent among the early congratulations was a warm personal note from Jack Warner.

Back on that day of our first real meeting, my talk with Nixon was unusually personal. I told him about the high hopes I held for him and the firm and described the boredom and depression I had been feeling about my work. I felt I had to disclose my own politics (maybe to get a sense of how ideological he really was), so I told him that I was a birthright Democrat, that I had voted and worked against him, and that as recently as the previous year I had hosted a fund-raising party for Bobby Kennedy in my Brooklyn home. He waved all this away. He was happy to work with people of a political worldview different from his own who were willing to speak their mind. He had access to "more than enough" Republicans, many of whom had "less than scintillating" ideas.

I found myself more at ease with Nixon in that first conversation than I was with most of my longtime partners, and for a reason: We both wanted it that way. To me, Nixon was a figure out of history, still powerful and at the same time down-to-earth, candid, receptive to my offer of friendship and assistance. For his part, Nixon saw me as a useful ally in his adaptation to Wall Street and the law firm's culture and an eager potential participant in his plans for a political future. Those plans had already been well formed in the quiet of his mind.

So after I made my personal speech, Nixon relaxed and spoke openly about his own feelings. He thought he could develop a fair amount of business for the firm. There were Elmer Bobst of Warner-Lambert, Don Kendall of PepsiCo, and other possibilities. He would spend his time doing his dutiful best for his partners. But he wasn't going to "whore around," for example by lobbying Congress on behalf of clients. He intended to keep in touch with public issues, travel, occasionally speak out. He was not going to forfeit opportunities for public service.

He thought that what was right for him would also be good for the firm. We should search for young lawyers who were scrappers, he said, not children of the elite but people who had fought to make their way in the world ("like you and me"). He thought the most impressive man in the firm was Bob Guthrie, a small-town southern boy who had made good on his own. That was the model, he said, of the kind of person he admired, a man with ideas who didn't flaunt his brains, a fighter and risk taker, a "natural." Nixon also spoke admiringly about Dick Ritzel, whose father had chauffeured the sort of rich people whom the son now counseled as head of the firm's trusts and estates department.

Nixon's less-than-polished emotions came clear at the point during our conversation when I described a case I was handling, *Hill v. Time Inc.* The plaintiff, Jim Hill, Guthrie's old roommate from

Harvard Law School, had been the subject, along with his family, of an offensive article in *Life* magazine. Angered by the publicity, the Hills wanted a retraction and apology—or, failing that, damages. Guthrie had turned the firm loose to help the Hills by representing them on a contingent-fee basis against *Life's* publisher, Time Inc. Guthrie assigned the case to me. By the time I had my conversation with Nixon about it, the trial had taken place, the Hills had won a record verdict, and the state court appellate process was underway. Nixon listened carefully to my description of the case. The magazine wasn't out to injure the Hills, he remarked; it just didn't give a good goddamn about them. It was only interested in selling its goddamn magazine. That's what makes it so infuriating, he went on. All that fancy First Amendment talk—just a lot of pious "bullshit" while they exploit the hell out of you.

I took it upon myself to help Nixon fit into the firm and its law practice. Within the firm I could see that there were three schools of thought about the odd couple we made. The older partners were delighted that a youngish (thirty-nine), energetic type like me was drawing Nixon into law and the business of law. Most of the younger partners, Republicans, were in awe of Nixon and saw me as someone who might get them a piece of the political action. The more liberal young lawyers, a smaller group, narrowed their eyes at the Nixon-Garment association: What's all the hustling about? But they didn't actually ask. If they had, I would have happily said, "Hey, guys, relax. This is Main Chance Farm."

As part of my Nixon project, I arranged to introduce him to the local bar. A few months after he joined Nixon Mudge, I arranged a "meet Richard Nixon" party for area lawyers and judges.

Brooklyn was then home to a far more significant legal community than it is now, when much of the borough has become a wasteland of poverty-blasted housing and barren crack-infested spaces and many of its lawyers have gone over the side, following their clients to Nassau and Suffolk counties. In the 1960s, the office building at 66 Court Street, now converted into apartments, was a vast arcade of law firms and solo practitioners.

I asked two friends to help me put the evening together. One was Leo Glasser, who had continued as a professor at Brooklyn Law School. The other was Jerry Leitner, now a Brooklyn Law School professor and Brooklyn trial attorney. Leo and Jerry were sturdy Democrats, as were almost all the men on the list of invitees they assembled for me; Republican officeholders in Brooklyn were a rarity. I was understandably anxious about the turnout. What if only a handful of the one hundred plus invited dignitaries showed up? It would be an embarrassment for Nixon and a disaster for me.

Between the mailing of invitations and the date of the party, history intervened. John Kennedy's death on November 22, 1963, had the ironic consequence of restoring Richard Nixon to life as a national political figure. The two men had been locked in combat just three years earlier; now Nixon, spared Kennedy's fate, was seen as the survivor. Something of the triumphant Kennedy lived on in the defeated Nixon—a collection of memories, a kind of physical closeness, an unexpected metaphysical reward for being the living member of a historic duo. Kennedy's death made Nixon more of a celebrity. As Kennedy passed into history, Nixon pushed forward.

In mid-January, just before the party, the Gallup organization published a poll designed to gauge the impact of Kennedy's death. It showed, among other things, the order in which the Republican party's rank and file preferred various national Republican figures. Nixon led the pack, and among party leaders his strength was even more pronounced. A solid 30 percent of Republicans around the country were holding fast to this man. There was a base for another national campaign.

Nixon's visit to Brooklyn was a large success. Both floors of our apartment were packed. Many of the invited had felt free to bring family and friends. The guests were old political hands and understood that the party was a rally. The reception was alive with the noise, sweat, and excitement of a major political event. For the first time I watched Nixon in his natural element. I began to understand that there are two distinct types of human being, politicians and nonpoliticians. Politicians are happier in the company of enemies who are politicians than with friends who are nonpoliticians. I believe anthropologists call this species affinity.

Jerry Leitner knew all the judges, so he managed the introductions, moving each arrival along to Nixon for the ritual of back-slapping and political hellos. Din filled the place. Cars choked the usually quiet street. Neighbors, curious about the commotion, peered through the ground-floor windows and were invited in to meet Mr. Nixon.

As with all successful political events, everyone enjoyed the sense of being part of *something* important, even those who didn't know quite what. Most of them, of course, as history-hardened politicians, knew exactly what the "something" was, and they let me know: Beetle-browed, battle-scarred Nixon might yet become president of the United States. Whatever it was that potential presidents have, Nixon had it.

By now most of us have grown blasé or worse about aspirants to the presidency. Back then, though, we were informed by Theodore H. White's warmhearted dramatization of the previous presidential campaign. The presidency seemed the ultimate place of drama and power, and the idea of suddenly being so close to a man who might become president was intoxicating.

I was not the only one intoxicated. A guest that night was the famed criminal lawyer Samuel Leibowitz, who had bravely and skillfully defended the Scottsboro boys in the 1930s. Now a Brooklyn criminal court judge, Leibowitz had grown aggressively sour and pompous: "I know all your tricks, counselor," was his style. As he was leaving the party, Leibowitz suddenly stopped near the door and, in front of his Democratic colleagues, delivered a loud-voiced farewell speech to Richard Nixon. It summarized Nixon's political strengths, his entitlement to the presidency, and the concluding assertion that Nixon had been blatantly cheated out of his due on Election Day in 1960 by the chicanery of Mayor Richard Daley of Chicago. It was tasteless bluster—but I saw that most of the assembled Democrats were vigorously nodding their heads in agreement. I was viewing what I now recognize as the hysteria that overwhelms otherwise rational people when they are in the presence of a world-class celebrity. (In the Oval Office, in the presence of an actual president, I have seen every vestige of sanity and independence sink without a trace.)

Eventually the house emptied out. The booze was depleted, the food gone. Grace's little meatballs, it turned out, were a great idea.

Nixon explained that politicians like small but substantial foods that they can spear with toothpicks so they can eat, drink, talk, and circulate without juggling plates and cutlery.

It was now seven-thirty, and Nixon accepted my invitation to sit upstairs in the family room for a while with Leo Glasser, Jerry Leitner, and Grace. We could have a bite of food and drink and gossip about his Brooklyn coming-out party—his first political foray in New York since 1960. Nixon started the conversation with a small tour d'horizon, built of well-honed anecdotes and assessments of Khrushchev and De Gaulle. Then he summarized his views on the role of Asia in world affairs. We were a tiny audience, but the presentation was as careful as if he were on *Meet the Press*. (Did Horowitz need a vast crowd when he practiced piano?) Nixon questioned us closely about the judges he had just met. Who were they? How were New York's state court judges selected? What kind of political chores did lawyers have to perform to get on the list? Which way was "up" in New York politics? The Nixon vacuum cleaner was at work, sucking in whatever tidbits our little group could offer while he chewed hungrily on his food and sipped a scotch highball.

At eight o'clock, Nixon got ready to call a cab. Jerry said his wife, Jean, was coming to drive him into Manhattan for dinner at the Plaza Hotel with friends, and they would be delighted to drop Nixon uptown. But Jerry wanted Nixon to know that Jean was very pregnant—two weeks overdue, in fact, and she couldn't get into their sports car, so the car she'd be driving was pretty awful, an old family jalopy. . . . No problem, Nixon said. Jean arrived, and off they went.

Late that night, Jerry called to tell me what had happened. Nixon told the Leitners that he had heard a great deal about Brooklyn Heights but had never seen much of it except for political rallies at the St. George Hotel. Could he have a quick look around the area before heading for Manhattan? So the Leitners circled around to Court Street and pointed out the landmarks: the ancient courthouses, the commercial buildings crammed with law offices. Then they headed over to the famous Heights promenade for a quick view of the Manhattan skyline, cruised past some of the old brownstones on Montague Street, and headed onto the Brooklyn Bridge.

In those days there was no lighting on the bridge, and at night it was pitch dark except for the beams of passing cars. Halfway across, the Leitner car came to a shuddering stop. It was dead. It would have to be towed and was of no further use that evening. Anxious about his perilously pregnant wife and his famous passenger, Jerry tried to flag a ride. He failed. Nixon stepped out and took over, and the waving man's familiar face quickly brought a cab to a startled stop. Jean was transferred to the taxi for the trip to Manhattan. Nixon wanted to stay with Jerry and the broken-down car until help arrived, but Jerry persuaded him that his higher duty was to provide safe escort for pregnant Jean—which he uneventfully did.

The morning after, Nixon said to me in the office that his luck was as miserable as ever: "Think of the coverage if Jerry's wife went into labor on the bridge." I'm almost sure he was joking. A couple of days later Nixon sent a note to the still-pregnant Jean with a copy of *Six Crises*, dedicated to "Joshua and/or Janice Leitner." The note said, "In view of our little crisis last Thursday night, I thought that Joshua (or Janice) might like to have a copy of my account of some other crises I have experienced during my life. . . ." Two more votes for Nixon.

The day after the party, talking to Nixon, I made my first intervention in his thinking about the presidency. I reported the praise heaped on him by the Brooklyn Democrats and noted the large number of unsuspected supporters he had in that presumably unfriendly borough. I then went off the deep end by flatly predicting that he would become president of the United States. I was not speculating on possibilities but announcing his fate with Delphic certainty. Even now I wince a little to think of how aggressively I turned my cards over and declared myself a founding member of the nonexistent Nixon campaign team. Little did I know that in a mystical outburst I had said exactly the right, crazy thing to the mystical Richard Nixon. Nixon, man of destiny, had found his prophet. He waved off my effusiveness with a deprecatory remark but not a denial. If my intention was to seal my collaboration with Nixon, I had just scored a ten-strike.

I remember this moment with some clarity, which is no surprise. But, it appears, so did Nixon. Nine years later, shortly after his election to a second term, Nixon wrote me one of those letters of thanks, suitable for framing and office display, that presidents send their campaign helpers. But this particular letter had a remarkably precise reference to our conversation the morning after the party in Brooklyn:

> What really put the icing on the cake is that we carried Brooklyn! I remember when I visited you in your home in Brooklyn and you said that we had more friends there than we realized, I thought you were being a bit over-optimistic, to put it mildly, but again you proved to be right. I give you all the credit for that achievement.

Which would have been a nice conclusion to my tale except for one thing: Nixon did not carry Brooklyn in 1972. It was close, but no cigar.

There was yet another footnote to come, this one connected with Judge Leibowitz's comment about Mayor Richard Daley's "theft" of Illinois in the 1960 election.

In 1987, the Washington lawyer Edward Bennett Williams and I met for lunch to discuss a case in which we were co-counsel. After a while, Williams changed the subject. He and Nixon had known each other reasonably well and been on fairly good terms during the 1950s, when Williams represented a number of political figures, including Joe McCarthy. During the Nixon presidency the relationship soured for various reasons, particularly Williams's representation of *The Washington Post* and his close ties to the *Post's* publisher, Katharine Graham, and the Kennedy family.

But the years had passed, and by 1987 the battles with Nixon were old business and starkly irrelevant to Williams, who was now sick with metastasizing cancer and in the middle of a long, surgery-strewn struggle to stay alive. At our lunch, Williams was enjoying a quiet time between episodes of hospitalization and chemotherapy. He told me his illness had made him think about problems of survival. He had just read *Exile*, a book by Robert Sam Anson about Nixon's post-resignation struggle to live and recover a measure of national respect. Williams said he realized that the man he most admired among all his contemporaries was the unsinkable Richard Nixon. Could I arrange a meeting between the two of them so they could sit together, have a drink, put the past behind them, and talk a little bit, survivor to survivor?

By then I was not surprised at such a request and did not doubt that Nixon would agree to a meeting. He was almost invariably warm and generous to past adversaries, like a litigator after a bitter courtroom contest or a soldier in the aftermath of a bloody war. As for Nixon's former enemies, they usually found themselves welded to him by the smoke, noise, and pain of combat.

Williams and I flew to New York on June 4, 1987, for lunch with Nixon at his favorite Manhattan restaurant, Le Cirque. We made a brief stop at Williams's New York apartment so he could shower and change. He came out for a moment to show me the surgical railroad tracks crisscrossing his chest and abdomen.

We arrived at the restaurant first. Then Nixon walked in, precisely on time. As the two shook hands while standing at our corner table by the door, the action and talk in the packed, noisy room came to a total stop for an instant, like a freeze-frame photo.

For three hours, we consumed the standard Nixon banquet—salad, Dover sole, soufflé, and white wine. I listened and drank while they talked. Their political memories were sharp. There was no opining about war and peace or national political trends. Instead, old neighborhoods were revisited and old friends exhumed. Tales were told about departed kings like Lyndon Johnson, Jack Kennedy, Senator Richard Russell, Ike. There was some ruminating about Watergate: Williams speculated about the course of events if the tapes had been burned, and Nixon, forgetting I was there, regretted that he hadn't had Edward Bennett Williams at his side. The two of them talked a lot about "old Joe McCarthy." Both had known him well. Both reflected on the way he had stumbled on some correct ideas about communism but made such a corrupt mess of it that his name would forever be a synonym for political persecution.

And so the conversation went—no talk about sickness, or the campaign against death that both men were waging, just a quiet summing up of a quarter century of life in the arena of politics that both loved.

Then the subject of Mayor Daley and Illinois came up. Williams, a magnificent storyteller, told how he had gone out to Chicago, at Daley's request, for a final visit to the dying man. As their conversation ended, said Williams, Daley beckoned him closer to his hospital bedside and whispered, "Ed, this is the moment to tell me honestly what you think. Will God forgive me for stealing Illinois from Nixon?"

There was a dramatic pause at the table. Finally, Nixon cleared his throat and deadpanned, "Interesting, Ed, but Illinois just wasn't enough to do it. I needed two more states and it wasn't there, so there was no point worrying about Illinois." Nixon probably knew that Williams's whole Daley story was pure apocrypha: The mayor was in a terminal coma by the time he was taken to the hospital.

It didn't matter. There was a sweet, balm-spreading quality to this final peace conference between two of the fiercest warriors of twentieth-century politics. For the moment, their meeting seemed more important than what actually happened in that presidential campaign long ago.

೪ 4 ೭

NIXON GOES TO COURT

True to his word, Nixon devoted a good part of his time to the practice of law. In fact, the episode that created a close working relationship between the two of us was our collaboration as co-counsel in the case of *Hill v. Time Inc.*, whose jury verdict in the Hills' favor was being appealed by Time Inc. when Nixon arrived at the firm.

It was in the *Hill* case that Nixon made his first appearance before the Supreme Court. Though the Court reversed the verdict and ordered a new trial, the principle we urged eventually became governing law. The case also established Nixon's professional credentials as an appellate lawyer of distinction and thus served the collateral purpose of polishing his new public persona.

The events that gave rise to the case began on September 9, 1952, when three convicts escaped from the federal penitentiary in Lewisburg, Pennsylvania. A few days later, they invaded the home of James and Elizabeth Hill in a Philadelphia suburb. The convicts held the Hills, their three teenage daughters, and their twin sons, aged four, as hostages for nineteen hours. Except for the captivity itself, the convicts behaved in a decent, even gentlemanly, manner and left without doing additional harm to the family. Ten days later, they were apprehended in Manhattan.

In the immediate aftermath of the Hills' ordeal, especially while the convicts were still at large, there was a great deal of public and press interest in the incident. Some speculated openly that there had been acts of sexual violence toward Mrs. Hill and her teenage daughters. But the Hills tried to keep the publicity to a minimum; they emphasized the absence of violence and otherwise declined comment. They later moved to Connecticut and took pains to shield the family from reminders of the bizarre episode. They rejected all requests for interviews and offers of payment for their story.

Almost two and a half years later, the February 28, 1955, issue of *Life* carried a review of the new Broadway melodrama *The Desperate Hours*. The review, part of what *Life* labeled a "True Crime" story, described the play as a "re-enacted" account of the Hills' ordeal and nowhere suggested that the play was fictionalized. It was accompanied by photos of the Hills' former home: The magazine had rented the house from the new owners, transported cast members from the play to what was described as the "actual" house, and photographed them at the site in scenes from the play. Some of the large photos vividly depicted scenes of violence of the sort the Hills repeatedly said had not occurred during their captivity.

Thus the factual relationship between the Hill incident and *The Desperate Hours* was extremely thin. What made *The Desperate Hours* a gripping melodrama was liberal use of bloody violence, drunkenness, profanity, sex, and heroism. These elements were the antithesis of those in the actual Hill captivity. But because of the *Life* feature, curiosity and speculation about the incident flared up in the Hills' new community.

That was when James Hill phoned his Harvard Law classmate Bob Guthrie to ask for help and Guthrie assigned me to the case.

My first step was to ask *Life* for a retraction. *Life* refused. We filed suit. In pretrial discovery we found that the *Life* feature and the consequent reemergence of the Hill family into the public eye were the result of a common sort of journalistic coincidence: The tryout of *The Desperate Hours* took place in Philadelphia, near the neighborhood where the Hill incident had occurred. *Life*'s entertainment editor, Tom Prideaux, heard about this coincidence and got the idea for a review with an unusual "news" angle.

We also found out that in the view of *Life*'s editors, the magazine's "True Crime" format required that a highly explicit connection be made between the Hill incident and the *Desperate Hours* review. Accordingly, a series of drafts of the feature's text showed a gradual tightening of this relationship, until in the final, published version, *Life* said categorically, "Americans all over the country" who "read about the desperate ordeal of the James Hill family" can "see the story re-enacted in Hayes' Broadway play based on the book."

Life, in pretrial arguments, responded to the Hills' suit by asserting that the article, notwithstanding disputes about its accuracy, was protected by the First Amendment. To this claim the Hills replied that the article's central theme was a fabrication. As such, it was not constitutionally protected; instead, its false depiction of the Hills was an actionable invasion of their privacy for purposes of commercial exploitation.

The trial of *Hill v. Time Inc.* ran for two weeks before a pleasant enough New York State Supreme Court judge named Arthur Klein and a conventionally confused jury. Both I and my calmly competent trial assistant, Don Zoeller, then a recent Fordham Law night school graduate and later the senior partner of Mudge Rose, saw what our job was. We knew the judge and jury might well wonder why the Hills were so bothered by the *Life* article. *Life's* account did not insult them. So what was all the fuss about? We saw that we had to get the jury as angry as we were at Time Inc., and help them see the issue not as libel but as an act of commercial exploitation, an invasion of the privacy of private persons.

So we readily conceded at the trial that *Life* had not set out deliberately to harm the Hills. Who the Hills were, how they might feel about being drawn back into the public eye and identified as victims of the kind of ordeal portrayed in *Desperate Hours*—these questions were the furthest thing from *Life's* editorial mind. That was our point: To the squadron of *Life* staffers and editors who spent weeks meticulously devising, editing, and polishing their article, the Hills were simply names in the news, one-dimensional journalistic props, not flesh-and-blood people. In short, we bet our case on the theme of ice-cold institutional indifference.

We showed the jury how the editing process had worked. Entertainment editor Tom Prideaux's first draft had described the play as a "somewhat fictionalized" account. A *Life* researcher, aware that the drama was pure fiction, put a question mark over the word "somewhat." But the senior editorial hand in the process disregarded the warning, drew a slashing line through the qualifications, and made *The Desperate Hours* into a reenactment.

A *Life* researcher testified that the idea of photographing violent scenes from the play in the Hills' former home was considered by the *Life* staff to be a "good gimmick." Another *Life* researcher testified that it was her job to check—literally, with a check mark over every word—each fact in the story; but she admitted that when it came to checking whether the play was a "reenactment" of the Hill story, she simply took her editor's word for it. In the researcher's files was a *New York Times* article about the play, written in January 1955, a month before the *Life* feature, in which Joseph Hayes, the author of the play, had said, "Instead of researching any of the specific cases" of hostage taking, "I found it best to let my imagination play with the idea." Prideaux had met with Hayes. We asked Prideaux why he hadn't asked Hayes whether the play was in fact about the Hill incident. Prideaux said authors are not necessarily the best judge of what inspires them, adding, "It would have been a waste of time." In perhaps the trial's crowning moment of journalistic insensitivity, Prideaux testified that since there was a "connection" between the Hill incident and *The Desperate Hours*, *Life* felt "it was an obligatory thing to do, to point out this connection." And that, kiddies, is the kind of unguarded hubris that produces chillingly large punitive damage verdicts against the press.

Mrs. Hill did not testify, though she was present and was introduced to the jury so that no one could suggest she was being hidden away lest she somehow damage the Hills' case. Two psychiatrists testified that she had sustained lasting injury from the distorted publicity of the *Life* article. She had come through the original hostage incident well but had fallen apart when the *Life* article brought back her memories, transformed them into her worst nightmares, and presented them to the world as reality. Mrs. Hill's therapy had included the administration of thirty electroconvulsive shock treatments. The doctors testified that she was and would remain a psychological tinderbox. *Life*, calling no expert to refute this testimony, attributed Mrs. Hill's symptoms to menopause and malingering.

The jury returned an award of $175,000 in compensatory and punitive damages, the largest invasion-of-privacy award in the state's history (several jurors had wanted to award as much as $500,000). The next morning, I was actually dismayed that *The New York Times* did not feature a page one story about the miraculous triumph of the people over the press that Zoeller and I had wrought in the dismal precincts of Foley Square.

On appeal, the state courts affirmed the judgment of liability. Time Inc. then filed an appeal to the U.S. Supreme Court.

The Court's decision to hear the case established that large public issues were involved. It also summoned up what seemed to me an attractive picture—for the case and for Richard Nixon's future —of Nixon, who had apparently passed from the political scene, defending the right of privacy against one of the nation's largest publishers. I suggested to Nixon that he argue the appeal, the clients joined in the request, and Nixon eventually agreed to do so. At first Nixon believed, not unreasonably, that he ran a large risk by this decision, since some of his oldest ideological enemies now sat on the Court and would have their knives out for him. But he also saw that his emergence as a Supreme Court advocate could become part of people's perception of him as a "New Nixon," a disciplined advocate respectful of constitutional principles, not the bitter politician lashing out at journalists in his famous "last press conference" in California in 1962.

Moreover, the Hills were sympathetic litigants, an average middle-class mother and father who genuinely valued their privacy and that of their five children. Arguing on their behalf, Nixon would have the best possible vehicle for expressing his feelings about press abuses of privacy. If he did his professional best, how badly could he lose?

Nixon's preparation for his Supreme Court argument began in 1965 shortly after the Court agreed to hear the case. Just the previous year, in the landmark case *New York Times v. Sullivan*, the Supreme Court had decided that a public official suing for libel was obliged to meet extremely high standards of proof. The *Hill* case involved the first post-*Sullivan* look by the Court at the competing claims of individual privacy and institutional press freedom. Nixon could not afford to stumble before his old political adversaries or be seen as doing nothing more than continuing his war against the press by other means. This was a "crisis" such as had periodically marked his career, and during 1965 and 1966 I had the opportunity to see how he met it. The "how" was a type of preparation that even someone as detail-crazed as I was had to recognize as stunningly meticulous.

Nixon began by reading and virtually committing to memory the *Hill* trial record, the state court decisions, and copious quantities of background material, including federal and state case law, law review articles, and philosophical writings on libel and privacy. He read his way through the First Amendment analyses of law professors and philosophers such as Alexander Meikeljohn, Thomas Emerson, William Prosser, and Edward Bloustein. The famous Nixon yellow legal pads accumulated, filled with summaries, questions, and preliminary lines of oral argument. As his grasp of the issues tightened, requests came to me for memoranda on fine points that needed elaboration. He scribbled endlessly on drafts and galleys of our Supreme Court briefs. As the day of argument approached, there were almost continuous question-and-answer drills, simulating a court argument, with his law firm colleagues. He worked particularly hard grinding his points down to their essentials. His preparation was almost obsessive; he left nothing to chance. His behavior was a sign not only of professional pride but of his determination not to let recent defeats drive him from the public arena.

Much of Nixon's preparation for his argument took place on the margins of his political and personal life—lunches, dinners, and trips to clients' corporate board meetings. On airplanes, Nixon liked to have a companion to protect him from being badgered by well-wishers. At the start of a flight, before burying himself in his notes and yellow pads, he would instruct me to answer his questions but otherwise leave him alone.

On one trip during which I performed my mixed function of debate coach and security guard, Nixon was scheduled to speak in Miami to directors of a company called Investors Diversified Services. The evening before the speech, we went to the nearby home of Warner-Lambert's Elmer Bobst for drinks. We dined at a local country club with Bobst and his wife, then got into a car for a drive to the place where we were scheduled to spend the night, a new home in a Miami-area real estate development. Nixon took one look at the place, and his always-operational political instincts and suspicions told him that in the morning the developers would expect to get pictures of him in the house in order to use his name and photograph for publicity purposes. He ordered the driver to take us back to the Bobst home, about forty miles away. When we arrived, after midnight, the gates were locked. A high wall surrounded the estate. What now? Nixon told the driver to come back for him at seven-thirty A.M. and then said, "Come on, Garment. It's over the wall we go." So over we went, two New York lawyers, briefcases and all. We were able to get into the pool house, which had twin beds. We turned out the lights like kids at summer camp.

That night Nixon talked until he fell asleep. He told me his consuming interest was foreign policy. He talked about world affairs at length and said he felt his life had to be dedicated to great foreign policy purposes. This man, fiercely determined to stay in the political life for which he was in many ways so ill suited, told me he felt driven to do so not by the rivalries or ideological commitments of domestic politics but by his pacifist mother's idealism and the profound importance of foreign affairs.

That was the night's theme. Nixon said that accumulating money, belonging to exclusive clubs, and playing golf were just not his idea of a worthwhile existence. He had lived "in the arena," among great public events, and that was where he wanted to stay, even if it meant "a shorter life" for him. In particular, Nixon said he would do anything, make any sacrifice, to be able to continue using his talents and experience in making foreign policy. "Anything," he added, "except see a shrink."

When I woke up the next morning, Nixon had left to make his speech. Bobst appeared, unsurprised to find me on the premises; Nixon must have told him about our adventure. Bobst and I sat by the pool from breakfast through lunch and had a long, surprising conversation. Some of it was about Bobst's life. He was a minister's son, a thoughtful, kindly man who looked like Mr. Magoo and spoke in a formal basso profundo voice that managed to make "hello" sound like a portentous public pronouncement. He was known as a stickler for ethics in corporate life and had played a large role in funding cancer research. He was deeply interested in China and spoke at length that morning about its power and importance.

We also talked some about Bobst's hopes for Nixon. By now, Bobst was convinced that Nixon would be president and told me that he and Nixon had often talked about what Nixon would do in the White House. He said he and Nixon felt that "the most important thing" to be done in foreign affairs was to "bring China into the world." But the two of them disagreed on what to do about Vietnam. Bobst thought it was an unmitigated disaster from which the United States must quickly withdraw. Nixon insisted that the U.S. position in Vietnam was that of a "cork in the bottle," and pulling the cork quickly could have unknown, even catastrophic, consequences. As Bobst talked, however, it became clear that the real issue between them was merely whether to get out quickly or slowly. Nixon, said Bobst, accepted that Vietnam could not be "won" and that we would eventually have to withdraw.

I was not destined to find out any more about Nixon's foreign-policy vision, at least on that trip. On the flight back to New York, Nixon returned to his yellow pad. I did the eating and drinking for both of us and browsed through a paperback. There were no questions, no more summer-camp confessions.

Nixon continued his intense preparation for the *Hill* argument through the morning of April 27, 1966, when I anxiously summoned him from the lawyers' lounge in the Supreme Court just before the Court was scheduled to convene. He was still flipping through his yellow pads. When I tried to move him along, he laid a restraining hand on me and said, "Never rush into a public place." We strode slowly to our assigned seats, as if to the strains of "Hail to the Chief." At precisely 10:00 A.M. the nine justices appeared silently from behind their red velvet curtain and quickly took their seats. Chief Justice Warren called the first case. Then, shortly after noon, he called the appeal in *Time Inc. v. Hill.*

Time's lawyer, Harold Medina, argued that the *Life* article was basically an accurate depiction of the connection between *The Des-*

perate Hours and the real Hill case. Therefore the piece was a comment on the news and, as such, was constitutionally protected.

Nixon's main effort was to demonstrate that the magazine had consciously presented the fictionalized play as a "re-enacted" account of the Hill incident: The depiction of the Hills' involvement was a deliberate falsification, an admitted "gimmick" designed to justify the use of the former Hill home as a "True Crime" site for the magazine's review of the play. Nixon argued that *Life*'s article satisfied the stringent constitutional test for publishers' liability.

This was Nixon's first argument in any appellate court, but he sounded like a polished professional of the bar—his footing confident, his language lawyerlike, his organization clear. He had true "bottom," responding to dozens of tough questions. The Court obviously relished the performance. John MacKenzie, now the senior editorial page writer on the law for *The New York Times* and then covering the Court for *The Washington Post*, wrote that Nixon's presentation was "one of the better oral arguments of the year." According to Bernard Schwartz's biography of Earl Warren, *Super Chief*, at a Court luncheon shortly after the argument the justices expressed surprise that Nixon had done so well. Bruce Allen Murphy's biography of Abe Fortas notes that soon after the argument, Fortas said that Nixon had made "one of the best arguments that he had heard since he had been on the Court" and that, with work, he could be "one of the great advocates of our time."

Nixon and I came away from the argument feeling we had scratched out a narrow majority of justices. Justice Hugo Black, a First Amendment absolutist, had been hostile during the argument. By contrast, forceful statements on privacy by Justices Warren and Fortas were encouraging—but, after some thought, not surprising. Nixon observed that these two men had been in the political arena and knew firsthand how fierce and lacerating the press could be when it fastened on a target. They would see that for private persons, such unwanted and false exposure could be, in Nixon's words, "as traumatic as a physical blow."

We flew back to New York at the end of a day that had started a little after dawn. Aboard the plane, Nixon continued working. We parted at La Guardia. I went home, drank a couple of vodkas, and fell into an exhausted sleep.

I arrived at work at about ten the next morning and found on my desk a five-page, single-spaced memorandum addressed to me from Nixon. Upon finally arriving back at his Fifth Avenue apartment, Nixon had dictated a tape of detailed, self-critical comments on his argument and an assessment of points he would now handle differently. Rose Mary Woods had transcribed the tape early the next morning. It remains the most instructive example of Richard Nixon's tenacity and discipline that I have ever read, including the papers he produced in his presidential and postpresidential years. There was no reason for Nixon to believe that the case would be reargued (rearguments were rare). As far as we were concerned, the case was over. Nixon's memorandum was a pure exercise in intellectual self-criticism:

TO: Leonard Garment
        April 28, 1966

FROM: Richard M. Nixon

Now that the case is over, here are some of the points I believe deserved more emphasis in the oral argument. . . .

THE FACTS

I think it would have been most effective after completing my analysis of the LIFE pictures to turn to Justice Fortas and to have directly replied to the question he asked Medina as to whether there had been some "rather ugly incidents" in the play. Medina as you recall answered that question in the negative. I could have briefly recounted in a most effective way the murder of the trash man, the killing of two of the convicts, the wounding of the boyfriend . . . and the constant use of profanity in its ugliest form throughout the play. . . .

LIFE'S RESPONSIBILITY

I should have read that dramatic interchange in the record where you asked Prideaux if he had read the green [editing] file and he answered, "Yes." I could have then followed that up by asking the Justices to read the contents of the file which included Hayes' story as well as the current news events and then to reach their own judgments as to whether . . . any one of them would have proceeded to "assume that the play was a re-enactment of the Hill incident."

LIFE'S MOTIVE

I think it would have been helpful to give the Court an idea as to the true nature of the right of privacy and how it differs from defamation. . . . What I intended to point out if time permitted was that as distinguished from libel . . . intent to hurt the plaintiff through the use of falsehood is completely irrelevant in the tort of privacy.

Nixon's memo concluded with an analysis of the constitutional underpinnings of the right of privacy. He predicted the problems inherent in a free-floating rationale for a general right of privacy, first stated in *Griswold v. Connecticut* (1965). In that case, Supreme Court justice William O. Douglas, writing for the majority, could not cite any specific constitutional foundation for a general right of privacy, but claimed that such a right could be inferred from constitutional "emanations" and "penumbras." *Griswold's* muddled language brought new confusion to the discussion of the privacy issue. Nixon, in his midnight memo, wrote:

THE CONSTITUTIONAL NATURE OF THE PRIVACY RIGHT

. . . This kind of analysis, if followed to its conclusion, is both inaccurate and potentially dangerous from a Constitutional standpoint. In *Griswold*, it was essential to find that there was a "Constitutional right to privacy in marriage" since the issue there was the power of the state to impair that right. Unless it had been found that the right of privacy in marriage had Constitutional status, the Connecticut statute could not have been declared unconstitutional.

Here the question is not the power of the state to infringe on a right but the power of the state to recognize and implement a right.

The memo showed two things nagging at Richard Nixon's perfectionist soul. First, he believed he had missed opportunities to highlight factual arguments that would have helped place the *Hill* case farther outside the zone of constitutional protection defined by *New York Times v. Sullivan*. More important, he regretted his failure to give fuller and more precise expression to his shrewd insight that Justice Douglas's weak reasoning in *Griswold* was going to get the Court into deep and dangerous constitutional waters.

Griswold later became the key authority for the Court's 1973 decision on abortion in *Roe v. Wade*; and *Griswold's* confusion, criticized by both liberal and conservative scholars, has seriously undermined the legitimacy of *Roe*. In 1987, more than twenty years after the *Griswold* decision, the confirmation hearings on the nomination of Robert Bork to the Supreme Court reverberated with the problem that Nixon saw coming.

May and most of June passed without word from the Court. On June 20, the last day of the term, we had disappointing news: An order had come down restoring the case to the docket for reargument in the fall. Nixon interrupted his cross-country campaigning for Republican candidates in the 1966 midterm elections, a crucial part of his burgeoning presidential effort, and set aside three weeks to focus intensively on the altered array of arguments. Reargument on October 18 and 19, 1966, was another smooth, professional performance by both Medina and Nixon. I thought Nixon was even better and more relaxed this time. But the attitudes and apparent lineup of Court opinion had changed, from our point of view for the worse. As the questions and comments by the Court proceeded, it seemed clear that only the chief justice and Justice Fortas were holding fast to their earlier sympathies for the Hills' claim.

The decision came down on January 9, 1967, reversing the New York State court and remanding the case for a new trial. The vote was 5–4, with five justices writing separate opinions.

Justice Brennan wrote for the majority, holding that the trial judge's charge to the jury did not instruct the jurors with constitutional clarity under the now operative rule of *New York Times v. Sullivan*, which required a finding that the challenged material was published with legal malice—that is, with knowledge of falsity or reckless indifference to the question of truth. The principal dissent was written by Justice Fortas, joined by Chief Justice Warren and Justice Clark. This dissent argued that the trial court's charge, while not a "textbook model," nevertheless satisfied the *Sullivan* standard.

When I learned about the decision via a phone call from the clerk of the Court, I called Nixon at his apartment. He listened, asked one or two questions about the authorship of the opinions, and then said, "I always knew I wouldn't be permitted to win a big appeal against the press. Now, Len, get this absolutely clear: I never want to hear about the *Hill* case again." Without a pause, he turned to some business involving the 1968 presidential campaign.

During the years after *Hill*, I had the lukewarm comfort of seeing libel law turn around. The ironic effect of the disturbing *Hill* result was to stimulate debate in law school articles and case commentaries over what arguments private people should be able to make in cases like *Hill*. In 1974, in the libel case of *Gertz v. Robert Welch, Inc.*, Justice Lewis Powell wrote for the Supreme Court majority that the *Sullivan* rule was applicable only to public figures, not to private individuals. Under *Gertz*, the Hill family would have won in the Supreme Court.

Another decade passed. In late 1985 there appeared a book by Bernard Schwartz titled *The Unpublished Opinions of the Warren Court*, in which Schwartz analyzed major Warren Court cases in light of previously secret draft opinions and justice-to-justice memoranda. Anthony Lewis, reviewing the book for *The New York Times*, noted that the most acrimonious political struggle described by Schwartz was the clash between Justices Hugo Black and Abe Fortas over *Time Inc. v. Hill*.

Midmorning on a Tuesday in January 1986 I got a phone call from Richard Nixon. "Did you see Tony Lewis's review in Sunday's *Times*? Why don't you check it out? Maybe we'll find out what really happened in that case." It was the first time he had mentioned the subject to me in twenty years.

It turned out that at the Court's private conference on April 29, 1966, two days after the first oral argument in the case, the vote was

6–3 to affirm the judgment in favor of the Hills. The chief justice assigned the drafting of the Court's opinion to Fortas.

Few in Washington who knew Abe Fortas on the day he was appointed to the Court would have marked him as an enemy of the press. He came from a lower-middle-class Jewish family in Memphis, a brilliant boy and talented violinist with a large capacity for high-quality work. He won a scholarship to Yale Law School, where he was editor-in-chief of the *Yale Law Journal*, and became a Roosevelt New Dealer. After World War II he set up a law practice with the famed trust-busting attorney general Thurman Arnold and flourished financially and politically. He was prominent in the anti-McCarthy forces in Washington in the 1950s and argued a number of civil rights cases pro bono. The most famous was the 1963 *Gideon v. Wainwright*, in which the Supreme Court constitutionally guaranteed a right to counsel for indigent defendants in serious criminal cases.

Fortas also became the quintessential Washington insider, adviser, and confidant. His most important client in this respect was Senate Majority Leader and later President Lyndon Johnson. In 1965 Johnson appointed Fortas to the Supreme Court—over Fortas's very sincere objections—at a Johnsonian press conference called without Fortas's knowledge or consent. Thus was Fortas launched on a judicial career.

Even as a newcomer to the Court, Fortas was a strong, confident figure. His first year was a great personal success. The *New York Times* law reporter Fred Graham called him a "promising member of 'the club' " who was fast becoming "a power on the Supreme Court." *U.S. News & World Report* said he could be "counted among those who will set the tone and style of the Court in the future."

One member of the Court, Hugo Black, violently disagreed. Black had overcome his prior membership in the Ku Klux Klan to gain his Court appointment from Roosevelt in 1937 and, ever since, had worn the mantle of the Court's liberal. Black disliked everything about Fortas. Fortas's biographer Bruce Murphy says Black saw Fortas as a "pretender to the throne of leadership" on the Court. Schwartz's book portrays Black's intense antipathy to Fortas as even more than that, and in fact rather mysterious: It was apparent almost from the day Fortas joined the Court and intensified sharply thereafter. Perhaps the aversion was simply what it appeared to be: the ideological absolutist Black's detestation of the political pragmatist Fortas. Perhaps Black saw in Fortas a descendant of his ancient adversary Felix Frankfurter, a proponent of the doctrine of balancing competing constitutional interests, a philosophy deeply offensive to Black's fundamentalist soul. Perhaps it was something else. Whatever it was ultimately determined the outcome of *Hill*.

O ver the years, Fortas's attitude toward the press had grown more hostile, partly because of his bruising encounters with it on behalf of Lyndon Johnson. And in the *Hill* case, Fortas was truly stirred by the injustice he saw to the Hill family. Nixon's presence in the case was incidental to Fortas: Whatever political baggage the former vice president might be carrying, he also happened to be bearing the right message. Fortas, a political professional, also admired Nixon's skilled performance under pressure. Fortas produced a coruscating sixteen-page majority opinion draft in the *Hill* case. "Needless, heedless, wanton and deliberate injury of the sort inflicted by *Life*'s picture story," he said, "is not an essential instrument of responsible journalism." Fortas also wrote a passionate defense of privacy, what Schwartz calls "as broad a statement of that right as any ever made by a member of the highest court."

Fortas's choice of strong language turned out to be imprudent. Hugo Black welcomed the broad scope, intensity, and attendant weaknesses of Fortas's draft: They presented him with an opportunity to cut Fortas down to size. But for this job Black needed time, and he found a way to get it. Fortas, because of critical comments from various justices when his draft opinion was first circulated, found it necessary to make revisions. Black wrote what Murphy calls a "petulant" note to Fortas, insisting that because of the changes, Black, too, needed extra time—more than the current term allowed—to rewrite his response. Fortas agreed to reargument of the case in the Court's next term.

Meanwhile, Black continued his campaign against Fortas. Black said to other justices that Fortas's draft was "the worst First Amendment opinion he had seen in a dozen years" and added that "it would take him all summer to write his dissent," which "would be the greatest dissent of his life." The day before the reargument of the *Hill* case, Justice Black answered Fortas's sixteen-page memorandum of affirmance by distributing to his colleagues an opposing sixteen-page memo of his own, a blockbuster denunciation of Fortas and, as promised, one of the most forceful statements Black ever made of his judicial philosophy. For instance, Black said,

> After mature reflection I am unable to recall any prior case in this Court that offers a greater threat to freedom of speech and press than this one does. . . .

Black's lobbying and his extraordinarily hyperbolic memorandum, timed for the eve of reargument, had the intended effect, finally garnering the votes for a majority.

The irony is that after all the speculation about how the Court would respond to Richard Nixon, personal antagonism toward him had no effect on the case's outcome. The two justices who most detested Nixon's politics, Warren and Fortas, were unshakable defenders of his position in the *Time Inc. v. Hill* case. Instead, the personal clash that determined *Hill*'s outcome was the animus between Black and Fortas. In the course of their battle, Fortas's old-style liberal, pluralist notion of press freedom as a value to be weighed against other values gave way to Black's idea of press rights, which was much larger and more uncompromising in its claims.

Sullivan and *Hill* symbolized the politics of the time and prefigured the country's politics in the subsequent decades. *Sullivan*'s enormous expansion of press freedom occurred in part because the case involved chilling restraints imposed by a southern court and jury in the middle of the civil rights revolution. *Hill* was decided in the way it was partly because of the pro-press enthusiasm so recently generated by *Sullivan*. At the same time, political activists were becoming more generally antagonistic toward the government and other traditional bastions of power; the press mirrored this antagonism and asserted more power for itself in expressing it.

On the other side of the cultural divide stood citizens starting to be offended by what they saw as the arrogance of journalists and intellectual elites in riding heedless over the interests and values of more ordinary folk. The beginnings of this cleavage helped elect Richard Nixon president in 1968.

In the years that followed, the division deepened. For many journalists, children of *Sullivan* and *Hill*, Watergate made the idea of any press restraint anathema. This view led journalists to use *Sullivan* in a self-aggrandizing and ultimately self-destructive way. They acted as if they thought the First Amendment's writ ran without limit; many citizens thought otherwise. The resentment engendered by what was viewed as the superciliousness of the press and other such elites surely played a role in forming the country's increasingly conservative disposition during these years. It also led to a relationship between the press and other American institutions that is now seriously awry. Post-Watergate norms of journalistic behavior have generated widespread popular anger, and court decisions and jury verdicts reflect the growing sentiment. Thus, today the press finds itself in an environment so hostile as to threaten the liberty that Hugo Black was so sure he was securing.

In a more concrete matter, it should be noted that Elizabeth Hill took her own life in August 1971. Since James Hill gave me permission to discuss this matter, I can give my view of it. I do not say that the false and unwanted publicity of the *Life* article caused Mrs. Hill's untimely death; suicide is too mysterious an act for such assertions. It is not unfair, however, to say that troubled persons, clinging to their psychological integrity in an increasingly invasive world, suffer with special acuteness when they are forced into the spotlight of negative community attention. In many cases their ordeal brings them more than just transitory embarrassment or a general sense of resentment at a trespass. It brings, as Justice Harlan put it in agreeing with Fortas, "severe risk of irremediable harm." But this sort of reasoning rubbed a righteous jurist like Hugo Black the wrong way, just as the complexities and particularities of Abe Fortas provoked in Black a vast resentment.

Early one morning in 1970, a year or so after I joined President Nixon's White House staff, Abe Fortas came to see me. He said his visit had nothing to do with law or politics. It concerned the arts, a policy area for which I had White House responsibility.

His mission, Fortas explained humorously and deftly, was to see whether some way could be found to permit musicians to deadhead cellos and other large musical instruments on airplanes that had excess space. Still an accomplished violinist, he was at pains to point out to me that he could hold his fiddle in his lap and was therefore not self-interested on this issue. Would I help out? Sure, I said, but don't hold your breath while the Civil Aeronautics Board decides whether to waive its rules against such practices.

By then Fortas had resigned from the Court amid scandal. In 1968, after President Johnson had made himself a lame duck by announcing he would not run for reelection, he tried to appoint Justice Fortas to the post of Chief Justice. The nomination was blocked by revelations that Fortas had received a private honorarium while on the Court and had, to boot, given Johnson a great deal of strictly political advice. Then in May 1969 a *Life* magazine article revealed that Fortas had accepted a substantial honorarium from the financier Louis Wolfson, who was then being investigated by the Securities and Exchange Commission. Fortas was forced off the Court altogether. To the end of his days, according to his biographer Bruce Murphy, he maintained to friends and colleagues that the *Life* article had been Time Inc.'s punishment of him for his role in the *Hill* case.

When Fortas came to see me in 1970 I had never met him but did feel a personal tie because of the *Hill* matter. As we chatted, I mentioned the case. This produced a surprising outburst from Fortas. In all his time on the Court, he said, no case had affected him so much or so deeply offended his sense of fairness and equity. "It was a bad result and terribly unfair to the Hill family," he said. "I offer you my apologies for not being more effective."

Fortas and I became something between acquaintances and friends. He could be a shrewd and merry counselor (or a cold and difficult man if he chose), and from time to time I called on him for advice. I saw why President Johnson couldn't break his habit of turning to Fortas for counsel, even when Fortas had ascended to the supposedly cloistered life of a Supreme Court justice. Fortas's last big piece of advice to me came after Nixon was driven from office, and it was that I should try to persuade President Gerald Ford to pardon his predecessor.

In the months after he gave me that recommendation, I read Fortas's various public condemnations of Richard Nixon and reflected on the complex political style they shared. Each man had extraordinary gifts and each was a bundle of contradictions. Each would praise the other in private while attacking in public—or vice versa. During the 1968 fight over Fortas's nomination as chief justice, Bruce Murphy says, Nixon encouraged other Republicans to attack but would not himself attack Fortas or make Fortas an explicit issue in the 1968 presidential campaign. Fortas, meanwhile, was free with his praise of Nixon's skills as an advocate—that is, when speaking to other lawyers, who viewed such talk as a mark of professionalism and sophistication. Not so in public, where Fortas would follow convention and bury Nixon rather than praise him. For each, it was a matter of audience. And this method of conducting political business contributed to both men's undoing.

In December 1974, when I was leaving the Ford administration to return to New York and practice law, Fortas asked me to lunch. He was at his charming best. As we finished, he said, "You know, I have a tiny law firm but an interesting practice over in Georgetown, lots of freedom to do as much or as little as I want. Would you like to become my partner?"

I told him I was honored, pleased, and tempted, but I had had enough of Washington and was determined to go back home. "You'll return," he said, grinning elfishly. "Washington is just too much fun."

⳨ 5 ⳩

THE LONG MARCH

The concept of a Nixon come-back was born for me in that first long conversation in Nixon's office at 20 Broad Street in 1963. Later there would be the masses of people and elaborate machinery of a presidential campaign. But in the beginning there were just two men whose needs and skills happened to fit together, the first pieces in a multidimensional jigsaw puzzle. I recruited Nixon to the *Hill* case; concurrently, he recruited me to help him build a base camp for his next assault on the White House. I thus became the first of the "New Nixon" crowd.

By this time I had developed a talent more amorphous and useful than simple legal skill: I was good at introducing people to one another and getting them to work together in complicated enterprises—assembling human trains, tracks, and switches, even when I was not sure where I wanted to go. So, like the band manager I still was, I started rounding up a crew of disparate individuals with the talents to compose a Nixon campaign and the inclination to abandon normal lives for a plunge into the great unknown. The process of booking the right mix of players went forward from 1963 up to the day of Nixon's formal announcement of his second campaign for the presidency in February 1968.

The core of Nixon veterans from campaigns past—people like

Peter Flanigan, Maury Stans, Bob Haldeman, John Ehrlichman, John Lodge, Pat Hillings—was pretty much in place by 1965. From 1965 through 1968, I helped recruit new people: Tom Evans, John Sears, Frank Shakespeare, Bill Gavin, Harry Treleaven, Alan Greenspan, Martin Anderson, Roger Ailes, and Kevin Phillips, who joined Nixon's own writing recruits—Ray Price, Pat Buchanan, and Bill Safire. Finally, there were joint draft picks by Nixon and me—preeminently our law partner John Mitchell.

After individual testing, each player who passed muster was fitted into a particular slot, and the disjointed collection was woven into a fairly efficient campaign team. Nixon guided the whole operation along its course. Unlike me, he had a strategy: not to get locked in too soon. So day after day he mused and muttered, fussing with details, calling here and there, soaking up information, reacting to events, doubling back, breaking away occasionally for a foreign trip or business meeting, ceaselessly tinkering, bobbing, weaving, and maneuvering at his disciplined chess player's pace toward the 1968 endgame.

This time, Nixon must have said to himself over and over, there must be no screwup.

Nineteen sixty-four was the year in which Nixon tested and educated me in presidential politics. The process was informal and indirect. Between litigation assignments I would have tutorial visits with him on little or no notice. There was no agenda, just an occasional exchange of biographical fragments or some casual luncheon gossip about the comings and goings of 1964's Republican presidential contenders—Barry Goldwater, George Romney, Nelson Rockefeller, Charles Percy, John Lindsay.

During these meetings Nixon mostly listened with stoic patience to my increasingly uninhibited presentation of ideas, opinions, and incitements to Republican riot. Rediscovering my adolescent sense of mission, I offered exhortations with the certitude of the authentic amateur. Nixon was prepared to wait me out until I ripened into something that might be useful. He also introduced me to his political family—in order to give me a sense of the inside game and, more important, have the Nixon professionals look me over to see whether I could play some kind of campaign role.

First in this family was Rose Mary Woods, Nixon's executive secretary. Rose played mother hen to the whole budding brood of "New" Nixonites, shuttling the players in and out or on and off the idiosyncratic schedule of "the boss" to meet needs and priorities that only he and she understood. Always on duty, single-minded in her devotion to Nixon and his family, Rose held the organization together from the first days at 20 Broad Street, when the incipient operation consisted simply of him, her, and a Rolodex as big as the Ritz.

Woods grew up in working-class, Irish Catholic Chicago and became Congressman Richard Nixon's secretary almost as soon as he arrived in Washington. My guess is that she never thereafter passed a single day distracted from her devotion to her boss. Rose was the litmus test of Richard Nixon's guarded feelings toward the world around him. She flashed signals of acceptance and sounded bells of alarm that mirrored the man's mercurial moods and feelings. If you could read Rose Woods, you could read Nixon. If you crossed Nixon, you crossed Rose. If you crossed Rose, there was no court of appeal.

I liked and admired her from the start, partly because she responded so generously to my eagerness to be part of the Nixon entourage. "Don't bother to knock; go right in" was her usual response when I requested a moment of Nixon's time. I also liked her because she was funny, smart, and loyal. Her lively personality, warmth, golden-red hair, and creamy white skin reminded me so much of my mother that I felt not only needed but at home.

Rose and I remained warm friends until one dismal Watergate day in 1973. She had come under suspicion for playing a part in the famous 18½-minute tape gap. As harried and nervous counsel to the president, I wrote her a curt note telling her she would have to get her own lawyer. Worse, I signed the chilling, one-sentence epistle "Love, Len." We have since made up, but in the incomplete way of people who have suffered a failure of trust.

Other old-timers from Nixon's life casually filtered into mine as opportunities arose. In 1964, when Nixon heard I was heading to California to take depositions in a case, he suggested that I look up Bob Haldeman, then manager of the Los Angeles office of the

J. Walter Thompson advertising agency. He had been with Nixon in the 1960 and 1962 campaigns and knew him well. We met over lunch. Haldeman said that if Nixon tried again for the presidency, he had to do it differently. He had to be more selective in organizing staff and using his time. He had to realize that television was the key: looking good, rested, prepared, and, above all, cool. Today these are conventional campaign formulae; then they were fairly fresh.

In the same year, I was headed for Seattle in a utility-rate case when Nixon asked me to go through the same routine with John Ehrlichman. Ehrlichman's views were like Haldeman's, but Ehrlichman had a fine wit, which he displayed in telling me about his and Haldeman's loony adventures in campus politics and with Nixon. Later I would see that wit turn knife-like, when some unfortunate White House staffer dropped the ball.

Both men were friendly, intelligent, interested in Nixon and 1968—and noncommittal. They had already been through their struggles and disappointments with the Nixon-managed efforts of 1960 and 1962. They wanted to know whether Nixon could change his personal style, assemble a new staff, and learn to delegate authority.

Around the same time, I met Bob Finch, the third California veteran that Nixon asked me to see. Finch, whose natural warmth and decency emerged from under all the hard-boiled political chatter, was closest of the three to Nixon. Finch encouraged my belief that Nixon was something more than the sum of a bunch of nasty clichés.

Nixon began toying with the idea of making a run for the nomination in 1964. A Republican lawyer named Sherman Unger, who had been a Nixon advance man in 1960, was egging him on— though, in fairness to Unger, political cause and effect were impossible to sort out where Richard Nixon was concerned. Haldeman, Ehrlichman, and Finch were dubious about the on-and-off flirtation with the idea of a 1964 run: It was either too soon for him to re-emerge as a national candidate or too little and too late for a real campaign effort. Anyway, it was clearly the conservatives' year to run and Lyndon Johnson's year to win.

But in 1964 the skeptical Haldeman, Ehrlichman, and Finch were not yet part of Nixon's organization. It was therefore Nixon

alone who had to keep himself from antagonizing Republican conservatives by challenging Barry Goldwater in the spring of 1964. He
pulled himself back from the brink with inches to spare, announcing
his support for Goldwater's nomination shortly before the Republican convention in July.

A few weeks before the Republican convention, Nixon had
vaguely instructed me, "Just go out there and get the feel of it." I
was booked into a room in a downtown motel in San Francisco,
where there was actually nothing for me to do except hang out, look
at the Republicans assembled en masse, sample the city's splendid
food, and visit the suite of rooms rented at the Saint Francis Hotel
for a small Nixon delegation that included Haldeman, Ehrlichman,
and a former Nixon press secretary, Herb Klein.

They were in town ostensibly for reasons of nostalgia and because Nixon was to introduce Goldwater to the convention after
the nomination was completed. But they were also there to prepare
for the future. And who could say? Maybe something unpredictable
would happen in the combustible atmosphere that surrounded
Goldwater's imminent triumph over the Republican establishment.

We gathered in the Nixon suite to view the convention on television and await Nixon's arrival from New York, watchfully alert.
I, the lone newcomer but nonetheless an instant member of the
inner circle of a presidential candidate, was fascinated by every moment of my sudden plunge into politics. It was even more wondrous
because this was a time when politics and government still had the
power to promise a transformation of national life.

The televised convention proceedings started with a ninety-
minute reading of the platform, a stupefying ritual that allows time
for kibitzing, conniving, and tension building. This fake serenity
ended abruptly when, during President Eisenhower's farewell
speech to his fellow Republicans, he made a passing, almost paren-
thetical, swipe at the press. A commotion started in the Goldwater-
packed galleries. Horns honked, whistles blew, and clenched fists
were thurst angrily at the surrogates for all media, the news booths
that floated near the ceiling of the huge amphitheatre with their
taunting CBS, NBC, and ABC logos. An animal roar shook the Cow
Palace.

Animal roar number two took place soon afterward, while Nelson Rockefeller was speaking in support of a resolution to condemn Birchite extremism. The Goldwater troops in the galleries exploded in a sustained frenzy of rage, and the convention chairman's gaveling and pleading had not the slightest effect. Rockefeller stood there, grinning, tickled pink. All along, his only hope for derailing the Goldwater train had been somehow to provoke the Goldwaterites into riotous misbehavior that would demonstrate their craziness to the convention delegates and the country. Now it was happening.

In our suite at the Saint Francis, Haldeman jumped up and off went our little band, sprinting to waiting cars for a dash out to the Cow Palace to see whether a miracle might occur. During the six-mile, six-minute ride, communications buff Haldeman monitored the continuing tumult on a tiny portable television set, the first I had ever seen. When we arrived in the hall, the frenzied excitement was still in full storm.

My first live view of a political convention was a stunner. Ablaze with night-baseball lighting, the floor was a packed crowd of delegates, banners, balloons, newsmen, and every kind of convention paraphernalia. It was hectic, but not riotous. The galleries packed with Goldwater partisans were another story. An otherworldly cry of anger poured from the rocking, rolling, undulating mass of bodies, and it went on and on. If history could be changed by sheer noise, this was the moment. I couldn't remember a crowd sound to compare with it except for the pandemonium that followed Bobby Thomson's miracle home run at the Polo Grounds in September of 1951.

This time, no miracle occurred. The Goldwater marshals, spread out among the delegates and linked by walkie-talkies to coordinators watching the melee on TV in vans outside the hall, kept tight control of the floor. Gradually the uproar ran its course, the din subsided, and the exciting moment of possibility passed. The convention resumed and ran its predictable course.

The final moment of excitement and most enduring piece of political history came when Goldwater uttered his famous acceptance-speech declaration, "Extremism in the pursuit of liberty is no vice." Animal roar number three. In an instant Goldwater lost whatever minuscule chance he might have had to win the presidency. But his deliberately incautious declaration also ignited conservative fires that are still burning.

A careful observer would have noticed that during Goldwater's felo-de-se, Richard Nixon was almost literally sitting on his hands. Just minutes earlier, Nixon had introduced the nominee to the delegates in a pick-up-all-the-marbles "unity" oration painstakingly crafted with an eye to the inevitable outcome in November and the opportunity it would present four years later.

I had stayed in touch with Beverly Lourd, my old girlfriend and *Brooklyn Law Review* colleague from the late 1940s, who was now a well-known radical lawyer in San Francisco under her married name of Beverly Axelrod. Beverly and her husband, Marshal Axelrod, were the only people I knew in San Francisco apart from the Nixon group, so I divided my time. Mornings, I drifted alone around the convention meetings and lobbies, "getting the feel of things." Afternoons I went sightseeing with Beverly, who showed off the city like a proud parent. Evenings I hung out with the Nixonites at the Saint Francis. Afterward, Beverly would take me to meet her friends, mostly civil rights activists. We would listen to jazz, drive around, and debate politics. I was something of a carnival freak to Beverly's friends—a Nixon "insider" who was a pal of Mother Courage. But the spirit was not hostile; our disagreements stayed civil and friendly. Thus when Beverly asked me whether I could get her and her friends passes to the Cow Palace so that they could take in the big show, I—still a sucker for a left hook—agreed.

These tickets, plus others similarly inveigled out of unwary Republicans and secret sympathizers, were used to stage nationally televised civil rights demonstrations in the Cow Palace and the convention plaza. They were actually more like riots, marked by noisy interruptions, manhandling of demonstrators, screams, forced ejections, arrests. It finally began to occur to me that Beverly was something more problematic than just a particularly energetic do-gooder.

Looking back at the convention, I can see that the two incidents —the torrent of right-wing hate during Rockefeller's speech and Beverly's notion of a legitimate civil rights demonstration—mark the ideological boundaries of a time in the country's political history. Categories were established at San Francisco that have stayed drawn since then. There were the swelling demands for justice, along with an expanding notion of what justice demanded, and there were the anxieties and angers of millions of southerners and, later, middle-class whites. This fault line was blurred for a while by Goldwater's failed presidential candidacy. But, like the cleavages exposed by *Sullivan* and *Hill*, in time it became clear.

Back from the convention, I hunted talent. In 1965 I recruited Tom Evans out of a playground sandbox in Brooklyn Heights, where we were both babysitting our toddlers on the weekend. He was Arrow Collar handsome, the quintessential WASP, a Silver Star hero of the Korean War, and a leader of New York Republicans for Nixon in 1960, an act of considerable bravery in Nelson Rockefeller's well-policed domain. Evans joined my litigation department and became the informal administrator of Nixon's 1968 campaign.

John Sears, another of my litigation assistants, was a baby-faced Catholic intellectual made prematurely old by hard times and family tragedy. He had a penchant for after-hours metaphysical musings and a concrete genius for politics. I brought him by Nixon's office when he was being interviewed for a job at the law firm. Nixon spotted Sears's talent in roughly four minutes and drafted him, in 1965, as his full-time political assistant.

Nixon's first personal pick, hired in 1965, was the conservative editorial writer Pat Buchanan, an energetic young man who bashed his typewriter keys as if they were a platoon of Jane Fondas. Nixon soon balanced Buchanan with a moderate, Ray Price, who had been the editorial-page editor of the recently defunct *New York Herald Tribune*. Bill Safire, a New York publicist, became the balance wheel of what would be the most celebrated writing threesome in presidential history.

I remember my first meeting with Safire, in 1965, at Nixon's suggestion ("You'll like him. He's with Rockefeller now, but he's smart and funny and important to us, so get to know him"). Safire turned out to be a wisecracking New Yorker with an against-the-grain manner and a taste in clothes—garish plaid sports jackets and thick rubber-soled shoes—that seemed designed to cause heartburn and start fights. He was, as Nixon described him, smart, feisty, and funny. He was also full of instruction, puns, and inside-baseball gossip about New York politicians like Rockefeller, John Lindsay,

Bill Rogers, Jack Wells, and Len Hall, as well as about Nixon's prospects for 1968.

Each of the three writers picked by Nixon had a different style, and each was willing to blend his words with those of the others when Nixon wanted a bouillabaisse.

During a lunchtime stroll on Broad Street in 1966 I ran into my old saxophone-playing colleague from Henry Jerome's band, Alan Greenspan, who took me to lunch at the Bankers Club to talk about his interest in commodities futures and political futures, particularly Richard Nixon's. In due course I introduced the two men. Greenspan and I had a number of talks during that mating time. One I remember clearly—a long dinner at Oscar's, a darkly overdecorated and overpriced French restaurant on one of the narrow side streets that snake around the Wall Street area. Even then, Greenspan was impressively obscure, uttering perfectly formed sentences about money and finance that were largely unintelligible to me. What came across clearly, though, was his feeling for the poetics of an arcane topic, the federal budget. Talking about such stuff as historical numbers, fixed commitments, anticipations of future revenues, and the small area for discretionary federal spending, Greenspan brought the bewildering subject briefly to life with the nice metaphor of the budget as the "central nervous system" of America's politics. He helped me understand how the trained eye of an economist, like the fingers of a clinician, can detect hidden strengths and pathologies in the country's economic entrails.

I appreciated the fact that over the years Greenspan, like me, had made a useful connection between art and politics—in his case, between music and numbers. After meeting Greenspan and hearing the budget spiel, Nixon was also impressed and asked him to join Arthur Burns, a Columbia University economist, as one of Nixon's informal advisers.

Greenspan later brought a young colleague (everyone was young in those days) named Martin Anderson to see me. Anderson, like Greenspan an Ayn Rand acolyte, was a Columbia University economist who had just published a critical study of federal housing policy, *The Federal Bulldozer*. He became director of our issues staff and drafted a blizzard of position papers, some of which, like the proposal for an all-volunteer army, later became law.

A stray event brought us another important amateur. One of

Rose Mary Woods's many duties was to supervise the twice-daily mail delivery and see that it was not only processed and answered but read with care, so that the important stuff did not wash away in the effluvia. In 1967 Rose Woods spotted a nugget and sent it to me as chief assayer of odds and ends.

It was a letter from William Gavin, a thirty-one-year-old high school teacher. "Dear Mr. Nixon," it said,

May I offer two suggestions concerning your plans for 1968?

1. Run. You can win. Nothing can happen to you, politically speaking, that is worse than what has happened to you. Ortega y Gasset in his *The Revolt of the Masses* says: "These ideas are the only genuine ideas; the ideas of the shipwrecked. All the rest is rhetoric, posturing, farce. He who does not really feel himself lost, is lost without remission. . . ." You, in effect, are "lost"; that is why you are the only political figure with the vision to see things the way they are and not as Leftist or Rightist kooks would have them be. Run. You will win.

This first suggestion was enough to tell me that here was someone who not only understood the weird metaphysics of Richard Nixon but was able to cram it into a one-paragraph microchip. Gavin's second suggestion was also striking:

2. A tip for television: Instead of those wooden performances beloved by politicians . . . why not have live press conferences as your campaign on television? People will see you daring all, not asking and answering phony "questions" made up by your staff. . . .

I invited Gavin to visit me in New York. He later told me he had expected to see a Wall Street WASP in a blue pinstriped suit and was surprised to find a street-corner type like himself (in a blue pinstriped suit). Gavin was a pleasant-faced young man with a visible Irish Catholic sensibility. He reminisced with me over lunch at Whyte's on Fulton Street about the experiences we shared as city-bred strangers who loved mainstream jazz.

He agreed to send me, as the spirit moved him, anything he

wanted to say about the campaign. Several hundred one-liners later, Gavin was invited to a Christmas party at the Nixon apartment on Fifth Avenue and was startled by Nixon's memory trick of greeting him as "the one-liner man." A few months later I brought Gavin into the campaign full time as a speechwriter and luncheon companion.

He contributed, among other things, the elegaic "I see a face . . ." portion of Nixon's acceptance speech in Miami Beach. After that he rode in Nixon's personal campaign plane, landed in the administration, and eventually went on to work as all-purpose assistant to House Republican Minority Leader Bob Michel. He provided Michel with speeches, policy advice, and, of course, one-liners. A jazz fan, he became a one-man congressional lobby for Willis Conover, the Voice of America's voice of jazz.

And that was how the campaign machinery was put together— part Lego set and part jigsaw puzzle, one piece attached to another, until one day the contraption shuddered to life.

In the months before the 1966 elections, Nixon's time was mainly spent on the road, campaigning and gathering due bills from candidates and Republican party leaders. Because of the "loser" tag that he carried after his defeats in 1960 and 1962, he had to do well at electioneering this time around.

Nixon also intended to play the role of president-in-exile, preparing for the call to return from the New York wilderness to national leadership. He wanted to establish himself as counsel to the Republican party, not just campaigning for his client-candidates all over the country but appropriating to himself authority to shape national strategy. So he alternated his trips to East Anonymous, Illinois, with visits to European and Asian capitals and meetings with foreign and defense policy strategists.

In this connection Nixon once took me to lunch at the Recess Club, on Broad Street, with Hungarian physicist Edward Teller. Teller brought along his impressive ego, near-impenetrable accent, healthy appetite, and stock of pseudoscientific, mostly commercial ideas about the untapped resources of New Zealand, which he said could make their developers filthy rich. After lunch, Nixon and I deposited Teller in a taxicab and walked back to the Nixon Mudge offices. I remarked to Nixon about the large piles of dandruff sitting like epaulets on Teller's shoulders. "That's not dandruff," Nixon said solemnly. "It's Strontium 90."

In jet planes crossing the country on solo business trips, I would slide into the certainty that I was to fulfill my own (not to mention my mother's) early ambitions for great achievement. On top of my litigation load, I became the all-around campaign pest, plunging headlong into everything. I read, wrote, and talked politics nonstop, recruiting and proselytizing, extracting from my litigation associates the last drop of political assistance and bringing coffee and confidence each day to the handful of Nixon troops scattered around 20 Broad Street. I had stumbled on one of the world's surest homeopathic cures for depression.

During those years I came to know more of the odd pieces of Nixon's personality. He seemed never to forget a political face or—for better or for worse—a friend or enemy. He had experienced virtually every sort of political circumstance and had developed the ability to retrieve bits of information from this crowded past and make useful connections like an advanced computer. As a result, the moment someone opened his or her mouth and began to say something political, Nixon knew exactly where the speaker was heading and where the speech would end. From courtesy or necessity, Nixon had to hear his visitor out. The waiting made him acutely uncomfortable—to the point of visible pain, verbal discontinuity, and a profound aversion to having political conversations at all unless they were absolutely essential.

He came to prefer talking with just a few people, like his immediate family, fellow sports buffs, and foreign leaders who at least had new information to pass along. Also among his preferred companions were trustworthy, politically sentient (and largely silent) listeners, to whom he could draft and redraft his ideas via the rambling, repetitious, stream-of-consciousness monologues with which the world would later become familiar.

He found the tape recorder another useful device for recording events, impressions, and ideas, and for translating written speech drafts into texts bearing the cadence of his own speaking voice. But his closest friend was the always available, always compliant, always silent yellow pad. It not only enabled him to conduct a disciplined conversation with himself; it also served as a kind of door through which he could walk and shut out the world. When Nixon took out his yellow pad and unscrewed his pen, you knew it was time to move on.

These idiosyncrasies were just a few results of the mysterious process by which Nixon had somehow figured out how to make the disparate parts of his personality work. I knew there had to be much more tinkering in order to transform such an intensely private man into a successful public figure.

I remember other anomalies during those early comeback years. On one bizarre occasion on the road, in Minneapolis, Nixon was due to make an evening speech to the Hennepin County Republican faithful. When we reached the convention hall, Nixon decided to avoid the crowds around the elevator and walk up the stairs to the banquet room. We ducked into the stairwell, then found that we were locked in—and locked out, behind soundproof fire doors. We ran up, down, and around for ten minutes, trying to find someone to rescue us. Here was my first real-life political test, and—drenched in sweat, close to panic—I was hopeless. Nixon, the crisis veteran, kept his cool (barely) and asked me to help him bang away on the ground-floor door with our fists while shouting for rescue. It finally arrived. My career as an advance man was ended. Only afterward did I wonder why a veteran politician like Nixon would duck a crowd of admirers and thereby risk disaster.

I was dismayed when Nixon was foolishly suckered—or so I thought—into making careless "Old Nixon" lapses. Once when campaigning in New Jersey he gratuitously urged that Rutgers, a state university, discharge Professor Eugene Genovese for having made a pro–Viet Cong speech. I wondered how he could do something so stupid; but of course it was quite deliberate. Nixon was simply playing to a constituency slightly different from the Friends of Leonard Garment. I was later to learn that he delighted in irritating the media with acts of lumpen "tastelessness." "So much for their fucking sophistication," Nixon would say. In time, this and other elements of "complexity" would make him an object of grudging admiration by many intellectuals.

After the Genovese incident, Safire, Sears, and I drafted a redemptive speech, which Nixon delivered at the University of Rochester. It managed both to maintain his position on Genovese and mount a general defense of academic freedom. President Eisenhower wrote Nixon a letter saying the Rochester speech was too liberal. Nixon pointedly sent a copy of the letter to Safire and me.

Another time, at a press conference after a speech to the Boys Clubs of America, Nixon repeated the ludicrous charge by the organization's public relations man that the Marxist DuBois Club had ripped off the Boys Clubs' prestigious name. On my way to work I read Nixon's comment in the *New York Post* and rode up in the elevator filled with fantasies of barging into his office with "How in God's name could you do it? You've just gone and pissed away two years of hard work!" But I settled for a mumbled complaint to Nixon, who shrugged off the incident: "Well, Len, that's what happens when you listen to one of those damned press agents. Don't worry, it will pass." So it did, and—so brief is public memory—faster than I had thought possible. The Nixon haters had a few moments of happy nostalgia, there were a couple of columns of reflexive satire, and finis. The press line was now the cheerful "New Nixon," not the old reactionary from California.

This burgeoning new image of Nixon's brought me unanticipated experiences. One day in the summer of 1966, the black comedian Dick Gregory asked to see Nixon—God knows why—but settled, agreeably, for me. He wanted to say nothing in particular but a lot about everything to someone who was prepared to listen. This I did for twelve or more continuous hours of a brilliant, funny, touching, transcendentally strange monologue that alluded to war, poverty, race, space and time travel, extraterrestrial life, extrasensory perception, fasting, running, yoga, prebirth and postmortem infinity, karma, communication among animals, flowers, and trees, and the correct approach to the use of drugs. That was for openers.

Grace and the kids were on Cape Cod for the summer, so Gregory and I met in my living room, whose huge skylight provided a backdrop of clouds, planes, birds, and changing light, from late-afternoon sun to middle-of-the-night stars. I respectfully decline to say what we ate, drank, and/or smoked, but we managed to stay at it until early the next morning, when we tumbled out onto State Street, Gregory still talking, both of us famished, two men desperately seeking a diner.

After that, nothing about the whirlwind of sixties nostrums could surprise or shock me.

In spite of all my running around, I was marginal to Nixon's role in the 1966 congressional campaigns. People of different temperament from mine had to do the careful job of scheduling Nixon through the nooks and crannies of the various races. His principal helpers were Rose Mary Woods, John Sears, John Whittaker, and Pat Buchanan. They picked targets, assembled schedules, arranged transportation, did advance work for local rallies, distributed speeches, press releases, and newspaper columns, and attended to the growing mountain of political detritus that campaign momentum produces.

Bill Safire was, as usual, in and out—an idea here, a phrase there. But in the final days of the campaign, Safire played the key role in a drama that had as big a part as any in Nixon's successful pursuit of the presidency.

In 1966 Nixon's opportunities were Lyndon Johnson's headaches —crime, inflation, and the Great Society. By contrast, the situation in Vietnam was difficult for the hawkish Nixon to exploit. Nixon's opportunity on Vietnam, and the campaign team's moment in the sun, came when the October Disease, that presidential compulsion to pull a last-minute rabbit out of a hat, struck President Johnson just before the congressional elections. A conference of Asian nations was scheduled for mid-October in Manila, and Johnson announced that he would attend. The resulting Manila Communiqué was published in *The New York Times* in October 1966. Before the day was over, Safire read the document, spotted an opening, and went to work. He typed out a critique of the communiqué, identifying as its weakest point the proposal for "mutual withdrawal," arguably premature, of U.S. and North Vietnamese troops from South Vietnam. The Viet Cong would be left in place, and, Safire argued, they were fully capable of destroying the Saigon government. Next, Safire drove to New Jersey to see Nixon, who was campaigning there with Buchanan. Safire collected additional comments from the two of them, then withdrew to a New Jersey hotel and dictated to Rose Mary Woods a "Letter to the President," concluding with a series of questions about the Manila Communiqué.

Nixon vetoed the "open letter" idea as too gimmicky, but he

agreed with the substance of Safire's draft. After much Nixon fiddling and Safire redrafting, there emerged another draft, "Appraisal of Manila." But what to do with it?

Safire knew Harrison Salisbury, the assistant managing editor of *The New York Times*, and pulled out all the stops to persuade him to run the full text of Nixon's "Appraisal." Salisbury told Safire there was a chance the text could be run, but only if it was delivered before that day's afternoon deadline. For the next four hours, great excitement seized the area around Nixon's law-firm office. I watched Nixon, Safire, and Buchanan work over the final text and redraft pages. Secretaries ran back and forth. Messengers hovered. The next day in the *Times*, backing up a page one story about Nixon's response to the Manila Communiqué, was the full text of Nixon's "Appraisal."

It is rare for the full text of anything, including presidential speeches, to run in *The New York Times*. When the paper does run a full statement, particularly by a private person, the message to political professionals is, "This is very important." President Johnson read *The New York Times* in his White House bed first thing in the morning and had a purple fit. First he had his fit privately. Then he had it publicly, in a televised press conference. Although the true target of his presidential rage was the *Times*, his public target could only be Richard Nixon. So Johnson denounced Nixon bitterly and at length as a "chronic campaigner [who] never realized what was going on even when he had an official office. . . ."

The Johnson staff cringed. Mrs. Johnson cringed. The country cringed. Nixon and his people were stunned by this monumental break. Nixon, of all people, was now cast in the unaccustomed role of public-spirited underdog, manfully biting his lip while offering charitable words of sympathy to a "tired" President Johnson.

My only contribution during this historic episode was to put Nixon together with Mike Wallace, who chartered a plane and flew to New Hampshire to get fresh Nixon footage for CBS News after Johnson blew up. I also suggested, via Rose Mary Woods, that Nixon gently allude to his 1962 press calamity: "I know what it is to be under pressure and tired, and how easy and human it is to lose control for a moment."

Nixon at his pious best.

There was now daylight, and Nixon ran for it. Lyndon Johnson had made him national leader of the Republican party; the coming election was now not just a bunch of congressional and state contests but "Johnson versus Nixon." Nixon was chosen by the Republican National Committee to deliver the Republicans' televised election-eve speech on November 5, 1966. If the Republicans did as well as he expected on Election Day, he would get double the credit.

The 1966 elections were a triumph for Nixon beyond his expectations. Republican gains were bigger than predicted, and the candidates Nixon had campaigned for won pretty much across the board. On election night, about forty staffers, volunteers, and friends were invited to watch the returns in a suite at the Drake Hotel in New York. As results came in, Nixon, sequestered in a bedroom, kept a tally of the state-by-state results brought to him by John Sears. Nixon occasionally emerged to share his growing excitement with the group: "Have you seen those numbers? We're on the move. Have another drink on the house, everyone." Calls came in from grateful winners—including Governor-elect Ronald Reagan, who had just trounced Nixon's 1962 nemesis, Governor Pat Brown. Nixon relaxed enough to place a call to Walter Cronkite, on the air for CBS, and conduct a live assessment of the election's significance.

One by one the senior members of the staff were invited to visit Nixon, who was alone, stretched out on the bed, a phone in one hand and a highball in the other. For each visitor there was a personal word of thanks and encouragement. For me, the message was warm, but what I remember best was the strange part. Nixon, by then reasonably well oiled (it didn't take much to do the trick), said reflectively, "You're never going to make it in politics, Len. You just don't know how to lie."

I was bothered by his assessment but merely tucked it away with all the other things I did not understand about myself. Nixon knew that history's successful politicians are natural liars; lying in politics is a basic skill, like a strong left hand in stride piano. Looking back, I'm grateful that Nixon reached that judgment as soon as he did. It saved me a lot of trouble. He would have done better had he realized that he, too, fell short when it came to dissimulating with skill.

Among the political advice with which I continually pelted Nixon, I told him he should shore up his president-in-exile posture by resisting demands for comments on political trivia. He should, I said, avoid overexposure. Nixon went me one better: The Sunday before the 1966 elections, during a CBS interview, he announced one of his "moratoriums"—this time a "holiday from politics for at least six months."

What this meant was that other presidential candidates, particularly the front-runner, Governor George Romney, would be allowed time to put their feet in their mouths while Nixon dined with the famous in the great capitals of the world, letting pictures with prime ministers take the place of boring or dangerous words about the economy and Vietnam.

He went to Israel. A cocktail reception was given for him, but only one prominent invitee showed up—an Israeli general named Itzhak Rabin, whose empty schedule and polite curiosity earned him a place in Nixon's permanent memory bank under the heading "Friends." A couple of years afterward, Rabin, as Israel's ambassador to the U.S., did not find it difficult to establish a close working relationship with the newly inaugurated President Nixon. Rabin's successes in Washington, in turn, contributed to his eventual selection as prime minister of Israel.

For the remainder of 1966 and into early 1967, we geared up for the final stages of the presidential nomination contest. Some organizational activities went smoothly: Political managers, local leaders, and money would be there when needed. But Nixon still had to find a commander-in-chief for his Army of the Potomac. This search became his single most important, almost obsessive, concern. He knew that his biggest mistake in 1960 had been running his own campaign. It demoralized his nominal managers, sent confusing signals to his organization, and exhausted Nixon himself. Worse, although Nixon was highly disciplined when analyzing abstract issues, he was deeply ambivalent when faced with personal deci-sions. He made costly mistakes when he listened to his inner voice, which did not always have his best interests at heart. One critical consequence of Nixon's 1960 performance was that the men he wanted most for the 1968 national campaign, like Bob Haldeman and John Ehrlichman, refused to join until they were convinced that Nixon had kicked the habit of grabbing the controls at critical moments.

So Nixon tried to find a heavyweight manager, but with no luck. From time to time he would voice his frustrations to me. I would hear about the former attorney general Bill Rogers, Nixon's pal from the early Eisenhower days, a man with acknowledged ability to mediate debates between Nixon and Nixon and to make binding campaign decisions. Rogers was now senior partner of Rogers & Wells, a prosperous Wall Street law firm. "Rogers won't take it on," said Nixon. "He's the best, but he likes making all that money. And his wife would kill him."

Then there was the former Republican national chairman Len Hall: "Well, Hall has finally decided he's going with Romney—a hopeless candidate." I tried to comfort Nixon on the subject of Hall: "I think we're lucky. It sounds to me like he's getting old and out of touch." So Nixon continued his scouting and tryouts through 1967. Dr. Gaylord Parkinson, a Reagan manager from California, came and went quickly; the former congressman Bob Ellsworth of Kansas, very smart but too nice a man for the job, was temporarily thrown into the breach.

Even as Nixon was recruiting among the usual suspects, the man who eventually took charge and made victory possible for Nixon in 1968 walked unobtrusively into the campaign through the front door of Nixon Mudge. John Newton Mitchell was the senior partner of a prominent New York municipal bond firm, Caldwell Mitchell & Trimble, which merged with Nixon Mudge at the end of 1966. Mitchell was a Fordham Law School graduate who had never run a political campaign, but he had campaigned successfully for legal business and produced billions of dollars of state and municipal financing for a blue-chip list of clients that included governors, may-ors, and investment bankers around the country.

His national prominence was based on his knack for devising

new ways of raising money through the use of public credit. One of his satisfied customers was New York's governor, Nelson Rockefeller, for whom he invented the "moral obligation" bond—a financial instrument that produced huge amounts of money for Rockefeller's pet projects and even huger headaches for the future generations of New Yorkers who had to live with the unsecured state debt thereby accumulated. Because of his experience in mining money for public projects, Mitchell was steeped in operational politics. He could look at a map and tell you the names of the individuals who exercised political power down to the precinct level, for these were the people whose cooperation he needed for his financing work.

Mitchell announced that he was coming to our expanding law firm in order to build a bigger bond practice, which he did, but I think he came primarily because of the larger possibilities of a political partnership with Richard Nixon, who he knew, from his life in the heart of American politics, had a substantial chance to become president. This prospect, I thought and still believe, was exciting to the publicly unexcitable John Mitchell.

Most Americans who were alive in the 1970s remember at least vaguely what John Mitchell looked like. His most prominent feature was a pipe clenched between his teeth. Slightly paunchy, slightly bald, with a fine Roman nose poised over jowls that were set into rolling motion by his characteristic chuckle, Mitchell passed unnoticed in a Broad Street crowd. His manner was controlled. He rarely raised his voice, preferring throw-away sarcasms to express disagreement. An old hip accident made for a limp that looked like a swagger. A small neurological injury produced a hand tremor that he concealed by constantly holding, filling, scraping, and tamping down his pipe. (His wife, Martha, also contributed to the tremor.)

There was an engaging informality and disarming modesty of manner about John Mitchell that made me like him from the start. But it required the determination of a dentist to draw secrets out of him, particularly if they showed him in a good light. He was, for instance, the commander of the Pacific Theatre Naval Squadron that included John F. Kennedy's *PT-109*. His demeanor and history drew powerful people into his orbit. He exuded a calm, confident, professional competence, a quality as rare as it is valuable in the hyperventilated atmosphere of politics.

Though most of the events in political campaigns have many fathers and mothers, Nixon's selecting Mitchell as campaign manager was my idea. Five years later, after the 1972 presidential election, the newly reelected Nixon sent me a nostalgic letter in which he remembered the process: "I also recall that you were the one who had the brilliant idea that John Mitchell could take over the campaign in 1968, a job which he was superbly fitted for and which he carried out with such distinction." In retrospect, of course, it is not clear just how brilliant the idea really was, particularly for Mitchell.

I remember the Mitchell moment. It was the end of 1967, and we were in Nixon's office. He was nattering to me about the perennial campaign manager problem. Suddenly the lightbulb clicked on over my head and I announced, "The answer to our problem is sitting twenty feet away from us, in the next office, a guy who looks, walks, and sounds like a campaign manager, knows more about politics than all the other guys you've been talking about, and his name is John Mitchell." Nixon reacted by doing something he did only when he heard a fresh thought about politics—in other words, very rarely. He abruptly stood up—shot up, actually—and started pacing the room. Mitchell. But of course. The purloined letter. We talked briefly about Mitchell's qualifications, particularly the fact that his membership in the law firm ensured loyalty, but Nixon did not need much instruction or argument.

"But will he do it, Len?"

"Certainly. My guess is he had precisely this in mind when he agreed to merge."

"All right, sound him out. But do it gently. Then we'll see how it goes."

The occasion came a few weeks later at a black-tie dinner held at New York's University Club to celebrate, some months after the fact, the merger of Mitchell's firm with ours. It was a robust event, loaded with food, drink, big talk, and high hopes. Responding to an exuberant toast to his future, Nixon said, "And if I become President, Garment goes on the Supreme Court." Promises, promises.

Toward the evening's end, I spotted Mitchell weaving his way to the men's room. I followed him. There, standing in the next stall, I popped the question: "Say, John, how would you feel about managing a presidential campaign?" Pipe in mouth, Mitchell leaned back and said, "Are you out of your fucking mind, Garment?" Which, I learned, was Mitchell's way of saying yes. The rest of the story is in all the books. Nixon assigned Mitchell the test of assembling the team for the primary in Wisconsin—which turned out to be natural terrain for Mitchell, who had recently done bond work in the state. He displayed his formidable political and administrative skills. That was it, though the formal announcement that Mitchell would run the campaign was not made until shortly before the primaries.

Mitchell was right for the job because he was not a man to suffer interference with his professional prerogatives from anyone, Nixon included. This was what Nixon wanted. Mitchell was also Nixon's professional equal, or better, inside the firm, and he made clear that he would not hesitate to return to full-time bond work if his leadership was undermined or his public autonomy as campaign manager impaired.

Ultimately, John Mitchell's failing was that despite his modest manner, he was not really a modest man. Although he talked self-deprecatingly, he had a fatal belief in his ability to handle any job even remotely related to politics. He was in the habit of making long lists, thirty to forty items, and giving each the same degree of attention. Mitchell thoroughly confused the substantive complexities of governing with the roustabout world of operational politics and thought he was master of both.

It is true that just after the 1968 election, when Nixon asked him to become attorney general, Mitchell resisted. The reason, though, was not any doubt in Mitchell's mind about his professional capacity to serve as the nation's chief law enforcement official; rather, the problem was his concern about his wife's emotional stability. Nixon, thinking he needed Mitchell to run the Justice Department as much as he needed him to manage the campaign, deployed everyone, including me, to overcome Mitchell's resistance.

Nixon succeeded and Mitchell got in over his head, tragically so. He did many generous and useful things about which history has been silent. But he was asked to serve as political adviser to a very political president and at the same time fulfill the constitutional responsibilities of an attorney general; he was given, in other words, the task of reconciling irreconcilables. He was not nearly so tough as most people (including himself) thought, and in the end he was no match for his own bad judgment, his president's worst side, and the small army of Chuck Colsons, Gordon Liddys, and John Deans scurrying around the halls of the Nixon administration.

In 1967 Nixon's campaign picked up speed, and my all-purpose profundity, dispensed to anyone who would listen, was "The man and the times have finally come together." This was so in ways I did not understand back then.

The years of Nixon's comeback constituted one of the most confusing times in American history. They had some of everything: assassinations of national leaders, wars, the Pill, pot, peyote, LSD, civil rights, women's rights, communications and sexual revolutions, campus demonstrations and violence, fire and death in the cities, generational convulsions, and the splendor of a manned space flight. Abbie Hoffman and the rest of the Chicago Seven gave a loony, long-running seminar on public disorder in Judge Julius Hoffman's courtroom; the exponents of Black Power—Stokely, Huey, and Rap—scared the wits out of white America. There was no shortage of social commentators to explain what was happening, but most of us stood around, mouths agape, mumbling about "national crack-up" and a "crumbling center."

As it happened, the campaign years 1967 and 1968 were the most frenetic of the 1960s, as much Marx Brothers farce (particularly the stateroom sequence in A Night at the Opera) and Greek tragedy as conventional presidential politics. In the eye of the storm, Nixon clung unwaveringly to his centrist strategy and made adjustments only when the need was compellingly clear.

I, on the other hand, ran around like Chicken Little on speed. I continually inveighed against the campaign's passivity and its failure to react decisively (and, as would have been the case, catastrophically) to events. I lobbied for new programs and big speeches and wrote excited memoranda on breaking news and long-range projects. Years later, during one of those famous taped conversations with Nixon, Ehrlichman described me, with justification, as a "nuclear overreactor." I suppose my principal contribution was to introduce a leavening touch of disorder to a tightly corseted enterprise. Perhaps this was no small thing; as we now know, Nixon needed everything available to win the presidency, including at least one strange soul like me.

In January 1968, a month before Nixon formally announced his candidacy, the New York newspaper *Newsday* ran an article on the activities of the "New Nixon" team. The piece was accompanied by a large photograph, taken in Nixon's New York apartment, of the younger principals of that team. In the photo, Nixon stands in the front of an Indian-file line of young men. He is avuncular, happily proud of his harvest, and looking—well, sort of "New." First in the line of determinedly cheerful campaigners is me; then Ray Price, Martin Anderson, Dwight Chapin, Pat Buchanan, and Tom Evans. A smaller photo shows the Washington campaign staff, including John Sears, Bob Ellsworth, former *Fortune* magazine writer Richard Whalen, and a quiet fellow named Drew Mason.

The point of the photo and the article was that Nixon had assembled a fresh staff, and that everything about his campaign would be new and spontaneous. There was no John Mitchell in the picture, or other heavyweight elders of the effort. And no decidedly nonspontaneous media technicians. At the time the *Newsday* picture was taken, Bob Haldeman and John Ehrlichman were still on the West Coast, waiting to see how the preliminaries came out.

One man in the picture, Dick Whalen, was another city boy recruited by Nixon to the writing staff. A thirty-six-year-old Irish Catholic from working-class Queens, Whalen already had a distinguished career in political and economic journalism. Stubby, energetic, and opinionated, Whalen peered out at the world through thick glasses that were anything but rose-colored. Unlike Ray Price, Whalen was not a close friend of mine, but we had important things in common besides our urban bloodlines. Most important, we both felt the Vietnam War was hopeless, distracting the country from dealing with the Soviet Union and preventing us from coming to terms with domestic problems caused by deformities of race, culture, and economics.

Whalen's intelligence and passion seemed well suited to developing a campaign rhetoric without clichés and appropriate to the storms whipping around us. We both wanted Nixon to think and talk more seriously about matters of substance, and Whalen, even more than I, refused to roll over and take no for an answer. So we worked together well and closely. The strategy was simple: I did the downfield blocking while Whalen supplied polished and forceful campaign prose that reflected his angers and beliefs.

One day in September 1967 I read a newspaper account of a speech given by Daniel Patrick Moynihan to the board of the Americans for Democratic Action. It caught my eye because it was titled "The Politics of Stability," a subject of relevance after a summer of urban riots and a spreading backlash that had already made George Wallace a significant actor in the politics of 1968. The speech, read twenty-five years later, stands up extraordinarily well. Moynihan argued that it was past time for liberal Democrats to recognize their responsibility for dealing with the national crisis of stability and to make alliances with political conservatives who shared this concern. Liberals, in Moynihan's view, had to divest themselves of the idea that the nation, especially its cities, could be run from agencies in Washington. And they had to overcome their destructive condescension on the issue of race, which took the form of "sticking up for and explaining away anything, however outrageous, which Negroes, individually or collectively, might do."

Moynihan concluded with eerie prescience that the time had come for confronting the realities of black and white. "It will not be pretty," he said, but if liberals did not lead under these circumstances, the direction of events would fall to those "whose purpose [is] more to destroy than build."

In 1967 Moynihan's fellow Democrats were not prepared to listen, but I was happy to do so. I wrote to Moynihan and expressed interest in the speech. He sent me a cordial note and a copy of his reading text, which I turned over to Whalen. Each of us wrote to Nixon recommending that he use his coming speech to the National Association of Manufacturers to echo and elaborate on Moynihan's ideas.

Whalen drafted Nixon's N.A.M. speech, which argued that the failures of 1960s liberalism stemmed from the fact that people had despaired of their individual efforts and turned to government to protect them; the results were disappointing and deeply flawed. Nixon called on the business community to recognize the serious threat posed by the nation's social crisis and to begin dealing with the economic needs and aspirations of the urban poor in a systematic way. The speech contained not a single applause line and was received in pin-drop silence. When Nixon finished, he was literally cheered by the large crowd of usually stolid businessmen.

The speech helped organize Nixon's thinking about social issues and made him more comfortable talking about them. Its most important effect, however, was to establish the link between Nixon and Moynihan that eventually brought Moynihan to the White House as Nixon's urban adviser. Less than a year after the N.A.M. speech, Nixon was asking Moynihan's private advice on his inaugural address, and Moynihan, echoing the words that first brought him to Nixon's attention, was telling him, "The black poor desperately need to be reassured that you have no intention of running away from the great goal . . . of a free and open society in which equality of opportunity for blacks increasingly has the outcome of equal achievement as well." Nixon's inaugural address contained that message.

The subject of race was one of the large internal footballs of the campaign. Despite the objections of hard-liners, Nixon addressed racial issues in calm and sober terms, though there was no shortage of law-and-order boilerplate. The most heated internal debate about race took place just after Martin Luther King's assassination in 1968, when Nixon had to decide whether to attend the funeral. Most of his political strategists, as well as President Eisenhower, opposed his going, fearing the loss of southern delegates.

Bill Safire, Ray Price, Dick Whalen, and I were of one mind: Nixon, whether for moral or political reasons, had to go. We talked to him. Safire reminded him of the damage he had sustained in the campaign of 1960 when Dr. King was jailed: Kennedy responded, Nixon did not, and Nixon's friend and supporter Jackie Robinson walked out of the campaign, along with masses of potential black votes. Nixon ended the discussion by phoning John Mitchell and telling him the "libs" had carried the day. He would attend the funeral—but would not march in the postfuneral procession. When the event finally took place, he went to the funeral and began the march, then quietly dropped out as the parade turned a corner.

The other favorite debating topic was Vietnam. In late February 1968, Nixon asked me to get the writers together to start thinking about a Vietnam speech. Whalen and I thought Nixon should start talking about the end of our involvement in the war; Price and Buchanan thought otherwise. But all of us agreed it was still too soon to judge the effects of the recent Tet Offensive, not to mention too risky to try to outfox Lyndon Johnson.

Volunteers turned up with offers to help Nixon find a way out of Vietnam. One was Nixon's friend Elmer Bobst, who since 1965 had been urging Nixon to separate himself from the war. Another individual who appeared in 1967 was Roger Hilsman, President Kennedy's assistant secretary for Far Eastern Affairs and now a professor at Columbia University, who visited with Whalen and me over drinks at the Biltmore Bar and offered a detailed "peace with honor" strategy for Nixon. We passed Hilsman's ideas along to Nixon, but there was no reaction.

Then, in mid-March 1968, Nixon decided to make a radio speech outlining a new position on Vietnam. He would present a plan to reduce the American commitment without severing it, while drawing the Soviet Union into negotiations on a broad agenda that would include Soviet assistance in ending the war. The speech was scheduled for delivery Saturday night, March 30. At noon that day, we were notified by the networks that President Johnson had asked for television time for Sunday night. Nixon naturally canceled his own speech. Johnson, in his televised address, outlined his own peace proposal for Vietnam—and added, as a postscript, that he would not run for reelection in 1968.

For Democrats, Johnson's announcement turned the world upside down, at least temporarily. But the Nixon campaign rolled along, and Nixon's nomination was a certainty before the Republican convention opened in Miami Beach in mid-July. The convention's only dramatic event was Nixon's selection of Spiro Agnew as his running mate. John Mitchell saddled Pat Buchanan and me with the depressing assignment of drafting Agnew's seconding speech— his "audition"—and then trying to explain the choice of Agnew to the world. We gave it our loyal all. Agnew proceeded to make matters progressively worse with his love of alliteration and his peculiar penchant for politically poisonous prose, viz., "If you've seen one slum, you've seen them all."

The convention also saw the unveiling of the hard-nosed Haldeman-Ehrlichman operation—an abrupt, though probably essential, shift of authority from the happy and anarchic little band that had run the campaign from 1966 through the 1968 primaries. Dick Whalen had a nasty nose-to-nose with Ehrlichman over access to Nixon's carefully guarded floor in the Doral Hotel, one of those felicitous "Fuck you, fella"/"Up yours" exchanges. After Miami, when the troupe flew to Mission Bay in San Diego for campaign planning, there was a dinnertime run-in between Whalen and John Mitchell, who gave Whalen a boozy rerun of Ehrlichman's lecture on "dime-a-dozen writers." The next morning at breakfast, Whalen told me he was packing it in: The California crowd was a bunch of second-raters and automatons, dangerous men without serious political convictions.

He was part right, part wrong. There were all sorts among the Californians, and besides, no one ever won a campaign without enough second-raters and automatons to ensure that things get done. In his campaign memoir, *Catch the Falling Flag,* Whalen records my parting words to him at our breakfast: "The trouble with you, Dick, is that you care too much. You're really a Jew at heart." In any event, a half hour after our breakfast, from my second-floor window, I saw him marching up the path, suitcase in hand, toward the main gate and out of the campaign.

If I was glibly ready to extend to Whalen the courtesy title of Jew, the story was more complicated when it came to identifying myself as one. I had never lost my sense of Jewish identity, even through all the WASP-saturated years on Wall Street; but the Jewishness was hidden by a thoroughly acculturated style and sensibility, and I had nothing at all to do with organized Jewish life. As for the tropes and twitches of "polite" anti-Semitism that I regularly encountered with law firm clients, I shrugged them off like mosquito bites.

The Six Day War, in 1967, changed that. At the time the war

took place, I was the only Jewish senior adviser on Nixon's campaign staff besides Murray Chotiner, who was anathema to liberal Jews (which was to say almost all Jews) and was locked away in the campaign closet.

When the war began, Nixon was in Egypt on one of his frequent refresher trips to foreign places. He had already scheduled a visit to Israel, and through friends in New York I helped organize his itinerary there. Nixon sensed that Israel's preemptive strike would bring the war to a quick end, so he flew to nearby Greece and perched there to wait it out. Thus he was the first prominent foreign political figure to visit Israel after the war. He was given the run of the country, and I arranged a number of war-related additions to his schedule. When he returned to the United States, I drove out to Kennedy Airport to brief him for his crowded airport press conference. I also brokered an invitation for Nixon to address a large audience of American Jewish leaders at the Pierre Hotel.

Nixon's speech at the Pierre was an anecdote-spiked political report on Israel's newsworthy places and personalities as he encountered them immediately after the drama of the war. He riveted the overflow audience. The meeting's chairman, the famous old Zionist figure Dr. Emanuel Neuman, praised Nixon's sympathetic analysis and described him as a new and vigorous leadership "voice" on Mideast issues. This was an unusual success for Nixon, who had never been exactly the beau ideal of American Jews. I don't know whether it was shock, pleasure, or a still more primitive emotion, but my eyes brimmed over at the sight of all these paradigmatic figures, the Jewish uncles of my childhood, receiving Richard Nixon's sympathetic account of Israeli courage and skill with such unrestrained admiration and affection. For Richard Nixon, yet!

A new responsibility was thereupon added to my duties: I was now Nixon's informal liaison to American Jews and to Israelis. I held this shadow portfolio for the remainder of the campaign and during the years of the Nixon presidency. I was suddenly back home, albeit part time.

These bubblings of race, religion, and culture during the campaign prefigured the work I was later assigned to do in the White House—working with the French nutritionist Jean Mayer on food programs, coordinating civil rights efforts, listening to Vietnam-generated fury, dealing with Jews and Israel, working with artists. Through designation by Nixon and self-anointment, I was the campaign emissary to alien worlds, that conglomerate of minority interests that most mistrusted or hated Nixon. I had no illusion that they could be won over, but there was a political point in blunting the edge of their hostility. This was something my history qualified me to do. I had access, I knew the signals and language, I could distinguish the serious people from the hustlers, and I really liked the job.

But what occupied most of my time during the campaign was another task altogether. As part of my role in the Nixon effort, I had a hand in the early development of the new, more powerful, and less-than-benign industry of modern political advertising. Here is the whole blameworthy story:

Once John Mitchell was in place in the spring of 1967, the next step for Nixon was to launch a media campaign strong enough to bring victory in New Hampshire and other primaries and thus overcome the "loser" image for good. To do so, he had to fight his press image as a sharp-edged, Uriah Heep–type television performer, a brooding and unpleasant private personality.

When I first got to know Nixon, it struck me with particular force that there was a disjunction between the man I knew and the public image that I, as a liberal Democrat, had retained from Nixon's years in public life. He was odd-looking, to be sure, but also an intelligent, interesting, self-deprecatingly witty man. Nixon saw even further: He knew this contrast would be a political asset in his return to public life. It would give him, in addition to his 99 percent name and face recognition, the capacity to surprise—to set the low public expectations against his large private abilities and permit the press to discover, gradually, some realities that they would dub the "New Nixon" running again for president. The passage of time, as well as the media's general fascination with novelty and perpetual hunger for fresh copy, would enable Nixon to use his defeats, traumas, and exaggerated defects to give his comeback campaign a running start.

So Nixon practiced law, traveled the world with his family,

played elder statesman, and smiled a lot. He chatted engagingly on television about the "great issues," played the piano, and joked about himself in public with Jack Paar and Johnny Carson. He made himself pleasantly and selectively available to the press. Before long, there were mostly "New Nixon" stories.

This was all quite silly, because the Old and New Nixons were simply different parts of a densely complicated personality. But now he displayed it with greater discrimination and advantage to an increasingly neutral audience. A disciplined student of his past mistakes, Nixon was finally figuring out how to get some breaks from the press.

At that point Nixon asked me to put together the campaign's advertising. In his view, I had the requisite credentials: I was trustworthy, politically ignorant, and an energetic recruiter. I had experience in persuasion (trial lawyer) and show business (jazz saxophonist). Missing among these were any professional qualifications for the job, but this lack was exactly what recommended me. Nixon wanted me to look around without a lot of fixed notions and locate some experienced people who would work under my direction with him and the men who already knew his predilections and peeves—Price, Buchanan, Safire, and me. Nixon's guidelines were simple: Don't hire an advertising agency. They're dinosaurs and they devour money. For now, keep it small, creative, informal.

It sounded to me like he wanted me to re-create the Modern Jazz Quartet or the Harlem Globetrotters—and that is essentially what happened.

The first media professional that Nixon and I brought into the campaign was Frank Shakespeare. He was not only an experienced television executive, in restless self-exile from high-level conflict at CBS, but a staunch political conservative with passionate beliefs about ideological politics and modern television. He had run through the list of candidates for 1968 and found that Reagan and Nixon were the only ones who made sense to him. He prudently concluded that Reagan was untested, so Nixon was his choice.

In July 1967, through William F. Buckley, Shakespeare arranged a meeting with Nixon at 20 Broad Street. They talked politics and television for ninety minutes. Nixon then asked him to call me about a role in the campaign.

At our first meeting, lunch courtesy of CBS at "21," I found that Shakespeare had a set of forcefully articulated moral and philosophical principles and the look of a man with bigger things in mind than a place in a political campaign organization. His unfurrowed brow and bland, pleasant Holy Cross face were illuminated by an intense blue-eyed gaze that suggested passions more complex than those of commonplace ambition. We quickly became the closest of friends. The excitement of winning the presidency allowed us to put aside little differences like ideology and religion, and our odd coupling persists to this day, deepened by time and age.

At our initial lunch, Shakespeare delivered an illuminating two-hour lecture on the impact of modern television. It was transforming not only politics, he said, but the way the culture received and used information. Understanding the nature of the medium would be especially crucial to Nixon's 1968 campaign, for television, if misused, was the cruelest of all media. The first thing we had to do was examine Nixon's previous filmed appearances and determine what format would present the best of Nixon to television viewers.

Shortly afterward, a few of us—Shakespeare, Ray Price, Tom Evans, and me—assembled in a CBS screening room, where we watched six or seven hours of Nixon TV appearances that Frank had requisitioned from the company's film library. We saw that Nixon the stump speaker—lawyerlike, earnest, intense, perspiring, forced —was Nixon at his absolute worst, all wrong for the cool television medium. On the other hand, Nixon more or less at ease, talking informally, one on one, was close to the "personal" Nixon whom we found surprisingly congenial.

Ray Price wrote a memo of the group's recommendations on Nixon's use of television. "The greater the element of informality and spontaneity," he said, "the better [Nixon] comes across." Our goal, he went on, was "to remind supporters of the candidate's strengths, and to demonstrate to nonsupporters that the Herblock images are fiction." He summed up, "It's not the man we have to change, but rather the impression."

Price, Shakespeare, and I agreed in the early summer of 1967 that the format for Nixon's television advertising and the centerpiece of his campaign should be question-and-answer sessions with panels of local citizens, which we would film, edit, and broadcast on local television. We now needed a professional team to develop the details. My MacDougal Street roommate, Red Werner, worked at the J. Walter Thompson advertising agency as a copywriter. He mentioned that his boss, Harry Treleaven, had once dabbled in Republican politics, having prepared the successful 1966 congressional campaign of a young Texas politician named George Bush. Treleaven and I had met and spoken briefly in the spring of 1967, but he did not seem eager to take on the Nixon campaign. I left for an August holiday with my family out at Amagansett, on Long Island. The last day of the vacation, Grace sent me down to the beach with the kids to get them out of the way while she finished packing. There I came upon Treleaven sitting on the sand, drinking a beer, and staring out at the breaking surf that sparkled in the late-afternoon sun. We chatted again about the Nixon campaign. We agreed to meet back in the city to talk seriously.

If there is such a thing as a genius for political advertising, Harry Treleaven had it. A quiet and private man, he was unpretentious and self-effacing almost to a disabling fault. He was vaguely Republican and vaguely Christian Science, but he seemed to care intensely only about things like good taste and good work. Treleaven was one of those people obsessed with their craft. He enjoyed the manipulative aesthetic of advertising's words, pictures, and music in the same intense way he enjoyed the late-afternoon light bouncing off the ocean waves at Amagansett. He rarely tried to explain his professional judgments beyond saying, "I don't know why, I just get a kick out of it." I remember Harry in the final weeks of the 1968 campaign, a smallish, fine-featured man with thinning gray hair, in standard button-down shirt and Brooks Brothers gray, raindrops dripping off his nose from a sudden storm on Sixth Avenue, straining to tell me, through the wheeze and cough of chronic asthma, something more important than life itself about a dinky sixty-second campaign spot he was reworking with the filmmaker Gene Jones for the tenth time. I remember thinking, "Another obsessive nut." But that's what I loved about him.

On November 21, 1967, Treleaven delivered what he called his first stab at a Nixon advertising strategy. It turned out to be our permanent guide. Cuteness, obliqueness, slickness, "gimmicks that say 'Madison Avenue at work here,' " were out. He also had a correction for the rest of us:

It's not a "New Nixon" that's now at the top of the polls. It's the old Nixon with his strengths looking stronger and his negatives blurred by the years. . . . In short, it's the attitude of the voters that's new—not Mr. Nixon. The advertising, therefore, should not strain to create a brand new image—because the old one's doing pretty well. . . .

In the fall of 1967 Nixon was in Philadelphia being interviewed on *The Mike Douglas Show*. There he discovered twenty-six-year-old Roger Ailes, a product of Cleveland, Ohio, and even more a product of the television era. Ailes had already been the producer of Mike Douglas's nationally syndicated show for three years, supervising five ninety-minute programs a week. These shows covered the wit, wisdom, and sentiments of both prominent and ordinary people on every conceivable issue and gave Ailes a fingertip familiarity with America's TV soul.

Nixon first met Ailes when the two chatted in the makeup room before Nixon's appearance. Nixon ritually complained about a political system that required a man to use "gimmicks" to be elected president. Ailes replied that television was not a gimmick but a fact of American life. Unless Mr. Nixon accepted this he could forget about 1968. Ailes went on bluntly to detail the things Nixon had done wrong on television in 1960 and how he should address his problems in 1968. Within days, Nixon told me about Ailes and asked me to get him to New York, introduce him around, and see if he was interested in joining the campaign. Midway through the primaries in 1968, Ailes took charge of Nixon's television.

My own role in the media operation was hiring, backslapping, and quality control. I assembled the operating quartet in one large office and ran the enterprise like a newspaper city room—making sure we listened to one another's phone conversations, attended one another's meetings, kibitzed, joked, shared pastrami sandwiches, and embellished one another's campaign gossip. It was, for me, the best part of the campaign, joyful in fact, close to the camaraderie of a small jazz group and a deliverance from the routines of Wall Street law practice. I was back in show business. I particularly enjoyed the editing process itself, in the color-filled high-tech studios with bearded technicians, hip jokes and jargon, and banks of monitors flickering in glass-paneled control rooms. Nixon's head would speed forward or backward in a blur as we reviewed his videotaped answers, shortened some, and snipped out others altogether, dropping them down the chute of history.

In Hillsborough, New Hampshire, we filmed material for the nation's first primary. It was fairly close to the conversational Nixon. He handled questions from locals in schoolrooms, firehouses, and community centers, all with an old-timer's ease. The traveling press corps protested their exclusion from these sessions and ran stories about our manipulative secrecy, but we got the material we wanted and aired five-minute sections that were relaxed and informal. When Ailes joined us, he created a more formal setting for these interviews. He presented Nixon in a press-conference format that combined elements of informality with distance and suspense —though the chances of a case-hardened politician like Nixon stumbling seriously over any question was near zero. In fact, Nixon was especially effective against hostile questioners. The press was allowed to watch the shows on monitors in a separate studio and to interview the panelists and audience after the show.

These shows were the main part of our advertising campaign. They were supplemented by conventional print advertising and the one-minute spot commercials that were Treleaven's special passion. Harry used Nixon's best feature, his voice, over photographic montages of American political scenes to present Nixon's views on his principal campaign themes—Vietnam, law and order, race, the economy. The spots were politically ineffective, their messsage blurred by all the soft imagery and artwork. But they pleased Treleaven and were acceptable to Nixon, who hated sitting in a studio shooting and reshooting commercials but was willing to sit in his apartment study reading short scripts into a tape recorder.

By present-day standards, these spots were straightforward and noncontroversial. We did one attack spot, which juxtaposed a smiling Humphrey at the chaotic Democratic convention, accompanied by "Happy Days Are Here Again" background music, with scenes of violence, poverty, and war. The Democratic campaign organization protested, and Shakespeare and I instantly yanked the commercial. The Democrats, though, were no slouches at this game. My favorite 1968 spot was an anti-Wallace ad made for the Humphrey campaign by Doyle Dane Bernbach. In it, a voter pulls the lever for the Wallace-LeMay ticket and the voting booth blows up.

Our ad group's heroic period did not last long. At the Miami convention and the Mission Bay meeting just afterward, the political managers pushed us aside. Giving inescapable evidence of this shift, Nixon invited me to join him, his family, Rose Mary Woods, Ray Price, and Bob Haldeman in the presidential suite for a network filming of the presumptive nominee watching television during the convention delegates' balloting. We sat there, mute, conscious of being singled out for the eye of history by Mike Wallace's film crew. We knew we were there because we were the only people in the campaign who at that historic moment had absolutely nothing to do.

The television group operated mostly on automatic pilot after the convention. For weeks we ran excerpts from Nixon's convention address, in line with Treleaven's theory that we should run whatever seemed to work until people got sick of it or new commercial spots were ready for airing. Meanwhile, Kevin Phillips—a young demographer whose hiring I recommended to John Mitchell after scanning a manuscript Phillips had handed me in lieu of a résumé, something called "The Emerging Republican Majority"—sat in a little room near Mitchell and me, consulting his printouts and his vast memory bank and telling us, on the basis of his house-by-house knowledge of voting sensitivities, where to air or not to air particular commercials.

Then, in October, Humphrey began breathing down Nixon's neck. Humphrey gave a dovish Vietnam speech in Salt Lake City that started Democratic holdouts moving back to him. Organized labor got off its hands. The press began concentrating once again on "Old Nixon" stories. Southern Democrats who had vented their spleen by supporting Wallace in the early weeks of the campaign now started returning to their traditional Democratic home.

A friend of Shakespeare's from CBS had produced a cut-rate documentary for the campaign that told Nixon's life story through old family photos and a Nixon voice-over narration. Getting Nixon to sit for this piece of sentimentalism, all about death and struggle and lessons learned from the early days in Whittier, was worse than pulling teeth, and he refused to look at the finished product. His family viewed the film and thought it was "too personal," so we were forbidden to use it. But in the closing days of the campaign, Nixon's mysteriously disappearing lead made it necessary to throw everything into the breach. We were reluctantly allowed to use the film—if the Nixon family's friend Billy Graham personally approved it. So on a rainy Saturday afternoon in late October, Graham, sniffling in misery from the flu, joined me in an otherwise deserted TV studio on Manhattan's West Side, peered into a Moviola editing machine for a half hour, and then, from a public phone in the hallway phoned Nixon, campaigning somewhere out in America, to assure him that the documentary was tasteful enough to be aired. We ran it nationally, day and night, at a cost of hundreds of thousands of dollars, in the final, desperate days of the 1968 campaign.

With two days to go, the polls indicated that the race was too close to call. We assembled in Los Angeles to prepare for two crucial two-hour election eve telethons. Roger Ailes, the meshugganer, had gone off with some friends for an existential leap out of an airplane, his first try at parachuting, to break the tension of getting ready for the climactic TV production. He tore several tendons in his foot. ("We'd be better off if he broke his goddamn neck," Treleaven sniffed.) Directing the four hours of telethons with his foot in a bucket of ice and his head in a Percodan fog, Ailes did his best work of the campaign that night.

So did Nixon. During the half-hour break between the eastern and western portions of his marathon performance, Nixon called me into his dressing room. He was wrapped in a bathrobe and towel, eating a cheese sandwich, and looking like Rocky between rounds. He asked for my comments. I gave him sage advice: "Just hang in there, Dick." Which he did, except for a strange comment he made in one of his final glazed-eye answers about "getting down to the nut cutting."

That wrapped up the advertising and the campaign. The next morning we returned to New York to see what all our efforts had produced.

In a sense, we never found out. No one knows whether the

telethon, the "man in the arena," the "self-portrait," or anything else the Nixon ad group did significantly helped Nixon win the presidency. No doubt we helped Nixon make a TV presentation in the 1968 campaign that was more effective than its counterpart in 1960 or 1962, because it was more natural than the sharp-edged image of the earlier campaigns. This has to be counted a plus, since every advantage had to be exploited and every disadvantage blunted in a race like the one that produced such a paper-thin Nixon victory. Still, once Nixon's lead began shrinking, everything Nixon and the media group did to stem the downward drift failed to work. Perhaps most illuminating is the fact that Nixon had about 43 percent of the national vote in the spring of 1968 and 43 percent on Election Day in November 1968.

Clearly, the overall effect of the advertising was not large compared with the real determinants of the election's outcome: the turbulence of 1968, Lyndon Johnson's prolonged interference with the Humphrey campaign's freedom of action on Vietnam, voter turnout and turnoff, and other subterranean complexities beyond the control of Madison Avenue.

I think this is the way history would have regarded—or, more accurately, disregarded—the Nixon advertising effort but for Joe McGinniss's book *The Selling of the President*, which bestowed fame, fortune, and legendary status on the Nixon advertising campaign and its perpetrators, the members of our media quartet.

The book argued that the "New Nixon" had been created and sold to America by a group of manipulators—Frank Shakespeare, Harry Treleaven, Roger Ailes, and me. McGinniss called us the first to adapt the manipulative techniques of commercial advertising on a large scale to presidential politics.

Joe McGinniss dropped into the Nixon campaign in a haphazard way. As McGinniss himself tells the story in his book, in July of 1968, after the traumatic blows of the Martin Luther King and Bobby Kennedy assassinations, he left his column at *The Philadelphia Enquirer* for a while to write a book about presidential campaign advertising. He asked an acquaintance at Doyle Dane, the Humphrey agency, if he could follow the agency's people around.

His sophisticated friend answered with a horrified no. McGinniss figured, what the hell, and called the Nixon camp. He explained his project, he says—and, to his surprise, Treleaven and I said yes. No questions asked, no ground rules imposed.

Years later, McGinniss told the writer Janet Malcolm a somewhat different story about how he had gained entrée. The Nixon people, he said to her, "were almost touchingly naïve. They said, 'Oh, gosh, really—a book? Yeah, sure.' " McGinniss hated Nixon and thought we were doing something sinister, he told Malcolm, but felt no obligation to apprise us of those facts. "And when they were talking about what they were doing," he recalled, "and turned to me and said, 'What do you think of that?' I'd say, 'Yeah, that looks good,' if it was done effectively." In other words, Malcolm sums up, McGinniss was an "enemy infiltrator."

But whatever he said, the fact is that we foolishly allowed ourselves to be lulled by his friendly assurances and our own gullibility —plus at least a touch of vanity (we secretly liked the idea of having a "historian" write about our momentous efforts). So we gave the office keys to a man who, we learned afterward, was on record as a sworn enemy of our campaign. In mitigation, this was long before investigative journalism became a blood sport.

McGinniss, no doubt holding his breath and pinching himself every night at his good luck, spent his days in friendly companionship with the four Nixon naïfs. He laughed at our gibes, sympathized with our difficulties, offered judicious and helpful suggestions, shared our meals, memoranda, meetings, and private Nixon taping sessions, and inconspicuously jotted down notes on everything he saw and heard in a small reporter's notebook. Eventually he wove it all into *The Selling of the President*, published in 1969, one of that year's super bestsellers.

Treleaven is introduced in the book as a man who "loves artificial things." Frank Shakespeare is runner-up to Nixon as archvillain of the book, God's angry conservative. McGinniss quotes remarks by Roger Ailes:

Let's face it, a lot of people think Nixon is dull. Think he's a bore, a pain in the ass. They look at him as the kind of kid who always carried a book bag. Who was 42 years old the day he was born. They figure other kids got footballs for Christmas; Nixon got a briefcase and loved it. He'd always have his homework done and he'd never let you copy. Now you put him on television, you've got a problem right away. He's a funny-looking guy. He looks like somebody hung him in a closet overnight and he jumps out in the morning with his suit all bunched up and starts running around saying, "I want to be President." I mean this is how he strikes some people. That's why these shows are important. To make them forget all that.

Snaking through all this anecdotage is McGinniss's real argument: In 1960, television cost Nixon the presidency by portraying him accurately. So in 1968, Nixon was determined to control his television and project a new, false image. His professionals created panel shows with controlled audiences and TV spots conveying preplanned impressions. But Nixon disliked television, and the old pols gradually took over the campaign and shoved aside the new men. The "Old Nixon" gradually broke through the media cocoon constructed for him. His big, early lead vanished; he barely won.

In fact, McGinniss's own description of the 1968 Nixon advertising campaign portrays it as a relatively innocent affair. "It was run," says McGinniss in the book, "by men who shared [Nixon's] vision" and thought they were revealing the genuine Nixon. This was a candidate who did have ideas about public policy and who looked his best when fielding tough issue questions in rehearsed settings. McGinniss reported these things but refused to acknowledge them in his judgments, because his professed concern about the use of television in politics actually ran a distant second to his hatred of Nixon. The hatred made his book into an internally contradictory mess.

As Kathleen Jamieson puts it in her authoritative 1984 study of political advertising, *Packaging the Presidency*, "McGinniss seems to be doing to Nixon . . . what he accuses Nixon's admen of doing to Nixon—creating images that do not comport with reality."

The campaign of 1968 was in fact the last gasp of the old politics; it was not the start of something new. But the thesis of the McGinniss book was greeted with storms of praise. It perfectly fit the journalistic zeitgeist of 1968, which loved the identification of a corrupt Nixon with corrupt television and corrupt advertising.

And because the McGinniss book was so popular, it played a major part in producing precisely the phenomenon it had excoriated with so much moralistic steam. It introduced into the conventional wisdom the idea that television advertising techniques were all-powerful and absolutely essential to a modern political campaign. It convinced candidates that they had to buy large and expensive quantities of air time and hire expensive media strategists and television consultants.

Roger Ailes, for example, had planned to return to network television production in 1969 but was swamped with offers to run campaigns in the 1970 elections. He, and scores of others like him, set up campaign consulting firms, and a new industry was born. Campaigns began phasing out other types of campaigning, like volunteer activities, that used to involve more people in politics. Political television advertising, once out of the closet, became more cynically manipulative and corrosively negative. It also created an insatiable demand for campaign funds. It helped produce a political culture that is nastier, meaner-spirited, and emptier of ideas than it once had been.

Thus McGinniss accelerated the deformation of American politics by creating a self-sustaining myth about the power of political advertising. The press, by and large, wanting to believe that television and Nixon were capable of the worst, accepted McGinniss's argument uncritically and thus helped make it come true.

Nixon wrapped up his final telethon in Los Angeles. His last answer of the show ended the 1968 campaign—or so we thought as we drove back to the Beverly Wilshire Hotel, slightly numb but exhilarated and thirsty.

The festivities had only begun when someone, probably the media consultant Ruth Jones, mentioned the idea of "drive time," radio commercials that could catch people in their cars on Election Day. Why hadn't heard I about this sooner? The party recessed, and David Eisenhower was roused from his bed and brought to my suite. Still in his pajamas and rubbing his eyes, David read a bunch of thirty-second and ten-second spots into a portable tape recorder. Elsewhere in the suite, Ruth was booking national radio time. The commercials would run everywhere in motoring America the next day.

At last, there was nothing left to do. I, always happiest when I had driven myself and everyone around me to distraction, was now able to go to sleep.

The next morning we boarded the *Tricia*, Nixon's big jet, for the flight back to New York. Floating high over the country, the entire campaign family was together for the first time, sealed off from the voters five miles below in an airborne metaphor of the separation that takes place on Election Day between the candidate and the country. For the first time that year, we were merely observers; the process was on its own.

After some booze and nervous babble, the functional staff groups—writers, media, advance men, secretaries—trooped forward to Nixon's compartment for thanks and, for us media advisers, a not-unhappy farewell. Then we gradually settled into our own private thoughts, drawing apart, thumbing through magazines and newspapers. A TV set in the staff compartment began giving fuzzy accounts of voting turnout in places like Kansas and New Hampshire.

At mid-point in the flight, somewhere over heartland America between Mississippi and Indiana, the golden light in the West receded, and the dark from the East fell over the cabin. We were approaching home. Down below, lights twinkling on in towns and cities made the countryside look like a vast theatre just before the curtain goes up. Everyone on the plane became a poet in that quiet final hour.

We landed at Newark Airport in a blaze of excitement and television lights. A car took me to Brooklyn Heights, where Grace was waiting. We voted, then went to the thirty-fifth floor of the Waldorf-Astoria to watch the returns. Tonight the future had arrived, and stopped.

At midnight I sent Grace home; it was going to be close. For the next few hours I watched the returns with Frank Shakespeare in a hospitality suite down the hall from Nixon. Rockefeller, Jacob Javits, Strom Thurmond, and other political figures came and went, but Nixon was not ready to see anybody. Bob Haldeman, John Ehrlichman, and campaign aide Dwight Chapin monitored the television next door to Nixon's suite. Mitchell, Finch, and Chotiner audited reports from the field. At about three A.M. Nixon concluded that he had won. At about four, he rounded up a dozen of us, including Mitchell, Haldeman, Rose Mary Woods, Finch, Price, Buchanan, and me, plus newcomer–old-timer Bryce Harlow, to wait out the expected victory.

Relaxed and convivial at first, Nixon joked, rambled, ribbed, reminisced, drank a couple of beers, ate a sandwich, smoked a cigar, and occasionally sent Mitchell or Haldeman to get details on open states. After a while an anxious mood descended on the group. The final result was just hanging there, like a post-term baby. Texas reported "mechanical difficulties"; there would be no official result until morning. Illinois was even more ominous: Mayor Richard Daley was up to his traditional trick, withholding votes from his Chicago vote cache until the downstate results revealed the deficit, which would then be made up by hook or, more likely, by crook. This could be a stomach-churning reprise of 1960.

I was supposed to be part of the effort to stop Mayor Daley's traditional chicanery. In early 1968, during the primary season, Nixon asked me to assemble a group of volunteer lawyers under the catchy name "Operation Eagle Eye" to thwart a replay of the 1960 vote snatch by the Daley organization. I flew to Chicago and briefly saw some lawyers and local press to set the operation in motion and publicize it; that night I was supposed to meet with local Republicans who were to provide logistical support. But I totally gummed up my mission. I stopped by the popular *Irv Kupcinet Show* to make what I thought would be a brief pitch for the "Eagle Eye" operation, but I ended up camera-trapped for three hours in Kupcinet's "conversation pit," debating with Senator George McGovern, Gore Vidal, Alan Lomax, Allard Lowenstein, and Kupcinet himself on all of Nixon's positions—Vietnam, race, youth, economic policy, and on and on. My miserable performance would have been even worse had it not been for periodic interventions by McGovern, who understood the sweat-soaked predicament of an amateur and rescued me whenever I was about to sink out of sight.

It was just as well that I was trapped before the cameras; I knew zero about the perpetration or prevention of voting fraud. John Mitchell and his Chicago apparat took up "Eagle Eye" in a more professional manner.

Finally, as we sat with Nixon through the dawn hours in the

Waldorf, waiting for the centipede to drop the final shoe labeled Illinois, we saw the fruits of Mitchell's work. Mitchell's strategy to counter Daley had been to arrange the withholding of a large cache of Republican-controlled votes in downstate Illinois. So, hour after hour, John Mitchell and Richard Daley dueled, each withholding his ultimate weapon as the sun rose over a still-sleeping America.

About eight A.M., Nixon, out of patience, told Mitchell to place a call to Mike Wallace, who was live on CBS television, and challenge Daley to release his votes. We watched the TV screen as Mike took Mitchell's call and put Mitchell's challenge to Daley. The Illinois votes were released, the state went to Nixon, and, around noon, Humphrey conceded.

Shortly after the election, I was invited to join the president-elect and campaign team for a celebratory first flight on *Air Force One* (Lyndon Johnson's postelection treat for Nixon) to Key Biscayne. Instead, I kept a dinner date with Mike Wallace—displaying both fidelity to a friend and condescension toward ordinary politicians. While the Nixon team divvied up the spoils in sunny Florida, Mike and I had a glorious evening in New York.

We reminisced about the campaign years—from our first meeting in the mid-1960s, two hustling New York Jews wisecracking over lunch at Whyte's on Yom Kippur, through my visit with Frank Shakespeare to Mike's room at Roosevelt Hospital in 1968, where we conveyed candidate Nixon's offer to make Wallace his press spokesman, with plenipotentiary powers, for the campaign and the presidency. Mike was then recovering from a hemorrhoidectomy and so gave new life to an old joke: "Tell Mr. Nixon he really knows how to hurt a guy," he said, grinning and grimacing in his pain. He weighed our offer but eventually said no, electing instead to take his chances with a berth on an experimental CBS news show called *60 Minutes*. Nixon's offer to Wallace, who was well known as a journalistic maverick, was for me convincing evidence that Nixon's early vision of his candidacy and presidency was vastly different from the one that emerged later.

By keeping my postcampaign dinner date with Wallace rather than heading for Key Biscayne, I was expressing something more than a desire to reminisce. Aggressive types like me are drawn to activities like litigation, politics, or mountain climbing not by the intellectual or moral virtue of the enterprise but by the primitive joy of striving and succeeding: Nothing rivals combat as a way of organizing life's conventional and depressing aimlessness. Thus, when the four-year sprint for the presidency was done, I felt . . . serene. No plans, ambitions, or thoughts about Washington or the law firm or much of anything else. My future would emerge. Things would fall into place. Nixon would see to it. After all, I had been with him from day one.

I also had a concrete reason to believe there was a special bond between Nixon and me that ensured a place for me in his presidency if I wanted it.

True, once the presidential campaign went on the road, I rarely saw Nixon. His airborne managers, Bob Haldeman and John Ehrlichman, wisely exercised control over every minute of Nixon's dawn-to-dark schedule. He would occasionally phone me to shmooze when he was back in New York over a weekend or refreshing his tan at Key Biscayne; those conversations were, I'm sure, indistinguishable from scores of similar calls he would make to other friends and advisers.

But during the dark times of October, as Nixon's lead steadily shrank, he made nighttime calls to me of a very different sort. They would come to my home, between midnight and two A.M. or even later. Sometimes Nixon himself was on the line. Sometimes it was Ehrlichman, announcing, "The old man wants to talk with you for a bit." Nixon would usually apologize for the late hour, ask after my family and the morale of the New York staff, how John was doing with Martha, some such thing. Then began what was less a conversation than a monologue, centered on his anxieties of the day. These were mostly about his narrowing margin over Humphrey and the impact of an expected bombing halt in Vietnam.

The Democrats are going home, Len, he'd say. The Wallace vote is hurting us. Watch for an L.B.J. stunt right before the election. Don't let your people panic. I would offer an occasional opinion, but he didn't need that from me. What he wanted was reassurance. I was Nixon's chief optimist and good-luck charm, the man who had declared, way back in early 1964, that he was destined to be president. Then Nixon would drift further, into a procession of sad and lonely thoughts, mingling past and present, that needed to be expressed, not necessarily heard. The monologue would gradually grow less clear, slower, indistinct, and finally end, often in midsentence. There would be silence and then a dial tone.

Together with Grace, I worried over these calls. She was no stranger to nocturnal phone calls: John Mitchell's wife, Martha, was a frequent telephone visitor. Martha would invariably call on nights when John and I were at a late dinner meeting and assure Grace that their two husbands were catting around town somewhere. Grace and I were the least surprised people in the world when Martha started to reach out and touch everyone in Washington with her bizarre phone communications.

But the Nixon calls were more serious. Was he drinking? Was the pressure too much? Could he be cracking up? Then the next day would bring news that Nixon was back on the trail, alert, lively, crisp, making everything perfectly clear. I would feel a sense of relief at grave danger averted.

Nearly twenty-five years later, in 1991, I was visiting with John Ehrlichman over dinner in Santa Fe. I asked him whether those phone calls were some kind of hallucination. "That was an interesting little routine," Ehrlichman answered. At the end of a long campaign day on the road, he said, Nixon's imperative need to get some sleep ran into his chronic insomnia. The usual solution was a Seconal, a stiff drink, and a phone call to me. I was the friendly, disembodied presence to whom Nixon could unload his daily deposit of anxieties until he was finally carried away by alcohol, sedation, and exhaustion into the Land of Nod. It was more cries and whispers than train whistles in the night, but it served its purpose.

Ineffable feelings of closeness or no, it happened that after the president-elect and his party returned from Key Biscayne, I was no longer part of the inner circle. I did not see or hear from Nixon, now ensconced in the Pierre Hotel with the men who were helping him assemble his administration. I reasoned that he would get around to me sooner or later.

Meanwhile, I was interviewing minority candidates for jobs in the new administration. My young assistant Christopher DeMuth knew James Farmer, the former president of the Congress of Racial Equality (CORE), and had worked in Farmer's campaign against Shirley Chisholm for her Bedford-Stuyvesant congressional seat. DeMuth introduced me to Farmer, who became an assistant secretary at the Department of Health, Education and Welfare. I also raised the idea of bringing Pat Moynihan into the administration. Haldeman asked me to sound him out. I met him for the first time at the Laurent Restaurant, where a long and rollicking dinner ensued. Moynihan said he was willing to be secretary of transportation. But that job was already committed to Governor John Volpe of Massachusetts, so Moynihan and Nixon fashioned an alternative: Moynihan would become Nixon's adviser on urban affairs and director of a new Urban Affairs Council in the White House.

An Israeli diplomat named Shlomo Argov, searching for a friendly face in the administration-to-be, took me to an orientation lunch at the Plaza Hotel. It was one third history, two thirds Mideast humor (he knew his customer). Soon afterward, the gloriously eloquent Argov was named deputy to the new Israeli ambassador, Itzhak Rabin. During our years in Wasington, Argov was my working colleague and a close family friend.

And so it went in those postelection days—a little of this and a little of that, while I read newspapers, talked to the press, visited with law firm colleagues, lunched with Ray Price and Bill Safire, and waited to hear from Nixon about my future. The great day finally arrived, and the call came from the Pierre: "Mr. Nixon would like you to come right over." My heart beat a little faster. In the cab, I realized that I still had no idea what I wanted to do: John Erlichman had already been announced as counsel to the president, the job my law partners had wanted me to have, and the top slots at the Justice Department were filled. But I believed Nixon would know what was best for me.

The Pierre had been chosen as transition headquarters because it was close to Nixon's apartment a few blocks up Fifth Avenue. Nixon's office at the hotel was a comfortable suite, with Rose Mary Woods perched outside, buried in paper as usual. Nixon was relaxed and warm, as if we had last met and talked that morning. He went briskly to his first order of business—not Leonard Garment but John Mitchell. "We have the same old problem, Len," he said, "and I need your help. It's Martha. I need John as my attorney general, but he won't do it. He's worried that Martha can't handle the Washington pressure. You've got to talk to him and make him understand how important this is. He trusts your judgment on things like this." I said sure, I would give it my best.

Now it was my turn: Len, Nixon said in more or less these words, I've been thinking a lot about what you should do. I want you to come to Washington (good!) and move into the firm's office there (what?). You'll be right across the street from the White House; I'll see to it that you have a White House pass, attend meetings, handle personal assignments for me that I don't want to run through the bureaucracy (what does *that* mean?). You will be part of my kitchen cabinet (oy!). You've reached an age and level in the firm where you can start accumulating some real money for Grace and the children (who cares?). Get a nice house. Entertain in style. Learn the ropes. In no time you'll be the "Clark Clifford of the Republican party."

That last phrase is verbatim.

Beginning with fellow Missourian Harry Truman, whom he served as political adviser, confidential messenger, and organizer of presidential poker parties, Clark Clifford came to signify a rare kind of Washington insider power. His influence was only marginally affected by the comings and goings of presidents, cabinet officials, and members of Congress. Mainly from his law firm perch, occasionally within the government itself—he was Lyndon Johnson's last secretary of defense—Clifford exercised his unusual talents, combining impeccable connections and a penetratingly shrewd grasp of law and politics, all in a tall, handsome Savile Row package. His only notable stumble took place when he was eighty years plus and became a player in the B.C.C.I. scandal.

Me, a Republican Clark Clifford? Fat chance.

It wasn't until later that I understood what troves of influence Nixon was offering me. At the time, I was puzzled and embarrassed. After all the years of devoted exertion, after bringing the bat and ball, recruiting the players, and renting the stadium, how could I be the only guy left sitting on the bench when the game started? But I thanked Nixon for his thoughtfulness and left the room, feeling downcast.

Over the years, I wondered about Nixon's initial exclusion of me from his new administration. But after finally talking to most of the participants in the early personnel decisions, I know that the various paranoid theories I invented were wrong. Nixon saw me as a freelance operator, a political naïf who had never displayed any aptitude or appetite for the actual politics of governing. Probably my casual decision to pass up his invitation to go to Key Biscayne and stake out my claim reinforced his opinion. So he probably thought he was doing what was best for me. After all, in light of the life he had lived up until then, he was offering me what he must have thought was a career scenario made in heaven. And so it could have been, if I had been more sophisticated about power in Washington and less determined to be where the most obvious action was.

I went to Washington, moved into Nixon's immense former law office overlooking his new public quarters across Pennsylvania Avenue, and temporarily shared a suite at the Watergate Hotel with Frank Shakespeare, now director of the United States Information Agency. I returned to New York for family weekends, went to gala Washington parties, and kept on interviewing job aspirants. At one point consideration was given to naming me director of the Office of Economic Opportunity, a tough spot to fill because the nominee had to have both an interest in social issues and a willingness to drastically downsize this artifact of the War on Poverty. Arthur Burns, who had been named counselor to the president, had me over to the White House for an interview lunch. Dr. Burns, one of the great men of public life, soliloquized through most of the lunch about the new administration and the old problems, his white hair perfectly parted in the middle, looking so much like a children's-book owl that I had trouble concentrating. He gently probed my general politics, then finally asked what I thought about O.E.O.'s mission and priorities. I answered something like, "Well, Arthur, I don't know much about the place or its programs, but it has to be kept in business for political reasons. So I would improve the staff, trim the community action programs to the bone, and shift emphasis to the one thing I know produces results for poor people: the legal services program."

Gong! Wrong answer. Though Burns was too polite to say so,

this was just what he wanted to avoid. O.E.O.'s legal services program was one of the new administration's biggest political headaches, because it had promoted a proliferation of class-action lawsuits designed to achieve political change for whole communities rather than case-by-case legal relief for individuals. The friendly lunch ended on a distinct "Don't call us, we'll call you" note of finality. The Illinois congressman Don Rumsfeld was drafted to command the O.E.O. battlefield and skillfully handled the job with the help of a senior deputy named Dick Cheney. Rumsfeld was succeeded by Frank Carlucci. All three later became secretary of defense, a logical progression. And I ultimately became the reigning White House expert on the legal services program, helping to persuade Nixon, for his last bill signing in office, to create an independent Legal Services Corporation.

Apart from failing my first federal job interview, I did a lot of general moping. Each day I had what I thought of as my wretched little breakfast across Seventeenth Street from the White House, where I read the news about my various campaign colleagues, recruits, and assistants who were now running the world. Aching with envy, I dragged myself one block to my grandly inappropriate office, from which I had an unobstructed bird's-eye view of the White House buildings and grounds. I ached some more.

Nixon kept his word about making me an "insider." I got my White House pass. Word went out to the press that I was consulted by the president on various important matters of state (not so). I went to White House meetings. But the meetings were mostly public relations conclaves. My contacts with the president himself were virtually nonexistent, and my assignments, mostly from Bob Haldeman, were what I saw as peripheral odds and ends, in areas like minority hiring and the arts. On the Washington legal front, not much was happening: My business productivity hovered around zero. I was not going to be the Clark Clifford of the Republican party. I still had next to no idea of what Clark Clifford did. Periodically I flew back to Brooklyn and drove Grace and the kids crazy.

Finally, one weekend, Bob Guthrie, my Mudge Rose mentor, took me to his home in Hilton Head, South Carolina, and urged me to cut my losses: "Face it, boy. You're not meant for Washington. Come home and start doing something you know how to do." Time was running out. Clients were already beginning to call me, asking me to intercede for them with government agencies whose very existence was news to me.

Then, on May 24, 1969, I picked up *The Washington Post* to find a page one story headed PRESIDENT'S IDEA MAN: OUTSIDER WITH INSIDE TIES. It was a combination of friendly leaks and not-unfriendly speculation, painting me as what Nixon wanted me to be—the Clark Clifford of the Republican party:

> There are times in the White House when the discussion among President Nixon's staff reaches a point where someone will say: "What does Len think about this?" So someone will pick up a phone, dial 298-5970 and get Leonard Garment. . . .
>
> Garment's name appears on no White House roster. . . . Yet . . . in the course of a week, he talks to the President two or three times by telephone. He has visited the President four or five times on unannounced calls since the Administration took office and he has seen the President socially uncounted times. . . .
>
> Mudge Rose is in a position to increase its business substantially. . . . "They must have a partners' meeting every morning to decide on what new business to take," a competing lawyer says.

That was it. If I did not take action, my fate as a maladapted eminence grise was sealed. Within hours—or was it minutes?—I was on the phone to Peter Flanigan, the highest-ranking of my personal friends at the White House. "Peter," I said, "I'm either going into the government, back to New York, or, sooner or later, off to jail." Peter hung up, then quickly called back: "The president would like you to join the White House staff."

Nixon had at first offered me what he thought was a generous piece of the spoils of office. Now I finally had my hands on the only spoils I could understand, a real job in the administration.

❦ 6 ❧

THE NIXON WHITE HOUSE:
ARTS AND CRAFT

When I went across the street to the White House, my public-service intentions were mixed: an appetite for activity, a flight from law practice, continued competition in the assimilation sweepstakes, curiosity about the mysteries of presidential power, ambition to share in that power, and a formless desire to do something "useful." But I see this only in retrospect; at the time, my motives were not so clear to me. Thus, when I finally crashed the White House party, I was left with the problem of what to do.

The president had given me all the trappings of a high-ranking assistant, but no specific responsibilities. I would have to invent a job out of what was available in the distant swamplands of Republican politics, such as civil rights, Jews, and cultural affairs, activities that no sane and reasonably ambitious person in my position would have touched in 1969.

The process of invention was slow. Nobody pushed me to do a thing. Since I, though "special consultant to the president," had nothing special to consult about, I just sent him acres of policy memos. I was not part of any organized staff activity—no surprise, since the most constant inner-circle activity in the upper reaches of the White House was muscle flexing. Haldeman and Ehrlichman were not your conventional political operators. They were formidably intelligent and bristled with energy and self-confidence. These qualities proved to be essential to Nixon's acquisition and exercise of power. Despite his political skills and tunnel-digging determination, Nixon was surprisingly soft in the clinch, whether the issue was dropping staffers or bombs. He needed tough, cold-blooded executives to put his plans into play.

The relationships among Haldeman, Ehrlichman, Kissinger, and Nixon were singularly devoted to the breeding and tending of power. They were not friends, not even a little. Indeed, if the members of Nixon's German general staff shared an emotion, it was an intense dislike of Nixon, which he returned. But without a lot of piety and false idealism to get in the way, this strange quartet did a better job of governing in the early Nixon years than most of their predecessors or successors.

Haldeman and Ehrlichman were not ideological or temperamental twins. Haldeman usually greeted me in the White House, half affectionately and half derisively, as "Lenny Government," so amused was he to find a dim-witted Democratic do-gooder on the team of political knife wielders that Nixon had assembled.

Ehrlichman, by contrast, took me seriously and occasionally suggested that I call the president and drop in to chat with him about things in general. Years later, Ehrlichman told me he had hoped I might provide a moderating balance to the agitators of Nixon's darker side, who seized any opportunity to pour poison into his susceptible ears. But when Ehrlichman told me to go see Nixon, I thought he was merely being polite, and I felt foolish bothering a busy president with idle, if benign, chatter. I did not know how much chatter in the Oval Office was just as idle and nowhere so benign. So I spent my time feeling mostly relieved that I had, once again, a secure setting in which to "secretly" watch the great show and continue my search for a proper relationship to the world.

In the spring of 1969, strange as it seems to our own disillusioned decade, Washington glowed with drama and expectation; the White House was center stage. It was and is a surpassingly dangerous place; but its serene setting, in a small private park fenced off from the surrounding urban hubbub, makes presidents and their staffers slow to find this out.

They take good care of you at the White House. You always get a smart salute from the uniformed marine tending the door. In the basement are dining rooms, kitchens, darkrooms, a barbershop, an exercise room, and facilities for sandwiches, soda, and hanging out. The meticulous care given White House inhabitants is epitomized by the White House telephone operators, legendary for their ability to handle crushing waves of phone calls during real or manufactured national excitements and to locate anyone, anytime, anywhere in the world. Everyone who has worked in the White House has a favorite operator story. Once, when I had been out of government for five years, I had to locate the head of a large investment house, a client of my law firm, because a hospital on whose board he sat had been seized by a sudden labor crisis. He was on vacation, on a yacht somewhere in the Mediterranean. Unreachable. I called the White House and asked, not thinking to identify myself, "There's a crisis. Could you please locate Mr. X?" "Yes, Mr. Garment," the operator answered instantly, and proceeded to do her job.

The main floor of the West Wing is the prime real estate in the White House, fought and wept over by the White House staff because of its proximity to the president, who sits a few feet away in the middle of the web of offices and facilities. Across Executive Avenue, whose parking spaces are as precious as the West Wing's main-floor offices, is the massive Old Executive Office Building (O.E.O.B.). Its inhabitants—people in the Office of Management and Budget, the Office of the Vice President, the National Security Council, the Council of Economic Advisers, the speechwriting staff, and such—always feel a bit déclassé compared with their West Wing brethren.

In this building there are news-clipping collectors, television news watchers, letter answerers, spooks and counterspooks, carpenters, painters, bodyguards, cooks, physicians, a bowling alley, banking facilities, and God knows what else. The long, dark halls, the nooks and crannies sliced up by partitions in attempts to accommodate the demands of the building's inhabitants, the attic spaces and secret rooms add to a sense that the O.E.O.B. is secondarily a working building and primarily a place to play hide-and-seek. No wonder some White House actors saw the building as a sanctuary from prying eyes—a good place to organize an undercover operation or hatch a conspiracy. The Watergate plumbers used Room 193, on the

O.E.O.B.'s basement floor, as the command center for their demented activities.

During President Nixon's White House years, he worked in the suite immediately to the left of the O.E.O.B.'s entrance. The Oval Office, by contrast, was where he ceremonially presided. Word was put about that Nixon had chosen his O.E.O.B. office to make his staff in the building feel less second-class, but the evidence is that he actually preferred this office. Here he had his comfortable furniture, his favorite brown plush easy chair and ottoman, his collection of pipes, photos, and memorabilia, his musical sound system—and, eventually, some of his less aesthetic taping equipment. It was in this office that John Dean delivered his March 21, 1973, "cancer on the presidency" oration to Nixon. In fact, Bill Safire has written that at the very moment Dean was talking, Safire, who had resigned and was leaving the White House, paused at the office door for a moment, undecided whether to go in and say one last good-bye to Nixon. He passed up the chance, thus missing his opportunity to alter history or become an unindicted co-conspirator.

I was assigned to a spacious and sunny O.E.O.B. corner office just down the hall from Nixon's suite. I had a connecting room for two secretaries and one for a staff assistant. My office bore the weird number 188^1/$_2$, testimony to the hopelessness of the efforts to make the building fit its inhabitants. My next-door neighbor was Charles Colson.

For the six years I spent on the White House staff of President Nixon and, briefly, President Ford, the day began in predawn darkness. A Chrysler sedan—warm in winter, cool in summer, an army driver at the wheel, *The New York Times*, *The Washington Post*, and the White House news summaries on the backseat—waited at my home. We drove north, up Route 95, over the Key Bridge, past the dawn-shrouded shape of the Lincoln Memorial, along a silent Constitution Avenue, through the southwest gate of the White House, and up to the basement door of the West Wing. The White House day officially started with a seven-thirty A.M. senior staff meeting over coffee in the Roosevelt Room. Haldeman, Ehrlichman, and Kissinger had already met in Haldeman's office to sort out the president's problems for the day; then Ehrlichman convened the larger Roosevelt Room meeting, proceeding around the table for brief staff reports.

Ehrlichman, as it suited him, could be charming, brusque, funny, knowledgeable, or painfully acerbic. He was always in charge. His heavy dark eyebrows did their familiar fidgeting dance as he called the roll, cut off speeches, handed out assignments, and shut down the meeting at eight A.M. For months, my occasional contributions to these meetings consisted mainly of puns—which, while modest, were not altogether without redeeming value. One of the administration's persistent problems, for instance, was its inability to obtain the much-desired resignation of the chairman of the Federal Home Loan Bank Board, a gentleman named Louis Lapin. Huge amounts of taxpayer-financed time were devoted at the staff meeting, day after day, to the Lapin Dilemma. Finally I suggested that people should resign themselves to their problem; as they all knew, "Lapins make lousy leavers." Groans, but no more Lapin complaints.

Many of the figures who gathered around that early-morning table at one time or another during the Nixon years are now well known: Henry Kissinger, George Shultz, Don Rumsfeld, Al Haig, Mel Laird, Peter Flanigan, Bryce Harlow, Herb Stein, Dick Cheney, Ann Armstrong, Caspar Weinberger, Frank Carlucci, Paul O'Neill, Arthur Burns, Elizabeth Dole, Jim Schlesinger, Bill Timmons, Brent Scowcroft, Virginia Knauer. Sprinkled among these eminentoes-in-training were more anonymous worker bees, a few of whom became public figures only when institutional loyalty, White House isolation, and a defective sense of self-interest combined to get them a fleeting moment of Watergate fame and possibly a not-so-fleeting jail term. Some of these were eminently decent young men, like the lawyers Egil "Bud" Krogh and Ed Morgan, who performed their staff assignments with energy and skill—Krogh in law enforcement, Morgan in school desegregation—only to have their lives desperately messed up while carrying out assignments for Nixon, Ehrlichman, or Colson. For Krogh, it was the Ellsberg break-in; for Morgan, the backdating of Nixon's deed of vice presidential papers to the government.

Ron Ziegler, who managed to be close as a glove to the president but who had no operational assignments and escaped Watergate miraculously unharmed, was occasionally at the Roosevelt Room meeting, but more frequently he sent his deputy, Jerry Warren. Chuck Colson also sent a deputy, presumably having better (i.e., worse) things to do with his mornings. Murray Chotiner, charter member of the original Nixon political family and throwback to Nixon's most controversial years in politics, made an occasional appearance. He was one of my favorites, a shrewd landsman who could pass for any middle-aged Jewish uncle with a paunch—in particular for my uncle Abe Garment, a waiter in the Little Oriental Restaurant on Pitkin Avenue in Brooklyn.

Then there was Harry Dent, formerly Strom Thurmond's assistant, now a White House political adviser and the operational executive of Nixon's "southern strategy." I eventually became Harry's informal counterpart, proponent of the Nixon "northern strategy." To become president, Nixon had promised a great deal to the South; now, in office, he had the power and desire to deliver considerably less. Nixon's idea was that Harry and I would battle out issues of politics and race hand to hand, by fair means and foul, thereby miraculously achieving a functional balance that would be tolerable to southern conservatives and northern liberals. It was, shall we say, not easy, necessitating John Mitchell's famous dictum, "Watch what we do, not what we say."

After the morning meeting, people went to the White House mess for breakfast and hard-core gossip. Then the staff went off to bully cabinet officers or jolly members of Congress, plan arms negotiations and covert operations or fiddle with the federal budget and U.S. economy. I usually drifted back to my office, content to drink more coffee, scribble those memos, finish the daily and weekly media, case the O.E.O.B. and West Wing, visit speechwriter chums, and kibitz with policy staffers. I placed and answered phone calls, talked to reporters and supplicants for White House information, and had lots of lunches.

Gradually, a job took shape along the lines of my babbled speech to Arthur Burns when he interviewed me for the directorship of the Office of Economic Opportunity. I gradually became White House counsel to power-impoverished parts of the federal government, resident advocate for the great unwashed of the executive branch, ombudsman for the door-pounding outside world. Word got around. Business boomed.

It boomed, in fact, in places I didn't even know existed. One day I got a letter, bucked to me by the president himself, from an impressive-sounding group of scientists operating out of Miami under the respectable corporate name of Vanguard Research, Inc. They wanted White House support for their application to the National Science Foundation for a grant to help find the Abominable Snowman—or, more precisely, not the Snowman himself, a Russo-Asian denizen, but the North American Sasquatch (aka Bigfoot).

There was a seconding letter from the editor of *The Bigfoot Bulletin*, who testified that while he had not actually seen Bigfoot, he had found "tracks as well as hairs and feces that cannot be identified as belonging to any known creature." I stifled the temptation to tell him about some people I knew who might fit the bill, and I tried to be helpful. But the National Science Foundation had other priorities.

With all this activity, I soon needed a helper. Morris Liebman, an eminent Chicago lawyer of my acquaintance and a man-about-politics, was a compulsive matchmaker. He introduced me to Brad Patterson, the executive director of the President's Commission on Equal Opportunity. Before working with me, Brad had served as a National War College lecturer, deputy cabinet secretary, and executive assistant to Sargent Shriver at the Peace Corps. He knew how and by whom policy was formed in the federal government. If he didn't know a policy-relevant fact, he knew how to get it quickly. He knew precisely how papers moved everywhere in the government: in what sequence, through whose hands, and the home phone numbers of the people attached to those hands. Brad was trusted by every professional in Washington. He was the reason I was able to cover a large number of policy areas without getting into public trouble.

As I went along, I enlisted other individuals: an incredible secretary named Eleanor Conner, Carol Harford for cultural issues, pickup teams of executive branch and volunteer staff for assignments like school desegregation, fair housing, and reform of American Indian policy. But, as actors say at Hollywood award ceremonies about their producers and mothers, it was Brad Patterson who made it all possible. As a result of his help, settling into my new line of work was not hard. Indeed, it was the least of the difficulties I experienced in moving from private to public life. My major problems were back home.

· · ·

During the great distraction of the Nixon comeback and campaign years, the difficulties in my marriage seemed to abate—or I wasn't back home in New York often enough for there to be any problems, at least for me. Now, though, it was clear that I was staying in Washington, and the question of what to do about the marriage had to be confronted. It was not that Grace and I did not get along; in most ways we did, famously. But both of us were depressives who had concluded that by marrying we could at least cheer each other up full-time and who wound up making things progressively worse for each other, full-time. I had access to various kinds of temporary relief: work, travel, friends, psychiatry, crazy plans to make Richard Nixon president of the United States. Grace was stuck with psychiatry, keeping house, looking after the kids, and, when they could walk and talk, ferrying them to their own psychiatrists. When she finished her chores, she would go to the bedroom, close the door, lie on her bed, and weep, night after night, inconsolably. And not only at home: I remember a winter weekend in the 1950s, before the kids were born, when a bunch of us—my brothers, their wives, and some close friends—went to the Music Inn, a lodge near Lenox, Massachusetts. These were people Grace knew, liked, and was easy with. She joined us for a cheerful-joke-filled breakfast the first day, then went to our room and never came out. I made the conventional excuses about "illness." For three days she slept, stared at the ceiling, and cried.

One of her doctors later described Grace as "anhedonistic," clinically incapable of pleasure. But this description missed the true quality of her depression. When she wept, it was never about anything in particular except for one thing, a lost life, which no one could return to her.

As long as I was living in New York, it was clear that we would stay stuck in this rut. My going to Washington in 1968 changed the equation. Once there, I returned to Brooklyn infrequently; Grace came down only for the inaugural, and with the kids for a weekend. I began to assess the marriage more abstractly—more clearly, I thought, than before. I was logical, disinterested, and lawyerlike: the time had come. It's now or never. Break it off; it will be best for everyone. Grace is sealed in cement, paralyzed. Everything has been tried; nothing works. Force her to act. Free her, free yourself, save two lives. The kids will survive. Show some guts. Do it now. I worked out various speeches in my head based on this argument. It got to the point where I was pretty good at imagining the scene— the quiet talk, Grace nodding her head as she absorbed my arguments and accepted my logic, smiling, relieved, grateful that I was getting it all out in the open, finally making her deal with it. The details in my head were blurred, but the feeling was clear—warm, civilized, friendly, nice.

So one weekend early in the summer of 1969, I returned to Brooklyn Heights to talk to Grace about a separation. Once home, I stalled as long as I could. On Sunday afternoon, before heading back to Washington, I asked Grace to walk with me out to the backyard, out of earshot of the kids, for a talk. I mumbled about "something serious." We sat on some railroad ties that formed a large, square border around our willow tree. This was not just any tree that grew in Brooklyn. It was full-grown and forty feet high, acquired by the two of us joyously, expansively, crazily in 1965. We had it carted in by truck from a Scarsdale nursery, the mammoth roots and branches tied back in bundles. Six perspiring workmen accompanied the tree, pushed it through our garage opening, and carried out the pyramid-building operation necessary to plant it. The willow tree was supposed to be the first stage of an ambitious landscaping plan but turned out to be the last, because we ran out of money. The tree was a reminder of all our expectations and misadventures, the oversized projects lovingly and confidently launched because they transiently excited our imaginations, the ceaseless efforts we made to search out solutions for problems we couldn't define.

The tree was also a reminder that with all the craziness, headaches, and tears, there had been lots of good times. So I knew, as soon as I began my rehearsed spiel, that I had picked the wrong spot. I was talking about separation, but I was thinking about the house, the tree, the kids. Grace said something about Washington giving her, and all of us, a chance for a fresh start. She began crying. I began crying. That was that. We would all go to Washington. I flew back hugely relieved, wondering how I could have thought of leaving my family. And, give or take a few bad moments, the next six years were relatively happy ones for all of us, probably the best of Grace's life.

I was back on our old street in Brooklyn Heights recently, visiting our friends Joe and Mary Merz, the architects of the Brooklyn house. I went over to the old house and, peering through the gate, could see that the willow tree was gone. It turned out that the tree was too big for a city backyard. Its roots had begun to choke the adjoining underground structures, and it had to be extracted like an infected tooth. But it served its purpose.

Later in the summer of 1969, Michael Straight, a friend of mine and a client of my old law firm, made an offer I couldn't refuse. Mike owned a house in Virginia called Green Spring Farm. It was being vacated by its present tenants, a young C.I.A. officer, Fred Hitz, and his family, who had been assigned to Africa. Would I like to rent it? The offer carried uncertainties. There was no lease, because Straight was in the process of giving the property to Fairfax County as part of a complex land and rezoning swap. The tenancy was not only terminable on thirty days' notice but subject to rights of access for the Straight family. I would be part tenant, part house sitter. Still, when I saw what I would be getting for a manageable rent, my eyes popped. It was seven acres of gorgeous landscaping, with access to a bass pond, a grass tennis court, and horse barns. There was even a nice old caretaker couple, John and Mary Quast, who "lived in a shoe"—actually, a kind of fairy-tale cottage near the pond—and looked after the property. The house itself was a tidy little brick Colonial built around 1780; the history of the house was also the history of the way a part of Virginia lived for two centuries. After all the sturm und drang of the previous year, it was good to be able to surprise Grace and the kids with the glories of Green Spring Farm. In August, without prior notice, I unveiled it to their delighted eyes. Everything about it spelled "fresh start" to the Garment family.

Indeed, "fresh start" is the reason, I came to realize, why many people are drawn to Washington—why they come and stay or, if they leave, often return. It is a place of fresh starts, where the "real life" back home is suspended. Washington inflicts its own wounds, of course, but somehow life in political Washington has the quality of a perpetual open-air theatre whose curtain rises with *The Wash-*

ington Post and falls each evening with the eleven o'clock TV news. Maybe the reason so little good fiction has been written about Washington is that Washington life itself has so many elements of make-believe and improbability.

Take Green Spring Farm, for instance. In 1969, when Fred Hitz departed, Mike Straight needed a tenant and I needed a house. At the same time, Mike and I were working together on a federal arts project. Five years later, in 1974, when I had narrowly escaped the taint of Watergate, personal scandal nevertheless threatened me—and the cause was Green Spring Farm. In the summer of 1974, *The Washington Monthly*, an influential liberal magazine, published an article suggesting that the Green Spring Farm lease was a "sweetheart" contract and that the quid pro quo for my low rent may have been the high-level federal arts job that I had arranged for Mike Straight. It was lucky for me that this was Watergate endgame time; Washington had more exciting things to worry about, so this scandalette vanished without a trace. Fifteen years later, in 1989, I was back in Washington and bought a house. We found that our next-door neighbors, and soon our good friends, were Jim and Debbie Fallows, just returned from Japan. Jim had been a speechwriter for Jimmy Carter; he was at that time a noted writer on politics and Washington editor of the *Atlantic Monthly*. (Moving up in the world, he is now the editor of *U.S. News & World Report*.) Going through old files one day, preparing to write this memoir, I came upon the yellowing pages of the *Washington Monthly* article on the scandal of Green Spring Farm. The author was, naturally, Jim Fallows. That's Washington.

The arts project that Mike Straight and I were working on was, as it happened, my first White House enterprise: I was developing a Nixon arts policy. In 1969, this idea seemed an oxymoron, but eventually it took shape and became a serious accomplishment, for which I received a large amount of undeserved credit. The foregoing assertion is not an exercise in modesty, real or feigned. It is an illustration of an interesting fact of public life: Many of the worthy or unworthy things you actually do in government will escape notice or proper attribution, while you will frequently be praised, blamed, or given a place in history for activities with which you have only a glancing connection.

Early in 1969, while I was still at the Mudge Rose offices in Washington, Peter Flanigan asked me one day to find a replacement for Roger Stevens, the chairman of the National Endowment for the Arts (N.E.A.). Stevens, Washington's all-purpose panjandrum of culture, was a popular figure. So, I asked, why don't we leave him in place? Nixon wants a couple of Democrats in his administration, and the N.E.A. job is really no big deal. Flanigan knew and respected Stevens, but said it was important to show that Republicans could do more in government than manage defense and economic policy.

I began my hunt by enlisting the help of Michael Straight, who was extremely knowledgeable in the arts. Straight had written skeptically in *The New Republic* about the way the N.E.A. was distributing its microscopic allocation of federal funds. N.E.A. policy was idiosyncratic, Straight argued: Money was spent on things like individual prizes and artists' housing in New York City, when the emphasis should be on systematic support for arts institutions and for efforts to expand the base of constituent and congressional support for federal arts funding.

Straight's argument made sense to me, in light of the little I knew about the infant Endowment, founded in 1965. In their first few years, both the N.E.A. and its sister organization, the National Endowment for the Humanities, were surrounded by clouds of gauzy rhetoric and not much hard cash. They were nothing more than stunted imitations of the elite European institutions that administered government support for the fine arts. In 1969, when Nixon took office, the combined budget of the endowments was about $15 million, a scruffy sum for the task of elevating the American soul. But Mike and I had time on our hands and a license to tinker.

We began to patch together a plan to make the endowments into significant institutions. My main contribution was knowledge of Nixon. I knew from the campaign how he liked to surprise people, not just out of perversity—though he certainly enjoyed confounding his critics' assumptions about him—but also from a belief in the strategic wisdom of Wee Willie Keeler: "Just hit 'em where they ain't." I also knew that Nixon, like many historical leaders, believed there was a connection between great cultures and great civilizations and that patronage of the arts and letters by aristocracies or governments strengthened this connection.

Finally, I knew the least likely fact of all: Nixon was a closet aesthete and had strong, traditional views about what was good or bad in painting, music, architecture, and writing. He hero-worshiped great performers—Rudolf Serkin, for example—and habitually turned the volume up on his home phonograph and played classical music or Richard Rodgers as an accompaniment to the plain prose of his political dreams. A cynic might say that Nixon was a vulnerable customer for a couple of cultural shingle salesmen like Straight and me.

There was also an operational argument in all this. Nixon was facing months and probably years of thunder on his left. He would do well to use whatever offsets were available, even if small, to mollify his liberal adversaries and dilute their anger. I had an intuition that if we made the case that a dollar of intervention in the arts would buy multiple dollars of political peace, Nixon might agree—as long as we could provide him with a prudent initiative in capable hands.

Here my expertise ended. For the rest, I turned to Straight, Charles MacWhorter, and Nancy Hanks.

Mike Straight was the model of an American aristocrat. He was rich, Leslie Howard–handsome, elegant, quiet, self-effacing. He played tennis every day, drove beat-up cars, wore tattered shirts with perfectly tailored suits, and had faultless manners to match his unfailingly generous disposition. He was born in Southampton to Willard Straight and Dorothy Whitney Straight and grew up in a family steeped in money, culture, and liberal politics, with friends like Franklin Roosevelt and Felix Frankfurter. At Cambridge he became a pal of John Maynard Keynes. Later he was part of Ben Cohen and Tommy Corcoran's speechwriting team in the Roosevelt administration, and later still an economist, novelist, art critic, political commentator, collector, and patron. He was a dauntingly complex figure, cursed mainly by not really having to do anything and, therefore, being compelled to try everything—like my cousin George Swetlow, but with money and without the ethnic angst.

The second member of our arts planning group was Charlie MacWhorter, a lawyer with AT&T and one of Nixon's oldest political friends. Charlie, an elfin figure, was the man on the campaign bus or plane who provided the candidate and the press with bits of local political color, which he drew from a vast trove of information he had collected, the way kids collect baseball cards, over a lifetime of volunteer political activity in the Republican party, starting with service during the 1950s in Richard Nixon's congressional office. Over time it became clear to me that MacWhorter was the type of political secret agent who patiently accumulates credits for large causes—the arts, opposition to Vietnam—by doing small errands for the mighty.

The third central figure was Nancy Hanks, president of the Associated Councils on the Arts, a handsome, energetic, and exuberant woman who had worked for years with the Rockefeller family on their various public policy projects.

Mike, Charlie, Nancy, and I went through the usual list of Republican suspects, looking for a new N.E.A. chairman. There were the very rich, the very distinguished, the established patrons—each of whom, fortunately, declined, principally because the total Endowment budget was less than what they spent on their household help. Finally, I looked around and saw, perched there, our perfect candidate, Nancy Hanks herself. After characteristically insisting on a list of ironclad guarantees from the Office of Management and Budget, she said yes.

Then, to my surprise, New York's Jacob Javits, Nancy's Republican home-state senator, whose consent was necessary for her Senate confirmation, said no. He had his own candidate: John Walker, the retired director of the National Gallery of Art—and he was serious. I proceeded, for the first and last time in my Washington years, to outmaneuver Jack Javits. I sent word that if the nominee couldn't be Nancy, it would be not John Walker but Mike Straight, the only Democrat Nixon would accept as chairman.

Mike seemed ambivalent but agreed to go along with the ploy, predicting that Javits would fold and withdraw his opposition to Nancy in order to avoid being responsible for the naming of a Democrat as chairman. When Javits relented, and I called Mike to tell him, he seemed not only genuinely pleased but relieved. Nixon named Nancy chairman at a September 1969 press conference in San Clemente, pledging his personal support for the expansion of the federal cultural effort.

Nancy and I agreed that Mike should be named deputy chairman. But when I talked to him about the mechanics of Senate confirmation, he informed me that his F.B.I. clearance would not be routine. I learned part of the reason then, part later.

In the 1930s, when Straight was at Cambridge hobnobbing with Keynes, he also knew Anthony Blunt and Guy Burgess, who were agents of the Soviet Union. They recruited Straight into the Communist party, then instructed him to break publicly with the party, go underground, return to the United States, and find ways to gather information in important places.

After going home, Straight first worked as an unpaid volunteer in the State Department, then got his job as a speechwriter for F.D.R. He says he never had access to, let alone transmitted, any classified information, but he did not break decisively with his Communist past.

In 1951 in Washington, with the Korean War on, Straight came upon Burgess, who was in the British Foreign Service—the Far Eastern Affairs Section, no less. Straight settled for delivering a warning: "If you aren't out of government within a month, I swear I'll turn you in." In May, Burgess disappeared, soon turning up in the Soviet Union.

Straight might never have come forward with his story. But in 1963, President Kennedy created an Advisory Council on the Arts that was meant to lead to an arts endowment. White House aide Arthur Schlesinger called Straight and said Kennedy planned to name him the first chairman of the new endowment. Straight felt compelled to tell his story to the F.B.I.—where his first interrogator was a sympathetic young agent, Jimmy Lee, the son of his mother's head gardener—and to British intelligence services, which had long suspected Blunt, by then Sir Anthony, of espionage. In 1964 Blunt, informed that Straight had told the whole story, confessed.

That explained why, in 1969, Straight seemed reluctant to be named to the high-profile chairman's job and happy when I told him the job would go to Nancy. I checked with the F.B.I. about making him deputy chairman, and they had no objection: I later learned that since 1963, when he first went to the F.B.I., Mike had been helping British and American intelligence pursue Soviet espionage agents.

In most matters, Straight's politics were predictably liberal. But while he was at the N.E.A., whenever he encountered an attempt to manipulate the arts for political purposes, he turned fierce—gagging, as it were, on any reminder of the rallying cry of his Communist years, "Art is a weapon." Hardened by history, Mike did more than anyone else during those years to keep the Endowment clear of the shoals of politics.

Once the Hanks-Straight team was in place, they proceeded to exploit the president's promises. Their strategy was simple: They would emphasize the provision of support for mainstream arts institutions, proven art works, and clearly qualified grantees. This type of support would in turn promote constituent and congressional support for a steady buildup in the arts budget. As for the White House, we began by doubling the arts budget, then compounded it year after year, as Nancy captivated Congress, budget officials, governors, mayors, and the press, while Mike watched the store. By 1976, when Nancy finished her second term as chairman, the federal arts budget had grown from $8 million to almost $90 million and was still climbing.

Apart from intervening with budgeteers like Cap Weinberger and Paul O'Neill, my role was to play fireman in controversies of taste that from time to time Nancy sent along for handling. These problems were comparatively small, since Nancy and Mike, to avoid explosions on the right, had drawn a tight net around the grant process. But occasionally I helped. For instance, there was the immense Alex Liberman sculpture *Adam*, an abstract configuration of red-painted metal 29 feet long by 26 feet wide that graced the front of the classic Corcoran Museum across the street from the White House. *Adam* drove Nixon slightly crazy whenever he stepped out onto the White House grounds for a moment of tranquillity and caught a glimpse of it. "Get it out of my sight," Nixon implored me. He knew he could not just order its removal, the way he would order an invasion or a bombing run. In a matter like this he could order himself blue in the face and nothing other than public embarrassment would result, unless someone outmaneuvered the endlessly resistant federal bureaucracy. I talked to Nancy and Mike. They quietly arranged for the National Park Service to lift, load, and relocate *Adam* to remote Hains Point, a patch of green and trees at the edge of the Potomac River.

Not long afterward, on an evening's cruise down the Potomac on the presidential yacht *Sequoia*, we rounded a bend in the river—and all of us, Nixon included, suddenly saw *Adam*. I cursed my bad luck and held my breath. Nixon, though, nodded his head to no one in particular and said, "This is where it should have been in the first place." A good moment for the arts, a better one for craft.

Also instructive was the completion of the Hirshhorn Museum, stymied by resistance from the snobbish Washington arts establishment, which was appalled that a national museum on the Mall would bear the name of the nouveau immigrant art collector, Abe Hirshhorn. Nixon, no fan of the modern art that made up Hirshhorn's gift to the country, would happily have seen the project go down the drain. Moynihan and I thought Hirshhorn's priceless gift had to be saved. Working with movie mogul Taft Shreiber, a friend of both Hirshhorn's and Nixon's, a major Republican contributor, and an admirer of modern art—we assembled a board of directors, most of whom owned important collections of modern art and were major contributors to the political campaigns of Richard Nixon. Moynihan agreed to be the museum's chairman. With these inducements, Haldeman and Ehrlichman were able to persuade Nixon to sign the authorizing documents. The Hirshhorn Museum rose from the near-dead and joined the ranks of the great Smithsonian museums that line the approach to the Capitol.

The problem of politics and obscenity in the arts bedeviled us then as it does today, but compared with the country's current headaches in the area, ours were minor. On one occasion the American Film Institute, a federally funded organization located in the federally assisted Kennedy Center, scheduled *State of Siege*, a Costa-Gavras film about the killing of an American hostage by leftist terrorists in a Latin American dictatorship. It seemed to me crazy or worse to run a film extolling terrorist murder in a federally funded facility. I told my friend George Stevens, the director of the Institute, that I intended to withdraw the president's name from the list of sponsors of the film's benefit premier and that I would do so noisily. Stevens calmly canceled the film, publicly announcing his judgment that running a pro-assassin movie at a center named for an assassinated president was less than appropriate.

Most painful was the dispute surrounding *Mass*, an antiwar oratorio that Leonard Bernstein wrote to celebrate the opening of the

Kennedy Center in 1970. Bernstein invited me to sit with him at the dress rehearsal, where, down front in the empty Opera Hall, I listened to both his splendid creation and his fervent plea that I persuade the president to attend the gala premiere. I tried to explain to Bernstein why it was impossible to persuade Richard Nixon, after a week of antiwar protests, to dress up in black tie to attend an antiwar protest set to music. Bernstein, his handsome head leaning in close to mine, his arm around my shoulders, was singing passages in my ear and pleading, "Lenny, Lenny, don't you realize how important this is?" I was of two minds: No and Definitely No. Bernstein, whose *Mass* so inextricably mixed art and politics, would not —simply *could* not—comprehend why *Nixon* would mix art and politics. Never before or since have I seen the impenetrable wall between the two worlds so clearly.

There were scores of such skirmishes; Endowment panels were even then capable of recommending remarkably foolish grants for a publicly accountable institution. But for the most part, Nancy and Mike, particularly Mike, contained or smothered pernicious aberrations. Within the private arts world, an unarticulated consensus took shape to spare the nasty words and save the delicate child.

There were genuine satisfactions in running interference for federal support of culture in those years. One of the best moments came on a trip to Europe with my pal Ron Berman, a sturdy Renaissance scholar who was the chairman of the National Endowment for the Humanities. A middle-distance runner from Brooklyn (which got him his scholarship to Harvard), Berman kept a tight grip on his Endowment's programs, concentrating on libraries, academic archives, university presses, televised histories like *The Adams Chronicles*, and the acquisition of talented program managers like Roger Rosenblatt, who headed Ron's education section.

Just before I decamped from Washington in December 1974, Ron invited me, still the government's official culture maven, to join him at festivities in the Louvre celebrating an exhibit of Assyrian bronzes. We walked through the exhibit, then sat down to an official lunch. There, Assyrian bronze curators and other Middle East art experts lectured Ron condescendingly on the ABC's of the bronzes. After lunch, Ron proceeded to his reply—a breathtaking tour de force, including everything from a contextual analysis of the historic and aesthetic antecedents of the bronzes to their general impact on the plastic arts. I proudly hugged him after the event, proclaiming an epic victory for Erasmus Hall High School.

Nancy Hanks died in 1983 at the age of fifty-five, after an extended battle with cancer. By then, a fin-de-siècle sadness hovered over the once-exuberant federal arts project. The seeds of this disappointment had been sown during our own years in charge of the Endowment. Nancy, with her passion for growth, persistently sought to enlarge the arts constituency by doing what politicians do best: doling out money with less and less discrimination in order to get more and more money. Side shows—experimental and provocative forms, political arts, new and exotic grant categories—gradually edged into the main arena, attracting crowds of trouble from increasingly vocal enemies. Ironically, Nancy, the establishment politician, was the figure who allowed the arts endowment to become a bazaar in which proven artistic excellence had to elbow its way through crowds of mediocrity and sensationalism. And Mike Straight, who had learned about art and politics the hard way, was the one who repeatedly warned Nancy (and me) that she was buying peace in her time with a sacrifice of quality that would ultimately threaten the Endowment. He was dead right.

By the time I returned to Washington in 1980 to practice law, the endowments were in serious trouble, the result of a loosening of standards during the Carter administration, the growing power after 1980 of politicians who wanted to destroy the endowments altogether, and the activities of visual artists who seemed bent on painting an even bigger bull's-cye on the N.E.A.'s heart. There were incessant controversies over grants and subgrants, involving works such as a virulently political AIDS mural featuring New York's Cardinal John J. O'Connor, a photo composition titled *Piss Christ* featuring a crucifix in a container of artist Andres Serrano's urine, and a theatre work involving symbolic excrement spread over performance artist Karen Finley's body and a yam thrust in her vagina. These cases were insigificant in number, but the aggressive defense of them by the elite arts community symbolized for many (me, for one) a descent into infantile chaos of the once-disciplined, tightrope-walking federal effort to sponsor aesthetic excellence and disseminate it to the nation. In 1989–90, when Congress debated extending the endowments' authorization, these controversies paralyzed the proceedings. To quiet the noise, the administration and Congress set up a bipartisan commission, Washington's usual solution to political embarrassment. John Brademas, the president of New York University and an original congressional draftsman of the Endowment legislation in 1965, was named one of the commission's cochairmen. I was the other. There were ten additional appointees—Republicans, Democrats, left-wing liberals, and right-wing conservatives, a heterogeneous and fiercely opinionated group of arts aficionados.

We held public hearings and private debates for two months, then amazingly and unanimously agreed on recommendations: The N.E.A. should be reauthorized and should place no specific restrictions on the content of the work it funds. But the Endowment's grant-making procedures should be drastically changed to curb artistic craziness and conflicts of interest among grant panelists. The message, *sub silentio:* If you liked fecal art, fine, but on your own time and not with federal money.

Though there are signs of recovery at the Endowment, some things are hard to change. If structural distinctions are not drawn between public support for validated American art treasures and private support for art still in the aesthetic laboratory, and if "freedom of expression" keeps being reflexively brandished by the press and arts community as a substitute for the hard, compromise-filled work of sustaining a political consensus for the arts, then the federal arts experiment will fade and fail—not all at once, but gradually and inexorably. But the arts will survive. The nation will certainly survive. Somewhat saddened, so will I. After all, I still have my saxophone and my clarinet.

While I was in the Nixon White House, I played the latter more than the former. The clarinet seemed a more credible instrument to whip out casually for a "spontaneous" display of middle-aged virtuosity. By contrast, the tenor saxophone—a large, monstrously shaped looping product of Adolph Sax's fevered dreams—bespeaks premeditation. I had the world's best chance to strut my dimly remembered stuff at the White House on April 29, 1969. The evening was the cultural high point of the Nixon administration, though not because I played clarinet. We were giving a black-tie presidential dinner to celebrate the seventieth birthday of Duke Ellington. Willis Conover, jazz impresario of the Voice of America, had been trying for some time to arrange a jazz evening at the White House. He talked with Charlie MacWhorter about an Ellington party, then brought the idea to me. I thought it was wonderful and passed the idea on to the White House social secretary, Lucy Winchester, who concurred. Voice of America would record the proceedings and, though forbidden to broadcast them in the United States, would transmit them to the rest of the world.

That evening, amid the fragrance of budding White House magnolias and the waning but still-ambient warmth of the presidential honeymoon, many of the great figures of American jazz gathered to pay homage to Ellington in words and music. During dinner the "Strolling Strings" from the U.S. Army band played Ellington songs. After dinner, a band of America's best played a concert of Ellington compositions specially arranged by Gerry Mulligan. Joe Williams and Mary Mayo sang. Nixon presented the Medal of Freedom to "Edward Kennedy . . . [stage pause] Ellington" and played "Happy Birthday" on the piano in his usual key of G. Ellington bestowed his traditional four kisses (two for each cheek) on a startled Nixon, then improvised a charming song, "Pat," for Mrs. Nixon. It was one of the happiest, most relaxed public occasions of Richard Nixon's life.

At midnight, Nixon bid his guests a buoyant good night and invited everyone to stay on for a jam session and dancing. As the ebullient crowd milled around the East Room waiting for the chairs to be cleared, Nixon sent word that I should bring the pianist Earl "Fatha" Hines upstairs to the family quarters for a nightcap. Hines and Nixon sat around for a while, reminiscing. Hines, the pioneer artist, talked about the early joys of his long life in jazz. Nixon, the political utilitarian, told about what he learned from the years of piano lessons and practicing he endured as a kid. By the time Hines and I got back downstairs, the chandeliered East Room had been transformed into the old Cotton Club. Improbable couples had formed—Duke Ellington with Rose Mary Woods, the dancer Carmen de Lavallade with George Shultz—and were dancing to the music of Dizzy Gillespie, Gerry Mulligan, Clark Terry, Bill Berry, Jim Hall, Dave Brubeck, Billy Taylor, J. J. Johnson, Urbie Green, and (very briefly) me, accompanied by a rhythm section from the Marine Corps band. Years would pass before Benny Goodman forgave me for not instructing him to bring his clarinet; but if he played, how could I? It was a night of rare amity. This was not exactly a crowd of Nixon fans, but the Host Syndrome frequently transforms guests, as the Stockholm Syndrome does hostages, into admirers or even adulants until time restores their equilibrium. Which it did in this case. Frank Stanton, head of CBS, offered to finance a recording of the event, to be distributed in the U.S. as well as abroad, with the proceeds going to a fund for musicians. But all the evening's performers had to consent, and one would not: Fervently against the Vietnam War, he did not want to give away any form of aid or comfort to Richard Nixon and Nixon's White House.

Willis Conover and I carried a film print of the Ellington concert to the Moscow Film Festival in mid-July 1969. We were part of a U.S.I.A. delegation charged with presenting American works at the festival. The delegation included Mike Straight; Jack Valenti, aide to President Johnson; TV commentator Nancy Dickerson; and the designer Mollie Parnis. First we flew to London, where, for the long flight to Moscow, we boarded an Aeroflot plane. Entering the plane was like entering Russia itself. No sleek interior design, no svelte flight attendants, no fungible airline food. The plane's cabin was more like a dimly remembered, overdecorated room in my Aunt Bessie's cavernous Coney Island apartment, crowded with furniture, old rugs, the smell of cabbage and potatoes cooking, and hefty neighbors in babushkas helping out with household chores. I felt like I was going back home . . . way, way back.

At the Moscow airport, hours passed while our baggage was scrutinized and passports were transferred from one bureaucratic hand to another. The main focus of official interest was my clarinet, which Willis Conover had suggested I bring so I could play with some of his jazz musician friends. Indeed, some Russian musicians, looking like ersatz hippies, had appeared at the airport to welcome us; their presence only added to the bureaucrats' suspicion. Why were these odd-looking scientists and engineers (for these were their day jobs) meeting an official American delegation? Why was an American politician carrying a clarinet case? I doubt that these microscopic pre-glasnost mysteries were ever cleared up to the Soviets' satisfaction.

Eventually we made our way to Moscow and the Hotel Rossiya. There were stout, silent watchwomen behind desks on every dimly lit floor, Pentagon-length corridors stretching to the horizon, nonexistent civilian communications, and an ever-present sense of eyes, ears, microphones, and satellites tracking our movements and conversation. Late that night, Mike Straight invited me to accompany him to nearby Red Square, an immense, dramatically floodlit, cobblestoned space over which loomed the towers and turrets of the Kremlin. We stood there silently, watching the goose-stepping Red Guards. Straight's mind seemed far away; I didn't know, back then, just how far.

Political management dogged each step of the festival. On the second evening, our delegation visited the Café Pechora, Moscow's main jazz club on Kalinin Prospekt, where I played with the Russian musicians who had met us at the airport. All of them were fine instrumentalists. They did not speak much English, but they knew, from records, all the current bop tunes. So we had the kind of euphorically good time that comes with an unexpected coupling. The K.G.B. agent assigned to cover Russian jazz types—and known, congenially, to all of them—swung along with the music, occasionally jotting a confidential note on his little spy pad. ("Korsky out of tune," I imagined him scribbling. "Also, too many choruses on 'Stella by Starlight.' Firing squad.")

Conover recalls that the Russian musicians were vastly unimpressed by my official connection with the president of the United States. It was my ancient, minuscule association with Billie Holiday and Woody Herman that bowled them over.

The trip to Moscow was more than a cultural lark. When I was appointed to the delegation, I was still a private citizen. By the time we left for Moscow, though, I had been in government for a couple of months, and some official assignments had been tacked on to my Soviet trip. In early July, Israeli defense minister Moshe Dayan had asked that I be sent to Israel for a visit, and National Security Adviser Henry Kissinger had decided I should go there after Moscow. I was to meet the Israeli leadership and get acquainted with the political configurations so that I would be equipped to carry private communications to the Israelis from Nixon and Kissinger. More specifically, while I was in Moscow I was to meet with Assistant Secretary of State Joseph Sisco, who would be in Moscow on official business. Sisco, who was in charge of U.S. Mideast diplomacy, would give me a private message to carry to Prime Minister Golda Meir.

Kissinger also briefed me on what I should and should not do in my meetings with Soviet officials. The Russians, Kissinger explained, would, as they always did with a newly elected president, search out opportunities to gather whatever information they could about Nixon's policy inclinations and personality. The press had touted me as a friend and adviser of Nixon's since 1963; the Russians would therefore check me out carefully. If the chance comes your way, Kissinger told me, convey the impression that Nixon is somewhat "crazy"—immensely intelligent, well organized, and experienced, to be sure, but at moments of stress or personal challenge unpredictable and capable of the bloodiest brutality. Today, anyone familiar with Nixon's foreign policy knows about the "madman" strategy. But in June of 1969, as I sat in Kissinger's office in the White House basement, his instructions were more than a small surprise. Still, I got the drift of what I was supposed to do.

Our delegation was already at the film festival when something happened that suddenly intensified high-level Soviet interest in me. In the early summer of 1969, well before the festival, the president's urban adviser, Pat Moynihan, had recommended to Nixon the creation of a commission on national goals. This is the kind of project modern presidents find irresistible: It provides an aura of vision and presidential reach, an offset to the crummy, dog-eared, day-to-day business of real politics. Nixon said yes. But presidential counselor Arthur Burns disliked the idea intensely. In a compromise, Moynihan and Burns agreed on a director for the effort: me. This was approximately like putting Homer Simpson in charge of the space program. But my friend Moynihan believed he could direct the study through me, and Burns thought I did not have the expertise to get the project off the ground. Thus I was, each of them thought, the perfect choice.

By July 14, our film festival delegation was in Moscow. That day the *International Herald Tribune* carried a front-page story, widely distributed in Moscow, in which Nixon publicly announced the creation of the National Goals Research Staff. At a White House press conference, Moynihan, with characteristic rhetoric, described the group's charter in cosmic terms. It would study and report on emerging trends in demography, education, economic growth, environment, technology assessment, and the use of social indicators to identify America's emerging social needs. It would present comparative arguments for a national debate on how to achieve long-range growth without jeopardizing the quality of life. And the staff's director would be Leonard Garment.

What Soviet officials saw was a Five Year Plan, with me in charge of it. I must be not just an amiable friend of President Nixon but a man who would wield massive power over the American future. So Georgy Arbatov, a senior adviser to General Secretary Leonid Brezhnev and director of the then-powerful Moscow Institute for United States studies, sent a message to me through our ambassador, Jacob Beame, asking me to meet with him and his colleagues. Beame said I must accept the invitation. He also said he would send along a couple of the embassy's best note takers, so that the meeting would be accurately recorded and reported to the State Department. Suddenly the lighthearted Moscow cultural trip had turned into the kind of nightmare where you find yourself addressing a large, august audience with your pants around your ankles.

What to do? Well, I first told our ambassador that I wanted complete informality and so would go alone. (Nobody near us/to see us or hear us . . .) You can't do that, Beame replied. They are a tricky bunch. We want to safeguard you. We have already agreed with Arbatov that they will have no more than five people present. We want to match them. I stood my ground, asserting the dispositive power of a presidential assistant. I have my reasons, I said mysteriously. I go alone or not at all. At the appointed hour, I appeared at the Moscow Institute, an old Russian house decorated with the familiar Russian trimmings. The conference table was covered with mineral water, Russian soft drinks, cigarettes, and fruit. Sadly, I noticed, no vodka. The Soviet delegation was of course not the five people promised to our embassy but eight or ten chunky, impressive-looking professionals, including what I'm sure were several K.G.B. veterans.

I pray that the newly opened Soviet archives never disgorge the Institute's notes of that meeting and reveal the pearls of confusion I cast before my interrogators during the three or four hours I was there. Arbatov led off: Why was the world's major anti-Communist power, with a Republican, free-enterprise administration, undertaking a major project that contemplated economic and demographic central planning? Was this not an admission of capitalism's internal contradictions? And so on.

The clutch of Soviet technicians and spies leaned forward, concenrated and serious, to hear my response. I took a deep breath and plunged in. Since they spoke fluent English but not fluent American, I began with an idiomatic, convoluted introduction that would have made doubletalk artist Al Kelly proud. I talked very fast. I told the whole story of my life—my Russian father, the family's struggle out of poverty, working in the dress factory, my religious awakening, the early interest in socialism, then music, then law, my passage into the dangerous American culture. Addressing Arbatov's questions, I offered aphoristic gems like "All circles can be squared" and "There is no such thing as contradiction, only a constrained grasp of complexity." Phrases dimly remembered from Marxist literature infiltrated my semideranged discourse.

My Soviet hosts began to wilt. They muttered to each other in Russian. I gained strength. I had not forgotten my instructions from Kissinger about making the Russians think Nixon was crazy. Actually, after I had talked for an hour and a half they were already thinking he must be loony to have me as an adviser. Now it was time to move in for the kill. I reviewed my years of work and friendship with Nixon. Arbatov and company's adrenaline machines started up again. I said things about the president of the United States that would have turned every hair on every head in our Foreign Service white with fright. Nixon is, I observed with clinical cheer, a dramatically disjointed personality, capable of acts of generosity and thoughtfulness but equally capable of barbaric cruelty to those who engage him in tests of strength. He is also, I threw in, more than a little paranoid because of years of bashing at the hands of political and media enemies. At his core, I said, he is predictably unpredictable, a man full of complex contradictions, a strategic visionary but, when necessary, a coldhearted butcher. So it went. Talk, talk. Scribble, scribble. I was, as jazz musicians say, cooking.

Finally it was over. Arbatov and his fellows bid me a warm adieu, delighted to have found that Mr. Bumble was also Mr. Big Mouth. They had reason to believe the meeting had been wonderfully productive. And so it had been. Because, strange to say, everything I said about Richard Nixon turned out to be more or less true.

After that meeting, Arbatov occasionally called me in Washington; our meetings, of which Henry Kissinger's National Security Council staff had to be notified in advance, were cordial and mutually uninformative. But when we discovered the Soviets building submarine facilities at Cienfuegos in Cuba, Nixon and Kissinger clamped down on such meetings.

One day during this crisis of detente, Kissinger learned I had a lunch date with Arbatov at the Hay Adams Hotel. "Don't go to lunch with Arbatov," he said.

"O.K.," I said. "I'll call and cancel."

"No," Kissinger said. "Don't call. Stand him up."

I could picture the Soviet America-watcher sitting in the lobby at the Hay Adams, gradually getting the idea.

The National Goals Research Staff was terminated after just one report because John Ehrlichman decided to create a Domestic Council that would subsume its functions. The report, *Toward Balanced Growth: Quantity with Quality,* was assembled by Professor Raymond Bauer of Harvard with minimal participation by me. Bauer worked wonders with little money and a skeleton staff, skillfully anticipating emerging issues such as consumerism, environmental degradation, and U.S. population movements. The report was received by the press with a marked lack of interest. The group's burial was also a quiet one, sparsely attended.

Meanwhile, back in Moscow, the film festival itself was, well, okay, but not as much fun as an evening at the Cineplex Odeon and a Chinese meal. Crowds of plain-dressed thousands filled an immense triple-tiered theatre to see the entries. Spontaneous enthusiasm greeted only the Ellington film, which was shown to a full house of Russian free spirits at a small side-street theatre reserved for unofficial screenings. In the middle of all this, my clarinet mysteriously disappeared from a closet in my hotel room. I spent a day making anxious inquiries. Officials spent a day shaking their heads. The next afternoon I returned to my room and found the clarinet sitting on my bed. All it lacked was a "kosher" stamp from the K.G.B.

Toward the end of the festival, a U.S. embassy official called and asked me to go to the embassy building. If I had a sweater, he told me, I should bring it along. I arrived at the embassy and was taken to the top floor. There I was ushered into an ice-cold Plexiglas room-within-a-room called the "Bubble." It was reserved for meetings that had to be protected from Soviet listening devices. The cold temperature was related to the antibugging equipment and the room's windowless construction.

There, with a handful of State Department associates, was Joe Sisco, whom Kissinger had told me I would be hearing from in Moscow. Sisco was a refreshing departure from standard State Department style. He was smart, cheerful, almost aggressively informal. He came quickly to the point: I was to go to Jerusalem and carry a message personally to Prime Minister Golda Meir and to no one else. He placed before me two pages plastered with warnings like TOP SECRET and EYES ONLY. I read the message quickly; it was an arcane commentary on Secretary of State William Rogers's plan for a Middle East settlement and other related matters. "What do I do with it?" I asked. "You sit here and memorize its contents," Sisco said. "It doesn't leave this room." Jesus, I thought, this is something I'm not good at. Especially under the watchful eyes of the several State Department officials who were sitting around the table looking at me, amused by this latest example of befuddled White House amateurism. It was, fortunately, too cold to perspire, and I settled down to read the message over and over.

Sisco finally broke the silence: "Look, you don't have to memorize it word for word. Just get the gist clear in your head and run through it for me." That done, I was ushered out of the diplomatic space capsule, out of the embassy, and into Mideast history. Standing in the bright summer sunlight, I made a few cryptic notes about the message and folded them into my wallet. I would soon have to pack for my first visit to Israel. I kept repeating in my head, "The USG advises the GOI (small Yiddish joke) that little cooperation is expected from Moscow on subject matter and venue for negotiations in the near term. . . ."

Wheels up and off to Israel, I reflected that my true-life week had been stranger than any of the fiction I had seen at the film festival. But it was only a taste of things to come. I was headed for a place where the blood flowed in the open, not in the underground chambers of the Soviet secret police. And I was moving from kindergarten to first grade in my political education.

John and Jenny Garment's wedding picture, 1918. My father, formal and fastidious, stares into the future. My mother looks down the camera's throat with the confidence that carried us through our storms of adaptation.

Sonia Swetlow, the Garment family's all-purpose aunt, midwife, and flaming feminist. Posing with her large portmanteau, which held the tools of her gynecological practice, Sonia announced her identity. If there was ever an Uncle Sonia, he was gone before I was born, and was never replaced.

Me at five, in my sailor's best, excited by the camera, the hooded operator, and the first flood of experience.

George Swetlow, cousin and pseudo-stepfather, around the time he was black-belting me around his gymnasium on Eastern Parkway. I grew a mustache in his memory (and to cover up the side effects of a lot of dental work).

ABOVE: The Garment family—Marty, my father, me, my mother,
Charlie—in a rare moment of domestic bliss at the Waldemere Hotel,
Livingstone Manor, Catskills, 1934. BELOW: Camp Kee-Wah, 1935.
I am in the bottom row, second from left. Bosom buddy Lennie Puretz
is on my left. Al Cohn (third row, second from left) made a cameo
appearance for this photo but mainly hid out in the infirmary,
studying music and preparing for jazz greatness.

ABOVE: At the 1939 World's Fair with Frank Press, the smartest kid at Tilden High School. As the world teetered on the edge of war, the two of us confidently, ignorantly planned our brilliant careers. LEFT: In Little Rock, Arkansas, 1944, with my protector, Tony Perna. BELOW: At Nola's Rehearsal Studios in New York, 1944, getting Henry Jerome's new band ready. I'm on the far left. On the far right is Alan Greenspan, before he acquired his federal reserve.

ABOVE: Jerry Hellman kisses
his Oscar for *Midnight Cowboy*,
judged Best Picture of 1969.
RIGHT: Auburn-haired, green-eyed
Gloria Hellman introduced me to
her brother, Jerry, then to her friend
Grace Albert, whom I married.
BELOW: Grace, shortly after
our marriage.

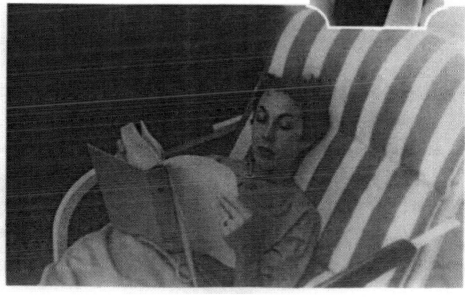

Why Are These Men for Nixon?

Newsday, Saturday, January 27, 1968

The one-word answer to the question in this 1968 headline: excitement.

© 1968 SUSSMAN/NEWSDAY, UPI/BETTMAN

From left: Filmmaker Eugene Jones, Nixon advertising director Harry Treleaven, me, and a technician in Jones's editing studio, reviewing a campaign commercial. Joe McGinniss is probably skulking off-camera but within earshot, making notes.

ABOVE: In February 1969, President Nixon had his Mudge Rose law partners to dinner in the President's Dining Room at the White House. For Nixon it was an occasion of nostalgia and gratitude, if not excitement. I am on Mrs. Nixon's left, with John Mitchell on her right. Two seats to Mitchell's right is the firm's extraordinary leader, Bob Guthrie. And at the other end of the table . . . BELOW: Grace is on President Nixon's left. On his right is John Mitchell's redoubtable wife, Martha.

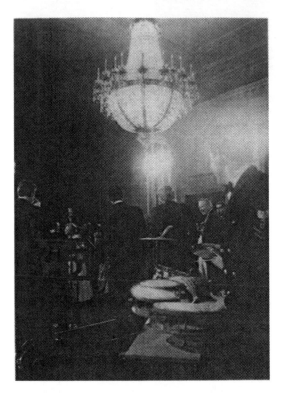

March 1969, the East Room of the White House, around midnight, on the happiest occasion of Nixon's presidency, the seventieth birthday party he gave for Duke Ellington. A jam session is beginning. In front of the band, dancing, is Rose Mary Woods. On my right is Dizzy Gillespie.

Russia in 1970, somewhere between Moscow and Tbilisi, and freezing. I am not singing "White Christmas"; I'm trying to explain why USIA director Frank Shakespeare and I left our fur hats back at the hotel. None of the KGB agents in attendance offered us theirs.

ABOVE: The atmosphere was cordial in this May 1970 meeting, but Roy
Wilkins, one of the last of the country's heroic black leaders, told us that
failures of white leadership were spurring a movement toward black
nationalism. BELOW: The Cabinet Room, July 8, 1970. President Nixon is
presenting his historic Indian reform proposals. I am at the lower right,
reveling in the moment. Most of the work on the proposals was done by
Bobbie Kilberg, sitting against the wall at the left, and Brad Patterson,
seated on my left—with, characteristically, his back to the camera.

ABOVE: Here, on May 22, 1973, I am handing out copies of President Nixon's first statement on Watergate, a highly legalistic document. But where's Waldo? Hint: The top of my balding head is partly visible at the center of the media melee. BELOW: Order has been restored in the White House pressroom. Under Ron Zeigler's watchful gaze—"Does Len actually believe what he's saying?"—I explain the inexplicables of Nixon's May 22, 1973, statement. Bedlam resumes.

Mrs. Meir sent me this photo around the time of Nixon's resignation. Our friendship was one of the permanent prizes of my life, outlasting the pains of Watergate.

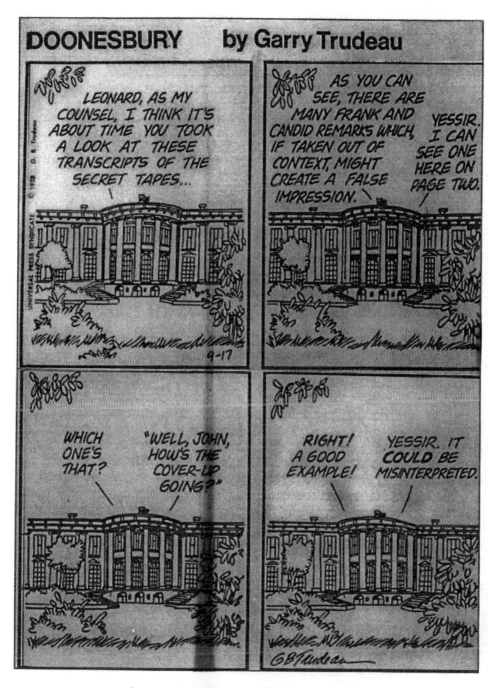

By the time this eerily prophetic cartoon appeared
in September 1973, jokes were the least of my problems.

In the Third Committee of the United Nations, the electronic voting teller
has just announced the passage of the Zionism-is-racism resolution.
I am in the U.S. delegate's chair. Pat Moynihan, standing behind me, is
about to cross the floor to embrace Israeli ambassador Chaim Herzog.

Moynihan and I leave the
White House after a battle
in the bureaucratic wars with
Henry Kissinger. I urged Pat
to look cheerful. He did. The
press therefore declared him
the winner—a temporary
condition. AP/WIDE WORLD
PHOTOS

ABOVE: This was one of seemingly endless occasions on which Bud McFarlane testified during Iran-*contra*. My contribution as his lawyer was to look suitably serious. KENNETH JARECKE/CONTACT PRESS IMAGES INC. BELOW: President George Bush was indeed a friend. During this meeting I made two suggestions: that he should say more about the post–Rodney King riots that had just occurred in Los Angeles (he did) and that he should keep Pat Buchanan out of a prime-time spot at the Republican convention (he didn't).

To Len Garment
With best wishes, Your Friend,
G. Bush

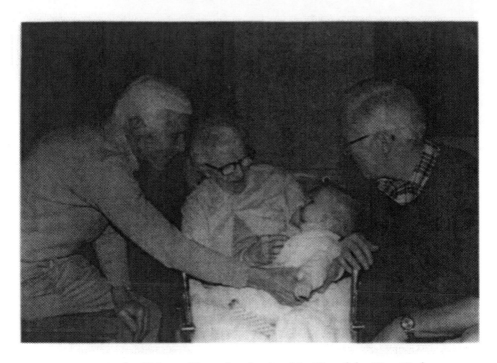

ABOVE: At the Hebrew Home for the Aged in Riverdale, New York, my mother, age ninety-two, examines brand-new baby Annie for the first and, sadly, the only time. My brother Marty is on the left. BELOW: Suzi and me, Fire Island, summer 1996. I'm featuring the mustache I grew in honor of George Swetlow. In the course of writing this book I came to like George less and my mustache-free father more, so I shaved the thing off. Suzi's first comment: "Welcome home." PHOTO BY BEN FERNANDEZ

My daughter Annie, now age fourteen.

Nixon, Suzi, and me on June 10, 1987, at a party given by Vice President Bush. Nixon was beginning to look presidential again.

TOP: Paul, a few years back,
when he was assistant
principal clarinetist with the
Atlanta Symphony Orchestra.
ABOVE: My daughter Sara
in Brooklyn, where flowers
grow on stone stoops. RIGHT:
At Annie's bat mitzvah, doing
one of my favorite things.

≥ 7 ≤

NIXON, KISSINGER, AND ISRAEL

When I visited Israel for the first time, in 1969, I was forty-five years old. The trip turned out to be something of a substitute for the Bar Mitzvah I'd skipped at age thirteen. In the thirty-some years since I had dropped out of Rabbi Cohen's Hebrew school in Crown Heights, my Jewishness had consisted primarily of hanging out on weekends with my brothers and our gang of Upper West Side Jewish wiseguys; then came Richard Nixon and my status as his campaign's designated liaison with the Jewish community. Thus it came to pass that at the end of July 1969 I found myself landing in Israel at a floodlit Lod Airport as the president's personal representative to all things Jewish.

For this initial trip, Nixon and Kissinger had instructed me to bear friendly tidings to Israel and submit to the Israelis' expected embrace. Then I was to become their official friend at court.

Virtually every American Jew entering Israel for the first time is struck by the same thing: the ubiquity of Jews. Police, soldiers, baggage handlers, customs officials—Jewish. If you have grown up in an American-Jewish world, where Jewish life is lived in niches, seeing all these Jews in such uncharacteristic roles is a jolt. You find Jewishness suddenly at the sovereign center of things, right down to the advertising billboards and lavatory markings. The sight produces a rush of chauvinistic elation: Hey, the whole place is ours!

I was rescued from the airport bedlam by someone who introduced himself as Mr. Jacobi. He was a senior official of the Israeli Foreign Ministry, whose assignment was to guide and tutor me. He was a stocky, quietly genial man who looked a lot like Eric Blore, the English butler in the Fred Astaire movies. At first Jacobi's behavior seemed extraordinarily offhand and casual; later I learned that he was simply bored by the official visitor drill that he had been through at least a hundred times.

On that first trip and on subsequent trips over the years I grew to marvel at the patience of the Israeli leadership and bureaucracy in dealing with American visitors like me. We arrived in wave after wave, expecting to be greeted, briefed, praised, entertained, interviewed, shown the sights, introduced to war heroes and cabinet ministers. It makes me tired even now to think of the number of these meetings that Itzhak Rabin—as general, ambassador, Knesset member, cabinet official, two-time prime minister, and Famous Civilian—had to endure in the almost fifty years after he first led Israeli troops into battle in 1948. But, like universal military service, this was and is a part of Israel's wall-to-wall survival routines, compulsory and probably perpetual. Israeli officials endure it, albeit with universal complaining, as a necessary component of their public life. I remember how intensely my friend Shlomo Argov focused on his never-ending task of making me understand precisely how it felt to be an Israeli living at the edge of extinction, threatened always by Arab enmity, Western indifference, and history's random craziness. This, Argov would say, is what Western leaders do not comprehend "in their bones."

Jacobi took me to my hotel in Tel Aviv. There was not a great deal to see between the airport and the city, but Jacobi noted each spot that had even the vaguest connection to the history of Israel and the Arab-Israeli conflict. When we finally reached the hotel, he told me that my first scheduled meeting was an eight A.M. breakfast the next morning with Defense Minister Moshe Dayan, who would come and pick me up. I left a call for seven and went to sleep.

My phone rang at a pitch-dark five A.M. The man on the other end identified himself as Moshe Dayan, said he was in the lobby, and apologized for the early call. He said there was an emergency and he had to go to the Defense Ministry, but he wanted to keep our breakfast date. Could we talk now? He had brought coffee and rolls. Bathrobed and bleary, I welcomed the hero of the Six Day War into my room. He explained that air engagements, part of the constant, low-level War of Attrition, were in progress between Israeli and Egyptian planes, and he had to get to his office to follow events. I remember thinking, as I came awake, that Dayan was strangely shaped, with a small head perched on a body awkwardly heavy around the hips.

For him, our five A.M. encounter was just another brisk start to another day of interesting business. He was cheery, smiling, warmly engaging; while sipping coffee he took time out to ask about my itinerary and suggest a couple of sightseeing additions. Then he spent half an hour describing what was happening in the skies over Suez. When he had to leave, he offered me a calmer meeting at a more reasonable hour; think nothing of it, I demurred, stumbling back to bed.

Later in the week, Dayan invited me to his home in Tel Aviv for a drink and a talk. His main and surprising subject was Palestinian refugees, whose history and cynically manipulated plight were matters of evident and real concern to him. Around us I saw the evidence of another of Dayan's passions, archaeology, which he practiced on solo expeditions among the Bedouin tribes. Hundreds of pieces of pottery, along with other artifacts of intermingled Arab and Jewish history unearthed by Dayan on the West Bank, were displayed in the house and in the large sculpture garden behind it. The pieces gave texture to the theme of his conversation: We can live with the Palestinians if the Arab nations will let them live with us.

Dayan was very cordial, but during my entire visit to his home I felt superfluous and even a little embarrassed. There was a lot of bustle: His handsome daughter, Yael, was just back from Paris. Household help moved in and out. Phone conversations, one every few minutes, were conducted in Hebrew. Beyond the distraction, I got the sense that Dayan was simply doing his duty, politely reciting remembered lines to someone who did not know even the most elementary things about Israel. I was relieved when he bundled me off with an ancient piece of Dayan-discovered West Judaean pottery, inscribed by him to commemorate our new friendship.

Jacobi picked me up at Dayan's home for the main errand of my visit, a trip to Jerusalem and a meeting with Prime Minister Golda Meir. As we drove, he resumed his military travelogue. Here was a battle site from the 1948 war, following partition. There, from the 1967 war, was the famously troublesome Latrun Salient, former Arab territory jutting into the heart of Israel. Jacobi pointed out critical defense points that had held the line against invading Arab armies. Rusting remnants of smashed Arab and Israeli equipment had been left all over the place like teaching aids. For an hour we drove steadily uphill toward the plateau city of Jerusalem, with its stone architecture silhouetted against the blue sky. If the light is right, the beauty of the approach is awesome; I half expected to hear the horns of Heaven heralding our arrival. I understood, as many had before me, how natural it was that this city should have been ordained the birthplace of the world religions and that so much blood had been shed over so many years to settle claims to it. But the opportunity for reverie was brief: We went straight to Mrs. Meir's office at the Knesset, where I was to deliver my message.

The message from Joe Sisco and my instructions from Nixon and Kissinger had their roots in a fierce internal struggle over the direction of the administration's Mideast policy. I was introduced to the complications, before I went to the White House, by Harold Saunders, the Mideast specialist on Kissinger's staff, who came to my Mudge Rose office to give me a general briefing. There had been a truce after the Six Day War of 1967 but no formal ceasefire. Recently, said Saunders, shooting between Egypt and Israel had begun again in earnest. There had been artillery duels between Israeli and Egyptian positions along the Suez Canal, air combat in the Canal region between Israeli and Egyptian fighter planes, and sporadic Palestinian raids into Israel from the Gaza Strip and Jordan.

By the spring of 1969, when Saunders spoke to me, the Soviets had delivered large arms supplies to Syria and Egypt and introduced thousands of Soviet advisers and other personnel into Egypt. These actions had increased the air of crisis. In another development, Secretary of State William P. Rogers had made known the State Department's official preference for a cease-fire based on the restoration of boundaries that would not reflect "the weight of conquest." This euphemism meant that Israel was to return, with minor exceptions, all the territories it had occupied since 1967. An effort was being made to persuade Moscow to cooperate with the United States in pursuing this plan.

Soon after Saunders's briefing I joined the White House staff. In the summer I made my trip to Moscow, where I picked up Sisco's message for Mrs. Meir: The Soviets preferred not to cooperate with the United States but wanted to keep the Mideast pot boiling.

It turned out not to be that simple, though; nothing ever is in the Middle East. A fundamental complication was that Richard Nixon, upon assuming the presidency, had given formal responsibility for Mideast diplomacy to Secretary of State Rogers and cut Henry Kissinger out of the action. Nixon had his reasons. First, Kissinger was Jewish, thus suspect to Arab nations, and not yet well enough known to overcome this disability. Second, Nixon saw the Mideast as a colossal political pain in the neck; he wanted to concentrate his attention and Kissinger's on Vietnam, detente with the Soviets, NATO, and of course China, the prize shimmering in the distance. Finally, Rogers, a person of consequence in Washington, was not content to play the part of diplomatic ornament.

By giving Rogers formal authority over the Mideast, Nixon thought he could solve these problems simultaneously. Rogers would have a major foreign policy task. He could try out his and the State Department's idea of a comprehensive Mideast settlement and serve as a lightning rod for the sure-to-follow wrath of Israel and of American Jews. Nixon and Kissinger, meanwhile, would keep an eye on the region, prepared to intervene if Rogers bungled the assignment. There was never much chance that this convoluted division of authority would work. But the chances for failure were increased by the personalities of Nixon, Rogers, and Kissinger.

Nixon respected and trusted Rogers as he did few people in Washington. Rogers's loyalty and political judgment were proven; he had been advising Nixon since the "Checkers" crisis of 1952. On the other hand, Nixon had no great regard for Rogers's foreign policy skills; indeed, from Nixon's point of view, one of the attributes that had recommended Rogers as secretary of state was that he didn't know enough to get in the way of Nixon's intention to hold all the strategic strings. Except for the Mideast, Nixon intended that Rogers would be a foreign policy spokesman to the press and Congress, a diplomatic hand-holder to the world, and an urbane front man for the serious business in the back room.

In theory, the beneficiary of the arrangement would be Henry Kissinger, into whose hands Nixon had placed the task of backroom management. But from the beginning, Kissinger expressed dislike for Rogers with an intensity that was startling. It seemed disproportionate, even unseemly. In not-so-private conversations Kissinger assailed Rogers's foreign policy competence and spoke scornfully about his character and emotional stability.

Part of the reason for the displays was, I suppose, therapeutic—Kissinger blowing off steam. But Kissinger rarely acted in a purposeless way, and even the steam came from a boiler in the deepest regions of his personality, regions that were not unfamiliar to me. Kissinger in the Nixon White House was a brilliant, witty, foreign-born fellow with a heavy German accent; more important, he was a Jew, not a papier-mâché Jew but a real one, carrying a profound historical and psychological involvement with Jewishness and all the attendant baggage. He had triumphed almost miraculously over this circumstance, making his way through the politely, pervasively anti-Semitic world of the eastern foreign policy establishment—the world of John McCloy and friends. Through extraordinary intellect, energy, determination, and manipulative skill, Kissinger had made his way to the exalted post of national security adviser to the president of the United States. Though he paid a price, of a size one cannot guess, the White House supplied the world's best stage for Kissinger's talents.

But Kissinger wanted what his talents justified: to be senior counselor among all the cabinet-level officials of the national security establishment, officials who were without objective doubt intellectually inferior to him. He could not perform this function because he did not have his own large bureaucratic domain or the independent power and public prestige that went with it. More than that, Kissinger was treated at the White House as an exotic wunderkind—a character, an outsider. His colleagues' regard for him was genuine, but so were the endless gibes at his accent and style, and so were the railings against Jewish power that were part of the casual conversation among Nixon's inner circle. The message was easily read. Precisely the qualities that enabled Kissinger to strengthen and extend Nixon's powers—the European sophistication, the urbane brilliance, the self-mocking wit, the skill with the press, the unmistakable Jewishness—barred his way to the summit of U.S. foreign policy power, the post of secretary of state. By excluding Kissinger from Mideast negotiations, Nixon officially confirmed the way the national security adviser was regarded within the administration.

"Moronic bastards" and "goddamn anti-Semites" were among the milder ways Kissinger characterized his colleagues to me. Though I had wound my own way to the White House via comparatively easy compromises with the world of non-Jews, I didn't need a lengthy explanation of Kissinger's venomous explosions. He had survived Germany, losing a dozen relatives in the death camps. He had taught at Harvard, lectured and written influentially, advised presidents, smiled with fools, suffered slurs from enemies and snubs from inferiors, ingratiated himself with platoons of political hustlers, aided Rockefellers, signed on with the Republican party, and become a confidant of the Bundys and McCloys. But, to put it crudely, just as a black man can never change his skin, Kissinger could never—in fact, would never—shed his Jewishness. Which meant, according to conventional wisdom, that he could never meet the fundamental test for a secretary of state: that he be an absolutely trustworthy defender of American strategic and economic interests in the Mideast against an intransigent Israel supported by the not-so-mythic political and financial power of American Jewry.

The conventional wisdom failed to take account of the talents of Henry Kissinger. He soldiered along, did his jobs superbly, and played the requisite White House games. He built his constituencies and bided his time, waiting on events, miraculous or otherwise. In the end it did take a miracle of sorts, Watergate, to force Nixon to dislodge Rogers so that the now-indispensable Kissinger could become secretary of state. Kissinger's large ability to shoulder burdens of ambivalence, tested and proved on issues like the Mideast, could not have been much strained by the fact that the likelihood of this miracle had increased as the political plight of his president grew more desperate.

Thus the reason for Kissinger's warfare against Rogers was not so mysterious. And it must not be overlooked that Rogers, from start to finish, fully reciprocated Kissinger's hostility, infuriating Kissinger still more by seeming to behave like a gentleman no matter what the provocation. Moreover, since Rogers had his personal arrangement and relationship with Nixon and the sympathetic support of the State Department bureaucracy, he was in fact able to maintain control over U.S. Mideast initiatives during 1969 and most of 1970. During these years the interpersonal warfare raged, hidden from public view. It produced an incoherent Mideast policy that sent mixed signals to the Soviet Union, the Arab states, and Israel, a prescription for stalemate. Stalemate was what we got.

My first assignment as inhabitant of this swamp was to play the bit part of the slightly dim but trusted messenger, Nixon's Rosencrantz. I was given a few lines to memorize but not told the whole plot. In time, I learned more of the story and came to play a slightly larger role; but even now, more than twenty years later, with scores of books written, including one by every major player, the history of those years is choked with disagreements about facts and motives —just what a student of Mideast politics would expect.

I was ushered into Mrs. Meir's office and her presence. I don't remember whether we drank coffee or tea, but I do know we both smoked a lot—me Marlboros, Mrs. Meir an unfiltered brand, though maybe I'm just imagining this because she seemed so much tougher than those sissy cowboys with their filtered cigarettes. Hardly a beauty, she radiated a warm intelligence that reminded American Jews of their nurturing, nagging mothers. (Just ask Henry Kissinger.) Her cigarette voice, deep and raspy, gave her words a special edge. She did most of the talking. She explained post-1967 Egyptian-Israeli tensions in reverse chronological order: the 1956 betrayal in Suez, the 1948 War of Independence, the Holocaust, the preceding centuries of Jewish exile and persecution. Once again I had the feeling that I was hearing the standard recitation given to those whose knowledge of Israel was primitive but who were friendly and potentially useful.

Two or three times during the meeting, Mrs. Meir's phone rang. Each time, her talk in Hebrew was brief and calm, as if she were confirming a luncheon date. "We shot down another Egyptian plane," she informed me as she hung up after one conversation, paused to chain-light another cigarette, and resumed her narration without missing a beat.

The "secret" message I had brought from Sisco in Moscow, that the Soviets would continue to stir the pot, was of course non-news to her. She had already become convinced that the Soviets were not serious about getting peace negotiations under way and wanted to play the growing Mideast crisis to the hilt in order to elbow their way back into the region after their embarrassment in the Six Day War. As blunt in this first meeting as she was in our final one eight years later, Mrs. Meir said she was sure the president and Henry Kissinger understood the Soviet intention, even if Secretary Rogers and the State Department did not. Her main message to me was that she needed to meet Nixon in the flesh, as soon as possible, to present her case directly to him. In the War of Attrition, which I could see unfolding before me, she said, Israel could take care of itself—provided the United States delivered the Phantoms, Skyhawks, and other military equipment already under contract.

In addition to these specifics, there was another message underlying everything she said. The bottom line was that Israel was not about to return to the vulnerable 1967 borders, or anything like them, anytime soon, if ever. At that meeting and in one way or another at every meeting I was to have with her, she said something like this: There have been monstrous crimes against many peoples, but the greatest crime in the history of mankind is the Holocaust. This is something the world wants desperately to forget. We will never let that happen.

The next day, a small Israeli spotter plane flew Jacobi and me to Sharm al-Sheikh, the strategic outpost at the tip of the Sinai peninsula. On our way we banked low over the Sinai desert so that Jacobi could point out places close to Israel that had once been filled with Egyptian troops but were now an empty junkyard of enemy equipment, a wide and comforting buffer against any future Egyptian surprise attack. We had lunch at Sharm, where sitting next to me was a young Israeli soldier who, it turned out, had been Richard Nixon's personal escort officer during his visit to the Golan Heights shortly after the cease-fire in 1967. The soldier had been flown to

Sharm and deposited at the lunch for one reason: to ask me to please remind President Nixon about candidate Nixon's admonition to him on that day in 1967: "Israel must never give up an inch of the Golan Heights." (Nixon did remember, and, give or take a millimeter or so, he never forgot.)

Next we went to Eilat, where we stopped for a swim and a drink before returning to Tel Aviv. Jacobi and I stood around up to our chests in the pleasantly cool sea, dipping water on ourselves like two middle-aged bathers at Brighton Beach, while Jacobi talked about the problem of the delivery of fighter planes under preexisting Johnson administration contracts. The U.S. State and Defense Departments were being obstructive, he said. Rogers was polite but unfriendly. Kissinger was friendly but passive. Was there some way to break the log jam? Someone the president would listen to? As a matter of fact, there is, I said. Nixon will listen to John Mitchell, his attorney general, all day long about anything. Jacobi pursued this: Would I perhaps take this matter up with Mitchell? Sure I would.

Later on, back in Washington, I reported to Kissinger and Saunders, then went to Mitchell and asked for his help. I said it would be good foreign policy and good politics for him to get involved. Mitchell, after puffing on his pipe and muttering about "that bunch of jerks" at State, agreed to talk to Nixon. Mitchell was hardly a Zionist. His main motive was to garner political support from the American Jewish community. But I have no doubt that this practitioner of New York ethnic politics also felt a natural sympathy toward Israel and a natural hostility toward both the elite establishment world of Bill Rogers and the Arabist leanings of the State Department. By September, Mitchell was taking an active part in Mideast issues, and he eventually played an important role in expediting the movement of planes, weapons, and financial assistance to Israel. His involvement became so extensive that he began getting summaries of routine intercepts of Israeli embassy phone calls. One day, after I had talked on the phone with then Ambassador Rabin, I saw Mitchell, who heckled me: "I think you're giving Rabin bum advice, Len. Why don't you just let him make his own mistakes?"

Returning from my maiden voyage to the Mideast, I transmitted Mrs. Meir's wish to meet Nixon. Her desire was also conveyed—

redundancy was a hallmark of Israeli requests—through half a dozen other channels. In September 1969 she paid a state visit to Washington. Not surprisingly, the president and the prime minister bonded quickly and permanently; how could Nixon resist this mother of all mothers, Hannah Nixon squared—smart, spiky, and resolute in her simple schoolteacher frock?

Since I was not part of the official Mideast policy team, I did not take part in the White House and State Department talks that accompanied the state dinner and thus felt somewhat out of it. But Mrs. Meir soon made a follow-up visit to Washington, and one Sunday she phoned to ask me to come to her suite at the Shoreham Hotel for a talk. I said I couldn't make it: I was babysitting my two kids that afternoon. She said, "Bring them along." So Sara, then age eight, and Paul, seven, met their first prime minister and stuffed themselves with an entire box of Israeli chocolates while watching TV with Mrs. Meir's security guards in the anteroom of her suite. Mrs. Meir and I continued the conversation begun in Jerusalem. She gave her reactions to Nixon (positive), Rogers (negative), and Mitchell (curious). She expressed her annoyance at the limited nature of Kissinger's role in the Mideast policy process. Her forebodings about State and its Arabist orientation were greater than ever: "They are as predictable as the tides," she sighed. But getting to know Nixon had made her breathe a little easier. "I feel comfortable with him," she said. "We talk the same language, and we see the Soviets the same way." Then we talked, as we always did and always would, about military supplies. I promised to bustle over to Justice to hustle John Mitchell.

In December 1969, Secretary Rogers went public with his plan for Mideast peace. It prescribed that France, Britain, the United States, and the Soviet Union would in effect impose a peace on Israel, forcing the Israelis back basically to the 1967 borders. If carried into effect, the plan would bestow on the Soviets a huge prize, renewed influence in the Middle East, at virtually no cost.

The plan, you could say, did not go down well with the Israelis or, for that matter, with Nixon and Kissinger. I was following events from a distance, being by then more involved in domestic issues. But I knew enough, from White House gossip and informal briefings by Ambassador Rabin and his deputy Argov, to know that (a) the

Israelis were furious and (b) Nixon and Kissinger were, albeit reluctantly, giving Rogers his head.

Mrs. Meir soon made an emergency personal visit to the United States. First she was to stop in Washington to register her unhappiness. Then she would begin a cross-country speaking tour. When Mrs. Meir had finished her Washington visit, Kissinger called me down to his basement office. Our conversation went like this:

H.K.: You've been following the latest chapter in Bill Rogers's Middle East insanity?

L.G.: Uh-huh.

H.K.: Golda was here yesterday. She is beside herself.

L.G.: I can understand why.

H.K.: The president has a little errand for you. Call Rabin and arrange to meet Mrs. Meir at La Guardia. She's flying out of New York on her speaking tour. Meet her out in the open on the tarmac. Tell her we'd like her to speak out on the Rogers Plan.

L.G.: Who's "we," and what do you want her to say?

H.K.: The president and me. Tell her wherever she goes, in all her speeches and press conferences, we want her to slam the hell out of Rogers and his plan.

L.G.: Are you serious?

H.K.: If you doubt it, check with the president.

Which is of course what I immediately did, by calling Bob Haldeman. He put me on hold for twenty seconds, then came back on the line: "That's affirmative. The president says go ahead."

No one besides me seemed to think there was anything particularly unusual or interesting about my mission, which was to ask a foreign head of state to undercut the U.S. secretary of state at the instruction of the president of the United States. I called Ambassador Rabin and said I had to see the prime minister on the tarmac at La Guardia before she boarded her cross-country plane. No questions were asked. I flew to New York, where Mrs. Meir had spent the night, and in due course she greeted me, standing alone near her plane. I gave her the Nixon-Kissinger green light to slam Rogers and the plan everywhere she went. "Fine," she said calmly and shook my hand.

In the days that followed, I read with fascination the news accounts of Mrs. Meir's devastating cross-country assaults on the Rogers Plan, which never recovered from the hostility she mobilized. At the time, it seemed an awesome display of the creative duplicity one finds at the upper reaches of government. On reflection, I suppose it was as efficient a way as any to persuade a secretary of state that his plan wouldn't work. It was certainly less painful—and, for Nixon, less embarrassing—than a face-to-face confrontation.

The Rogers Plan did not die immediately. Like Rasputin in his last hours, it continued to stagger along, even after Nixon had handed Mrs. Meir the dagger, revolver, and poisoned cakes to kill it. One modification after another was presented to the Israelis by the State Department, sometimes in a new box or decorated with gaily colored ribbons. But the Arabs never got serious about face-to-face talks, let alone recognition or a peace treaty. The Russians never stopped playing games. The Israelis invented a hundred new versions of the word "no," and the whole affair took on the quality of a well-nourished obsessive-compulsive neurosis.

In the summer of 1970 Soviet intransigence finally brought the Rogers Plan to its knees. In the fall of that year an abortive assault on Jordan by Soviet-armed Syria, and the Jordanians' consequent "Black September" attack against Syrian-allied Palestinians on the East Bank, administered the coup de grâce. The Arabs were left in disarray, the Soviets were discredited, and the U.S.-Israeli military collaboration proved itself a valuable counterweight to Soviet mischief in the Mideast. Nixon and Kissinger soon took direct charge of U.S. policy in the region, and three years of surface calm ensued.

During those quiet years, my Jewish portfolio gathered dust apart from my organizing occasional meetings for American Jewish leaders with Nixon and Kissinger. The principal force behind these meetings was a Detroit businessman and philanthropist, Max Fisher, who had amassed a large fortune in the oil business, by 1959 sold his multimillion-dollar business, and turned to politics, philanthropy, and, in his avocational time, making more millions.

Max's politics were steadfastly Republican. His exploits in forging an alliance between Israel and a succession of Republican presidents deserve—and have gotten—a whole book.

I worked with Max on various minor crises, such as the Jackson-Vanik Amendment, which imposed trade sanctions on the Soviet Union for restricting Jewish emigration, and the French sale of jet fighters to Libya. But it was not until the Yom Kippur War of October 1973 that American-Israeli relations again became a matter of Israel's life and death. By then, because of the departure of John Dean from the White House on April 30, 1973, I had become acting counsel to the president. Kissinger was now both national security adviser and secretary of state.

The war began on October 6, 1973, with a coordinated surprise assault on Israel by Egypt and Syria. Egypt's Anwar Sadat launched the war; he did not expect to win. He wanted only to shed enough Israeli and Egyptian blood to gain legitimacy in Egypt and the Arab world and thus to be able to shape his own diplomacy. Once Sadat's push began, however, it was more successful, and lasted longer, than American or Israeli experts had thought possible. It was also much more costly than expected in both Israeli casualties and equipment losses. A debate quickly began within the U.S. government over how to titrate the resupply of military equipment to Israel, like doses of medicine, to keep Israel alive but not anger the Arabs or embarrass the Russians. The doctors conferred, the lawyers argued, and the experts played games, haggling over quantities of supplies and the methods and timing of deliveries as if the White House were a Middle Eastern bazaar. Nixon had to mediate the running debate and to handle the diplomacy, which reached its dramatic climax two weeks after the war began, on October 20, when Henry Kissinger flew to Moscow to talk with Soviet General Secretary Leonid Brezhnev about a cease-fire.

During this same two-week period, another war was reaching a climax—the battle for the Watergate tapes. It, too, peaked on October 20 with the decisive and, for Nixon, disastrous Saturday Night Massacre, in which Special Prosecutor Archibald Cox was fired and both Attorney General Elliot Richardson and Deputy Attorney General William Ruckelshaus resigned. I was present, like the Civil War photographer Matthew Brady, on the bloody White House battleground. Though busy enough, I had time to take some snapshots.

In *War and Peace*, Tolstoy describes the Battle of Borodino, which probably marked the beginning of Napoleon's end. The observer Pierre first sees the battle from a remote hilltop. Soldiers, horses, and equipment move about like toy figures in tranquil geometric patterns in the field below. But when Pierre rides down the hill to see the action at close range, he enters a grotesque nightmare of hysteria, noise, and confusion. A cannonball lands close by, severing a soldier's leg; everywhere Pierre sees blood and bodies and hears the screams of wounded men and animals. The lovely pastoral painting seen from the hilltop is, up close, a charnel house.

It wasn't quite that bad in the White House from October 6 to October 20. But it was definitely more patriotic gore than ruffles and flourishes. From a distance, the White House did not look much different from earlier times: just more people, paper, and bustle. But up close, the two wars continuously colliding with each other transformed the place and determined the fate of its chief occupant.

When the war erupted, the president had already been brutally battered by the Watergate-related events of 1973, but he still held the reins of domestic and foreign policy. Staggering under his assorted crises, Nixon nevertheless filtered the information, set the directions, and made the major strategic and tactical decisions, particularly those affecting his own survival.

Sometime in September, at Nixon's request, Fred Buzhardt, former Defense Department general counsel and now Nixon's special counsel, and I had spent a pleasant Sunday afternoon at Attorney General Elliot Richardson's graceful Virginia home overlooking the Potomac, listening to Richardson's crisply professional, utterly hair-raising summary of the bulletproof bribery case that the Justice Department had assembled against Spiro Agnew, vice president of the United States. The next morning, Buzhardt and I met with Nixon and advised him that Agnew was a dead duck and would have to resign or face indictment and trial. Nixon began consulting regularly with White House lawyers over the progress of Agnew's plea bargain negotiations. The president also had to start sorting out candidates for Agnew's job.

In addition, Nixon was engaged at the time in a personal review, unpleasant in every conceivable way, of the nine critical Watergate tape recordings that had been subpoenaed by Special Prosecutor Archibald Cox. Federal district court judge John Sirica had directed the

White House to produce the tapes. Sirica's order was now on appeal in the U.S. Court of Appeals for the District of Columbia, but the court's decision would come momentarily, and it was expected to go against the president. Nixon would have to know enough about the tapes to decide whether to comply, appeal, or try to compromise. So he went up to Camp David, donned big rabbit-ear headphones, and sat there for hours with Rose Woods and young White House staff aide Steve Bull, trying to decipher the endless, wandering, scratchy, cup-clattering, embarrassing, and legally compromising Watergate conversations. The tapes included the one that later turned up with the historic 18$\frac{1}{2}$-minute gap.

In the middle of all this, the Yom Kippur War began, adding more White House kibitzers, conflicting advice, and decisions to be made by Nixon. This particular crisis was played as a Feydeau farce. People ran in and out of offices and conference rooms clutching cables and memoranda, arguing for delivery to Israel of more or fewer aircraft and more or fewer "consumables," a word meaning bullets, bombs, and such, normally used only by technocrats but in those days tripping easily off even my tongue. The most heated arguments were over how to deliver the equipment without excessively offending friendly Arab nations. The first approach was to have the Israelis pick it up in their own planes, with the Israeli markings painted out. Then, as the quantities to be transported increased, people started talking about private charters; but the problem of war-zone insurance presented an apparently insurmountable obstacle. As the Israelis' losses grew and the supplies on hand and in the pipeline decreased, they went from asking to begging for help. I would hear despairing pleas from Rabin's successor, Ambassador-who-never-slept Simcha Dinitz, or his deputy, Mordecai Shalev, or from Mrs. Meir herself, calling from Israel. I would convey their concerns to Kissinger or his deputy, Brent Scowcroft, who had of course already received the same message from the same people.

Various accounts of this crisis have either the State Department, the Defense Department, or the White House putting up the most resistance to Israel's requests for help. To this day I am not sure who was primarily responsible. All the principal decision makers —Nixon, Kissinger, Defense Secretary James Schlesinger—wrongly believed that Israel would win quickly. They thought an "oversupplied" Israel might not yield easily enough to the pressure that Nixon and Kissinger planned to exert on the Jewish state at the postwar peace table. They were worried, not unreasonably, about Soviet as well as Arab reactions, including a possible oil embargo, if America made an "unbalanced" response to the Israeli requests for aid.

The differences among the principals, I know, were mostly matters of degree; the arguments they made reflected the predispositions of their deputies and departmental bureaucracies. There were no proper heroes or villains in this story. The man at the head of the strategic table during the days of U.S. resistance to Israel's resupply pleas was, as usual, Henry Kissinger; he was also there when the resupply process finally began in earnest. But it was Nixon who overruled the anxious naysayers and made the key decisions, on October 12 and 13, to use America's giant C-5A cargo planes to deliver tanks, Sidewinder missiles, and other military equipment directly to Israel. Reasoning that the United States "would take as much heat for sending three C-5As as for sending thirty," and convinced that the real issue was not the number of planes but how to ensure a successful airlift, he swept aside all the hemming, hawing, and compromise proposals of Kissinger's crisis-management group. When Kissinger conveyed his colleagues' hand-wringing diplomatic reservations about the number of C-5As to be used, Nixon angrily brushed them aside. "Goddamn it," he said, "use every one we have. Tell them to send everything that can fly."

The journalist Walter Isaacson has written a book, *Kissinger*, that includes a step-by-step account of the resupply debate, drawing on tape transcripts, contemporary notes, and post facto interviews. Even now, more than two decades later, the story is more pulse-pounding than Tom Clancy's best; there was even a climactic moment in which Israeli crowds, gathered in the streets, cheered and sang "God Bless America" as the great American rescue armada finally swept out of the skies into Tel Aviv. There were of course rational foreign-policy reasons for Nixon's decision to go all out. He had repeatedly promised Mrs. Meir help in any crisis, and Israel's losses of men and equipment were increasingly grave. Nixon was also looking to the postwar negotiations, and in anticipation of them he wanted to bolster both Israel's morale and its trust in the United States. The Soviets had mounted a major arms airlift to Egypt and Syria and were mobilizing seven airborne divisions. They were also supporting the bizarre Egyptian demand that Israel return the occupied territories as part of a cease-fire agreement. Nixon was determined to rebuff these Soviet efforts to worm its way back into the Middle East.

In addition to these calculations, I think another set of factors contributed even more powerfully to Nixon's decision to send Israel "everything that can fly." These other reasons had to do with the Watergate crisis.

Nixon may have been commander in chief when dealing with the two weeks of the Yom Kippur War, but the concurrent crises of Watergate and the disgrace of Vice President Agnew put him in a drastically different position. For part of the day he was leader of the Free World; for another part he was a presumptive criminal, surrounded by crowds of lawyers arguing, quibbling, hedging, nagging. Most frustrating, we lawyers kept coming up empty when Nixon told us what he really wanted to do, which was to get rid of his nemesis, Archibald Cox. Why couldn't we figure out how to end Cox's harassment of him? Why couldn't he just fire Cox and be done with it? With the Mideast burning, hard-won foreign policy gains threatened by Congress, and the American presidency going down the drain, couldn't we do anything more than counsel restraint? Nixon was like a modern Gulliver, bound hand and foot by ropes of his own creation ("God almighty, why didn't I burn those tapes?") and those fashioned from his lawyers' anxieties.

This was his situation when he began to hear the same irresolute, technical, anxiously self-interested, swinish lawyer talk from his Mideast crisis team: "Only one C-5A by day, sir, maybe two by night, or there will be hell to pay." No wonder Nixon was, as he puts it so mildly in his memoir, "exasperated." When he broke from his Mideast advisers' suffocating restraints, he was exhilarated, finally free to make an explosively clear-cut decision, flex his muscles, exercise the full measure of presidential authority, and confound the worriers and word mincers. For a glorious moment, he was the Nixon of old.

The reprieve was short, for the Saturday Night Massacre soon followed. But through the deafening media din that followed the firing and resignations, you could make out a few fragments of news on the sequel to Kissinger's Moscow meetings. Despite minor crises, in due and patient course, Kissinger's step-by-step disengagement of Israeli and Egyptian troops prepared the way for a Syrian disengagement—and for a breakthrough peace treaty, in the Carter years, between Egypt and Israel, and an eventual peace with Jordan. The treaty made good on Israel's promise to exchange occupied lands for real peace, including recognition, the safeguard of secure and acknowledged boundaries, and, as Golda Meir said to me the day we first met, "not one bit less."

No wonder Richard Nixon was Golda Meir's presidential pinup. He had kept his word to her in spades. Nor was her affection for him a passing fancy. Years after the Yom Kippur War, in her autobiography, she said of Nixon that "Israel never had a better friend" in the White House.

This history has some bearing on charges past and present that Richard Nixon was an anti-Semite.

As a general matter, if you show me a Christian or for that matter a Jew who does not have some traces of anti-Semitism in his or her soul, I will show you a human being whose body contains no germs. Anti-Semitism is one of those viruses that live latent in the human organism and flare up during moments of social or personal weakness. The relevant questions are about the quality and quantity of the anti-Semitic sentiment in an individual, how operational it is, and how it shows itself.

If you build from these considerations an anti-Semitism continuum running from 1 to 100, my personal experience would put Nixon somewhere between 15 and 20—better than most, worse than some, much like the rest of the world. It is certainly true that Nixon in his prime was a champion hater, but he was, to my knowledge, an equal-opportunity hater. If there was one group he hated with a particular passion, it was the left. Within that group, he reserved a particularly intense hatred for the journalistic left. Most of all, he hated people who caused personal hurt to himself and his family. For reasons of history, many of these people were

Jewish, but I do not think that was the defining personal characteristic that got Nixon's personal bile flowing.

The people whose companionship he most preferred—Bebe Rebozo, Bob Abplanalp, and Billy Graham, for example—were not Jewish. In this regard, too, Nixon was like most people, who like to spend their unbuttoned time with others who share their ethnic or cultural ties. But there were also Victor Lasky, Murray Chotiner, the Florida restaurateur Si Halpern, and other Jewish "pals." Moreover, a large number of the people he chose for his closest assistants in the White House were Jews, including Henry Kissinger, Arthur Burns, Herb Stein, Dick Nathan, Murray Weidenbaum, Bill Safire, Steve Hess, and me.

It is always possible that still-to-be-released tapes will provide evidence of truly ugly anti-Semitism in Nixon. But during Nixon's time in the White House, the stories about his anti-Semitism spread without benefit of such evidence. In one particularly hurtful incident, a story by Seymour Hersh appeared on the front page of *The New York Times* in 1973 reporting on the leaked transcript of a taped conversation between Dean and the president that was not public. It had been made available to the prosecution on a highly restricted basis, and the prosecution—or one of the judge's clerks— had to be the source of the leak. The *Times* story quoted Nixon on tape, in conversation with Dean, describing investigators from the Securities and Exchange Commission as "a couple of Jew boys." As I read the phrase, my heart, which was sinking regularly those days, dived into my shoes.

Late that night, tucked into bed, I got a call from the White House switchboard. The president wanted to see me; a car was on its way to pick me up. I arrived at the darkened mansion around midnight, presented myself to the guards, and rode the tiny elevator to the family quarters. Julie met me at the door and took me into the Lincoln Sitting Room. There the president sat in his easy chair, puffing a pipe and emitting smoke from his ears. I do not remember him in such a fury before or after that night. He said something very like, minus the more colorful expletives, "I did not use those words, Len. I swear it. It's an absolute goddamn lie. I know my own language. I never in my whole life used the term 'Jew boy.' You and Fred play that tape first thing tomorrow. You'll see I'm right. Then get Clifton Daniel"—he was the *Times's* Washington bureau chief —"in to hear it. I want a page one retraction from the *Times.*"

I found myself in the strange position of arguing, albeit half-heartedly, against Nixon's disclosing the conversation with Dean in this way; after all, we were still insisting on the constitutional confidentiality of the tapes. But there was no denying this choleric man. At the time, I was puzzled by the intensity of Nixon's rage. I think I understand it now. The *Times* was doing what caused Nixon the greatest conceivable anger: putting in his mouth the language of the lumpen bigot of southern California and reviving all the hateful stereotypes used against him during his early years. Nixon as white trash. The next morning, Buzhardt and I listened to the tapes. Nixon was correct. The phrase "Jewish boys" was there, and it was John Dean, not Nixon, who used it. The prosecutor's transcript had put words, in a more virulent form, in Nixon's mouth (just as it had Nixon calling Judge Sirica a "wop" when in fact he had praised Sirica's toughness as a judge and referred to him admiringly as "the kind I want").

I phoned Clifton Daniel, calmly explained the mix-up, said it was unfortunate and unfair, described how much it had upset Nixon, and said the president had directed me to play the tape for the *Times* and ask for a retraction. "Interesting," Daniel said; he would discuss it with New York and get back to me. For the next few days, Daniel and *The New York Times* went through every dodge known to journalism and the law to avoid retracting their extremely damaging mistake. Finally it came down to Daniel's insistence that he wouldn't listen to the tape in question unless he was also permitted to hear a number of other tapes. Why was that? I asked. Well, Daniel said, Nixon may have made the remark that the *Times* had reported, or a similar remark, in a different conversation with Dean around that time. I said no tape even vaguely meeting Daniel's description had been given to the prosecutors. Daniel said the *Times* would have to think about it. The *Times* did nothing.

By this time it was the spring of 1974. Nixon was all over me in a nonstop fury for the next few days; then some other crisis distracted him. But the incident stayed with me as similar incidents do with other persons who have been in government and emerge unable to fully trust the press ever again.

ಌ 8 ಌ

AMERICAN DILEMMAS

Richard Nixon came to office reasonably serious about the campaign promises he had made to help the poor and minorities. He sponsored Pat Moynihan's Family Assistance Plan, offered help to minority businesses to the tune of billions of dollars, and intervened in behalf of the Philadelphia Plan, which conditioned federal contracts on agreement by the construction unions to break their historic color line. But in 1969 and 1970 the country's principal racial crisis—indeed, its principal domestic crisis—was the desegregation of the southern public school systems.

Fifteen years previously, in *Brown v. Board of Education*, the Supreme Court had ordered school desegregation "with all deliberate speed." In the Deep South, many school districts had embraced "freedom of choice" plans, in which parents could theoretically send a child to any school in a given district, in order to evade the Court's decree. Now a new Supreme Court decision, *Green v. County School Board of New Kent County*, said that freedom of choice would be permitted only where it was demonstrably effective at integrating schools—i.e., almost never. Otherwise, school districts had to use more far-reaching desegregation techniques.

The courts were out of patience, the South out of time to devise proper school desegregation plans or face federal funds cutoffs.

Southern congressmen, encouraged by winks and nods from candidate Nixon during the 1968 campaign, were calling in every political chit to try to force the administration to extend the deadlines.

In November 1969, in *Holmes v. Alexander*, the Court said that "now" meant just that—at the very latest, desegregation plans must be on record by the fall of 1970. So at the end of January 1970, the administration was struggling to figure out how to get southern states to comply while keeping the South at political bay. Constant battles between Bob Finch, secretary of H.E.W., and John Mitchell at Justice produced a chaotic stalemate. Ad hoc interventions by the White House added to the confusion. The air was filled with talk of massive resistance to the Court's decision, leading to a constitutional confrontation between the Court and southern jurisdictions.

One day early in 1970, with the White House sensing the magnitude of the school segregation crisis but drifting aimlessly toward it, John Ehrlichman suggested that he and I sit down in my office for lunch with Clarence Mitchell, the legislative director of the N.A.A.C.P. John knew Mitchell's reputation and had heard my account of Mitchell's extraordinary exploits in civil rights lobbying.

I had met Mitchell some months before, when Attorney General John Mitchell began an abortive effort to weaken the enforcement provisions of the Voting Rights Act of 1965 and Nixon nominated a southerner, Circuit Court Judge Clement Haynesworth, to the Supreme Court. Clarence Mitchell persuaded me that both were bad ideas. He was correct about the Voting Rights Act but wrong about the highly qualified Haynesworth, whose nomination, I am embarrassed to say, I recommended that Nixon withdraw. (He didn't, although the nomination was rejected by the Senate.) Mitchell and I also worked together to beat back congressional resistance to the Philadelphia Plan.

It is hard to write about Mitchell without adopting a tone of eulogy. He was the civil rights movement's chief legislative lobbyist from 1950 to 1978; unlike most lobbyists, he was born poor and died poor. He was in many respects deeply conservative, radical only when it came to enforcement of individual rights under law. A large man, invariably dressed in a dark suit and vest, white shirt, and unmemorable tie, he radiated simplicity. When he presented his case he would sit there, big hands resting on his knees, eyes liquid and sad, his voice unusually soft, almost purring.

He had the manner of a minister; but he also had the trained mind of a lawyer and marshaled facts and technical arguments with professional precision. The combination made Mitchell the most powerful moral advocate I've ever known. Man to man and lawyer to lawyer, he persuaded me, as he had persuaded hundreds of legislators, to be a partner in his causes.

The three of us spent a couple of hours together at lunch. Mitchell talked about some civil rights issues coming up in the next few months. Ehrlichman asked questions and occasionally offered an anecdote to indicate his personal sympathy for Mitchell's positions. But Ehrlichman was a member—along with John Mitchell, Bob Haldeman, Bryce Harlow, Harry Dent, et al.—of Nixon's inner circle of tough political realists. At staff meetings in the Oval Office there was no way Ehrlichman was going to offer any soft sentiments to the group concerning civil rights. Clarence Mitchell understood this. He also understood Ehrlichman's implicit message: Garment, as the president's civil rights consultant, was free to be a front-line advocate. Ehrlichman would help in private discussions with the president but would have to avoid hand-to-hand combat.

The meeting was a turning point of sorts. Clarence Mitchell, with his patient and conciliatory manner, convinced Ehrlichman that there was at least one national black leader whose motive was to advance civil rights, not to cause political damage to Nixon.

Finally the White House did what a White House is supposed to do in a national crisis: It took charge. On February 16, 1970, the president created a working group of eight cabinet-level officials, half of them Nixon "moderates" and half Nixon hard-ass conservatives. The chairman was Vice President Agnew, to make the South happy; the vice chairman, George Shultz, to get the work done. But what work? The statement creating the group included instructions to nurse southern school districts through their agony by reducing disruption to students, preserving neighborhood schools, minimizing busing, and enforcing the law uniformly, North and South. These directions were as vague as they were constitutionally dubious.

Agnew and his ideological mentor and speechwriter, Pat Buchanan, at least had the wit to know that the directive was useless for the single purpose in which they were interested: maintaining the political support of southern conservatives. Four days before the formal announcement of the cabinet group, they unilaterally launched their own school desegregation strategy. Buchanan drafted a speech for the vice president, then sent it to Nixon (copy to Agnew) with a vintage Buchanan memo:

> The other day, one of the President's assistants phoned a friend in Charleston, South Carolina, to inquire how the administration was faring in the South after the latest court rulings ordering immediate integration of the public schools. . . .
>
> His South Carolina friend paused a moment and said, "I am looking out my window right now at the old Fort Sumter out there in the harbor, and if the federal government didn't have the atomic bomb, we'd be firing on it. . . ."
>
> The second era of Reconstruction is over; the ship of integration is going down . . . and we ought not to be aboard. For the first time since 1954, the national civil rights community is going to sustain an up-and-down defeat.

The memorandum was powerful, ringing with code words and built on the phony premise that the courts had ordered what Buchanan called "compulsory social integration." The memo advocated precisely the confrontation with the Supreme Court that Pat pretended to fear from George Wallace.

Five days later, Agnew sent Buchanan a guarded reaction:

> Obviously, the President's charge to me in his directive creating the Cabinet level committee . . . would not allow me to give the suggested speech as it now appears. Nevertheless, the political situation in my judgment demands that we move to some extent in the direction of indicating disfavor with the apparent consequences of recent court decisions. . . .

Agnew authorized Buchanan to rework the speech—and scheduled it for delivery in Atlanta on February 21. Three days before the scheduled date, Ehrlichman said the president wanted me to work with Buchanan as he rewrote Agnew's speech. We spent the night in Buchanan's office debating his new draft.

Pat and I had a civil enough relationship during the Nixon years. Technically, I outranked him on the White House staff, so he had to put up with my tactics that night, which were to argue the law, correct his facts, offer line-by-line redrafts, tell stories, jokes, anything to keep him from producing a coherent text. Pat was clear about his objective. "This speech," he declared in a moment of chilling indiscretion at around three A.M., "will tear the scab off the issue of race in this country." His announcement helped keep me awake as we shouted our way through the night. While Buchanan hammered away at his self-described "smoking typewriter," I wrote a memorandum of my own to send to Nixon along with Buchanan's insufficiently battered draft. Bill Safire, in his book *Before the Fall,* correctly describes my memo as a filibuster, an effort to persuade Nixon to take the speech away from Agnew and Buchanan altogether.

I had been shopping around for advice, talking principally to southern moderates involved in local desegregation efforts—educators, lawyers, businessmen, and politicians I knew from the presidential campaign. They made clear that local attitudes were more complicated than the "us against them" lineup assumed in Washington debate. Many southerners were looking for a way to meet the deadline dilemma without tearing their communities apart. This was the main point of my February 19 overnight memo to Nixon.

It would be a mistake, the memo said, to throw down the gauntlet to the courts, which would have to pick it up. Instead, our strategy should be to present

> a reasonable statement of the problem, of the human dilemmas created by judicial abstractions, of the need for new approaches . . . based on the lessons of 16 years' trial-and-error experience.

I argued that the speech outlining this approach should be not Agnew's but the president's and made the case that moderation was a plausible political strategy:

> Over the past two weeks I have talked with dozens of Southern leaders . . . involved in carrying out school desegregation plans.

They are doing an absolutely heroic job. . . . They deserve our support. . . . If we can manage to introduce some judicial realism into the situation, and get administrative running room for particularly difficult situations, we will be rendering them (and their communities) an enormous service.

In the morning, I asked the president's principal speechwriter, Ray Price, to prepare some notes to attach to my memorandum so that Nixon would get a sense of the tone he could achieve in a presidential statement. Here are a couple of Price passages:

We want to achieve a set of conditions in which neither the laws nor the institutions supported by law any longer draw an invidious distinction based on race. . . .

We also have to recognize that in a free society, there are limits to the amount of coercion that can reasonably be used; that profound social changes take time to accomplish; [and] that we can not afford to sacrifice the education of an entire generation on the altar of an abstract idea, no matter how desirable.

That afternoon, the president talked with his writing staff about the school desegregation speech. Bill Safire made detailed notes and in his book describes what happened:

Nixon . . . decided to do it himself, and the Agnew Atlanta speech was aborted. . . . "I'll have to speak in a sound way, on that fine line, representing the decent body of opinion, rejecting extremism on both sides. You know"—the President leaned forward and made the point to us that Garment had made to him in his memo that morning—"it could influence the next court decision. . . . You're not going to solve this race problem for a hundred years. . . . Desegregation, though, that has to happen now . . ." and, turning to Haldeman, a fellow Californian: "Bob, that's the only way they're going to get into Palisades High and Whittier High."

Nixon ended with the argument in my memo that most intrigued him:

You have to remember . . . that somewhere down the road I
may have to carry out this law. I can't throw down the gauntlet
to the Court.

That evening there was some sort of reception in the White
House East Room. I had already gotten word informally from Price
and Safire, but it was good to hear Haldeman's typically terse affir-
mation as he walked by me: "You won."

The next morning, Ehrlichman asked me to organize a comprehensive briefing for the president on school desegregation. Ray Price
would work with me. I could consult with whomever I wanted. But
only the president and Ehrlichman were to see the product. Thus
the task of preparing the public case for desegregation began in earnest. All the resources of the federal government were at my dis-
posal.

I enlisted three lawyers: a White House staffer, Bruce Rabb; a
Labor Department attorney, Tom Stoel; and an outside lawyer,
Douglas Parker, a friend and co-worker at Nixon Mudge. They read
the cases and commentaries, analyzed the state of desegregation
law, and tried to forecast trends. Professor James Coleman, a national authority on race and education, came over from Johns Hop-
kins University to describe the condition of underfinanced southern
school facilities, especially in rural areas, and suggest ways that
federal funds could ease these problems. The constitutional scholar
Alexander Bickel, a friend and a professor at Yale Law School, commented generally on the work and offered suggestions for a legislative approach, under the enabling clause of the Fourteenth
Amendment, that might provide some administrative discretion. I
spoke regularly with Pat Moynihan to test ideas and solicit names
of useful people. I talked with White House southern strategists and
civil rights leaders like Clarence Mitchell to get a sense of the political limits on the president's freedom of action. I examined housing
maps, school locator diagrams, transportation patterns, even aerial
photographs whose Byzantine quality made my eyes blur and my
head ache.

I had few illusions that the president would get cheers for making a centrist statement, but I wanted to separate the southern mainstream from the extremes and thus enable the massive school

desegregation of the Deep South, scheduled for September 1, to take place as peacefully as possible.

On March 5 I submitted a book of two hundred plus pages to Ehrlichman. The summary memorandum pointed out that an atmosphere of crisis had suddenly arisen, as the desegregation deadline neared and the sometimes alarming realities of the process became clear to people in the South. On one side we faced the danger of proceeding irresponsibly fast. On the other hand, many southern communities were already desegregating. Their leaders had put themselves on the line in committing themselves to the process and feared being undercut by a major administration retreat.

The president could not do nothing. He might propose legislation to allow more administrative flexibility; Bickel was working on a draft. In the meantime, the president had to present an administration position that separated him from the idea of racial balance in the schools while affirming support of *Brown's* basic principles. The statement would unequivocally commit the administration to desegregation, promise that the South would be treated equally with the North, say that southern desegregation efforts to date would not be scrapped, and state that the administration would not allow desegregation to mean the destruction of the public schools.

The primary objective of the statement would be reassurance—to blacks, southerners, southern community leaders, and parents. The job had to be done quickly: The 1970 school openings were now just months away.

That, more or less, is what the memorandum argued. For almost three weeks the president studied the materials and consulted White House critics of my proposed approach and of Ray's draft statement, which was included in the package. These critics were, in descending order of vehemence, Pat Buchanan, Harry Dent, and Bryce Harlow. Price and I, knowing that the political White House was chopping away at his draft, resisted undisclosed revisions that might seem small but could be disastrous.

Nixon juggled the northern and southern pieces of his puzzle. On March 16 he instructed Ray and me not to ground the final statement on "moral wrong" but to emphasize that southern opposition to desegregation was "legally wrong." He said northern white liberals condemned the South yet often sent their own children to all-white private schools; they were as wrong, in their way, as intractable southerners, and we should say so. He also tentatively accepted Professor Coleman's argument about the decrepit condition of southern schools, especially the rural ones, and of racially impacted schools in the North. Nixon told Price and me he wanted his statement to announce that we would ask for $500 million in fiscal year '71 and a billion dollars in fiscal year '72 to upgrade education in racially impacted schools of both regions.

The Buchanan-Dent-Harlow faction then proposed revising the statement to eliminate this commitment of funds. I objected to this by memorandum to the president:

> [D]esegregation has always been a one-way street, with the government demanding everything of the South. . . . Your idea of coupling support for desegregation with real financial help strikes an honorable bargain.

At Pat Moynihan's suggestion, the president met with Professor Coleman to resolve this issue and discuss desegregation generally. Ehrlichman, Price, and I were also present as Coleman described with absorbing specificity the miserable condition of rural and inner-city schools and argued the need to start attacking the isolation of black children in the immense racial ghettos of the North.

A stocky, balding, simple-spoken Kentuckian, Coleman made a powerful impression on the president and clinched the short-term case for including emergency funding in Nixon's statement.

Nixon then took detailed control of the statement's preparation. The final statement was close to Ray Price's original draft—though it also bore the marks of Nixon's lawyerish fussing, line by line, over tone, emphasis, and political balance.

Nixon issued the statement on March 24, 1970. Pat Buchanan reacted to the final product by saying to Bill Safire, "A golden opportunity lost," reflecting southern segregationist disappointment that the president had not confronted the courts. Northern liberals criticized the statement as too pinched, equivocal, and Solomonic where it should have been Draconian.

It was hard to know what each extreme expected, other than

wishing for some viscerally gratifying presidential position that would guarantee a constitutional confrontation. Nixon was satisfied that he had said what had to be said. So was I.

The internal debate over the direction of the administration was not over. On the eve of the president's State of the Union address in January 1971, Pat Buchanan sent Nixon a memo trying to steer him back in a conservative direction. Nixon's first-term moderation, the memo said,

> leaves the Republican True Believers without a vocal champion. One has to guess that this political vacuum will not go unfilled, that the old political faith will not go unchampioned for long.

Nixon asked me to give him, as quickly as possible, my response to Buchanan's arguments. I offered a different political analysis from Buchanan's:

> The President's natural—and strongest—position is not on the Right but in the middle—and the middle is exactly where he is. The important thing now . . . is to hold our course consistently enough and long enough so that it's clear we're not wobbling and being buffeted or panicked by the kind of reaction [Buchanan's] carefully thought-through polemic represents.

A quarter century old, the memos are eerily current. They offer an ideological road map to Buchanan's future: Empowered by the souring of America's middle class, he became increasingly a player in his own right in the presidential politics of 1992 and 1996. As for the moderate course, the likelihood of its success disappeared, as did much else, with Watergate.

As if life weren't complicated enough on the desegregation front, another major southern controversy raged concurrently in the Senate. It boiled over on April 8, just two weeks after Nixon's school desegregation statement, when the Senate rejected the nomination to the Supreme Court of Circuit Court Judge G. Harrold Carswell, whom Nixon had named as a replacement southerner after the defeat of Clement Haynesworth's nomination.

Before Carswell was named, I gave the president Clarence Mitchell's detailed early warning about the inevitable outcome and made my own recommendation against the nomination, but to no avail. During the Senate debate, Bryce Harlow, the president's chief congressional lobbyist, told Nixon that even Republican senators thought Carswell was "a boob, a dummy." But hell knew no wrath like Nixon twice scorned. Returning from lunch just minutes after Carswell's defeat, I went to Harlow's West Wing office. Nixon was across the street, working in his office in the Old Executive Office Building. Harlow wryly mused to me about the probable state of the president's mood at the moment: "If you go across the way, Len, you will undoubtedly see a plume of blue smoke curling up from under the door. He is burning mad, determined to do something. What it is, I don't know, but it will be awful, just awful; and he will wind up doing severe damage to himself, as he usually does at such times."

I asked Harlow what Nixon should do.

"Well, now," he said, "I've actually given some thought to that, and I have an idea. He should call the Republican senators who voted for *either* Haynesworth or Carswell and invite them for a ride on the *Sequoia* tonight, give them a couple of drinks, say his piece, clear the air, and get on with the business at hand."

That's a splendid idea, I said. Why don't you suggest it?

"I just might," Harlow replied, "but you and Ray Price will have to join me." Harlow handwrote an elegant note, Ray and I countersigned, and a messenger took the sealed envelope across to Nixon's office and slipped it under the door. Nothing more was heard until the next day, when Nixon went before the White House press corps and delivered a splenetic denunciation of the Senate, drafted by Pat Buchanan.

And that was that, except that Nixon shunned Harlow for the next two or three weeks. The conventional wisdom at the time was that Nixon's enraged reaction to the Carswell vote was just a cold-blooded sop to southern conservatives; to judge by our experience with him, it was more than that.

• • •

In the aftermath of the president's desegregation statement, the task was to manage the final stage of the crisis, the actual implementation of desegregation in the fall of 1970. The President's Cabinet Committee on School Desegregation had the job of organizing the white and black leadership of southern cities to prepare their communities for the coming massive change. Secretary of Labor George Shultz served as executive officer of this effort. I was encouraged to be invisible, though I occasionally emerged to attend selected meetings and discuss strategy with Shultz and his staff. I did make one contribution. At some point during the drafting of the president's statement, my colleague Brad Patterson had given me a document that came in over the transom. It was a one-page flyer published by a group of local leaders in Greenville, South Carolina, who called themselves the Citizens' Committee of the Greenville County School Board. The committee had undertaken to marshal support for the school board's desegregation plan, formulated in compliance with a federal court order. A paragraph in the flyer described the committee's objective:

> Your Citizens' Committee, your Ministerial Association, your Chamber of Commerce, your Human Relations Committee— in cooperation with school officials, civic clubs, churches and other Greenville organizations—urge all citizens to work together for a greater Greenville County. Together we can create superior public schools in Greenville. Together we can be a model community that leads the region in education, in economic progress, in spirit.

From my earlier conversations, I knew in general that there was a large body of southern leadership sentiment eager to find ways of avoiding a dangerous showdown with the courts. But here was something quite specific. I invited the leaders of the Greenville Committee to come to Washington for dinner in the White House mess and explain the details of their initiative to Brad and me. The principal spokesman for the group was a Greenville banker, Brown Mahon, a small man spotted by age, with thinning white hair, rimless glasses, a starched white shirt, and a tidy banker's reassuring way of presenting information. Mahon made clear that he was a conventional southerner who was uncomfortable with school desegregation; but his personal sentiments were overridden by his commitment to public education and obedience to law. These same principles, he explained, had brought together a highly disparate interracial group whose work had enabled Greenville to open its desegregated schools without trouble.

The idea of using or creating counterparts to the Greenville Committee in other communities eventually led to an administration approach that emphasized local organization rather than rhetoric, court orders, and H.E.W. funds cutoffs. Following the model suggested by Brown Mahon, which I passed along to Shultz, biracial committees were formed in the seven Deep South states most affected by the Supreme Court's September 1, 1970 deadline. It was a laborious process, involving a heroic marathon of meetings with hundreds of potential commission members by Shultz and his two principal staffers, Robert Mardian and Ed Morgan. Then Nixon himself met with these same people in the Oval Office. The potential committee members—blacks, whites, integrationists, segregationists, businessmen, union organizers, decades-long adversaries in the segregation wars—had to be persuaded state by state, meeting by meeting, to find common ground in their shared concern for the preservation of public education, obedience to the law, and the safeguarding of children from violence.

In its final weeks the process was as elaborate as a political campaign, deploying Nixon advance men, campaign literature, local speakers, and saturation advertising. I persuaded Billy Graham, a friend from the 1968 campaign and one of the South's authentic heroes, to film a series of short exhortations to peaceful compliance. These were run and rerun during donated television time in the weeks and days before the schools opened. The pieces of the year-long puzzle had come together.

Every political act has unintended consequences. I witnessed the most costly such consequence of the desegregation campaign of 1970 when I found myself, some fifteen years later, seated with

Senator Howell Heflin of Alabama and a number of archconserva-
tive acquaintances of mine from the Nixon years at the "guests of
honor" table in the main ballroom of a hotel in Mobile, Alabama. It
was a black-tie dinner celebrating the completion of a multibillion-
dollar boondoggle called the Tombigbee Waterway, a mammoth
canal linking the Mississippi River to Alabama and the Gulf region.

"What in the world are *you* doing here?" Heflin asked.

Well, I explained: In August of 1970, when I was scrounging
around for free television time to promote desegregation, I put the
arm on, among others, Kenneth Giddens, head of the Voice of
America, who owned the CBS affiliate in Mobile, Alabama, a crucial
local target of the administration's pacification effort. He generously
contributed time and expertise but exacted a small price. There was
this little old Tombigbee project that was a passion of local boosters
like Giddens, though not a spade of earth had yet been turned. Could
I, Giddens wondered, intervene with the Office of Management and
Budget to support the small congressional appropriation that was
necessary to keep the waterway idea alive?

Bryce Harlow and the White House lobbyist Bill Timmons
helped me persuade a reluctant O.M.B. and Congress to make the
token appropriation. I totally forgot about the whole thing. But it
stayed alive. Through the years, it grew like that giant fungus in
Michigan until it was completed in the mid-1980s at a mammoth
cost. My feelings of fiscal guilt are mitigated by the knowledge that
this is the lunatic but necessary way pork-barrel politics works all
the time, everywhere.

Our desegregation campaign culminated in a full-day meeting of
all the state committees in New Orleans on August 24, 1970. Nixon
told them that desegregation would occur on the Supreme Court's
timetable. The federal government was committed to helping ease
the difficulties, but the real choice to be made was local: "You can
have good schools, inferior schools, or no schools." Later that day
Nixon declared on television that the Supreme Court's decisions
would be carried out in a manner "treating this part of the country
with the respect that it deserves." When September 1970 finally
arrived, in the most intransigent, violence-ridden areas of the Deep

South, the largest number of students and schools in American history was peacefully desegregated. There was no reason to break out
the champagne, but a cold peace in the South was better than a
bloody war, and that much at least had been achieved by the year's
strenuous labors.

More school desegregation took place during Nixon's first term
than in all the preceding eighteen years following *Brown*. Historians
consider this Nixon's most important domestic achievement;
Nixon said publicly that it was his most important achievement,
period. While not reluctant to accept my share of credit, I was just
one of the cogs in a complex machine assembled under Nixon's
direction and maneuvered by him through a forest of structural
obstacles, racial fevers, and political conflicts. Nixon defined his
objective as getting the job done. He backed and filled, catered and
compromised, spoke in contradictory ways to different constituencies, yielded here, stiffened there, drew on every play in his volumi-
nous book, but did, in the end, get the job done.

Apart from desegregation, there were two civil rights issues in
1970 that can be fairly described as historic. One raised the issue of
tax-exempt status for segregated private schools. The other was voting rights. On both of them, Nixon surprised many accomplished
students of Nixonian ambivalence and disappointed most of the
conservatives in his administration.

In 1970, segregated private schools depended for their existence
on the tax-exempt status of private donations. On July 10, 1970,
after weeks of internal White House debate, the commissioner of
Internal Revenue, Randolph Thrower, unilaterally revoked the
schools' tax exemption. In White House discussions, the question
had come down to this: If donations to private religious schools and
institutions were tax-deductible, why shouldn't the same treatment
be given to private schools that were segregated not by religion but
by race?

Peter Flanigan presided over the struggle, collecting arguments
pro and con and convening meetings to debate them. I argued the
case for revoking the exemption, but under normal circumstances I
wouldn't have had a prayer, in view of the two constituencies that

would be upset by revocation, religious institutions fearing erosion of their traditional exemption and aggrieved southern conservatives. What changed the outcome was the support I got from Bryce Harlow. Bryce prepared a decision paper for the president; Flanigan and I joined him. Our position was that we couldn't have it both ways on school desegregation. We couldn't argue that we had to impose the severe dislocations of desegregation on the entire southern public education system because of the great constitutional wrong involved, yet at the same time allow an escape hatch for families that could afford private schools. Such differential treatment would surely undermine our effort to obtain voluntary compliance from affected southern communities.

Nixon agreed with us. He was able to get away with it, I think, in accidental part because he had so recently and convincingly demonstrated his sympathy for the South with his ferocious denunciation of the Senate after the Carswell defeat. Whether Nixon arrived at his tax-exemption position spontaneously or calculatedly I don't know; neither, probably, did Nixon. A decade later, in the Bob Jones University case, the new Reagan administration faced the same kind of choice. Reagan's Justice Department tried to reverse the I.R.S. ruling. The reaction was disastrous, the result failure.

The tax-exemption episode was pure Harlow. He had an unusually sharp instinct for what Lincoln the lawyer called the nub of a case, the real issue hidden in the spiderweb tangle that life and lawyers weave. He was also the product of years of experience at the presidential elbow: He had been one of President Eisenhower's senior advisers. Finally, before he joined the Nixon White House he was a universally respected lobbyist in a time when that was not an oxymoron. Harlow was naturally sympathetic to the sentiments of his southern political friends, but he knew we were engaged in the business of writing history. He was also profoundly concerned about the danger of a constitutional confrontation. Harlow's passion was American political history, particularly the Civil War. His idea of a vacation was a visit, map in hand, to the battlefields and burial grounds scattered around his home near Harpers Ferry, West Virginia, where John Brown had waged his one-man insurrection against slavery.

Near the end of Harlow's life, my wife Suzi and I visited him at his home in Harpers Ferry to reminisce about political adventures and to gossip about current Washington calamities. We spent most of the day listening to him, by now in an advanced stage of emphysema, whisper about the Civil War battles that had taken place nearby. "On your way back to Washington," Bryce said as we left, "stop at Antietam and visit the burial grounds. You'll find good writing about history all over the place. And when you come back next time bring my friend Moynihan along. I'll give you all a personal tour of some battlefields."

There was no next time, but we did stop to read the writing on the stones at Antietam, and I better understood the source of Bryce's passion for thoughtful moderation on matters of race.

The other major civil rights issue of that time was the fate of the 1970 Voting Rights Act, an extension of the 1965 Act. It had cleared both House and Senate but seemed certain to be vetoed—not because of its central features but because a provision had been added to it granting the vote to 18-year-olds, beginning with the 1972 election. John Mitchell and the White House political staff, including Bryce, argued that the newly enfranchised 18-to-21-year-old vote would go overwhelmingly Democratic and destroy Nixon's chances of reelection in 1972. Harlow and Mitchell were confident that Nixon would veto the bill. Yet mysteriously, on June 22, 1970, five days after final passage by the House, he signed it. White House aides told the press that the signing would go down in history as Nixon's biggest political blunder.

Rowland Evans, Jr., and Robert D. Novak, in their account of the first two years of the Nixon administration, *Nixon in the White House,* give me backhanded credit for Nixon's puzzling, presumably self-destructive, decision. "Leonard Garment," they say, "insisted that a veto would be sinful. . . . A presidential veto would simply prove what militant youth had been parroting—that the system was beyond reform and should be scrapped." They also hypothesized that Nixon "might have taken to heart Len Garment's warning of fire in the streets should a Negro voting bill be vetoed, if only as a temporary expedient."

None of this was the real explanation. It is true that I made the various arguments Evans and Novak cite. But what probably decided the case was an odd coincidence. During the internal White House fight, Lee Auspitz, one of the founders of the Ripon Society, a liberal Republican policy and politics group, visited me, bearing his usual collection of ideas, documents, and other scholarly odds and ends. He mentioned a recent study of college-age voting preferences which contradicted the general assumption that eighteen-year-olds would vote Democratic. The assumption was not true with non–Ivy League students or with noncollege youth.

On request, Auspitz promptly sent me the printouts, which I passed along to Ehrlichman and the president. The bill was signed. I suspect that Nixon had figured it out for himself, without a study.

The pattern of civil rights enforcement in Nixon's first term was for the most part operationally progressive but obscured by clouds of retrogressive rhetoric. One day Nixon would warm the hearts of his conservative constituents by railing against busing, though he knew that as a matter of constitutional law he could not do anything about it; the next day, so to speak, he would assemble his cabinet to hear Whitney Young and Vernon Jordan plead the Urban League's urgent case for financial help, then and there ordering George Shultz and me to round up the funds. One day he would promise Strom Thurmond the moon and stars; the next day he would, figuratively, give the same Thurmond the back of his hand.

This is the way it went for four years, a model of semistaged confusion, patchwork parts engineered to keep opposing groups guessing where Nixon would come down. There was no permanent peace; there could be none. But neither was there war.

The civil rights programs that stir most controversy in the 1990s, those promoting affirmative action, were, like support for the arts, made significant under Richard Nixon. The reasons were not so mysterious. Nixon liked the idea of job creation for minorities. Moreover, the oxen gored by affirmative action included unions and universities, not exactly Nixon's core constituency. The agency in charge of much of the affirmative action effort, the Equal Employment Opportunity Commission, was then in the hands of a tough-minded, very competent, and disciplined lawyer named Bill Brown.

So in bulletins to the bureaucracy and speeches to the public I innocently recited the litany of our support for "goals and timetables," benign outreach programs to remedy cases of actual discrimination.

The internal administration debate over affirmative action continued even through Watergate. In January 1974, the Supreme Court was considering the case of Marco DeFunis, who had been rejected by the University of Washington's law school despite grades and test scores that were better than those of a number of black students who were admitted. The administration had decided to support the law school's affirmative action program; the question was whether to argue for a broad affirmance by the Court or a comparatively narrow one. My position was characteristically cautious; Stanley Pottinger, the assistant attorney general for civil rights, pressed for a broader holding by the Court. In one meeting, the two of us made our arguments to Solicitor General Robert Bork, who would decide the matter. My notes record the following exchange:

> Pottinger: Your memo just tries to paper over the differences.
> Garment: And you just want to unpaper the differences to show how many there are.

We "papered" over the discernible differences and argued narrowly, but perhaps in the end it didn't matter. While we were having our high-minded debates, the E.E.O.C. and affirmative action agencies throughout the government drifted inexorably toward quotas and class actions—in retrospect, not a stunning surprise. Two decades later, working-class whites have come to feel—have in part, I think, been manipulated to feel—that they are the victims of affirmative action. Serious students of these programs are suggesting more refined approaches that aid sturdy, mobile members of the poverty class regardless of their race, gender, or ethnicity.

Yet even after seeing abuses of affirmative action in recent years, I still think the programs of the 1970s were justified, useful, and necessary. I had seen that exhortations to employers and banks, and declarations of general goodwill, were not enough, especially at the beginning. Affirmative action was the jump start that changed the exclusionary composition of the American workforce and business community and the public face of America. Black Americans finally became visible in the offices and workplaces of the country. The cultural distance between whites and blacks began to narrow.

If our biggest race-related problem nowadays were affirmative action, we could count ourselves lucky. Instead, a far larger problem, persistent poverty, remains. People enmeshed in this state are often but badly described as the "underclass," a term both euphemistic and nastily Nietzschean. In fact, it is hard to think of them as any kind of "class," so extreme is their social isolation and disorganization. They are small in number, something like three million persons, mostly urban, disproportionately black, and even more disproportionately belonging to family groups that include young unmarried mothers and have no fathers in evidence. To say these are high-risk individuals is to understate the case: They are potential addicts, suicides, criminals, and sociopaths.

Among the members of this group are both the most unfortunate of our fellow citizens and the most dangerous. You might think such a combination of traits would provide a powerful set of incentives to search sensibly for a solution, but this seems not to be so. Despite the efforts of leaders like Pat Moynihan, welfare reform has come to mean nothing other than controlling costs, in ways that give no reason to expect anything but a further increase in the morbid cohort of emotionally destitute, asocial, and potentially violent children.

Recently, I visited my musician son, Paul, at his apartment in a marginal section of Brooklyn. I was standing on the steps with Paul, his landlord, and the landlord's son, a five-year-old wearing a T-shirt that said, I NEED A HUG. A beautiful little girl, black, maybe eight years old, sat on the next stoop watching us. In a burst of sappiness I turned to her and said, "Hey, we *all* need a hug." She shrugged and answered, "What *I* need is a dick." Paul sighed at my naïveté. "You may have worked with a lot of jazz musicians," he said, "but you don't know shit about race today."

Maybe. And maybe the kid on the stoop came from a solid two-parent home and was just mimicking obscene rap lyrics. But what she said was like a punch in the stomach. In my White House years, dealing with civil rights, I did not envision this change. None of us could. And what comes next? Where the federal government has failed, do we really think the states are more likely to succeed?

. . .

With the Indians, the outcome has been just as unexpected, but considerably more hopeful. When the American Indian Movement started staging protest demonstrations in symbolically powerful places in 1969, I knew what most New Yorkers knew about the Indians' social problems, which was virtually nothing. Through most of the 1960s, because of national preoccupations with Vietnam, civil rights, and urban violence, the Indians were passed over by the media. They had the back of the back of the bus to themselves.

On November 19, 1969, with protests escalating against the Vietnam War, word came over the O.E.O.B. news ticker that ninety men, women, and children had occupied the semideserted Alcatraz Island in San Francisco Bay. They claimed title under the 1868 Treaty of Fort Laramie and declared they would resist removal. Brad Patterson remembers that my first reaction was, "Why don't we just give them the damned thing?"

Official life is not so simple. Robert Kunzig, who ran the General Services Administration and thus exercised jurisdiction over the twelve-acre federal rock, wanted to send the Coast Guard in immediately and use force to remove the trespassers. But I asserted authority as a senior White House official, ordering that no force be used until we had a chance to review our options. The last thing I wanted was a federal shootout with a garrison of Indians, including children, in the middle of San Francisco Bay just as hundreds of thousands of antiwar protesters were rolling in and out of Washington.

The Coast Guard was told to hold its fire. The outraged Kunzig swore he would never talk to me again. I should have been so lucky.

Alcatraz was a natural stage for protest theatre and had already hosted one Indian occupation in 1964, shortly after the deteriorating penitentiary there was officially shut down. The 1969 occupation was better planned. It was launched in coordination with local media and thus became the immediate focus of TV and newspaper attention, with boats, helicopters, television crews, and reporters swarming around the island. Also, the timing was brilliant: After years of complex, ambiguous troubles with civil rights and Vietnam, here was a nice, morally clean–looking protest. Most people already felt at least a dim guilt over the Indians' historical abuse and their dismal modern condition. If they didn't, press coverage of the Alcatraz occupation began to enlighten them. Within days the trespasser population of Alcatraz tripled as Indian and non-Indian students from nearby campuses, religious representatives, environmentalists, protest groupies, and miscellaneous weirdos made their way to the island.

I asked Brad and Bob Robertson, director of the vice president's National Council on Indian Opportunity, to draft conciliatory public statements and provided negotiating guidance to the G.S.A. official who was briefing the press. Beyond this, my major functions during the crisis were to approve the series of settlement proposals we made and to put up with daily ribbing by fellow White House staffers at the morning meeting ("Now you understand, General Garment," Kissinger said, "why I tilted to Pakistan").

I also had the job of staving off the law-and-order stalwarts in the White House and Justice Department who repeatedly flexed their muscles during what became a long siege. This I did mainly by dangling gory scenarios before them: "Do you want an American My Lai on your head?" In May 1970, with the Indians still at Alcatraz, the killings at Kent State and Jackson State ripped the campuses apart. After that, my argument for federal abstention became easier to make.

We launched one proposal after another: a grant for the design of a new Bay Area Indian Cultural Center, a gift of abandoned land on a nearby military facility for an Indian educational center. Nothing worked—because none of the proposals included a transfer of title to the island under the 1868 Fort Laramie Treaty. Boats filled with movie stars and political celebrities—Dick Gregory, Jane Fonda, Jonathan Winters, Ethel Kennedy, Bernadette Devlin—came and went, raising inflated hopes but only modest funds.

I had a nasty fight with Ethel Kennedy over the fact that I refused to use federal funds to feed the occupiers. One day her attorney, Edward Bennett Williams, phoned to warn me wryly that "Ethel is on the warpath." He was right: Mrs. Kennedy soon called to accuse me of "genocide." I told her she was free to use her own [expletive] money; I had enough trouble resisting pressures for a forcible [expletive] removal without dissipating my meager authority by spending federal funds to feed [expletive] lawbreakers. Brad, a model of civility, blanched through his mountain climber's tan and literally held his hands over his ears as Ethel and I got into high gear.

Over the months, the occupation gradually lost momentum, glamour, and point. More than a year passed. The media went away. Editorial comment turned sour; supplies dwindled. More hippies, drugs, and booze drifted in. It ended on the sunny morning of July 11, 1971, when federal marshals went out to Alcatraz and removed the unresisting handful of Indians, mostly women and children, who were still on the island. By then it was seen as an act of mercy.

Paradoxically, although the protest failed to achieve its goals, it proved the catalyst for a historic change in American Indian life. The public sympathies generated by the drama made it possible for the White House to set in motion a sweeping set of proposals to improve the prospects of American Indians. In early 1970, the Nixon White House put together a legislative plan aimed at enabling Native Americans to reestablish functional, self-governing communities. We had John Ehrlichman's invaluable backing. Most important, we had Nixon himself, who credited his high school football coach, a full-blooded Cherokee named Wallace "Chief" Newman, with giving him his basic life training in how to confront adversity and survive loss. Aside from gratitude, Nixon felt an empathy for Indians, America's home-grown victims, losers, and survivors. I sensed from the start that he would support us.

I asked a few White House staffers interested in Indian affairs—Brad Patterson; Bob Robertson; C. D. Ward, the assistant to the vice president; and a White House fellow, Bobbie Kilberg, who was working for Ehrlichman—to dig around in the departments and agencies, particularly the Bureau of Indian Affairs and H.E.W., and assemble what they could in the way of concrete proposals. I thought these could be discussed with national Indian leaders and lead to a presidential Message to Congress on Indian affairs. I told my collaborators that for a moment we had a rare combination of political circumstances: a sympathetic atmosphere, an absence of internal competition, and an unobstructed policy shot. We had to move quickly before this extraordinary alignment of forces ended. The staffers produced their individual pieces with wartime speed, and Nixon's speechwriter Lee Huebner assembled them in a draft message with almost exactly the right tone.

I was fiddling unproductively with Lee's draft one evening when Pat Moynihan came by to take me to dinner. I handed him a copy and he read it, looking like a cartoon of himself, gray hair in orderly disarray, half-glasses perched at the end of his nose, lips pursed in a schoolteacher's anticipatory disapproval. I was no longer surprised by his bottomless bag of political knowledge, so as he commented, I simply scribbled his suggestions in the margins of my copy.

When he finished reading, he said, "All it really needs is a stronger opening. May I borrow your typewriter?" Five minutes later the text was ready, and Nixon's July 8, 1970, Message to Congress on Indian affairs began with Pat's untouched words:

> The first Americans—the Indians—are the most deprived and most isolated minority group in our nation. On virtually every scale of measurement—employment, income, education, health—the condition of the Indian people ranks at the bottom.
> This condition is the heritage of centuries of injustice. . . . Even the Federal programs which are intended to meet their needs have frequently proven to be ineffective and demeaning.

The message went on to endorse expanded self-determination, economic aid, and the creation of an Independent Indian Trust Counsel Authority to take over legal representation of the Indians from agencies whose interests often conflicted with those of their so-called clients. Finally, in a symbolically crucial concession, the message supported restoration to the Taos Pueblo tribe of Blue Lake and the 44,000 surrounding acres of sacred lands.

The part of Nixon's Indian Message that Congress enacted most quickly was the return of the Blue Lake and its surrounding forests and mountains. They had been a religious shrine for centuries before the Europeans' arrival; but nature-loving, Indian-hating Theodore Roosevelt had incorporated the lands in a national forest preserve in 1906. Indians of all tribes viewed this as one of the most egregious acts of federal imperialism, so Nixon's support for the Blue Lake restoration was a particular triumph for them. In July 1970, they held a ceremony of gratitude at the lake.

My prize for helping gain Nixon's support was an all-expenses-paid trip to Santa Fe in a small Air Force jet and, three hours later, a swell horseback ride to Blue Lake. The procession of horses, led by an Indian on horseback and shepherded by other Indians on foot, moved carefully up the long, narrow, muddy mountain trail in the Sangre de Cristo Mountains near Santa Fe. I was wrapped in a yellow poncho, which provided scant protection against the chilly, wind-driven rain that had been coming down in sheets since our arrival. On one side of the trail soared a majestic forest. The other side fell away abruptly into a deep ravine. Every so often my horse slipped on a patch of wet rocks, which would spin off into space. How in God's name had I gotten involved in this? Me, of all people, a middle-aged, nature-hating New Yorker, a two-pack-a-day smoker who dreaded heights, scrupulously avoided physical danger, and had been thrown by the last horse he rode, a mangy hand-held pony in a Coney Island amusement park in 1932?

Finally we arrived at the lake. Strong hands helped me off the horse and laid me on the ground. I was given food, drink, and time to recover. The rain stopped, the sun came out, and the lakeside religious ceremonies that then took place made up for the morning's miseries. The high mountain air was crisp and bright. Indian chants sounded over the blue crater lake, which in the sunshine reflected the forest, sky, and white puffs of cloud like a giant mirror. As the prayers ended, a twinkling of trout rose everywhere to feed, dimpling the lake's surface. They seemed, at that moment, to be joining in the festivities.

Most of the administration's Indian reform initiatives, though, got bogged down in the congressional stalemate machine. Meanwhile there emerged among the Indians a mimetic form of post-sixties militance known as "Red Power," which found its principal voice in the American Indian Movement (AIM).

AIM was organized in 1968 in Minneapolis. Its constituency was mainly young and urban, and its most useful function was to protect urban Indians from police harassment by organizing patrols to monitor police sweeps through Indian sections of Minneapolis and other cities. The rest of AIM's program, by contrast, was ad hoc—diffuse and utopian to the point of incoherence. It called for restoration of complete tribal sovereignty and reinstallation of the "traditional" hereditary leadership. Since none of this was going to happen, AIM leaders did not waste time working for it. Instead, they concentrated on protests to ventilate grievances and popularize their own charismatic personalities.

In the spring of 1971, as the Alcatraz siege was petering out, AIM, which had not played a significant role in the incident, occupied Mount Rushmore in the Black Hills of South Dakota, a site sacred to the Sioux. After twelve hours, park rangers removed the AIM protesters, but not before Russell Means, one of AIM's founders, made his national debut by urinating on Mount Rushmore to express his contempt for the desecration of the Black Hills by the U.S. government.

Means was a big, classically handsome Oglala Sioux, born on South Dakota's Pine Ridge Reservation. He spent time on the road with other nomads of the 1960s, but then threw away the California clothes and styles and recast himself in the role of Ancient Sioux Warrior—braided, bejeweled, booted, and transported as if by magic from the colorful past into the bleak twentieth century. Means played his role, it must be said, with verve and courage, whether his convictions were synthetic or serious. And the times were right for his alleged agenda: to shake up Indians and whites.

In January 1972, a few months after the Mount Rushmore occupation, Means took center stage in Gordon, Nebraska, a town where five drunken whites had kidnapped a local Sioux cowboy, stripped off his pants, and deposited him, half naked, in the middle of a dance at the local American Legion hall. There he was beaten severely. Two brothers named Hare, part of the original gang of kidnappers, stuffed him into a car trunk, where he died. The Hare brothers were arrested but released without bail. Russell Means and AIM cofounder Dennis Banks organized a two-hundred-car protest caravan. They got the quick firing of the local police chief and official assurances that the prosecution would proceed (it did). AIM, Means, and Banks became heroes to large numbers of American Indians who had never before seen this kind of victory.

• • •

In August 1972, at the annual festival of the Rosebud Sioux tribe in South Dakota, the idea developed, under AIM sponsorship, of a cross-country caravan of tribal and urban Indians that would originate in San Francisco, Los Angeles, and Seattle. It would drive east, gaining momentum, picking up recruits from different tribes along the way, stopping for religious ceremonies, press briefings, and ad hoc sit-ins at strategic locations. The different streams of the caravan would converge in Washington just before the 1972 national election to engage political leaders of both parties in a discussion of Indian issues.

The Indians named this trek the "Trail of Broken Treaties Caravan." The name was intended to evoke the memory of the nineteenth-century "Trail of Tears." This was the route Indians were forced to travel, often in winter, without adequate food or clothing, during the ruthless federal deportation of the southern tribes—Cherokee, Choctaw, Chickasaw, Seminole, Creek—to newly designated Indian territories west of the Mississippi. The horrors of Indian removal remained as much a part of visceral Indian memory as the Holocaust is for Jews, and the Trail of Broken Treaties Caravan was an attempt to force that memory into American minds.

The Trail of Broken Treaties (T.B.T.) caravan began working its way eastward in early October. The organizers of the caravan had declared their intention to avoid offensive public behavior and lawbreaking, but it didn't take much to start a fire under the protest. T.B.T. organizers failed to arrange food and housing for the hundreds of people descending on Washington. Meanwhile, at the Interior Department, the assistant secretary for lands management, Harrison Loesch, wrote a memo ordering the Bureau of Indian Affairs "not to provide any assistance or funding, either directly or indirectly," to the caravan. T.B.T. sympathizers in the bureau leaked the memo to the Indians before they arrived in Washington. It became their "bloody shirt," an excuse for their own disorganization.

The caravan started drifting into Washington on Wednesday, November 1. Early on Thursday, November 2, after a day and night of total confusion, the Indians were instructed by T.B.T. leaders to pack their sleeping bags and go to the Bureau of Indian Affairs auditorium. Federal officials began an effort to find more housing, but in the afternoon the Indians voted to reject the government's offers and stay in the B.I.A. building until "acceptable" housing materialized.

The vote reflected the thinking of Means, Banks, and the other AIM leaders who calculated, not unreasonably, that an Indian encampment in the B.I.A. building would have far more news value than wandering around congressional offices—mostly empty, this being the week before a national election.

At Interior, Loesch ordered the General Services Administration security police to evict the Indians from the B.I.A. building at five P.M. Meanwhile, though, the White House decided to get more involved in the proceedings, and a meeting of federal officials—including Brad Patterson, since I was out of town—was scheduled with T.B.T. leaders for eight P.M. The planned raid on the Indians was suspended.

Or so we thought. Unaccountably, G.S.A. security did not get the word. Right on the old schedule, at five P.M., G.S.A. guards appeared in the B.I.A. building lobby—helmeted, booted, plastic visors in place, nightsticks in hand—and ordered the Indians to leave. There were scuffles, yells, pushing, shoving, clubbing.

The security guards withdrew, having raised the Indians' temperature by twenty degrees. The Indians barricaded doors with desks and file cabinets and climbed through windows onto the roof to report on police activity. The squat four-story building, surrounded by a moat and large grassy lawns and now brightly floodlit for national and world television, took on the appearance of a federal fort under Indian siege, except for the obvious difference. A mundane protest had been casually transformed into a potential catastrophe.

The eight P.M. negotiating session opened in a tense and rancid atmosphere. The Indian attendees announced that they would not take part in a meeting with Loesch present, so, livid but rational, Loesch left. Brad played for time, going around the table for statements of individual views. This went on until after midnight. One Indian calmly said, "You know, Mr. Patterson, a lot of us are going to die tonight." This reassuring remark had a history: A hundred years earlier, the Sioux warrior Crazy Horse, during the battle at

Little Bighorn, had shouted to his braves, "It's a good day to die." Custer found out he meant it.

After the meeting, Loesch and Bob Robertson said they wanted U.S. marshals to attack the building. Patterson dissented—and called Bud Krogh, the White House law enforcement staffer, who in turn called John Ehrlichman, who spoke to Nixon. Krogh reported back to Patterson that Nixon (and Ehrlichman) wanted the case taken to court in the morning. For now, force was not to be used.

By the next evening, the national press was paying close attention. A predictable gang of protest celebrities dropped by: Stokely Carmichael, Benjamin Spock, Marion Barry, others. Community supporters brought food baskets and blankets. The Indians erected a twenty-foot tepee in front of the B.I.A. The chief of the U.S. Marshal Service, Wayne Colburn, arrived at the B.I.A. to do the required reading of the district court's eviction order. He took one look at the smoldering scene and turned around and left. Just past midnight, a hundred Indians armed with clubs were standing on the steps of the B.I.A. building glaring at a large force of federal marshals—who, under strict instructions to do nothing, glared back. Inside the building, Indians conducted religious ceremonies and applied war paint. Russell Means helpfully explained to reporters in the halls that this ritual signifies "that the Indian who is going into battle is prepared to die."

I was summoned back to Washington that evening to deal with the trouble. I was told there was "serious" talk inside the building about setting it on fire on election eve—just three days away—to create a "funeral pyre." Informants inside the building confirmed the picture: Hundreds of men, women, and children had been encouraged by their leaders to whip themselves into a state of suicidal hysteria. They had brought in cans of gasoline to make Molotov cocktails. Rumors were circulating about heavy firearms smuggled in, dynamite stored on the top floor. I learned there were so many infants in the B.I.A. building that a nursery had to be set up to accommodate them.

Defusing the crisis would be like trying to talk a jumper off a high ledge. Also, the deaths at Kent State and Jackson State and the vast political consequences of these bungles were never far from my mind. So, right or wrong (as you might anticipate, plenty of people said "wrong"), I ruled out a federal assault on the B.I.A. building. In the next three days, many people would argue in favor of an assault, but few of them were in the White House, and none were among those with operational responsibility.

I knew my job was not to become a visible target in this mess but to find an intermediary among the T.B.T. leadership who spoke "American" and "Indian" and knew or could find out what was needed to break the deadlock. The man I was looking for turned out to be a young Indian lawyer named Hank Adams, not an AIM member but a volunteer who prepared publicity releases and policy statements for the group. Our initial phone conversation left me nearly brain-dead. Adams spoke very slowly, like a phonograph record playing at the wrong speed, and very softly, as if to evade wiretap detection. His sentences weaved, hovered, and never quite ended. He had a cough, a nervous laugh, and a stammer.

Still, I could see that Adams, highly intelligent and sophisticated about U.S.–American Indian history and law, knew every negotiating trick in the book. He, too, was looking for a way out, one that would not humiliate the Indian occupiers. I could also tell that finding a solution would require money: Every Indian in the B.I.A. building, I learned, was flat broke.

Soon I met Adams, who looked just like the voice on the phone —a slender, dark, nervously tentative young man squinting through scholarly horn-rimmed glasses. In the days that followed, Adams padded in and out of my White House office, constantly checking the room even while we were talking face to face.

The same weekend that I discovered Adams, I went to a dinner where one of the guests was Frank Carlucci, the deputy director of the Office of Management and Budget. He had previously served as a Foreign Service officer in revolution-ridden Third World countries and had run the Office of Economic Opportunity, where he and I had collaborated as troubleshooters. He was a man with experience at handling crises like the one at the B.I.A.—and he had something else that was precious: access to federal funds. I asked Hank Adams about Frank's joining me on the B.I.A. detail. Adams, who knew Carlucci from O.E.O. days, said yes, once a negotiation was under way on the prior issue of extracting the Indians from the building. I approached John Ehrlichman's deputy, Ken Cole, with the idea of Carlucci's joining me. Cole concurred.

Adams had been designated the Indians' official negotiator and said the White House should now take over the government side. Carlucci met with Cole, Krogh, Patterson, and me at the White House. The meeting voted to reaffirm the recommendation not to use force. Nixon and Ehrlichman agreed and formally directed that Carlucci and I conduct the negotiations. I asked Adams to come to the White House to start right away.

So on election eve, at eight P.M., Frank, Brad, and I met with Adams and a T.B.T. contingent of some dozen Indians in my O.E.O.B. office. The meeting began with Indian prayer ceremonies. Then came a discussion of Indian grievances, intermittently interrupted by telephone warnings to Adams of "imminent" catastrophe inside the B.I.A. building. Carlucci and I thought these calls were a pressure tactic, but we also knew that lodged in the building were real candidates for self-immolation and martyrdom.

The meeting lasted until long past midnight, ending with another prayer ceremony as strange as any event that had ever taken place in a White House office. The Indians, most quite ancient, their inexpressive faces dark, rubbery, and wrinkled as old tires, sat on the couches and on the floor, colorful blankets draped around their shoulders. A few had fallen asleep. I thought it would be condescending to get down on the floor, so I sat at my desk, trying to look amiable, interested, relaxed, and alert, like your friendly loan officer.

One of the religious leaders, Reuben Snake, presided. The prayers, keening chants, and ritual smoking began, and went on. And on. It was like something I had actually experienced long ago, at Jewish High Holiday services in a dimly lit, crowded, mildew-and-sweat-smelling Brooklyn synagogue, the liturgy foreign, unintelligible, endless, and boring, yet sweet and calming. At one point I actually shed tears, but less from emotion than from weariness and the foul, irritating fumes produced by the Indians' nonstop peace-pipe smoking.

Eventually the meeting broke up. I took Adams aside to ask how the evening had gone. He said we had made a good start. His comrades felt Carlucci and I were "sincere," which was what counted at this point. I asked Adams what tribe he belonged to. "I am a Sioux of the Assiniboin tribe," he said. "Funny," my voice said to him all by itself, "you don't look Siouxish." He winced and laughed. We had bonded.

Over the next three days a solution of sorts emerged. The government wanted to get the Indians out of Washington; the Indians wanted travel funds, amnesty for criminal acts, and some kind of face-saving formula. I wrote up a limited amnesty covering only the criminal occupation of the building. Carlucci wangled money from O.E.O. to get the hundreds of Indians back home. We agreed to organize a task force to discuss Indian grievances with all Indian organizations, not just the T.B.T. Indians; we thus denied the occupiers special standing.

The morning after the settlement, Carlucci and I visited the B.I.A. building. It had been literally torn apart: Toilets were smashed, sinks and plumbing were ripped from the walls, enormous mounds of official documents, letters, wires, and B.I.A. forms choked the stairwells. It was as if a massive, nonincendiary explosive charge had been detonated on the premises. The T.B.T. trekkers were in the process of leaving Washington the way they came, by bus, car, and van, taking with them stolen B.I.A. documents (dubbed "investigative evidence") and valuable Indian art works and artifacts. Federal techniques for removing Indians had changed dramatically. This time, when the U.S. government sent the Indians westward, it paid them per capita mileage and food allowances on the spot, in cash.

There was always something puzzling to me about the Indians' choice of a cross-country caravan to make their statement. Then I happened upon Joseph Mitchell's 1959 essay, "The Mohawks in High Steel," about the Caughnawaga Mohawk Indians, those fellows you see at construction sites tossing red-hot rivets around on open girders sixty or seventy stories up.

The Caughnawagas have the habit of stopping work in the middle of a high-steel job and driving great distances, sometimes cross-country, to start a new construction project, seemingly just for the hell of it. A white construction foreman described the phenomenon:

> Everything will be going along fine on a job. . . . Then the news will come over the grapevine about some big new job opening up somewhere; it might be a thousand miles away. . . . The Indians don't talk; they know what's in each other's minds. For a couple of days, they're tensed up and edgy. . . . They've heard

the call. Then, all of a sudden, they turn in their tools, and they're gone. . . . They won't even wait for their pay.

These are stable family men, mostly Catholic. When they leave a site, they summon substitutes to pick up the paychecks left behind and finish the original job. But they themselves are gone.

A century or two earlier, they would have been on their way to hunt buffalo and elk or find better grazing land or wage war. They would have been riding on ponies, not in battered cars and pickup trucks. But even in modern circumstances they somehow replay ancient dramas.

In the Trail of Broken Treaties Caravan you could of course find conventional motivations—self-aggrandizement, ideological passion, the desire to articulate legitimate political grievances. But the caravan, with its long journey, occupation of enemy territory, minuet of negotiations, and plunder, also called to mind the old rituals. The Indian participants—warriors, medicine men, peacemakers—played ancient roles, tiptoeing along the precipice between eighteenth-century history and twentieth-century reality.

Such patterns are common to Jews, blacks, Asians, Hispanics, and others: We are still what we were, perhaps concealed under layers of adaptation, but the product, for better or worse, of ineradicable tribal histories.

The Indians left behind not only a devastated building but a very bad taste in the mouths of many Americans, including a good number of previously sympathetic editorial writers and federal political figures. For my mother, of course, all that counted was the editorial verdict of *The New York Times:* "Only the sensitive response by the White House—particularly by Presidential adviser Leonard Garment —prevented a potentially disastrous confrontation." But the New York *Daily News* was editorially horrified at the soft-headed permissiveness of their hometown boy. Still, we had avoided the death or serious injury of civilians at the hands of federal soldiers or police, the type of tragedy that lifts the costs of social confrontation out of sight. Such disasters, the kind we later saw at Waco, did not happen at the B.I.A.; I thought and think that this was the crucial test.

We believed that further progress in Indian affairs would come via the comprehensive Indian reform proposals the White House had tabled before the T.B.T. caravan got started. But AIM had other ideas.

Russell Means, together with a group of ultraconservative "traditional" tribal elders who believed in an inherited, hierarchical Indian leadership, began attacking the existing government in Pine Ridge, South Dakota, for everything from thievery to excessively cozy relations with the B.I.A. There were fires, fights, arrests, and shootings. After months of these skirmishes, Means announced that William Kunstler, counselor to the counterculture, was coming to Rapid City to work with AIM. It was now official: The crisis had become a national event.

On February 27, 1971, one account has it, the Pine Ridge elder Frank Foolscrow, speaking for the "traditionals," gave Means and Banks the order: "Go to Wounded Knee and make your stand there." This story gives an air of spirituality to what followed. But in fact the occupation was planned by Means in advance. Hank Adams told me that in a 1970 conversation over coffee near Madison Square Garden in New York, Means called Wounded Knee an ideal location for a future demonstration.

It took a vast amount of blood to make Wounded Knee such a symbolic venue. In 1874, General George Custer, a Union hero of the Civil War, led a thousand Seventh Cavalry troops on a survey of the previously unexplored Black Hills of South Dakota. The beautiful, sacred Black Hills, named for forests so thick that the slopes appeared black, had been recognized in the 1868 Treaty of Fort Laramie as part of the permanent Sioux reservation. Custer's survey was an unlawful incursion. But Custer found gold, and the discovery brought a mass invasion of prospectors.

The army proceeded to provoke a confrontation with the Sioux near the Powder River. Thousands of Sioux, together with Cherokees, were led by the famed Crazy Horse and Sitting Bull. In an early battle, at Little Bighorn, the Indians under Crazy Horse wiped out Custer's Seventh Cavalry.

It was a temporary victory. Soon afterward, the Sioux capitulated, and there began some fifteen years of U.S. policies that nearly destroyed the once great Sioux reservation and its inhabitants. In

1889, word circulated among the Sioux of an Indian prophet whose Ghost Dance religion promised the Indians' resurrection. Ghost Dancers, engaging in days of excited ceremony and trancelike ecstasy, panicked nearby white settlers, who asked for federal protection. Custer's old Seventh Cavalry, now commanded by Colonel James Forsyth, was once again dispatched.

The cavalry, 470 men strong, trapped the leader Big Foot and 350 of his followers—men, women, and children—at Wounded Knee Creek. The army bivouacked the Indians overnight and in the morning began disarming them. In the disarmament process, soldiers entered Indian tents searching for weapons; Indians screamed in fright. One young Sioux shot a soldier; some say this was a signal to other Indians to start shooting. Whether it was or not, the cavalry responded quickly, killing half the Indian men with their first volley. Hand-to-hand fighting followed, but the heavily armed cavalry was in control.

Troops pursued and killed Indians who had fled into nearby ravines and ditches. Some 25 U.S. soldiers were killed; so were 275 to 300 Indians, two thirds of them women and children, almost all unarmed. As the killing ended, a blizzard struck. A number of the Indian wounded froze to death during the night. The body of Big Foot was found, frozen, when the weather cleared and the troops returned.

There exists a photograph taken at Wounded Knee shortly after the massacre. It shows U.S. soldiers near a long ditch dug for the burial of the Indian dead. The soldiers stand at ease, weary hunters after a successful shoot, their faces impassive. The ditch itself is partly filled with Indians, all face down. Next to the ditch another pile of Indians is waiting to be buried. In a phrase we have come to know, the bodies are piled like cordwood. U.S. soldiers who took part in the flamboyant revenge for Custer and Little Bighorn were awarded Congressional Medals of Honor.

Even public figures of the era had trouble explaining U.S. policies toward the Indians. When General William Tecumseh Sherman, commander of the army during the Indian wars, wrote about the misfortunes that befell the Indians, he could offer only that these wrongs were "in the nature of things, rather than a systematic desire to do wrong."

Thus, when AIM chose Wounded Knee as their next, and most dramatic, target, they chose a long-acknowledged blot on the national history, one that virtually everyone who examined it recognized as such.

On February 27, 1973, two hundred armed AIM members and supporters drove to Wounded Knee. They took over the town at gunpoint, looted the general store, occupied the local Catholic church, and took eleven residents hostage. By morning, Wounded Knee was surrounded by hundreds of U.S. marshals, F.B.I. agents, and B.I.A. police. Roadblocks cut off the primary routes of entry. The Indians, anticipating an assault, started work on defenses—digging trenches, piling sandbags, building dirt embankments.

The occupation settled in. At night, random gunfire was exchanged between the opposing forces. News and television reporters from around the globe were welcomed into Wounded Knee. AIM had quickly achieved its objective: another brilliantly cinematic news event, this time on the rugged scrub plains of Indian country, the vast natural stage where the great moral dramas of nineteenth-century U.S.-Indian history had been played out. The polls showed that the longer the occupation continued and details of Indian history were elaborated, the more sympathy was generated for the Indians' cause. It was a masterful coup.

Under the circumstances, it should have been clear to the men who gathered in the deputy attorney general's conference room to monitor the Wounded Knee crisis—at first intermittently, then every day—that an assault on the Indians at Wounded Knee would be a disaster for the government. But the message was not so clear to those whose professional training and responsibilities inclined them otherwise. They included the chief of the U.S. Marshal Service, Wayne Colburn; the senior F.B.I. representative, Joseph Trimback; and, occasionally, Deputy Attorney General Joe Snead, presumably speaking for his superiors in the Justice Department and White House. Thus there was constant, inconclusive debate about whether to use or withhold force.

In mid-March, pressure for an assault on Wounded Knee began to increase. The law enforcement people in the field were tired. Wounded Knee was becoming a clubhouse for white sixties radicals, and more were due to arrive when colleges let out in May. The Indian occupiers were increasingly contemptuous and provocative: They had assaulted a group of postal inspectors and paraded them around, handcuffed and at gunpoint, to be photographed by the press. Such incidents were likely to increase.

None of these concerns was without merit. While we debated, the heavy work was being done by the federal negotiators at Pine Ridge itself, a procession of senior attorneys from the Justice and Interior departments, including Deputy Attorney General Ralph Erickson, Assistant Attorney General Harlington Wood, Interior Department Solicitor Kent Frizzell, his deputy Dick Helstern, and Assistant Attorney General Stan Pottinger. They tried everything to persuade AIM to end the siege. They even voluntarily withdrew federal roadblocks, thus allowing the resupply of food and munitions to the occupiers. The law enforcement men in the field were, justifiably, not amused. Pressure for a full assault increased still further.

This was the moment when the U.S. Army, in a reversal of its historic role, came to the rescue of the Indians.

Soon after the Wounded Knee occupation began, I talked briefly with the army vice chief of staff, General Alexander Haig, in a West Wing corridor: "Would you do us a favor, Al? Make sure whoever is handling Wounded Knee for you knows that the Marshal Service and the F.B.I. have some real cowboys out at Pine Ridge who could wind up killing a lot of people. We may need an experienced military man to avoid a real mess."

"Don't worry," Haig said. "We've got the right man for the job."

Memory plays tricks, but I think he winked.

The army chief of staff, General Creighton Abrams, and Haig, both of them veterans of Vietnam combat, assigned Colonel Volney F. Warner as informal military liaison for the crisis. Warner, another Vietnam veteran and a native South Dakotan, was commander of the 82nd Airborne Division. He went to Pine Ridge, conducted an aerial and ground survey of the siege area, and talked to officials. When negotiations broke down and pressure for an assault came to a head in mid-March, Warner wrote Abrams and Haig a memo— which he recently showed to me—planning the assault on Wounded Knee if it should prove necessary. But, the memo said, satisfying law enforcement requirements simply doesn't justify the possible loss of life and potential damage to the public interest. . . .

Warner said no such thing in the meetings of our White House crisis group. In those sessions, he never frontally argued the anti-force position. He merely described in precise detail the probable consequences of alternative actions—and that was enough. In the climactic meeting, he briefed the group about the kinds and quantities of manpower and materiel the army would need if it had to take over and launch an assault: paratroopers, ground forces, helicopters, armored personnel carriers, tear gas, artillery, the works. He then gave an estimate of casualties in wounded and dead, counting U.S. troops, Indians, Wounded Knee residents caught in the crossfire. He explained the potentially lethal effect of tear gas on elderly Indians with pulmonary problems and on sick or malnourished Indian infants. Warner did all this with perfect calm. When he finished, proposals for an assault faded away.

Colonel Warner bought us negotiating time. The other major time buyer at Wounded Knee was my old Sioux friend Hank Adams. Much of the Wounded Knee story is a matter of record, but Adams's role has not been, until now. I asked Adams to work informally and quietly with federal officials and AIM representatives at Wounded Knee, to pass on to me privately any suggestions he had, and to keep in touch.

The internal warfare at Pine Ridge was so paralyzing that even getting Adams into Wounded Knee was a crisis. So was persuading harried federal negotiators that Adams might have something to offer. But once inside Wounded Knee, Adams gradually moved to the center of the negotiations. The dispute finally came down to the issue of disarmament. In Washington, I insisted that the Indians physically turn over their weapons before we began substantive talks: We would not conduct negotiations literally under the gun. The two sides eventually worked out an elaborate settlement choreography, which I approved. The Indians would hand over their weapons. There would follow substantive discussions of grievances.

In early April the meticulously detailed agreement was signed, and the federal siege was lifted on April 5. Now we actually had to carry out the disarmament—the same process that had sparked the first Wounded Knee tragedy. Russell Means came to Washington, where we were to supervise the disarmament sequence jointly. He promptly breached the agreement by insisting that we hold a "satisfactory" substantive negotiation before he telephoned Wounded Knee to begin the arms turnover. He held press conferences and testified before a hospitable, ignorant congressional committee. I offered to meet with him privately, but he declined. The siege at Wounded Knee resumed.

It turned out that Means's sabotaging of the April 5 agreement did not reflect his personal attitudes alone. A classmate of mine from Brooklyn Law School, Mark Lane, had turned up to advise the Wounded Knee occupiers. Adams later wrote in a long memo to the scholar Vine Deloria that Means had come under the influence of the "Wounded Knee Legal Offense/Defense Committee," of which Mark Lane was the guiding spirit. (Lane would later be involved, even more disastrously, in the Jonestown tragedy.)

According to some AIM leaders, Lane had devised a disarmament package that would in fact cause further delay. A telephone network started spreading rumors around the country that a federal assault on Wounded Knee was imminent. But federal negotiators, working with Wounded Knee headmen and chiefs, were approaching an agreement. Adams remembered that

> Kent Frizzell called me from Pine Ridge. He stated that he thought they had pretty much wrapped up an agreement. . . . He was requesting a letter from Leonard Garment of the White House . . . verifying [the provisions].

If tribal leaders at Wounded Knee wanted agreement, the feeling was not shared by everyone connected with the occupation. Adams recorded that in Rapid City, just after the final agreement had been arrived at, a member of the legal volunteers' committee gave him a tongue-lashing:

> He blamed me for the agreement, alleging that there wouldn't have been a settlement if I hadn't become involved again: "You know those old people trust you!"

As Adams left the AIM offices, Mark Lane was still there, recording a message to the people of Wounded Knee, a final desperate attempt to stop the settlement. But a voluntary evacuation had already begun. When the message was taken into Wounded Knee the next day, it arrived in an empty village.

Some notes on the later whereabouts of Wounded Knee figures:

When Hollywood types discovered the environment and native American history, they also discovered, in inevitable course, Banks, Means, and other AIM celebrities. Wounded Knee veterans appeared in the film *Incident at Oglala*, a docudrama about a Pine Ridge murder case made from Peter Matthiesen's splendidly written but hopelessly one-sided 1980 book, *In the Spirit of Crazy Horse*. Means and Banks played major roles in the movie *The Last of the Mohicans*. They took to acting as if they had been doing it all their adult lives.

The wandering Indian Hank Adams, his mediations quietly and successfully done, went back to the West Coast to work with Marlon Brando on Indian projects. Colonel Volney F. Warner, whom the Indians owed more than they knew, eventually became a four-star general. These last two, the Indian and the soldier, were the individuals who did most to prevent the second Wounded Knee from ending like the first one.

Pursuant to the final Wounded Knee agreement, a meeting was held at Pine Ridge on May 25, 1973, between a U.S. government delegation and Sioux elders. The Indians bluntly put the crucial question to Brad Patterson: Will you restore the Sioux Nation to its rightful status and lands as of the time of the signing of the 1868 Treaty of Fort Laramie? Brad had to answer no; he could not repeal history. The day was stale and disappointing, every grievance familiar and expected.

But America is nothing if not a land of surprises. In 1980, after more than sixty years of litigation, the U.S. Supreme Court decided, 8–1, that the United States had indeed violated the 1868 Treaty of Fort Laramie. The Court said the U.S. must pay fair compensation for the unlawful taking of property, including the Black Hills. Victory at last theirs, the Sioux litigants confounded everyone, including their own lawyers, by refusing to accept hundreds of millions of dollars in damages. They would take nothing less than the actual, physical return of their ancestral lands.

Not likely, since that would require tearing up vast sections of the American Midwest.

The nineteenth-century historian Francis Parkman had it right when he wrote that "the Indian is hewn out of rock." Though 95 percent destroyed, the Indians survived long enough to permit changes in American life and law that would make repair possible on Indian terms. Their resurgence in recent years makes it unlikely that the well-being of native Americans will depend for long on their historic status as victims of white injustice. Meanwhile, the Black Hills award, in a federal escrow account, is gathering interest.

And where was I during the historic ceremonies at Pine Ridge? Back at the White House, immersed in Watergate. After April 30, when I was appointed acting counsel to the president, I had to leave the prayers, peace pipes, and colorful wind-up of Wounded Knee to Brad Patterson and Bobbie Kilberg, who were in any event better qualified for the job. One of the many sadnesses of Watergate is that it dissipated the Nixon administration's ability to pursue the Indian initiatives it had more than started; John Ehrlichman, an indispensable agent of Nixon's Indian initiative, was soon gone from the White House.

During research for this book, I came upon a page one *Washington Post* article by William Greider, dated May 18, 1973, on the final talks at Pine Ridge. I happened to flip it over, and there on page 2 was an article about the first day of the Senate Watergate hearings. The headline read, WATERGATE: NOT EXACTLY HIGH DRAMA.

The Nixon team took care of that problem in short order.

℘ 9 ℘

WATERGATE

Nixon's presidency usually proceeded on more than one track. On February 20, 1972, the eve of his historic visit to the People's Republic of China, President Nixon gave a small private dinner for André Malraux, the elderly, distinguished novelist, historian, and cultural adviser to General De Gaulle. Malraux, an early visitor to revolutionary China, had recently met with Mao Zedong himself. The dinner would give Nixon a chance to mine the insights of the astute old Frenchman.

The guests sat down to dine by candlelight in the family dining room—the guest of honor, the president, Henry Kissinger, Secretary of State Rogers, Assistant Secretary of State for the Far East Richard Holdrige, and a State Department French-language note taker (though Malraux spoke English). Bill Safire and I were also there, though we didn't quite know why.

It was an oddly mystical evening. Nixon and Malraux both adopted a vague, obscure, allusive tone; their conversation was mostly aphoristic and even metaphysical. The rest of us had a lot of time to watch, listen, and nod our heads. I discovered—couldn't miss it, actually—that Malraux suffered from a gargantuan facial tic, which caused his every statement to be preceded by and interspersed with convulsive spasms. Yet, despite this heart-stopping conversational disability, he was monumentally poised. Distracted by the phenomenon, I hardly heard what he said. The next day, Safire and I discovered why we had been invited: The staff secretary, Alex Butterfield, asked each of us to prepare a summary of the table talk for the White House record. Unfortunately, neither one of us had made any notes. Within minutes we were sharing our mutual ignorance: "Do you remember anything?"

"Not much. What about you?"

"Something about Chiang's soldiers boiling Mao's supporters in railroad trains. . . . " After much brain racking, I produced a piece of literary evasion that managed to deal less with the content of the dinner dialogue than with "the contrast between Malraux's intense, spastic, pessimistic manner and the strong sense of physical well-being and enjoyment conveyed by the President." I noted that Malraux had said there was "something of the sorcerer" in Mao; Nixon answered that great leaders had "mystical qualities" and described in detail Lincoln's vision, in a dream, of his own assassination.

I sent the memo to Butterfield with a cover note: "I don't believe witchcraft is within the jurisdiction of the National Security Council, so I'm not sending a copy of this memo to H. Kissinger."

Meanwhile, on January 27, 1972, a month before this Olympian exchange, a meeting took place that had considerably more effect on Nixon's short-term future. This was the now-famed gathering, in Attorney General John Mitchell's Justice Department office, of Mitchell, G. Gordon Liddy, Jeb Magruder, and John Dean.

Liddy had been brought into the presidential campaign to satisfy Nixon's demand for a comprehensive political intelligence operation that would get the dirt on Democrats and find out what they had on Nixon. Now Liddy was presenting the group with his first proposal, outlined on briefing charts, which envisioned subverting the Democrats' convention and campaign with a million dollars' worth of kidnappers, wiretappers, prostitutes, and dirty-trick specialists.

Liddy's menu of political crime was not what Mitchell had in mind. The attorney general told him to try again. Liddy did, and the Watergate break-in six months later was part of Liddy's new, improved, scaled-down version.

. . .

Watergate had its origins in the reelection season of 1972, when Nixon's usual angers and suspicions were at a rolling boil. For three years, he and Kissinger, through painfully precise planning and negotiations, had constructed an intricately triangulated foreign policy: the opening to China, détente with the Soviets, and the grudgingly slow, bloody withdrawal of U.S. troops from Vietnam. Now the plans were moving toward a climax; yet at the end of 1971, as most people now forget, Nixon was running neck and neck in the polls with his chief challenger, Senator Edmund Muskie. Among the cultural elite, hatred of Nixon was increasingly intense; every so often a book like Philip Roth's *Our Gang*, portraying Nixon as the most loathsome political actor who ever lived, would come along to remind the president of this enmity. No sane man could have remained emotionally unaffected by these sentiments or unaware of their dangers.

Word went out to the political cadres to leave no tactical stone unturned, to use every trick in the book to ensure the second term that would fix Nixon's policy revolutions in place.

At the beginning of 1972 I was not privy to the knowledge held by the inner circle, thank God. I spent much time dispatching virtuous, ignorant little notes to the president, Haldeman, and Mitchell. I urged Nixon to run a high-minded campaign; cautioned Haldeman to beware ethical vulnerabilities, like the troublesome location of Mitchell's campaign office right next door to the offices of the law firm to which he would return after the campaign; and advised Mitchell to restrain the White House's tendency to paranoid behavior.

I was, you might say, slightly out of touch.

In the spring, things began to look up for Nixon. In March he made his triumphant televised tour of China. In April, when the North Vietnamese jeopardized his preparations for the arms control summit in Moscow by making a military push south through the demilitarized zone, Nixon risked all his détente chips by mining Haiphong harbor and sending B-52's there in force. One bomber hit a Soviet merchant ship, and Brezhnev grumbled. But the strategy worked: The summit went forward. It was one of Nixon's last lucky rolls of the dice.

In early June 1972, I took off with my friend Frank Shakespeare, director of the United States Information Agency, for an around-the-world inspection tour (known to the cynical as a junket) of U.S.I.A. facilities in the Mideast, India, and the Far East. Thus it came to pass that on June 17, 1972, the day the Watergate break-in took place, Shakespeare and I were belted into our seats in an Air Nepal helicopter groping our way, inches from the treetops, through cloud-shrouded Katmandu Valley in an attempt to break out of the fog for a close-up view of the north face of Mount Everest. Like the Watergate burglars—wrapped in their own deep fog—we failed to make it. But at least we came away with a perfect alibi. We then made a five-day tour of facilities in South Vietnam, which included gossipy dinners at the U.S. embassy with Ambassador Ellsworth Bunker and General Creighton Abrams. We heard not a single word about the faraway Watergate break-in. We first learned of the incident from a brief item in a Honolulu newspaper on our way home. My immediate thought: It had to be Colson and his army of screwballs.

Back in Washington, I found the break-in getting little official or media attention. I do not recall Ray Price, Bill Safire, or Brad Patterson voicing concern. In August 1972 I got another hint of the problem, a tiny seismic tremor signaling distant trouble. We were all in Miami Beach at the Doral Hotel for the Republican convention. I had no big campaign assignments, so I spent time soaking up sun and information about campaign politics. One afternoon at the pool, I noticed a sizable group of administration stalwarts huddled together at the outdoor bar. The shifting assemblage included, as I recall, Gordon Strachan, Bob Mardian, Fred LaRue, John Dean, Jeb Magruder, and Dwight Chapin, joined from time to time by Commander in Chief Charles Colson, dressed in a polyester sport shirt, faded Bermuda shorts, street shoes, and short black socks. They were whispering worriedly, chain-smoking, chain-drinking, and obviously not having any convention fun. With Nixon sure to win, what were they so worried about? Since I knew these were fellows whose major, endless campaign was for Nixon's favor, I thought they could simply be pondering some new political tricks to increase Nixon's electoral margin and their own second-term power. I later learned that while I half dozed in the Florida sun, my colleagues a dozen yards away were discussing the progress of the Watergate cover-up. I might easily have strolled over to bum a cigarette, asked a couple of questions, been given a couple of answers, and become a candidate for indictment.

Though I followed the sporadic news coverage of the early Watergate skirmishing after the election, it didn't amount to much; besides, there were Indian crises to keep me busy. I remained mainly in a state of happy ignorance. But someone in the White House was concerned—because this was the time when Deep Throat had begun to detail the operations of the administration "knife wielders" for the *Washington Post* reporter Bob Woodward.

Deep Throat got a lot of things wrong; he clearly had only a "hallway" familiarity with Watergate's complicated evidence. But he accurately described the frightened, almost spooky atmosphere of the White House at the time, and he contributed significantly to the undoing of Richard Nixon. He provided the *Post* with eye-popping stories, preceding disclosures by law enforcement people, that built momentum and drew in the rest of the press at a time when Watergate might otherwise have faded from public view. I'd say he accelerated the pace of Watergate by somewhere from six months to a year. If Nixon had had this added time, Watergate would have continued past the 1974 congressional elections. There might have been a changed political atmosphere, a changed makeup and mood in Congress, and a different outcome to the impeachment proceedings. Woodward and Bernstein and *The Washington Post* certainly didn't do it all, but they did a lot.

In writing this book, I was drawn deep into the community of searchers after Deep Throat. I read all the materials. I called, wrote, and visited all the potential sources. Not only did I fail to come up with a positive ID, but I ended with more questions than I had at the beginning. For instance, I have come to believe, for the first time, that there is something to the theories of researchers who think that people within the U.S. government were working actively to get Nixon out of office, an enterprise in which Nixon was, of course, a cooperating principal.

But at least I can now reply quite confidently to the often asked question, "Was there a single Deep Throat, or was Deep Throat a composite?"

The answer is, "Both of the above." I'm sure there was a chorus of Throats, with one Pavarotti leading the rest. This singular voice provided the narrative line that organized the jumbled first draft of *All the President's Men* into a coherent story. At the same time, the composite nature of the voice provided universal deniability: Everyone alleged to be Deep Throat could say truthfully, for one reason or another, "No, not me." As for the lead singer, not long ago an excellent source, one Bob Woodward, told me that Deep Throat's public role and public persona had changed radically since Watergate days; it was now so discordant with his former garage-skulking behavior that Deep Throat would never come forward to identify himself.

Someone, I'm sure, will someday nail down Deep Throat definitively. I hope it's me, but I'll be quite content if someone else scales this journalistic Everest first. Anyway, it's not me. Honest.

In February 1973, during a helicopter ride from the president's San Clemente helipad to *Air Force One* for a return flight to Washington, John Ehrlichman sat down next to me for one of our infrequent, brief conversations: You and I should talk soon about Watergate, Len, he said. It's getting a bit complicated. I may need you to do some litigating for the White House.

That was about it. I started examining news reports about Watergate more closely and trying to pick up clues from friends in the White House, but the result was still fragments and rumors. I waited to hear from Ehrlichman.

Back in 1968, when Nixon was first elected, my unexpressed hope and my law partners' expectation was that I could be named counsel to the president. As I have explained, it was never in the cards; since Nixon's idea of counsel to the president involved not much lawyering and a lot of politics, John Ehrlichman was the right choice. Still, though I didn't say so, I resented the job's going to an advance man and campaign latecomer. In time, when I got to like the independence of my own free-floating White House job, Ehrlichman began to use me as his own lawyer on major issues like southern school desegregation.

One spring day in 1970 Ehrlichman dropped into my office and asked if I would be interested in taking over as counsel to the president. He explained that he wanted to give full attention to his new Domestic Council and said he had already cleared the idea with Nixon. Later that day, Hobart Taylor, a friend of Nixon's and mine, came by to see me after visiting the president and reported Nixon's evident pleasure at having his old partner in the counsel's job.

If it was a pleasure, though, it was a passing one. There was not another word about the appointment, from Ehrlichman or the president. I asked around, but no one seemed to know what had happened.

Years later, when all the Watergate books emerged, so did the answer. In May 1970, almost immediately after my visit from Ehrlichman, Nixon ordered the Cambodian operation. The ensuing uproar and the killings at Kent State and Jackson State ignited anti-Nixon fury. College campuses closed down, and hundreds of thousands of demonstrators descended on Washington. Armed troops and sandbags lined the halls of the Old Executive Office Building. Buses barricaded the White House grounds.

At the time, one of my White House staff duties was something vaguely called "youth"—which, like "hunger," or "art," mainly meant raising money (for efforts such as summer job programs) and writing memos. But after Cambodia my responsibilities in this area expanded. I spent hundreds of hours with groups of students, teachers, and parents, listening, explaining, trying to persuade them that President Nixon was not about to compound his sins by dropping bombs on New Haven and Cambridge. Some of the encounters were painful. Parents and friends of the Kent State dead came by to vent their grief. I corresponded for months with Alison Krause's father; he and other Kent State family members were ceaselessly pressing for a grand jury investigation (which eventually occurred).

In one of these incidents Henry Kissinger called on me for a hand: An antiwar organizer had begun a fast in Washington, which he said would continue until the Vietnam War or his life expired. Shirley MacLaine, the actress and antiwar activist, had asked Kissinger to try to persuade the young man to end his fast. Henry went; I went with him. Henry, talking with the activist, was at his most eloquent. He seemed to have a perfect sense of the feelings and needs of his distraught one-man audience. I remember thinking that here, up close, for the first time, I was seeing Kissinger's intuitive, improvisational diplomatic genius at work. After two or three hours of his warm, patient, soothing, detailed discourse, the hunger strike was over.

These activities did not recommend me as White House counsel. In fact, around this time Bud Krogh and Jeb Magruder recommended to Haldeman that John Dean, a friend of theirs at the Justice Department, replace Ehrlichman. Dean had the nerve and political agility, they thought, to handle the "special" anti-antiwar political assignments that were now high on the White House agenda. In July 1970, Dean was named counsel to the president; he was told, though, that he would report not to Nixon but to Haldeman.

So Nixon, in a spasm of nostalgia, thought about naming me his counsel. But after Cambodia and the birth of a White House intelligence program that included personal surveillance, telephone intercepts, and letter openings, either he or Haldeman on his own vetoed the idea.

That was it until the spring of 1973. Midmorning of March 23, Ehrlichman asked me to come over to the White House to talk about Watergate. He said he wanted me to help him negotiate ground rules for White House witnesses in the coming Senate hearings. Senator Ervin, Ehrlichman said, would be a deadly television foe, reciting from the Constitution while grinding the president's witnesses into dust. The media would permit Ervin to get away with it, despite his years of pro-segregation partisanship, because Ervin's target was now Richard Nixon. My assignment would be to accompany White House witnesses to the hearings and figure out an effective way to make the public argument for fair treatment.

Later that day, Ron Ziegler phoned with a terse "Welcome aboard." I now became, along with Ziegler and Special Counsel Richard Moore, part of a group that met privately in Ziegler's White House office during March and April of 1973 to mull over Watergate "facts" and strategy. Ziegler knew a lot, but not about everything. Moore knew a lot, but less than Ziegler. I knew next to nothing. Up the hall a bit in the Oval Office, or across the street in Nixon's O.E.O.B. office, Nixon, Haldeman, Ehrlichman, and Dean had also been mulling, on a much more informed basis, for over a month, frequently at the same time Ziegler, Moore, and I were doing our puzzling. Ziegler literally ran between the two groups, and served as public spokesman when the occasional presidential bulletin on Watergate was issued to the White House press corps.

We now know from the Watergate tapes that during these weeks the president's group went endlessly around in vertiginous circles, hopelessly canvassing non-options that might protect all of them, like men trying to get out of a room without doors. Meanwhile, our own meetings reached out to various sources of information, including Paul O'Brien and Ken Parkinson, lawyers for the Committee to Re-elect the President. From them we learned that the criminal cases against senior administration officials were already substantial; it was too late for a general solution to the mess. These facts—that there could be no comprehensive rescue and that action would have to be taken against individuals—were clear to Moore and me, and I think to Ziegler, by the beginning of April 1973. Nixon also had this information. Why, then, we asked ourselves, did he not do something?

To add to the merriment, our ad hoc threesome heard the still-secret story of how the White House plumbers had burglarized the Los Angeles office of Dr. Lewis Fielding, Daniel Ellsberg's psychiatrist, in 1971. When I learned the news, I also learned that within days it would be made public by prosecutors or the Senate. I thought Nixon's only hope was to preempt the disastrous revelations by cleaning house.

At virtually the same time, on April 9, 1973, Ehrlichman called me and expanded his job offer. He said the president wanted me to get "up to speed" on Watergate in order to take the lead in representing the White House in negotiations about ground rules for the Senate hearings. Ehrlichman said that he himself would have to withdraw from formal participation, since he was certain to be a witness; and Dean, the White House counsel, was already a formal target. The White House needed an acting defense counsel who was completely uninvolved. Would I take the job for a while? Sure, I said—but only if the president asked me to do so. By now I knew considerably more than I had in my first Watergate conversation with Ehrlichman. I was not about to accompany Nixon into the swamp as his "lawyer" (whatever that designation meant in the

White House) unless he asked me personally. I also wanted to hear from Nixon about his knowledge of Watergate. Most of all I wanted to tell him face to face what I thought he had to do to survive.

Later that day I was asked to the president's O.E.O.B. hideaway office. Nixon and I talked for about half an hour. I made a few postconversation notes (and presumably it's all on tape). When I entered Nixon's office a few doors down the hall from mine, he was, as in the past, slouched in his old brown easy chair—he had brought it down from his pre-presidential New York quarters—with his super-shined black wingtips aloft on the ottoman, scratching away on the inevitable legal pad. That schoolboy intensity. The unwieldy head. The strange pull of his personality.

He welcomed me warmly. It was as if no time had passed and we were back in New York in the library of his Fifth Avenue apartment. Same man, same manner, same furniture, same wingtips, same yellow pad. He looked good, fit, relaxed. Not a worry in the world. "You're untouched by this," my notes recorded him saying. "Therefore I want you to come in and represent me and the White House—to be counsel, to advocate our position on executive privilege, to keep the [Ervin] committee from demagoguing, and so forth."

Nixon briefly outlined his view of the Watergate investigation. He described the scope of my assignment and assured me he was not involved in any part of the "crazy" Watergate break-in. He stated his concern about the fate of longtime friends and advisers like Haldeman, Ehrlichman, and Mitchell ("John's worries about Martha," he said, "made it possible for that bunch of nuts to take over"). He said he intended to cooperate with the Senate Watergate committee but felt it was essential to protect the principle of presidential confidentiality. I assured Nixon that I would steep myself in the facts and give him the best I had. The strategy I recommended to him, though, was designed not to contribute to his peace of mind but to shock him out of his false calm: I told him that based on what I already knew, I was convinced his survival depended on removing every official who was actually or potentially implicated in any aspect of the scandal (including, I said illogically, me). He had to sweep clean so that he could show the country an administration with a fresh face. His obligation was to protect not his friends and senior assistants but his ability to continue the presidential project of making peace with China, Vietnam, and the Soviet Union. I don't remember Nixon's making any comment or asking any questions that showed a trace of surprise during my little oration. No doubt he had anticipated most of it.

When we finished our discussion, Nixon asked me to go with him to a diplomatic ceremony in the East Room. On the path bordering the Rose Garden he paused and asked whether I was going to talk with "John." I assumed he meant John Mitchell. I said I couldn't do that: John was a prime target of the Watergate investigation. If I spoke with him, I might become a witness and be disqualified from further work on the case. This moment doubtless confirmed Nixon in his belief that I was hopeless when it came to the hard business of politics. He nodded his understanding and said with a small smile, "Well, Len, you just go ahead and steep yourself in the facts."

We arrived in the East Room, and I watched Nixon attend to the formalities of receiving the diplomatic credentials of a new ambassador from some tiny Third World country. He was thoroughly at ease, joking a little, appropriately grave at the ceremony's brief moment of solemnity. It was a marvel to see his ability to move from a discussion of mortal dangers to hosting a mundane official activity without the slightest hitch in stride. If I had been in his place, I would have been off somewhere pouring down my first double martini of the day.

When I acquired an official role in Watergate in 1973, my life changed drastically. Once again, as in the early campaign years, I saw and heard from Nixon often. Sometimes a call from the president would—unbeknownst to him—reach me when I was stretched out on a psychoanalyst's couch in an office near Dupont Circle, where I was once again coping with the usual depression. The doctor would hand me the receiver and whisper, "It's the president. Shall I step outside?" But there was no need for that. My shrink was C.I.A.-cleared, which was more than could be said for me.

In fact, as a result of one of the most unusual therapeutic events in human history, I snapped out of my depression and said good-bye to the psychiatrist altogether. The distraction of the century, for the country and the entire Western world, had begun. I was the last senior White House staffer who (a) had a license to practice law and (b) was not a potential indictee. I was a principal player in Watergate. My old friend Nixon needed me. I felt terrific.

I shouldn't have. The Watergate tapes later revealed that around the time of my April 9 meeting with him, Nixon was conducting a large number of factually detailed meetings and phone calls with Haldeman, Ehrlichman, Dean, Mitchell, and Henry Petersen, head of the Justice Department's Criminal Division, on the issue of how to get the president "out front" on Watergate without jeopardy to himself, Haldeman, or Ehrlichman. During my session with him he did not even hint at the advanced state of his knowledge.

I knew enough to start giving some warnings. Early on Saturday, April 14, 1973, I visited Henry Kissinger's office. After the president, Kissinger was the dominant figure in the administration. I also considered him a friend. For both reasons, I thought he was entitled to know something about the state of Watergate play.

Kissinger, in his memoirs, describes what I told him that Saturday morning:

> "Watergate" was about to blow up. . . . Garment said the "sordid mess" had many dimensions, only part of which he knew himself. It could not have developed without the co-operation of the highest levels of the Administration. Garment thought that Special Counsel to the President Charles W. Colson had probably been the "evil genius" behind it.
>
> Yet the scale of wrongdoing really made it impossible to imagine that Assistants to the President H. R. (Bob) Haldeman and John Ehrlichman . . . had been unaware. . . . And if Haldeman and Ehrlichman were involved, it was nearly inconceivable that the President had been completely ignorant.
>
> Whoever was the culprit, in Garment's view, only radical surgery and the fullest admission of error could avert catastrophe.

I gave Kissinger a bleak prognosis partly because I knew by then that the slow march of administration witnesses to the prosecutors and the grand jury had become a footrace: Everybody was anxious to begin negotiations in order to get immunity or the best possible plea bargain. Jeb Magruder had already implicated John Dean, Gordon Liddy, and John Mitchell in the break-in and cover-up, while Dean had presented evidence against Haldeman, Ehrlichman, Mitchell, and Magruder. Dean was also beginning to edge Nixon into his cover-up narratives. The prosecutors would have a picnic playing one desperate target off against another. In fact, we know from the tapes that on April 14, the day I gave Kissinger my warning, Ehrlichman, at Nixon's behest, urged John Mitchell to take full responsibility for Watergate. Mitchell, vehemently asserting his innocence, would have none of it. The strategies of the White House innermost circle were dissolving like sand castles at high tide.

That night, from one A.M. to five A.M., Justice Department prosecutors had presented a tearful Attorney General Richard Kleindienst, John Mitchell's successor, with evidence of crimes they said had been committed by his mentor and friend Mitchell and by other friends of Nixon's. The next day, after White House church services, Kleindienst went to the White House to review the information with the president. Nixon already knew the story; he had heard it from Henry Petersen. Still, Kleindienst was now making it official. Two days later, on April 16, the tapes record good staffer Haldeman reporting to Nixon on a conversation with me: I had told Haldeman that the president was now "in possession of knowledge . . . that he cannot [have] without acting." Nixon, on tape, was not particularly irritated by my statement of the obvious. He was much more annoyed that I had briefed Kissinger, then Haig, about the state of play: "What the hell did [Garment] do that for?" The last thing he wanted from me at this delicate moment was my brand of crisis management. Haldeman concurred, describing me as "the panic button type." He added wryly, "That doesn't mean he isn't right this time, incidentally."

On April 17, I repeated to Nixon my arguments about why Haldeman and Ehrlichman would have to resign. But by now I sensed that there was no chance Nixon would do the job promptly. Nixon saw, I realized, that matters would have to end with their resignations; but he clearly wanted to do things his own way—helpfully exploring with Haldeman and Ehrlichman one dead-end option after another, eventually pointing out why it wouldn't work, and calculating that after this process, when he finally dispatched his two

most knowledgeable assistants, they would leave without a dangerous bitterness toward him.

This, I believe, is one reason why the Nixon of the Watergate
tapes sounds so wandering, repetitious, contradictory, and at times
almost incoherent. At some points Nixon was doubtless stretching
his large intelligence obsessively to find a way out for himself and
his chief lieutenants. But in other conversations I think Nixon—
though not Bob or John—was aware of where he was heading and
created a smoke screen of circumlocution so that nobody else would
see his design.

In my April 17 plea to Nixon, I presented him with an outline
of what seemed to me an orderly sequence of White House remov-
als, based on the probative evidence then available to me. John
Dean, of course, led the list. Next came Bob Haldeman. Weeks before, Bob had asked me for advice. He said his tangential involvement in Watergate simply involved releasing $350,000 in old
campaign cash, which he had held in his safe, and arranging its
physical delivery to Fred LaRue, a close friend of John Mitchell's,
to assist in paying legal defense bills incurred by the Watergate
defendants. What did I think? "Get a lawyer," I said, and followed
with a brief explanation of conspiracy law, always an unhappy illu-
mination to laymen like Haldeman, who are astonished to find that
when the law deals with an agreement between two or more people
to commit a crime, someone can be caught in a criminal web and
have criminal intent attributed to him on the basis of seemingly (to
him) minor and even unknown acts.

Ehrlichman's vulnerability was less clear; I had not yet heard
about Herb Kalmbach's fund-raising discussions with him, Dean's
allegations, or his involvement in the Ellsberg break-in. I suppose I
wanted to lean over backward for a man I had come to admire and
who had helped me get some useful things done in government.
And I wanted to appear temperate to Nixon so he would not think I
was flailing around wildly, perhaps to the point of adding his valet
Manolo to my list of recommended firings. So I made a distinction
as to Ehrlichman in my recommendations, though I thought it was
only a matter of weeks before the tide would sweep over him, too.

Late in the afternoon of the same day, April 17, Ron Ziegler
made an announcement: Nixon had decided to make all White

House staffers available to testify before the Watergate grand jury—
and he wanted no immunity granted to any of them. I had prepared
the draft of this announcement, but my draft did not contain the
"no-immunity" clause. Ehrlichman added it without notice to me,
and Nixon accepted it, specifically for the attention of John Dean. If
Dean did not have immunity, Nixon and Ehrlichman reasoned, he
would realize that sooner or later he faced criminal sanctions; his
fate would then depend on Nixon's willingness to use presidential
powers to lighten his sentence. Presumably Dean, frightened by this
prospect, would be less likely to testify against Nixon to the grand
jury. But this turned out to be an extremely bad call on Nixon and
Ehrlichman's part. Just after Ziegler made the announcement, I met
Dean in the halls of the O.E.O.B. He asked me whether the "no-
immunity" clause was in the original draft I had prepared for Ehrlichman. I said it was not. Dean reacted with a spasm of rage at
Ehrlichman and Nixon. Only years later, when I read Dean's memoir, did the consequences of that brief conversation become clear to
me. Dean's fury did not subside. In short order he accelerated his
conversations with the Watergate prosecutors and started spilling
the beans, even without immunity. In this hapless fashion Nixon
was implicated in the cover-up, by his own miscalculation regarding
immunity, pressed on him by his first counsel, Ehrlichman, and
then by the powerful testimony of the counsel who followed. (Woe
unto ye clients.)

On April 23, Kleindienst advised Nixon that in the trial of Daniel Ellsberg for leaking the Pentagon Papers, which was then taking
place in California, the Department of Justice was legally obliged to
tell the judge about the Liddy-Hunt-Cubans break-in at the office of
Ellsberg's psychiatrist in Los Angeles. Time had run out for Nixon
to act on the status of Haldeman and Ehrlichman.

The two men's lawyers had advised them to fight for leaves
of absence, whose legal meaning would be ambiguous, rather than
agreeing to the incriminating finality of resignations. The advice
Nixon got from Henry Petersen, Bill Rogers, and me, among others,
was to ask for their resignations at once. Nixon knew by now that
he had no running room left. He directed Ziegler to prepare the two
men for their final meeting with the president at Camp David.

I was invited to join in the grim occasion and met briefly with

Nixon the morning of Sunday, April 30. For all I know, it may have been a bright sunny day, but what I remember was a sense of clouds, chill winds, and gloom everywhere. Nixon was shattered. He described his feelings to me, rehearsing what he was going to say to Bob and John: that losing them was like losing his right and left arms, that he had prayed the night before that he would not wake up to face this day.

Sometimes psychological echoes are too loud to ignore. Nixon was a man who had lost two brothers, Arthur and Harold; now he was about to suffer a not dissimilar loss. Furthermore, whereas the early deaths were not of his doing, Haldeman and Ehrlichman had to be cut down by Nixon's own hand for faithfully serving his political needs. No wonder it was terrible to contemplate. But Haldeman and Ehrlichman were political assistants, not family or close personal friends. They and Nixon were bound by the ambitions and codes of political men. So Nixon would do what he had to do.

In spite of Nixon's ghastly look that Sunday morning, I was reassured by his behavior. His dismissing Haldeman and Ehrlichman as he did, without the mitigating conditions that they and their lawyers had fought so hard to obtain, reinforced my sense that Nixon did not think himself personally implicated in the Watergate crimes. If he were personally culpable, I reasoned, he would have remained hostage to the two men. His emotional recoil from the dismissals—clothes rumpled, eyes red-rimmed by tears and fatigue —seemed to me the reaction of a man who may have been morally involved but was not criminally liable in the substantive crimes of Watergate.

I did not know that a few hours after I saw the president, Ehrlichman, as he has written in his memoirs, would tell Nixon bitterly that he wanted Nixon to explain to Ehrlichman's children why their father had been fired.

Since there is already an exhaustive library on Watergate, I will merely add details. A criminal investigation, led by the career Justice Department prosecutors Earl Silbert and Seymour Glanzer, ran nonstop until Elliot Richardson was confirmed as attorney general in May 1973. As a condition of Richardson's confirmation, special prosecutor Archibald Cox was appointed and took over the pursuit of Watergate criminality. Cox was impressively intelligent. He seemed like a scholarly, calm, objective professional, but he was in fact a fairly conventional Nixon hater. He began assembling a large collection of prosecutors and summa cum laude aides, a sizable number of them drawn from the Kennedy and McGovern Senate staffs. By the time Cox arrived, Silbert and Glanzer, though not exactly put to the lash by Henry Peterson, had already broken the Watergate cover-up and accumulated most of the evidence needed to prosecute Nixon's associates on charges of obstruction and related offenses. But when Cox came on the scene in the early summer, the focus of the criminal investigation changed. Now the point of the exercise was to nail Nixon.

Also in the game was the Senate Watergate staff, led by the Georgetown law professor and experienced prosecutor Sam Dash, who was both very smart and a palpably decent human being. Minority counsel (and, since 1994, Senator) Fred Thompson was no slouch either, but he suffered a huge disadvantage in staff numbers, logistical support, and the ability to control public information. In the late fall of 1973, the House Judiciary Committee added yet more manpower to the hunt: Under Chairman Peter Rodino, majority counsel John Doar began assembling his own team for impeachment proceedings. The House, Senate, and Cox staffs, plus other committee staffs looking into financial, real estate, and tax questions, came to number literally in the hundreds.

There was a strategic reason for the huge numbers of lawyers and other staffers. When the staff buildup took place, the Watergate tapes had not been revealed, let alone subpoenaed. There was every reason to assume that dislodging Nixon from the presidency would be a very hard job. Americans are reluctant to lose any president. Nixon had won a record reelection victory in 1972. He had an unparalleled collection of foreign policy triumphs, in days when that still mattered. He was a tough, smart politician with a high popularity rating and a solid base in Congress. And there was no concrete evidence of his involvement in the cover-up other than John Dean's testimony, which was equivocal and uncorroborated. Much more was needed. More could be found, the investigators reasoned, in areas of possible Nixon misconduct that were not directly related to

Watergate. Thus they probed alleged campaign finance violations, personal financial derelictions, illegal surveillance activities by the plumbers, foreign policy issues like the bombing of Cambodia, and so on. Cox, for instance, split his large staff into separate teams to handle his numerous criminal cases, such as the Watergate break-in and cover-up, the Ellsberg break-in, the illegal campaign contributions, the controversial ITT antitrust settlement, and the milk producers' political contributions.

The organizing objective of these investigations was to bleed Nixon to death. Nixon would try to induce public weariness with Watergate "wallowing"; the investigators would counter with a string of shocking news stories that would produce a continuous flow of political adrenaline. They had to maintain the anti-Nixon momentum, weary his staff, demoralize his supporters, erode his position with the public, and steadily weaken his still-powerful base in Congress. Perhaps he could be forced out of office. At the very least he would be prevented from functioning Nixon-style for the rest of his tattered term.

No doubt there were fair-minded, judicious men and women among the vast teams of Watergate sherpas who gathered in Washington in 1973 for the assault on Mount Nixon. I knew one, maybe two, myself. But I saw that most were basically motivated by three things: first, to take part in the sheer joy of getting rid of "Old Tricky," the bogeyman of their political adolescence; second, to see that the punishment given to Nixon and his cronies was severe enough to fit their public crimes; and third, to secure for themselves a place in the books that record history and create careers. Even for the most decent, motives had to be mixed.

In 1993, I visited the White House to see my longtime friend Bernard Nussbaum, then counsel to President Bill Clinton, who had been, back in 1973, one of the preeminent panters after Nixon's neck. He showed me around his West Wing office (it had been Ehrlichman's during the Nixon years) and singled out one prized memento, a large photograph of what looked like a college graduating class, row upon row of fresh, smiling faces anticipating their exciting date with the future. The photo was in fact of John Doar's impeachment staff, 104 strong, including young Bernie and the even younger Hillary Rodham. Similar group photos probably still exist of the hundreds of other happy Watergate investigators on the many other Watergate staffs.

Few, if any, of the throng of Watergate lawyers and investigators were in Washington simply to seek justice. For instance, the House Judiciary Committee presented its impeachment inquiry to Congress and the country as a meticulously objective exercise in political due process. On January 31, 1974, majority counsel John Doar began the committee's formal proceedings with the assurance that "every staff member was questioned whether or not they had taken a position on impeachment and if they had, other than that there should be an inquiry, then they were not considered for the job." Doar repeatedly affirmed that he and his staff were determinedly open-minded about the outcome of their exercise.

Yet not long after Watergate, in December 1976, in an article in *The Atlantic Monthly*, Renata Adler, a lawyer and well-known reporter and author, said otherwise. Adler worked on the House Judiciary Committee's impeachment staff and was, her article explains, a member of Doar's inner circle of "ad hoc irregulars"— seven people of whom five, including Adler herself, were very close friends of Doar's. These individuals, she says, did the "real work" of the inquiry, drafting briefs and arguments for impeachment and preparing public statements for Doar and various congressmen. From the beginning, Adler writes, there "never was any doubt among Doar and this small group" that "unless there was overwhelming evidence of Nixon's innocence . . . the object of the process was that the President must be impeached and removed from office." As for Doar himself, Adler recalls that he, months before he joined the House inquiry, was the second "non-radical person" she knew who called for Nixon's impeachment. But he thought he could not disclose this sentiment until congressional support for Nixon had eroded enough to permit the administration of the coup de grâce.

After Adler's article appeared, no one mentioned it. My friend Ray Price discussed it in his book *With Nixon* in 1977, but there was no public comment. I cited Adler's piece in a 1987 article about Watergate; still silence. When I taxed my journalistic friends with their nonresponse, they said only that Adler was "strange," or that her article also said bad and incredible things about Nixon, or that

Nixon was in fact guilty, so what was the difference? No one wanted to introduce troubling moral ambiguities into the historical record or undermine the impression that Nixon was pursued for pure motives and through pure methods.

There exist other such records of the spirit of the times. John Doar expected that Nixon would defend himself by claiming that he had only done what other presidents had done before him, so Doar commissioned the eminent Yale historian C. Vann Woodward to prepare a counterbrief. Titled "Responses of Presidents to Charges of Misconduct," and supposedly a comprehensive account of presidential misbehavior through the ages, it somehow managed to leave out Attorney General Robert Kennedy's authorizing, with J.F.K.'s knowledge, F.B.I. wiretaps of Martin Luther King, as well as President Lyndon Johnson's use of the odious King materials, his taping of the Mississippi Freedom Democratic party during the 1964 Democratic convention, and his spying on Richard Nixon's 1968 presidential campaign, allegedly for purposes of national security.

Up against the anti-Nixon numbers and anti-Nixon spirit was Nixon's legal "team." In addition to me, it consisted basically of the Pentagon's general counsel, Fred Buzhardt, drafted by Al Haig shortly after Haig took over as White House chief of staff; Douglas Parker, who had worked with me on school desegregation; and Charles Alan Wright, the only lawyer of national reputation among us, a much admired constitutional scholar at the University of Texas who came to Washington on call to advise the president and lead the presentation of constitutional arguments on his behalf. We could have taken *our* group picture in one of those amusement park booths that give you four photos for a dollar. There was, sad to say, not a single experienced criminal defense lawyer in the "firm."

Buzhardt, for years Strom Thurmond's man in South Carolina and Washington and thought to be a prototypical Dixie conservative, was a self-effacing model of personal decency and political moderation. I was comfortable with him from the start, and our friendship lasted beyond the White House foxhole. He was an authentically plain man. He spoke in a "How's that, again?" backwoods Southern drawl made even more exotic by a constant nasal overtone. He was hunched over and skinny as a split rail, his face pinched by bad dentures and a consequently restricted diet. I often worried about my own dental future, remembering my father's ugly pink clackers soaking in their bedside glass of water, so I asked Fred when and how he had lost his teeth. It turned out he had literally given them away for his country. As a West Point graduate during World War II, anxious to get into flight school and air combat, Fred was told that he would first have to go through months of periodontal surgery to get his mouth in shape for the wild blue yonder. Instead, he simply had all the offending teeth extracted in a marathon sequence of operations. I suggested that his autobiography be titled *A Yank at West Point.* He reacted with forbearance.

Eventually Fred took on Watergate's worst job: He became official listener to the presidential tapes. When we needed to find out what was on a particular tape, whether for the president or for delivery to Archibald Cox or Judge Sirica, Fred would don his Mickey Mouse earphones. He sat for hundreds of hours, playing and rewinding, making precise little penciled notes, smoking one carton after another of unfiltered Camels, sneaking off for a hasty lunch of soft food, working away until he suffered the first of the heart attacks that killed him not long after Nixon resigned.

Charley Wright also smoked unfiltered cigarettes. But unlike Buzhardt, for whom smoking was the single sinful pleasure, Charley reveled in his evening scotch, fine food, and good conversation. What he had in common with Fred Buzhardt was a tolerance for my puns and an enthusiastic devotion to the practice of law. While Fred was a shrewd small-town lawyer who had been elevated by industry, loyalty, and craftsmanship to one of the most powerful legal positions in the U.S. government, and was especially proud of his knowledge about the way law and politics intersected, Charley Wright was tall and slender and looked like a Texas sheriff who had happened to take a sabbatical at Cambridge and decided to pursue legal studies. He was a superb lawyer and knew it, forgoing false modesty as if such abstinence were the Eleventh Commandment. Charley loved to cite obscure footnotes from ancient cases. Fred retaliated by citing Scripture, chapter and verse.

The managing "partner" of our legal team was a nonlawyer, General Alexander Haig, who had given up the post of army vice chief of staff to replace Haldeman as chief of staff for the White House. The original idea was that Haig would not have anything to do with Watergate and would return to the army after helping with the post-Haldeman transition. Before long, though, he was mud wrestling along with the rest of us, barely able to tend to routine White House business. As Nixon dug deeper into his private shell, Haig became indispensable to managing both presidential business and Watergate business. He was the principal communications link between Nixon and his lawyers.

If anyone was qualified for this punishing assignment, Haig was. I say this even though our personal relationship was less than felicitous. There was much about Haig that I admired: his canny intelligence, courage, bureaucratic skills, the way he kept his office door and professional mind open, his capacity to work fifteen hours a day with savage intensity. My problem was that Haig was hardwired for combat, William Holden in battle dress, while I was the Brooklyn kid who got off the subway at the wrong Pennsylvania Avenue. The friction between us was constant, despite some synthetic middle-of-the-night Jack Daniels warmth. Certain qualities were Haig's lodestars—physical courage, unquestioning loyalty, fighting to win. These qualities were important to me, too, but I had a certain hesitation at the idea of risking my freedom, family, and reputation for Richard Nixon, let alone Al Haig. The tension came to a head one frazzled night in Haig's office when the booze had turned us in the wrong direction. I don't remember the precise casus belli, but Haig accused me of disloyalty, which brought us to the point of blows. Thank God for the presence of Major George Joulwan, Haig's principal aide and a bull of a man, who intervened and saved my life, or at least my genetically vulnerable teeth. He is now wearing four deserved stars.

The final member of the Watergate legal team, Doug Parker, was there against his will. A civil lawyer in every sense, Parker was counsel to the H.U.D. secretary, James Lynn, when I dragged him into Watergate. He had worked with me on difficult cases back in New York. In Washington, he had helped me not just on school desegregation but on other dicey problems for which meticulous lawyering and sober good sense were required. If I was anxious about Watergate, Parker was terrified, knowing as an astute lawyer that Washington had become a plague city. But he soldiered along, worrying twenty-four hours a day for both of us, enabling me to get some sleep. My first official directive after Haldeman and Ehr-lichman were dismissed was to order the F.B.I. to guard the two ex-aides' offices and files; Parker did the actual deployment, work-ing through the night. The next morning, in a cabinet meeting, Nixon threw a famous fit: "I want to know who gave that goddamn order. He's out right now, fired." No one spoke up; fortunately, I was absent, thus preventing serious presidential embarrassment. These days when I phone Parker, he still sounds vaguely apprehensive until he satisfies himself that I'm not calling about a matter hazard-ous to his life or liberty.

So why was the White House stumbling along with a handful of lawyers while "they" had a cast of hundreds? Part of our problem was appearances: The president had proclaimed his innocence and presumably did not need a large legal team. Another barrier was government rules: Though we brought in a few assistant U.S. attor-neys, the conflict-of-interest problem proved an enduring obstacle to our efforts to get adequate staff.

But there were other reasons. In early May, just after I became counsel to the president, I urged Nixon to let me try to find him outside counsel with the numbers and experience to handle Wa-tergate's large and predictably unpredictable problems. This idea was difficult for Nixon to accept, not only because of public rela-tions but also because there wasn't a private law firm he would trust with presidential confidences. Haig proposed Edward Bennett Williams and Joseph Califano, both active Democrats; Nixon vetoed these suggestions. Nixon finally agreed to let me talk to a lawyer he did trust—Bill Rogers, who would soon be leaving his post as secre-tary of state. Rogers already knew a lot about Watergate. Nixon told me to ask Rogers if he would assemble and lead an outside defense team.

In May 1973, I went over to the State Department, where Rogers and I talked for a couple of hours. As usual, I was somewhat dis-tracted by the difference between the semideranged incompetent of Henry Kissinger's fevered descriptions and the pleasant, calm, rational, superbly put together man before me. Indeed, Rogers's shiningly urbane manner somewhat obscured his professional toughness: He had logged thousands of rough-and-tumble hours in politics and public life, serving as attorney general for the demanding and infinitely cunning Dwight D. Eisenhower. In private life, Rogers had lawyered for *The Washington Post* and other companies of like size and importance. Though strategic foreign policy thinking may not have been his forte, he would have been a terrific outside counsel for Nixon.

Rogers listened politely and carefully to my proposal, but I could see from the start that his answer would be no. He wasn't quite ready to leave State, he said. He thought representing a president from outside the government would pose technical problems too daunting for him to undertake. He had been advising the president privately, as I knew, and would continue to do so whenever the president wanted his help. He added, for my benefit, that he suspected Watergate involved vast stretches of still-uncharted quicksand. This last, I think, was the real reason for his demurrer. He gave me some parting advice: "Watch your step, Len."

Nixon then decided, for reasons Buzhardt and I did not understand at that time, to manage his Watergate defense personally. He would be his own lawyer, working principally through Haig and doling out spoonfuls of time and information to Buzhardt and me while conferring personally and at length with the private lawyers for ex-aides Haldeman and Ehrlichman and with Haldeman himself. Nixon had concluded that the case was a political struggle, not a legal contest. He preferred to have the knowledgeable Haldeman at his side—and on his side—as he felt his way through the stages of the battle. Nixon saw his principal troops as his legislative staff and his supporters in Congress and the public, not his White House lawyers.

Nixon's strategy was to reduce Watergate to a credibility contest between Dean and Nixon, the hustler against the world statesman. Nixon was sure he would win. No one besides Dean could—or would—connect Nixon with the cover-up. Dean himself had no documentary corroboration of his version of his talks with Nixon. And there was no claim by anyone, Dean included, that Nixon was implicated in the Watergate break-in itself.

For various reasons, that was not the way things worked out. In April, May, and June 1973, saturation news coverage of Watergate informed the national audience about a dazzling array of Watergate "items" and coming attractions, including the approaching Senate hearings. There were stories about the Ellsberg break-in, destruction of files by Acting F.B.I. Director Pat Gray and the withdrawal of his nomination to be director, leaks about the authorization of the Watergate break-in at meetings involving Liddy, Magruder, Dean, and Mitchell; other leaks about details of the break-in itself and the cover-up; Dean's disclosure about Nixon's authorization of extraordinary domestic surveillance; Dean's revelation of the Colson–Dean–God-knows-who-else–concocted "enemies" list, which was portrayed as an attempt to anathematize patriotic American citizens; Dean's leaked stories of his forthcoming Senate testimony about his meetings with Nixon, and much more.

On May 17, 1973, which I came to think of as "Wheel of Fortune" day, Treasury Secretary William Simon informed me that the I.R.S. computer system had randomly selected the tax returns of Mr. and Mrs. Richard M. Nixon for an audit. The Nixons were in a vulnerable category because they had taken large deductions for the gift of Nixon's vice presidential papers and had paid virtually no taxes for two years. I called the I.R.S. commissioner, Don Alexander, who gave me the bad news in procedural detail. I notified Haig that the president would need private tax counsel and told Alexander to "audit away." The information was bound to be leaked, and it was. This was the first of a score of opportunistic infections, most involving financial charges, that breached the Nixon presidency's degraded immune system and worked progressive, irrevocable damage on it.

My own immune system was threatened as well. On "Wheel of Fortune" day, an hour after my conversation with Commissioner Alexander, Dan Rather called to advise me that CBS had taped a video interview with a man in London named Ratnoff who said that in January 1971 I approached him to buy bugging equipment. The alleged incident was said to have occurred face-to-face in a town in New Jersey I had never visited and never knew existed. This was my first taste of that spasm of dread and nausea that even a phony story produces for someone in government who knows that publication alone will produce a scandal. I shouted indignantly at Rather that the story was an "absolute, goddamn, fucking fabrication." To my exhausted relief, after half a day of back and forth, Rather chose to believe me. In those days, such a story would rarely run without corroboration. Now it could happen with ease.

That same day, May 17, the Senate Watergate hearings began.

. . .

Dash had organized a careful legal presentation and a dramatically incremental television production, beginning with mostly low-level campaign-committee witnesses who provided an organizational framework for the more prominent figures scheduled to appear later on. Almost everyone's early favorite—certainly mine— was Tony Ulasewicz, who had so many hush-money calls to make from pay phones around Washington that he equipped himself with a bus driver's coin dispenser. When the hearings started, TV stations that carried them were jammed with calls from viewers objecting to the preemption of their soap operas. But not for long. The Watergate story soon became meta-soap, with a clear story line and unforgettable characters.

To offset some of the negative effect of the Senate hearings, media coverage, and accumulated unanswered press and congressional questions, Buzhardt and I argued to Nixon and Haig that the time was overdue for us to say something comprehensive about the proliferating charges. Nixon doubted that a statement should be made, but Haig, Buzhardt, and I insisted that we needed a "theory of the case," a defense posture that put flesh on Nixon's bare-bones assertions of noninvolvement. The president agreed to let us try.

Price and Buchanan were assigned to do the basic writing while Buzhardt and I, with Haig's help, provided the policy lines. Nixon instructed us to draft initial statements that we could back up without any contribution from him. He said he would then revise the drafts on the basis of what he remembered. This seemed a weird order of battle, but Nixon was president. We had begun to learn that ours was not a genuine attorney-client relationship.

For two or three days we sat around an O.E.O.B. conference table belonging to David Gergen, who was in charge of the presidential writing group. Haig, Buzhardt, Price, Buchanan, and I drafted and redrafted passages. Nixon chose Buzhardt rather than Haig to carry these drafts down the long hall to Nixon's O.E.O.B. office. Once the drafts were delivered, we waited, often for an hour or more, to find out from Buzhardt what had passed muster and what had not. Gergen himself was not part of the drafting party but kept in touch with the deliberations, as he did with most Watergate goings-on, through conversational semaphores (at which he was adept), mostly with me.

I now know that when we were working on our statement, Haig knew there was a White House taping system, though he did not know how comprehensive it was; Nixon had ordered him not to tell the rest of us. I'm sure he also knew enough not to want to know more, which was why he seemed content not to be at the center of the action and scribbled away with the rest of the staffers in Gergen's office. Haig was happy to have Buzhardt—one of the shrewdest political lawyers in Washington, armed with attorney-client privilege and years of dealing with the national security establishment —tiptoe through the evidence with Nixon, accepting detailed representations of fact without pressing Nixon about their source.

Some of Nixon's handwritten comments on our drafts included strikingly detailed, seemingly verbatim, summaries of Nixon-Dean discussions. Nixon apparently had a secret cache of information that he would not show us, and increasingly it seemed probable to Fred and me that this information was of the type that might compromise our ability to represent him in court and in public if we knew its nature. Remembering that Nixon had told Henry Petersen in an April 15 meeting that he had John Dean "on tape," Fred and I began to suspect that Nixon, in revising our drafts, was consulting extracts from tape recordings.

I remember Buchanan's recommending, with the agreement of most of us, that Nixon take personal responsibility for the Ellsberg break-in and defend his actions publicly and aggressively. We thought that in a duel between the president and the leaker, Ellsberg, Nixon was a sure winner. I have a mental picture of Nixon personally discussing this issue with part of our group—again, after one of those long intervals—and telling us emphatically that much as he would like to do it, he couldn't, because he simply did not "recall" it that way.

One night as Buzhardt and I drove home, we talked about Nixon's strange methodology and agreed that he must have had a large cache of tapes that he was using selectively to "refresh" his recollection.

It was probably a combination of factors that made Nixon unwilling to reveal the taping system and the tapes' contents even to his lawyers and senior staff. He presumably thought that news of the secret system would quickly be leaked. He might have thought some of the talk on the tapes would cause staff disaffection. He may have been unsure about the legal implications of his lawyers and staffers having knowledge that could contradict their public representations. In this mix were added intangibles like misplaced confidence in .executive privilege, uncertainty about his political strength, and sheer confusion owing to the flood of events. All these things taken together leave Nixon's reluctance no great mystery; but the result of it was to isolate him from his so-called advisers and make us powerless to give sensible advice.

But like characters under hypnosis we plowed along. We worried, griped, and talked about quitting—but didn't. We were fascinated by the puzzles and excited by the daily dramas. More important, we were held in place by our identification with the odd, solitary man we served. For those of us who had been with Nixon since the fifties and sixties, the bond was understandable. But even to relative newcomers like Haig and Buzhardt it seemed somehow wrong to think about abandoning Nixon. It may have been loyalty or reluctance to part with power or admit failure. Still, even allowing for these reasons, there was also our conviction, not just rationalization, that despite Nixon's capacity for transgression, he had done and could yet do large presidential deeds far outweighing the misdeeds that now seemed to displace everything else in the political universe. So we chose not to confront Nixon about his tapes. We did what we could with the information he gave us. Like Haig, we did not want to know more than Nixon wanted us to know. It was partly caution but also deference to a president trying to save his administration while he still had the power to lead. In those days, before Watergate itself had soured American politics, the continuity of the presidency in a dangerous world meant a lot to the country and to us.

Our drafts eventually became a four-thousand-word "Statement," Nixon's first detailed defense of his position. The White House issued it on May 22. I drew the short straw and was shipped out front to brief the White House press corps on its contents.

Shirley Jackson once wrote a celebrated short story called "The Lottery," in which a community of otherwise normal people stones a neighbor to death. This is pretty much what happened in the packed White House press room as I tried to make clear why such things as presidentially authorized wiretapping, mail openings, secret intelligence operations, and breaking and entering were no big deal. The questioning, a verbal gang-bang, started at the decibel level of a scream and went up. Questions were shouted simultaneously. Answers were spiked with interruptions and insults:

How the hell can you take those positions, Len?

Well, let me answer . . .

Jeers. Boos.

What did you mean when you said there are unknown facts that you are still investigating? How could Nixon not know?

Well, there is the matter of memory . . .

More catcalls.

I have a White House photograph of the press conference—a huge crowd of reporters grabbing papers from someone. I know it's me only because of the familiar bald spot on top of my head. The journalists' questions, two hours of them, were broadcast throughout the White House. When the press conference finally ended, some of my colleagues passing me in the halls turned away in embarrassment as if I were a burn victim.

Nixon thought I had done well. He sent me a handwritten letter saying Al Haig had described me as a "tower of strength" during the whole process. Nice, but the truth of the matter is that I enjoyed the wild press briefing. A lot of hysterical shouting is, to a trial lawyer, simply a signal that he is doing his job effectively. Indeed, the May 22 statement, for all its obscurity, factual lacunae, and ignorant fakery, worked surprisingly well. Sated by their orgy of shouting and given a long presidential document to dissect, the Watergate press corps quieted to a whisper for a while. Then Dean started testifying, and the existence of the tapes was disclosed by Alex Butterfield. The debilitating Watergate media coverage resumed and never again let up.

During the respite that the May 22 statement brought us, Nixon began a more systematic review of the Nixon-Dean tapes in preparation for Dean's Senate appearance, which was scheduled for late June. On June 4, though I did not know this at the time, Nixon, Haldeman, Steve Bull (to set up the tapes), and, to a much lesser extent, Ron Ziegler began listening to tapes so that Nixon could decide whether their use would help or hurt him. Nixon's first instinct had been to preserve only his national security tapes, destroying the rest. At that time—at any time before the tapes' public disclosure in early July—such destruction would probably have been legal. During June, the discussion between Nixon and his former aide, Haldeman, about the "value" or "detriment" of the tapes went back and forth—until the chance to destroy the tapes without criminal vulnerability was gone.

The consequences of Nixon's hesitation began to appear on June 27, the second day of John Dean's cross-examination. Few mature Americans can have forgotten Dean's direct testimony—a bone-crushing 245 pages written by Dean himself and read nonstop in a calm, even soothing, affect-free voice for an entire day. He had the whole American TV and radio stage to himself and used it against Nixon with devastating effect, playing perfectly his role as the president's young counsel forced by an unhappy constellation of events to present his detailed account of White House crimes.

The daunting task of impeaching Dean's credibility fell to minority counsel Fred Thompson and the Watergate committee's Republican senators. To help them, Buzhardt had privately delivered various materials to Thompson and his staff. There were excerpts from Nixon's private fact summaries and tape extracts (though they were not labeled as such), which the president directed Buzhardt to read to Thompson over the phone. I knew nothing about this exchange; I'm sure Nixon ordered Buzhardt not to tell me. In addition, there was a list of thirty-nine groups of cross-examination questions, prepared by Buzhardt, Wright, Parker, and me. Finally, we supplied an accompanying narrative statement designed to help the cross-examiners by providing them with a coherent theory. The statement described Dean as the hyperambitious architect and director of the break-in and cover-up, working for his "patron" John Mitchell and attempting through false testimony to deflect responsibility to others, including the president. Charley Wright combined his authorial skills with his passion for mystery novels to write the story from facts and scraps of theories supplied by the rest of the lawyers as we passed the time watching Dean slaughter Nixon on television. Charley facetiously titled the narrative *Golden Boy*.

Seated before the television, watching the second day of Dean's cross-examination, we were first thunderstruck, then horrified as Senator Daniel Inouye started reading *Golden Boy* to the national television audience. I still don't know how the materials found their way into Inouye's hostile hands; back then we were pitifully naïve about the reliability of our supposed friends on the Watergate minority staffs. But Inouye, having received the documents and seeing the opportunity to neutralize the attack on Dean, struck boldly. He read the narrative slowly and dramatically to the TV cameras from beginning to end.

As a piece of advocacy, *Golden Boy* was not half bad. Even the gifted anti-Nixon journalist Mary McCarthy, writing in *The New York Review of Books*, said she was disheartened by the factual force of the attack on Dean and Mitchell. But it was a rhetorical disaster. It seemed a brutal, cynical betrayal of John Mitchell, the most loyal of the remaining Nixon loyalists—and a loyalist who still had the power to do grievous, even fatal damage to Nixon.

In the blink of an eye, the president and White House press office disavowed *Golden Boy*. The attack on Dean's credibility, though powerful, quickly disappeared in the welter of finger pointing. For damaging Mitchell I felt as mean and small as a schoolboy caught stealing money from a classmate's locker. I was also upset that the White House lawyers had been repudiated nationwide by their client, the president. I was less upset by something that turned out to be more important: The raw materials that Fred Buzhardt had privately telephoned to Fred Thompson, as well as the suggested cross-examination questions, drew heavily on the detailed information that Buzhardt had been given directly by the president. With so many investigators conducting depositions of the White House staff, how long would it be before one of them deduced the likely source of this information and asked the right person the right question?

On July 10, at ten A.M., at the direction of Al Haig, Larry Higby —an aide of Haldeman's sometimes called "Haldeman's Haldeman" —came to my office to tell me in detail about the secret taping system. Higby was scheduled to be interviewed in a few days by the Senate staff and needed guidance on how to handle questions about it. I was not shocked. I already assumed that Nixon had taped conversations from which he gave Buzhardt details for the May 22 statement. I also knew that previous presidents, going back to F.D.R., had taped specific conversations without notice to their guests— more prudently than Nixon with his self-activating monster. And the flood of Watergate events had partially anesthetized me, so that I had not thought much about the public consequences of Nixon's perpetual taping system.

Higby told me that besides himself, only Nixon, Haldeman, Alex Butterfield, and the Secret Service knew about the system. This, it turned out, was not right: Ehrlichman, Ziegler, and Haig also knew there was a taping capability. As far back as April, Ehrlichman had advised the president to listen to John Dean tapes to see how much of a problem Dean's testimony might pose. Still, talking with Higby, I saw that sooner or later someone would ask the "tapes" question. So I gave him the only advice possible: He was not required to volunteer information, but if he was asked directly whether there was a taping capability, he had to answer truthfully or face possible criminal charges. He shouldn't dance around the question. I put him through a trial run to illustrate what the prudent boundaries were. I don't recall whether Alex Butterfield, by then head of the Federal Aviation Administration, called me for advice on.dealing with questions about the tapes. If he did, I told him the same thing.

While Higby got by without revealing the tape system, But- terfield did not. Ironically, it was a Senate Watergate Committee minority staff lawyer who did the job; he had been alerted by Fred Thompson's highly detailed material and by John Dean's testimony that he believed he had been taped during his April 15 meeting with Nixon. The staff lawyer, Donald Sanders, was a devoted Nixon supporter. But on July 12, deposing Butterfield, he took the inevita- ble professional step, asked the direct question, and got the full story of the taping system's existence.

Nixon, in his *Memoirs*, tells how "shocked" he was by the news of Butterfield's revelation. He believed, he says, that any White House staff member asked this question would have invoked execu- tive privilege. In fact, on the question of the system's physical exis- tence, as opposed to the tapes' contents, I never entertained the idea of executive privilege or told anyone else to do so. I do not believe such a claim would have had the slightest legal merit; but this is an academic judgment, since none of the White House lawyers ever had the opportunity to discuss options before the crisis was upon us. If there had been reasonably open communications between the president and us, we would at least have had time to canvass the possibilities. But there wasn't and we didn't.

On July 12, while Butterfield was giving his deposition, Grace and I took off for northern Michigan to visit the kids at camp. When we arrived back at National Airport on Sunday night there was a message from the White House asking me to send Grace home and go to my office. Fred Buzhardt and Doug Parker were waiting with the news about Butterfield's disclosure; they had received a private heads-up, either directly or through Haig's office, from Senator Baker's staff on Saturday. They wanted me to phone Butterfield, who had called my office early on Sunday.

I reached Butterfield at home. He told me he had been asked about a taping system, had answered truthfully, and was told he would be called to testify about the matter before the full Senate committee. He wanted to know what would happen now. I told him he would be getting a subpoena, probably the next day. He sounded upset, but I told him he was in the fortunate position of having both no personal jeopardy and no alternative. The next morning Butterfield phoned from the barbershop. A process server had just delivered the subpoena. Butterfield asked me whether I would represent him. I said there were technical conflict reasons why I could not. But, I added, he didn't really need a lawyer. Since he was going to be on national television, it was more important for him to get a good haircut.

Fred Buzhardt quickly prepared a letter for the president to sign ordering the Secret Service not to testify about the tapes, but the damage was done. On Tuesday, July 17, the Senate committee unanimously instructed its chairman to use all legal means to obtain the tapes.

On the evening of the seventeenth, discussions of whether to destroy the tapes began at the Bethesda Naval Hospital, where the president had been confined with viral pneumonia since the previous Thursday. Before the meeting, Doug Parker and I reviewed the case law to determine whether the president was obliged to preserve the tapes. No subpoena had yet been physically served on him, but the committee had publicly made clear its intention to obtain the tapes, by subpoena if necessary. The answer was plain to both of us —and to Fred Buzhardt, with whom we reviewed the case law. The key decision, *United States v. Solow*, had been written by one of the most respected jurists in the country, District Judge Edward Weinfeld, in a 1956 case involving the same core facts: No subpoena had been served, but there was knowledge of a government body's intention to issue one. Weinfeld held that destruction of the documents was an obstruction of justice, the Second Circuit Court of Appeals affirmed the decision, and there was no court holding to the contrary. So the tapes could not lawfully be destroyed. This conclusion was not the end of the issue, since a president cannot be indicted while in office. But a presidential "felony" can be the basis for an article of impeachment.

On Monday and Tuesday there were virtually nonstop discussions among Haig, Buzhardt, Parker, and me about the significance of these conclusions. We also talked about various technical means for destroying the tapes (by electronic erasure, for example) and about who, other than Nixon himself, might undertake the deed. I made everyone slightly edgy by noting that even if Nixon could not be indicted, conspirators who facilitated a nonindictable felony, including lawyers and ex-generals, could.

By the time we all met with Nixon in the hospital, our views did not grossly differ. In talking to Nixon we simply emphasized different considerations. I focused on the legal and perceptual hazards. Buzhardt, a prudent lawyer, certainly understood the potential criminality of destroying the tapes, but as the most experienced political insider in the group, he concentrated on the practical consequences. Haig served as master of ceremonies; he displayed absolutely no appetite for a bonfire that might save the president but destroy his own career. Ziegler, though present, was largely silent; he would be the sounding board for Nixon and Haldeman after we left. For those who visited Nixon in that first session, a crucial factor was that none of us, as far as I know, had heard any of the tapes—with the possible exception of Buzhardt, who might have heard fragments by then.

We met with Nixon two or three times, first while he was still in bed, later in a small conference room in the presidential suite.

We talked about many things, including urgent destroy-the-tapes advice we were getting from a number of men—including Nelson Rockefeller, Henry Kissinger, and John Connally—whose recorded conversations with Nixon were not exactly *Reader's Digest* material. If anyone had taped these hospital sessions, the bunch of us— Nixon, Haig, Buzhardt, Ziegler, and I—would have sounded more than a little like the gang on tape in the Oval Office. Our discussions wove around inconclusively and at times incoherently. Our views overlapped, then diverged. We played devil's advocates for different positions. We tried, each in his own way, to smoke out Nixon's real feelings and intentions, but without luck.

Nixon's *Memoirs* seems to fix on me the principal responsibility for his failure to destroy the tapes. On the basis of the hospital conversations alone, that is not an unreasonable position, since I was the one who gave the legal opinion that destroying the tapes could be an obstruction of justice and thus a basis for impeachment. On the other hand, Haig later wrote that in those meetings I threatened to resign and denounce the president if he destroyed the tapes, and that certainly did not happen. If it had, I am sure Nixon would never have talked to me again, and justifiably so. In any event, Buzhardt did not disagree with the legal opinion I gave; he simply thought the president was politically strong enough to ride out the reaction, including Democratic charges of obstruction, and avoid impeachment. We all thought, on the basis of Charley Wright's near-categorical opinion, that we had a very powerful executive privilege argument. I don't recall that any of us had the nerve to raise the ultimate question: Who would actually put the tapes to the torch?

Haig sensibly refrained from expressing a view on the legal issues. But throughout, as at the first meeting, he was vocally concerned about the strong impression of guilt that would be produced by the tapes' destruction. Haig's memoir says he told the president to destroy the tapes; if so, he did it privately.

However, the decision on the tapes was not determined by the conversations that took place in the hospital. As Nixon himself remembers, at some point after our inconclusive exchanges ended, he called his former chief of staff. Haldeman's opinion, doubtless expressed with characteristically crisp confidence, was that the crucial Nixon-Dean tapes—including the March 21 tape, which Haldeman had heard in its entirety during a meeting with Nixon in early June—were Nixon's best defense. Haldeman said the tapes should therefore be preserved, though Nixon should first assert executive privilege and "not budge an inch."

Haldeman's judgment was stunningly wide of the mark. He completely misconstrued the impression the tapes would make. He even misremembered a crucial passage in the March 21 tape and thus wound up under indictment for perjury. At first, when I thought about his bizarre advice, the only explanations I could come up with were lame ones: Perhaps Haldeman gave Nixon the advice he knew Nixon wanted to hear. Maybe the aberration had something to do with Haldeman's devout belief in Christian Science, whose power to deny reality is enormous.

But evidence in the recently published Haldeman diaries suggests a different conclusion. The diaries show that Haldeman was always ambivalent toward Nixon, as any valet is toward his master.

When Nixon dismissed Haldeman on April 30, 1973, Haldeman wrote of the event, "It was the first time he had shaken my hand." That perception could not have been unaccompanied by a large amount of festering resentment. The influence of this resentment need not have been a conscious one, but it must be considered along with explanations based on Haldeman's tone deafness or ignorance of the law.

The objective fact is that Haldeman completely ignored the poison in the tapes, and Nixon, bolstered by his own wishes and misperceptions, acted on Haldeman's advice. By mid-July 1973, both the Senate and the special prosecutor had subpoenaed the tapes and related presidential records. Nixon refused all documentary demands, citing what he called his historic right and obligation to protect the privacy of presidential communications. The fat was in the fire. To Nixon's everlasting regret, the tapes were not.

Among Watergate revisionists it is conventional wisdom that the failure to destroy the tapes was the event, or nonevent, that led to the destruction of the Nixon presidency. If the tapes had been burned, they say, in the Rose Garden on national television or by shoveling them secretly into a furnace and announcing it afterward, the president would have survived. I have come to think that as a practical matter, as opposed to a legal one, they are probably right.

In 1973 I was still relatively new to presidential politics and did not really know how strong the pull of the presidency was, at least then. Nixon, in particular, had come to symbolize the kind of protective experience and personal strength that to the vast majority of citizens were of the greatest importance. Without the tapes, Nixon would still have faced the investigative batterings of Ervin, Rodino, Cox, and their myriad helpers. But he would have had more than a fighting chance. He would have been spared the constant repetition of grotesque White House conversations, the endless public embarrassment of missing or allegedly erased tapes, the March 21 tape that prosecutors considered criminal, and eventually the June 23 "smoking gun" tape, actually only faintly "smoking" but against which a demoralized White House and an enfeebled president could no longer defend because even his oldest and staunchest political comrades were now saying, "Enough."

The tapes did most of this damage. It's hard to argue with defeat, so I confess error. If I had foreseen the future, I would probably have stood with Fred Buzhardt and said something like: The tapes will kill you. Now you alone must decide what to do with them. If you destroy them, dissociate your staff from the decision and its implementation. Just do it: You'll have plenty of volunteer helpers.

If he had done something like this, would I have quit? Almost certainly not. But if I had given him this advice, would it have changed Nixon's ultimate decision? Almost certainly not. The important question is, why did Nixon accept Haldeman's judgment and preserve the tapes? I think the answer lies in the method and sequence by which Nixon arrived at his decision.

Nixon clearly did not want to destroy his tapes. He was intensely occupied, as most serious leaders are, by symbols of his place in history. The tapes were among those symbols, historically unique presidential memoirs and matchless evidence of the "real" positions participants took, particularly Kissinger and Nixon himself, during the historic meetings of Nixon's presidency. They were also financially priceless.

Moreover, the tapes were a kind of personal immortality, an actual piece of Nixon himself. In such objects—photographs, letters, locks of hair, Citizen Kane's "Rosebud"—the past is preserved against a disappearing present and an unknown future. Destruction of the tapes would have been something like an act of self-mutilation.

When Butterfield made his disclosure, Nixon was forced to choose. During the two or three days of inner-circle debate about the tapes' disposition, he knew the perils ahead. He knew that by his past delays he had already lost the chance to act with impunity and now faced a public and political reaction of large, unpredictable proportions. Yet he must also have flinched from an act so "unpresidential" as the deliberate destruction of presidential documents, however personally prudent it might be.

With these multiple reasons at work, he relied in the end on the simple, traditional mental safeguard against certain disaster: hope. He acted like the Russian peasant, in the classic joke, who gets money from the Czar to feed his family by promising that he will make the Czar's dog talk within a month. If he fails, he will forfeit his head. When the peasant returns home, his wife berates him for his lunacy. But he says, "Keep calm. The Czar is a busy man and may forget. He may get sick and die. There may be a war. And who knows? Maybe the dog will talk!"

Nixon banked on contingent events to bail him out. He ended up betting that the dog would talk. In doing so, he managed to create yet another Nixon-style "crisis," his very own home-brewed antidepressant.

After the Ervin Committee's decision to seek the tapes came Special Prosecutor Cox's subpoena; after that, since the tapes had not been destroyed, came the battles over the tapes in the District Court and Court of Appeals. Here Charley Wright performed his greatest Watergate trick, which was his writing of the tapes brief, centered on the constitutional principle of separation of powers. I say "trick" because Charley sometimes employed his gifts in a kind of magic act to confound his colleagues. In this historic case, with the deadline approaching, he just sat around the White House for days, watching Watergate-related television—what else was there? —and reading newspapers. He gabbed with other lawyers, doing no apparent work as the filing date drew near and turning away my nervous questions: "There's no problem, Len. I'm just thinking."

Two or three days before the deadline, he lifted himself from the sofa in my office, sighed, and broke open a fresh pack of Camels. "Excuse me," he said, "but I have to write that brief."

He had some research help from a young Texas lawyer named Tom Marinis, and he may have called for a few case books. But mainly, for the next few days, he typed away in a tiny office next to mine, finally producing a compact brief seemingly from memory. It covered separation of powers, executive privilege, and presidential privacy. It did not persuade the unpersuadable Judge Sirica; an appellate version fared only a little better with a divided court of appeals. But on their own terms, I thought Charley's briefs quite perfect—closely reasoned, uncompromisingly blunt pieces of constitutional advocacy, the writing simple and pellucid. We proposed small changes. Charley weighed each like a petition for certiorari and even ruled in our favor on a few of them. Nixon also had some ideas, which Charley, with an expressive smile, said were more "persuasive" than ours.

The style of Charley's oral arguments to Sirica and, later, to the D.C. court of appeals was also deliberately virtuoso. There was no outline of argument, no staff run-through. He simply carried into court one small card on which he had jotted a few quotes and citations. Driving to the courthouse for the appellate argument, I remember Wright casually asking me to suggest a figure of speech he might use to describe the consequences of eroding the president's control over private presidential papers and records like the tapes. I ad-libbed the not-so-remarkable metaphor of the sinking of the *Titanic:* A gash occurs in the side of an ocean liner, water pours in under the force of the ship's inertial momentum, and the supposedly unsinkable ship inexorably fills and founders. A half hour later, I was startled to hear my mumbled simile woven gracefully into Wright's argument—forming, in fact, the opening and closing of his thesis that a compromise of presidential confidentiality, even if small and well rationalized, would in time critically impair the privacy at the core of the presidential function and thus the functioning of the presidency itself. Today we know this argument was prescient; at the time, in the political excitement of Watergate, there was little chance that the courts would take it seriously, and they did not.

• • •

After these losses of Nixon's in the courts came the Saturday Night Massacre, Nixon's October 20 decision, in the midst of the Yom Kippur War, to fire Cox and terminate the special prosecutor's investigation. This was the self-administered blow that began the terminal stage of his presidency; and just as the Cox crisis made Nixon more aggressive in directing aid to Israel, so the Yom Kippur War helped convince Nixon that this was the moment to act against Archibald Cox.

In the same way that Daniel Ellsberg came to personify for Nixon a whole generation of enemies of the American presidency, Nixon haters who justified extreme action, so Archibald Cox came to personify Watergate in his mind. If I can get rid of Cox, Nixon seemed to be reasoning, Watergate will end. My mother would have described this line of thought as total "mishegoss," i.e., an extreme form of lunacy. But Nixon was not to be denied his seventh and final crisis.

On October 12, the same day Nixon was ordering the U.S. armada of aid to Israel into the air, came the news that the U.S. Court of Appeals for the District of Columbia had, as expected, decided against Nixon in the Watergate tapes appeal. Thus in a single twenty-four-hour period Nixon's situation was neatly set out: In the air over the Atlantic, his decisive presidential act had launched a huge fleet of U.S. planes in an operation larger than the Berlin airlift. On the ground, the life of his presidency was threatened by one man, a special prosecutor from Harvard still demanding production of the tapes.

During the week that followed, when Nixon had to make his decision about what to do in the wake of the federal appeals court ruling, the mammoth U.S. resupply of Israel took effect. The Israelis became the clear winners, moving beyond their prewar lines. At the beginning of the crisis, Nixon thought that at war's end he and Kissinger could get the Soviets to help him impose a comprehensive Mideast settlement. But battlefield exigencies had made it necessary to arm the Israelis to the hilt; Nixon wound up not simply saving Israel but, by rearming it, vastly enlarging its postwar freedom of action. This irony made it harder to take the next necessary step to persuade the Soviets to permit a cease-fire agreement by abandoning their support for obstructionist Egyptian demands. The Israelis, meanwhile, were amassing the maximum territory to use as negotiating tender in the postwar talks.

On October 19 Brezhnev asked Nixon to send Kissinger to Moscow for urgent discussions about a cease-fire. The president sent Kissinger the next day, with broad delegated authority. Then Nixon had to turn to the issue of Cox.

Nixon had devised a proposal that would give Cox edited summaries of the court-ordered tapes, with their accuracy validated by Senator John Stennis of Mississippi. The special prosecutor would then have no access to additional tapes. Cox could either acquiesce or be fired. I first learned about this general plan on Thursday, October 18, when Charley Wright and I were invited to join Fred Buzhardt, Al Haig, and Elliot Richardson in meetings on the subject that had started earlier in the week and would continue nonstop through Saturday, October 20. Not for the first time, Charley and I were brought in only after the strategy had been formed, to kibitz and add some "independent" content and cover to the deliberations. When we first heard about the plan, Charley thought it contained significant concessions and that Cox would go along. His opinion reflected a continuing confidence that the Supreme Court would ultimately support the assertion of executive privilege, that Cox, like himself a constitutional scholar, would understand this and therefore accept Nixon's proposal. I was not so confident about the Court, thinking it might see the case less as a constitutional puzzle than as a political test. (I was learning.) So while I hoped, I doubted Cox would accept the compromise proposal. I was sure that even if Cox accepted the idea of Senator Stennis's monitoring the tape summaries, he would never accept a limit on future requests for tapes. The most we could hope for, I said, was that Cox would resign without our losing Elliot Richardson.

Meanwhile, we had made no provision for the possibility that Cox would both refuse to resign and point to Richardson's confirmation pledge not to fire Cox for anything less than "extraordinary improprieties." The Nixon team, in deep denial, simply overlooked this detail; the need to believe that a solution existed overwhelmed the necessity for determining whether the ingredients were in hand.

There ensued twenty-four hours of frenzy. Senators Stennis, Baker, and Ervin were rounded up, rushed to Nixon in the White House by plane, train, and automobile, and persuaded to sign on to a vague agreement, amid a convulsion of misunderstandings, about what to do with the tapes. But on October 20 Cox rejected Nixon's plan and stood pat. It was the day Kissinger left for Moscow.

On the afternoon of the twentieth, Nixon called me into his office and asked me to speak to Elliot Richardson to try and persuade him to fire Cox. Haig had already tried and failed, but I was one of those who had recommended that Nixon appoint Richardson attorney general in April 1973, and Richardson and I had worked together closely and well since then. Nixon authorized me to tell Richardson that when dismissing Cox, he could make clear that he was carrying out a presidential order; I was also to try to get Richardson to defer his own resignation, which he intended to offer immediately, for just a few days, until Kissinger finished the Moscow cease-fire negotiations. With Nixon standing nearby, I phoned Richardson. But Elliot was adamant. He intended to resign that day, and that was that. End of phone call. Nixon, who had held his feelings in to check through the difficult preceding hours, now let down: "That pious goddamn bastard. More interested in his ass than his country."

Nixon thought his role in Kissinger's negotiations with Brezhnev was to look strong, and thought further that looking strong required acting strong on the Cox matter. This analysis afforded him zero maneuvering room. He passionately wanted to be rid of Cox. He also thought he could not retreat an inch from his compromise tapes proposal to Cox without damaging his presidential credibility. So when Cox publicly said no to Nixon's proposal, and Richardson said no to the order to fire Cox and even to Nixon's request to delay resignation, Nixon was stuck. He knew Richardson's resignation would be costly, but there was no way out. He could not retreat without seeming like a paper president to the observers in Moscow.

So Nixon fired Cox. Richardson resigned, along with his deputy, Bill Ruckelshaus. With the media and the country in a sustained explosion and the Nixon presidency in free fall, the third-ranking member of the Justice Department, Robert Bork, at the urging of

Richardson and Ruckelshaus, fired Cox and accepted the temporary task of holding the Justice Department together until the appointment of a new attorney general and a successor special prosecutor. Fred Buzhardt and I had the job of driving over to the Justice Department to bring Bork back to the White House, see that he assumed his temporary office of acting attorney general, and make sure he performed his official termination tasks before he could flee the jurisdiction.

Thus the damage of the Saturday Night Massacre was done. On a single weekend, the president had found himself in a nose-to-nose confrontation with two determined adversaries, Brezhnev and Cox. Nixon, in his debilitated condition, tried to face down both of them at the same time. It was too much. Out of deeply embedded beliefs or a love affair with power or what have you, Nixon had acted the way he felt a leader was obliged to act in a crisis. He wound up creating an even worse crisis, the worst of his political life. The death of his presidency was now only a matter of time.

Yet there was a seriocomic quality to the whole misadventure, summed up in a casual remark that Richardson drawled in Brahmin-speak to Bork, his successor, on Sunday night, as the frightful reaction began to build around the country and Nixon's political power hemorrhaged: "You know, Bob, the one serious mistake I made was that I did not make clear I would not fire Cox if he rejected the Stennis plan but refused to resign." Had he been asked why he did not make this clear, Richardson would doubtless have said, characteristically, "Well, nobody asked me."

On Sunday, the day after the historic "massacre," I stopped for a drink at the home of John Osborne and his wife, Trude; John was *The New Republic*'s official Nixon watcher and my closest friend among Washington journalists. In later years, whenever I saw John, he would describe that visit as one of the strangest events of the Watergate year. He said I appeared more relaxed, cheerful, and confident than I had been for months. Indeed, I was so "euphoric" that Osborne wondered whether I had been drinking, was on drugs, or had perhaps become unhinged from the pressure of recent weeks. I seemed oblivious to the storm gathering around the country. My guess is that I was principally feeling a vast ebbing of tension now that the long, wearying struggle between Nixon and Cox was finally finished, whatever the consequences. And I'm sure I half thought we might carry it off. Not a few experienced Washington politicians —including, with real trepidation, Senator Edward M. Kennedy and members of his staff—felt that if Nixon could hang tough for two or three weeks, he could "get away with" returning the Watergate investigation to his own Department of Justice. But the weekend produced an alarmed and hostile public reaction. The next business day after the Saturday Night Massacre, members of Congress tabled a flood of impeachment resolutions. Amid the torrent of adverse mail and phone calls, Nixon lost Republican leadership support. To stanch the political bleeding, Nixon had to appoint a new, strengthened special prosecutor, Leon Jaworski, who turned out to be every bit as tough as Cox. Under the pressure of the leadership, Nixon also abruptly raised the flag of surrender over the tapes, abandoning his appeal to the Supreme Court and agreeing to give the tapes to Judge Sirica. He called Haig, Wright, and me to his office and instructed us to turn over the subpoenaed tapes. We did so that afternoon, surprising Sirica and the country. Even then we were not free of illusion. We somehow convinced ourselves that the tapes were not really so incriminating and that this was a turning point in our fortunes. We still had not heard the tape of March 21, 1973—or, for that matter, any of the others.

The months after the Saturday Night Massacre were hectic and interesting in new ways. Fred Buzhardt and I were regularly in and out of Judge Sirica's courtroom, trying to explain or defend various physical problems with the tapes, determine relevance, and consider particularized objections based on national security and privacy. As part of this task, Doug Parker and I took part in a secret meeting one evening in the O.E.O.B. with two of Jaworski's senior trial assistants, Richard Ben-Veniste and Carl Feldbaum, and a group of eight court-approved electronics experts. We were there to agree on a technical protocol pursuant to which the experts would investigate and report to Sirica about the mystery of the 18½-minute gap in one of the subpoenaed tapes. The tape reel had been checked out of the

Secret Service's official depository to President Nixon, so if it was found that the gap resulted from human tampering rather than mechanical malfunction, the inference would be strong that the president was the guilty party.

We met in a windowless room at the end of several of O.E.O.B.'s winding corridors and spiral staircases. The site was so hidden from human eyes that we needed guides from the building staff to get us there and bring us out. The discussion about voltage levels, amperes, and ohms went on past midnight. The arguments among the experts became increasingly arcane, then bizarre. The American presidency hung in the balance, and we bleary-eyed attorneys were locked away in a chamber of the castle of Dr. Frankenstein, trying to monitor the excited scientists' audio-gibberish.

The lawyers ducked out for a breather. We began talking, chuckling, and soon we were sprawled on the stairwell floor, convulsed in sobbing laughter, handkerchiefs stuffed in our mouths so as not to betray ourselves to the technicians inside. It was like that with Watergate: Some days were more Buster Keaton than Al Capone.

Also, not every view of humanity offered by Watergate was a sour one. As Nixon's time dwindled, some White House staffers— many of them on Ron Zeigler's staff, most of them women—were real Spartans. Nixon and Zeigler, by hiring them, had given them a still unusual opportunity, and they delivered. They carried on without complaint, loyalty fixed—in contrast to many of my male colleagues, whose eyes constantly scanned the horizon for danger and opportunity.

Diane Sawyer was one of these Stakhanovites, constantly working. She did her rounds early in the morning and was still laboring when I left around midnight—editing, typing, packaging, dispatching hopeless answers to unanswerable press questions. She always had the same look: a skirt or jeans with a baggy sweater, a kerchief around her head, bottle-thick glasses, no makeup—a shleppy-looking, nearsighted Polish girl asking to be overlooked. Then she appeared with some press companion at the White House Correspondents' Dinner in the spring of 1973, dressed and decorated like *Vogue*'s Christmas tree, and several hundred mouths fell open. Diane went on to become journalistically famous and live happily ever after, or so I hope. She earned it.

Mainly, though, these months were a steady slide downhill to Nixon's resignation in August 1974. One event in particular made clear to Fred and me that we were approaching the end.

Henry Petersen had told Archibald Cox about Nixon's remark that he had John Dean "on tape"; when Cox inquired about this tape, we responded by letter, after consulting with Nixon, that the president was referring to a cassette. So part of the first subpoena for tapes was a subpoena for this cassette. There was, of course, no such thing; Nixon had merely been concealing the existence of the taping system. But now, in the fall of 1973, post-Cox, Fred had to testify to Sirica about the "missing" cassette. Fred spoke with Nixon about the problem, and Nixon suggested that Fred simply make a cassette from notes Nixon had and thereby dispose of the problem. After that conversation Fred came to my office looking worse than ever, a nearly impossible trick, and told me what the president had said. We knew Nixon's suggestion was talk from a desperate man about a collateral issue, but we were also weary from months of legal tightrope walking, and this one went over the line. Fred, a serious Baptist, said, "If I'm asked next week whether the president and I discussed his search for that cassette, I'm going to have to tell the whole story. It will be very bad. But I'm not going to lie under oath." (He didn't.)

The next day I made a yellow-pad list of all the pending investigations, serious and frivolous, of the president. It was long and formidable. The totality spelled a vast and, I thought, fatal erosion of presidential authority. Fred and Doug Parker worked on the list with me. We also included what we now knew about the 18½-minute gap and about subpoenaed tapes that seemed, justifiably or not, to be missing. We listed the president's suggestion about making a cassette and Fred's imminent testimony on the subject.

We decided to take our tale of woe to Haig, who was in Key Biscayne with the president for the weekend. He told us to come ahead. Saturday afternoon, Fred and I flew to Miami, drove to the Key Biscayne Hotel, and checked into the villa next to the one Haig and Ziegler were sharing. During the flight and at dinner afterward, Fred and I agreed to broaden our mission and propose to Haig, and to the president if he would see us, that it was time to start thinking about resignation. Allowing for the best and worst in the man, we were confident that Nixon would not impose a hopelessly paralyzed presidency on the country by fighting his case through a Senate trial.

We made our presentation to Haig and Ziegler, starting with the cassette story. I went over the list of investigative torpedoes that were trained on the president. Our judgment was that Nixon was not going to make it, but we made no demands or threats. I added that as a personal matter I felt I had outlived my usefulness as the president's lawyer but would be willing to take on my old responsibilities again. I would plead exhaustion . . . whatever. I would slide quietly out of Watergate.

Haig and Ziegler argued each issue, at times angrily but not without sympathy. They knew we had been flying blind and understood why we had lost confidence in our case. But it was too soon to talk resignation, Haig said. Nixon wasn't ready. The country wasn't ready. There were too many crises in the world. Ford was not yet up to the job. All true, we conceded, but Nixon had to prepare for what was coming.

We asked to see Nixon, but Haig said it would be better if he first took our views to him in the morning. We knew Haig would water them down in the presentation, but Nixon would know why we had come. The next morning, Fred and I drank coffee, read the Sunday papers, and made small talk until Haig returned. He said Nixon did not want to see us. He knew what the problems were and understood our views and feelings, but there was no point going over the same ground.

We agreed that I would gradually phase out of Watergate, and we spent the rest of our stay in Miami recruiting litigation assistance for the White House. We settled on a well-regarded local trial attorney, Sam Powers, who would soon start working full-time with Fred. In December, famed Boston trial lawyer James D. St. Clair arrived. "I'm going to deal with this as a straight lawsuit, not as a political problem," he announced. Good luck, I thought. Charley Wright was still on board, and a Supreme Court argument on a further demand for tapes was coming up. But by January 10, 1974, Charley was sick, sore, lame, and vomiting (as who wouldn't have been, considering the prospect of having to defend such a now-tattered principle as the presidential tapes privilege before the Supreme Court). St. Clair took over Charley's portfolio. When Nixon, in his *Memoirs*, discusses the Miami episode, he is generous to Fred and me. He says we had to proceed without much information, "undermanned, chronically overworked and regularly undermined by events and now by me." But this was nothing compared to the punishment Nixon was absorbing. I could leave quickly and quietly; for him, there was no exit except by resignation or death.

Others were absorbing punishment, too—particularly Bob Haldeman and John Ehrlichman, who knew I had campaigned to force them out. In January 1974, Phil Geyelin, the editor of *The Washington Post's* editorial page, and his deputy, Meg Greenfield, asked me to lunch. This was an off-the-record matter of utmost importance, they said; we had to find the most secret spot we could. We chose Trader Vic's, which was dark, subterranean, presumably secluded, and decidedly un-Washington. Once there, they asked me about the rumor they wanted to check out: Was Nixon going to announce his resignation in the coming State of the Union address? Not a chance, I said; that's someone's wishful thinking. *Yours.* I happened to glance at the next table, and there in the flesh was John Ehrlichman, with a luncheon companion and, just as corporeal, the Ehrlichman glare.

What I remember most about that day—apart from the glare, which I now recall nostalgically—is that back then, even amid the hatreds of Watergate, there were journalists who could be trusted to respect confidentiality and actually listen to an argument.

In February 1974, Nixon accelerated the end of his presidency by voluntarily releasing transcripts of the subpoenaed tapes and other tapes as well, gambling that he could deflate the tapes issue preemptively by revealing, explaining, and demystifying them. He would exercise control by deciding what material was relevant to Watergate and personally editing the transcripts. Harlow, Buchanan, and I—though I was no longer on official Watergate patrol—argued that the transcripts' release would be suicidal. But by this time the grand jury had named Nixon as an unindicted co-conspirator in the Watergate cover-up. A sealed briefcase of tapes and papers, plus the grand jury's charges, had been sent to the House Judiciary Committee for the impeachment inquiry. Nixon was desperate to avoid a further subpoena, this one for tapes he knew by now would be fatal.

So Nixon released a thousand pages of mumbled plotting, twisting, turning, and double dealing, all the numbing sleaziness of political men in desperate trouble, the whole mess compounded by countless transcription mistakes, arbitrary omissions, and, perhaps worst of all, innumerable references throughout to "expletive deleted." Every reader's imagination inevitably supplied language much viler than Nixon's commonplace obscenities. But the gusher of sanctimonious horror that the tape transcripts produced from politicians and editorial writers, as well as the effect on the public, stunned Nixon. A serious student of Disraeli, he had overlooked one of Disraeli's central dicta, that a national leader, whatever he did or said in private, had to present a decent face in public.

Ironically, with the preparation of the transcripts already in train, Jaworski subpoenaed a new batch of forty-six tapes with surgical specificity, relating each one to defendants and issues in the criminal conspiracy case. This second subpoena included what would come to be known as the "smoking gun" tape. This time Nixon went all the way to the Supreme Court with his executive-privilege argument in an attempt to avoid Jaworski's demand. But the previous presidential surrender of tapes ensured that there would be no significant consideration of his position. On July 24, 1974, the Supreme Court, to no one's surprise, unanimously affirmed the lower courts' decision that Nixon had to surrender the tapes. Before the decision, I had told the press that the president would feel compelled to abide by a "definitive" decision; this one, U.S. v. Nixon, was about as definitive as a Supreme Court opinion can be.

In August 1974, after the second batch of tapes had been turned over to Sirica and nine months after Buzhardt and I had visited Key Biscayne, an evidentiary feather broke Nixon's back. The White House released the "smoking gun" tape of June 23, which contained the actual words that almost everyone had already sensed Nixon must have said, in some form, to Haldeman or Ehrlichman or somebody, when the Watergate burglars got caught and the federal bloodhounds began to follow the money trail: Just tell them to knock it off, tell them it's national security, tell them anything, just make sure they knock it off.

Even now, conscious of the disagreeable things the tapes revealed and may reveal in the future, I doubt that the country gained more than it lost by their release. We now know whereof John Cheever spoke when he wrote his story of the magical radio that eavesdropped on the banalities and horrors of the ordinary conversations in a Manhattan apartment house. The Czech novelist Milan Kundera, writing about the issue of privacy, offered similar thoughts:

> [I]n private, a person says all sorts of things, slurs friends, uses coarse language, acts silly, tells dirty jokes, repeats himself, makes a companion laugh by shocking him with outrageous talk, floats heretical ideas he'd never admit in public, and so forth. . . . [T]hat we act different in private than in public is everyone's most conspicuous experience, it is the very ground of the life of the individual; curiously, this obvious fact remains unconscious, unacknowledged, . . . [I]t is rarely understood to be the value one must defend beyond all others . . . the indispensable condition, the sine qua non, for a man to live free.

Today we know how serious Kundera's worry is in a raw and intrusive culture like ours. But the question of Nixon's confidentiality was resolved in the "definitive" and formal terms of criminal and constitutional law. The release of the tapes meant that Watergate's epic narrative had for the moment run out of words, film, budget, hype, and story line. All that was left was the death watch in the less-than-gentle hospice of American politics. Pro-Nixon congressmen abandoned their erstwhile leader in droves as the 1974 midterm elections approached; anti-Nixon members of the House Judiciary Committee gloried in their television orations. In countless ways everyone was saying "enough," and Nixon heard it. Do not delude yourself for one moment that Haig or Kissinger or Barry Goldwater or anyone else had to tell Richard Nixon it was time to go.

I did not talk to Nixon during the last part of his presidency. When the June 23 tape emerged, I thought it was not so different from, or more harmful than, other evidence we had seen. But after talking with Fred Buzhardt and getting a sense of how fast Nixon's political support was ebbing, I decided to hold my peace. I changed my mind once, at a meeting with Bill Timmons and other political advisers, and raised the possibility that Nixon could go the whole route, right down to the Senate trial. The shudders that ran around the table persuaded me to resume my silence on the subject. Years later Senator Arlen Specter told me he had given Nixon the same advice. In the fall of 1973, after the Saturday Night Massacre, Specter, defeated for reelection as district attorney in Philadelphia, was interested in the job of outside counsel to Nixon, the post that eventually went to Jim St. Clair. Specter met with Al Haig and offered to represent Nixon, but only if Nixon would accept impeachment and defend himself in the Senate. No way, Haig said. No thanks, said Specter.

Indications of the approaching end abounded. As Nixon's time grew shorter, The Washington Post sent a reporter to Burgundy Farm Country Day School, which my children attended (and which one journalist of my acquaintance had described as "to the left of Mao"), to poll the kids on their predictable views of Nixon's possible impeachment. The reporter of course targeted the peer-pressured Garment children, and the Burgundy Farm staff cooperated with him. My kids, then thirteen and eleven, voted for impeachment.

I learned that the article was being readied for publication and called the Post's managing editor, Howard Simons. I believe I told him that if he printed the article I would drive straight to the Post and take the building apart brick by brick. Simons, one of the best men I ever met in American journalism, said that if such a demolition job became necessary he would help me do it. The article was, as they say, "spiked." It was the only occasion on which I ever intervened successfully with the press by arguing that fair play and privacy might sometimes be more important than the First Amendment.

The night of Nixon's resignation speech on August 8, Fred and I had dinner with Bill Safire at Sans Souci, the restaurant of choice for that White House generation. We returned to the White House to watch, along with Ray Price, who had drafted the speech, as

Nixon said good-bye to the presidency. Until the last moment we couldn't get the television set to work, but Fred located a screwdriver and got the picture going just as Nixon greeted his "fellow Americans." It was a poignant moment, particularly for Price and Safire, who had been with Nixon in both Washington and New York, and at least as much for me, who had been first aboard in the comeback campaign.

I was at home around midnight that night, lights out, when the phone rang. It was Nixon, his telephone voice sounding like the one I remembered from those late-night calls during the 1968 campaign. He was phoning old friends, making his disciplined rounds, saying good-bye, thanks for the help, sorry I let you down. He asked me what I thought the special prosecutor would do about him now. They'll indict me, won't they? I thought they would, knowing the pressure Jaworski's staff was putting on him to do so, but I did not say that to Nixon. I told him I didn't think so. They had more than their pound of presidential flesh. Well, Nixon went on, jail isn't so bad. It's a good place to think and write. Gandhi, Lenin—a lot of those fellows did their best work in prison. More demurrals from me. More thanks. "Give my love to Grace and the kids." Again, "I'm sorry I let you down, Len." *Click.* "Good night, Mr. President," I said to a buzzing line.

Nixon's farewell to his staff in the White House the next morning was genuine heartbreak. Nixon was scrambled, spontaneous, and moving, the muffled man emerging from tears, saluting father, mother, death, regret, rebirth. For a while, as he spoke, I thought he was looking at me. Then I realized he wasn't looking at anything, just staring into the middle distance between himself and the audience, the place where inner thoughts might be located when you're trying to say what you really feel.

The examination of the reasons for Nixon's political demise is still going on, but here is what I think happened. I think the beginning was Daniel Ellsberg's massive dump of the Pentagon Papers on *The New York Times* and *The Washington Post*. It was assumed at the time that nothing in the documents had any real relevance to national security, but a 1996 book, *The Day the Presses Stopped*, by the legal scholar David Rudenstine, perhaps the first person actually to have read the papers, says this is not so. Nixon was infuriated, with some justification, by Ellsberg's much-applauded treachery. He was concerned, correctly, that information in the papers would affect his credibility in negotiations with Vietnam, China, and the Soviet Union. But Nixon let his anger undermine his political judgment. With considerable urging from Kissinger, whose concerns were for U.S. foreign policy, Nixon decided to go to court to seek prior restraint on the Pentagon Papers' publication. He knew the burden of proof would be heavily against him, but he tried—and lost. Nixon then decided to go all out against Ellsberg in particular and leaks in general.

Thus the White House plumbers were born, headed by Hunt and Liddy, aided and abetted by the anger of the president and his talented, troublemaking Iago, Charles Colson. The memory of the plumbers' felonies, contemplated and consummated, particularly the bungled burglary at the office of Ellsberg's psychiatrist, no doubt inhibited Nixon when the somewhat less malign break-in at the Watergate was discovered.

I believe the Watergate break-in, a response to a general demand by Nixon for intelligence (not itself an extraordinary departure from politics as usual), was more or less authorized by a much-badgered John Mitchell, then pressed on Jeb Magruder by Chuck Colson and Gordon Strachan and conveyed to Liddy by Magruder and his assistant Robert Reisner. We do not know the precise extent of Nixon's role; the record does reflect his insistent pressure for political intelligence of this nature and his obsessive interest in the operational details of everything in the White House. Beyond that lies speculation, informed by common sense inferences.

The transition from bungled break-in to cover-up took place automatically, without discussion, debate, or even the whisper of gears shifting, because the president was personally involved, if not in the Watergate break-in then by authorizing prior Colson and plumber activities like the Ellsberg break-in and a crazy Colson plot to firebomb the Brookings Institution in order to recover a set of the Pentagon Papers. These were potentially more lethal than Watergate. Other factors contributed to the cover-up, but I have no doubt that the main motive was Nixon's sense of personal jeopardy. His decision was not irrational, though it turned out terribly wrong.

As events closed in on Nixon, I never contemplated abandoning his defense. As a matter of instinct, intuition, and common sense, I felt he was somehow "involved," but as long as there was no hard evidence that would make my own continued participation criminal, I would hang in, doing the best I could for a man I considered a friend and an extraordinary leader. Though Fred Buzhardt and I complained about not having access to information necessary to defend Nixon effectively, we were also protecting ourselves by letting Nixon decide what we could hear and see. That was why Nixon's suggestion to Fred in November 1973 that he should fabricate a cassette brought us down to Key Biscayne so quickly: Faced with knowledge, we felt we had to act.

My feelings about Nixon remained the same until his death—a tangle of familial echoes, affections, and curiosities never satisfied, in part because Nixon had kept me at arm's length and in part because I was content to have it that way. The Nixon who was despised by millions of strangers, and who aroused powerful ambivalence in close associates because of his nasty mood swings between grandiosity and pettiness, was not the Nixon I knew—or the Nixon known by Ray Price, his chief speechwriter, who spent as much personal time with Nixon and the Nixon family as anyone in the White House. Placed on the fringe of Nixon's life, I was exposed mainly to his attractive sides—his intelligence, idealism, and generosity. Only by "hearsay," mainly tape-recorded, did I "see" the fulminating stranger I was happy not to know.

Because we kept our distance from each other, more his doing than mine, I never got close enough to suffer a crisis of conscience about continuing to work for him, even as the days grew longer, his time grew shorter, and the evidence of his involvement in wrongdoing piled up. I knew he was not a cruel man or a warmonger. In my presence he did not talk or act like an anti-Semite or racist. Ridiculed by his enemies as an egregious liar, he probably lied less than most of his recent predecessors, because he was less comfortable and skillful than they were at doing so. He was physically clumsy, emotionally unpredictable, and frustrated, like most presidents, by the inertial drag of democratic politics. He was particularly infuriated by disloyalty, real or imagined. He was filled with a virtuoso collection of wounds and angers accumulated during childhood wars, political wars—especially with the media—and wars of survival.

Years after Watergate, when ex-President Nixon had an office at
26 Federal Plaza in New York, I would call on him from time to
time. Usually the visit was in connection with my work: I wanted
his help in drawing a precise bead on someone like Cap Weinberger
or Haig or Reagan staffers Don Regan or Jim Baker in connection
with some particular case or issue. Nixon also liked to shmooze
with me about politics. He was always hospitable, announcing his
views with, well, Nixonian authority. One of these meetings (I think
the agenda was the Mideast) went on for two hours. Nixon was
terrific, not only full of powerful insights but unusually warm and
funny. When we finished and walked to the door, I made my good-
bye very personal—something like "You know, I really miss you."
This was a mistake. Nixon literally shuddered. He walked away
from me and took a position behind his desk, head down, his face
working painfully as I took my embarrassed leave. It was a trip-wire
revelation of Nixon's memories of unrequited friendships, of disappointment, abandonment, personal loss, and, of course, death.

On the night we spent in Elmer Bobst's Florida pool house in
1965, Nixon said he would do anything to stay in public life—
"except see a shrink." Which was a sure sign, in Nixon-speak, that
despite himself he had indeed seen a shrink. It appears that when
Nixon was vice president, he occasionally flew from Washington
to New York to visit an internist and psychiatrist named Arnold
Hutschnecker.

Dr. Hutschnecker stuck to the letter of confidentiality with regard to Nixon but publicly intimated that he had helped the vice
president cope with chronic, debilitating psychosomatic symptoms.
Hutschnecker said Nixon had stopped the visits because his staff
feared political fallout.

When Nixon became president, Dr. Hutschnecker turned into
the shrink who came to dinner, visiting Washington and offering us
detailed policies for everything from war and peace to youth crime
and aggression. Some of these ideas were merely utopian; others,
such as a proposal to set up remedial camps for violence-prone
youth, were breathtakingly indiscreet. Eventually, the doctor faded
from the scene.

It was just as well. Had Nixon experienced even the highest-
quality psychotherapy, it would probably have interfered with the
mysterious concoction of character and personality that propels

men like him to great achievements as well as painful failures. Indeed, Nixon's unresolved awkwardness may be part of the answer to the question that in the end I find most interesting, the mystery of his deep penetration of the American psyche. It was a major reason why Nixon was able to sink and surface not just three times but many more. Perhaps despite his extraordinary intellect, memory, and ambition, he seemed like Everyman as president: ordinary, plain, disdained by the elite establishment, persistent, anxious, openhanded, manipulative, ambivalent, uncomfortable, idealistic, pragmatic, angry and mean-spirited, thoughtful and generous, a little bit of everything, like all the rest of us.

Yet Nixon was much more than ordinarily skilled in the gambler's arts of patience, nerve, and timing; he was a lover of challenge and the excitement of crisis, an adept, like Houdini, forever surprising skeptics with his ability to escape from the political equivalent of double-barred safes dumped into rivers or burial under six feet of crushing dirt. Nixon—his ambitions lofty, his style lumpen—in the end trumped his enemies. And from this, for all his careful avoidance of reminders of the "Old Nixon" during his final twenty years of disciplined self-rehabilitation, he surely derived his greatest, most savage satisfaction.

The descriptions of Nixon's career as tragedy are precisely wrong. It was more biblical than Shakespearean—the story of a man who sinned, suffered, died, and rose again. Without Watergate, Nixon would likely have finished his term, floundered around as a depressed man in search of a crisis, and died earlier than he did. As it was, he took up the supreme struggle of his political life and fought, won, and wrote about it time and again, until he was finally buried with great public honor.

In all the great contests of life Nixon was coach and player. I had the great fortune to watch for most of more than thirty years from the 50-yard line, and I was occasionally allowed to play. Coach Nixon kept me away from the more bruising encounters. He treated me almost as if I were a younger brother, to be protected, rather than a real player who might actually help him win a rough game. So I was always a peripheral character in the whirling dramas of the Nixon years. Indeed, I was often not precisely clear about what my job was or what message I was supposed to carry.

But if I was a little bit of Rosencrantz and Guildenstern, at least, in the end, I wasn't the slightest bit dead.

After Nixon left the White House, President Ford and his chief of staff, the former Illinois congressman and O.E.O. head Don Rumsfeld, generously saw to it that I stayed on the White House staff long enough to be thoroughly koshered by formal association with the new, clean, popular president. Even more generously, they gave me the highest-level staff designation, assistant to the president. I finally left the White House at the beginning of 1975, but not before making something of a contribution—I'll never know how much— to President Nixon's freedom and President Ford's headaches. The occasion was the presidential pardon for Richard Nixon.

On August 28, 1974, the day before President Ford's first press conference, I lunched with *The New Republic*'s John Osborne and saw another Washington friend, Eric Sevareid of CBS News. I asked them whether Ford should pardon Nixon. Both said yes. In the late afternoon, I called on Abe Fortas at his Georgetown home and put the question to him: Was it the right thing to do? Was it feasible? Should I weigh in personally and try to make the case to President Ford?

By all means, he said. This was the time for President Ford to act. The convulsion of a criminal trial for Richard Nixon was the last thing the country, deeply shaken as it was by Watergate and a presidential resignation, needed at this moment. This is "Ecclesiastes time," he said, a time for reconciliation, not the "horror" of a long political and legal bloodletting.

Fortas's judgment made up my mind. I talked to Al Haig, then still White House chief of staff, and wrote a memorandum that night to Haig and Philip Buchen, President Ford's counsel. I handed a copy to each of them in the White House at the staff meeting the next morning, together with a draft presidential statement by Ray Price. It said that a Nixon trial would be a long, distracting mess, ending, perhaps, in national tragedy (which I think was correct), and that the nation would accept the idea of a pardon from the new president (which was wrong). Later Haig told me he had let Buchen, not tainted by association with Nixon, take my memo in to President Ford. At ten-thirty that same morning, Haig called me. "It's all set," he said. There were lawyers' delays, but the announcement of the pardon came on September 8. Ford's presidency thereupon became hostage to his wise and politically generous exercise of presidential power. The pardon was probably a factor in Ford's loss to Jimmy Carter in 1976.

Grace took the kids back to Brooklyn Heights in September to put them in school and reopen the Willow Place house. We turned over our grand estate on Green Spring Road to its new owner, the state of Virginia, to which Mike Straight had made a gift of the property.

We had bought an old brownstone on Capitol Hill as an investment and rented it out. I moved into its cockroach-infested basement while finishing my temporary assignment with the Ford administration. I got used to my change of quarters rather quickly but don't know that I can say the same for my White House drivers, who had to watch me crawl out of the shabby basement every morning.

Grace drove down to Washington to help me pack my clothes and gear. Shortly after dawn on the morning we left, it was a crisp, bright day, with the Capitol dome, that beautiful American object, beginning to shine in the sunlight. A thousand writers have described this sight. Strange to say, I came closer to tears at that moment than at any time in the previous six Washington years.

❧ 10 ❧

GOING HOME

There was something slightly off-key about the air of determination with which Grace and I announced our intention to return to New York. Despite Watergate and because of it, our years in Washington had been good ones. We achieved some stability in our marriage, a rare occurrence. Grace was back at George Mason University working at a summa level to complete her long-delayed undergraduate degree. The kids were having a reasonably good time and avoiding serious brain damage at Burgundy Farm. I had managed to keep my reputation intact and got some decent job offers from Washington law firms, including that special offer from Abe Fortas.

But Grace and I never gave a moment's thought to staying. We told each other and our friends that we had no desire to hang around Washington with our noses pressed wistfully to the windows of government. We were going home, wiser and stronger, to resume the interrupted story line of our *real* lives. It turned out not to be so easy, for home was peopled by all our old demons. I eventually found a way out of the resulting unhappiness; Grace did not.

I teamed up with my friend, Saturday Night Massacre victim Bill Ruckelshaus, in a complicated career experiment. I joined the small New York law firm of Trubin, Sillcocks, Edelman & Knapp, and Ruckelshaus became counsel to the firm. I became counsel to

Bill's new Washington law firm, Ruckelshaus, Beveridge & Fairbanks. We confidently expected that we would quickly build a strong client base, create a two-city practice, merge the two firms, and . . . Well, nothing of the sort happened. I understood next to nothing about the Trubin firm's banking practice or the Ruckelshaus firm's specialized environmental work. In a matter of weeks I knew I had made a mess of my return to New York.

There were some consolations. For instance, limping around New York in 1975, I fell into the benign clutches of one of America's great cultural entrepreneurs, Harvey Lichtenstein, president of the Brooklyn Academy of Music, and joined his board. The Academy was moribund when he took it over. But Harvey, a large-headed, barrel-chested man who had, most improbably, trained as a ballet dancer, turned it into the acronymic BAM, with an image to match, and transformed it into a success. I remember our surviving a catastrophic flood from a burst water main only because Harvey convinced city authorities that he would kill if they did not come up with the funds to fix it fast. I recall Harvey on the way to a fundraising visit, standing hatless in a rainstorm, looking determined enough to will the money into existence out of thin air.

I eventually became BAM's board chairman and did little, which was more or less what Harvey wanted. The activity was certainly not enough to get me out of the professional doldrums.

There was nothing to do but pray for a miracle, and lo, it came. Lacking a better plan, I lobbied for the part-time job of U.S. representative to the United Nations Human Rights Commission in Geneva. My omnipresent friend Max Fisher presented my case to the White House, and I was named to the post. Meanwhile, early in 1975, Ford and Kissinger decided that it was time to confront the totalitarian ideas that ruled the U.N. and to split some of the Third World nations from their lock-step adherence to Soviet diktat. For this job they needed a new kind of U.N. ambassador, one who could make the public case for freedom. They thought Pat Moynihan, who had been ambassador to India and was now back at Harvard, would be ideal. Moynihan had recently set forth his views on the United States and the U.N. in a *Commentary* article titled "America in Opposition," in which he argued that the United States should actively fight the tyranny of the U.N. majority. The article came to

Kissinger's attention, and Kissinger urged President Ford to ask Moynihan to take the U.N. post. (It had once before been offered to him, by Nixon, but he had declined.)

In the early spring of 1975, Moynihan came to New York and told me he was undecided about the U.N. job. I said he had to do it. He asked how I was doing at work. I poured out my sad story, penitent to confessor: I had blundered horribly, and now I couldn't walk out. It was a depressing situation, altogether of my own making. Snapping his fingers, so to speak, Moynihan proposed a solution, in terms something like this: Now look here, old friend, I think your problem might be my salvation. I've been worrying a lot about whether to accept the U.N. job. I'd like to, but I'm unsure about what support I'll get from State and the White House. Now I think I have an answer. You are the official representative of the human-rights concerns of the United States. If you will take a leave of absence from your law firm and join me in New York, we can do something that has never been done: We can make the central objective of the United States at the U.N. General Assembly the advancement and protection of human rights. We'll just worry about being effective, not about being fired. Maybe getting fired should be our objective. You and I have worked with Kissinger for years. We know many of his tricks. Between us we are almost his equal. Say yes or I doubt that I will take the job.

I blubbered my thanks. Today I know that when Moynihan called me to make that dinner date, he already knew about my professional troubles.

Rejuvenated, I moved my headquarters from Park Avenue to the U.S. Mission to the U.N., joining Moynihan and his special assistant, Suzanne Weaver, a former Moynihan teaching assistant from Harvard now on leave from her job as an assistant professor of political science at Yale. I had met Suzi once before, at the White House. She was tiny, pretty, friendly, stratospherically intelligent, and excessively generous with her time and talents. The first thing she did when I came to the Mission was to give me her office, the one closest to Pat, and move herself and her Carlton-stuffed ashtray into the noisy, crowded staff office across the corridor.

In late August, Moynihan and I went to work assembling a plan for the General Assembly's Seventh Special Session on economic issues, due to convene in early September just before the regular General Assembly session. Moynihan and Kissinger met in Washington and agreed to try to gain the support of the major Western nations for a more generous approach to Third World economic development. They hoped that we could thereby break their pattern of submission to Soviet domination.

Kissinger's speech at the opening of the special session reflected this departure from the traditional Western resistance to economic aid, and he offered a series of concrete proposals. But the draft resolution proposed by the less-developed countries was a standard compilation of blue-sky demands and anti-Western vitriol. Moynihan concluded that we could never turn the situation around via line-by-line negotiations. We had to draft a totally new document that would incorporate the minimum positions of both the Third World and Western blocs and save face all around. As Pat put it, "We will have to fight their words with our words and be a lot smarter about it."

Over the weekend, in a series of sleep-free, smoke-filled sessions lasting about forty hours, Moynihan used his special talents to rewrite the entire Third World draft resolution, adopting its general language and format while amending almost every sentence in minute particulars that were difficult even for me to identify at first reading. For example, where the original draft said that "the accelerated development of the developing countries would best promote world peace and security," a U.N. euphemism implying a threat to the West, Moynihan softened the language to "world harmony and well-being."

Straining at a gnat? That was the U.N. Hundreds of such nearly invisible revisions changed the tone of the draft. Interspersed were the solid economic proposals that Kissinger had laid out.

In his memoir, Moynihan generously describes me as a partner in this process. In fact, though I was present throughout, I mainly stayed awake, chain-smoked, made coffee, scrounged around with Suzi Weaver for data, and caught and proofread revised pages that Moynihan yanked from his Smith-Corona. He was aided by Tom Enders, assistant secretary of the treasury, who came up from Washington to help us get Moynihan's marvelous machine moving. My unscientific theory is that the unusual physical size and titanic energy of these two men—Moynihan, the six-foot five-inch Hell's Kitchen expatriate, and Enders, smooth and urbane at six-foot eight —added to the feeling of inevitability that surrounded their project.

Our work done, we discovered that America's diplomats, representing the leading technological beacon of the free world, did not have a working Xerox machine. In the middle of the night we finally located one we could use at the embassy of pre-Khomeini Iran.

At the very end of the Special Session—to be precise, at five A.M. on the morning of September 16, the opening day of the thirtieth General Assembly—the delegates achieved unanimous agreement on the broadest economic development program in the history of the United Nations. That afternoon, Moynihan addressed the General Assembly and recited the American post-Watergate mantra: "This system works." At the end of the day Moynihan and I made our way to the Palm Restaurant on Second Avenue, where we celebrated. Exhausted and euphoric, Moynihan said that the auspices "could not be better" for our forthcoming human-rights work at the General Assembly. This time, Pat's gift for prophecy failed.

As Moynihan's memoir puts what happened next, "His Excellency Field Marshal Al Hadji Idi Amin Dada, V.C., D.S.O., M.C., President of the Republic of Uganda and Current Chairman of the Organization of African Unity, arrived on October 1 and the party was over." In the General Assembly, Amin called upon the American people, particularly African Americans, to "rid their country of Zionists" and urged "the extinction of the State of Israel." The General Assembly gave him a standing ovation.

Nevertheless, the State Department, which had dismissed Amin as a psychopath, held its collective tongue—with the exception of the public delegate to the General Assembly, the N.A.A.C.P. legislative chief, Clarence Mitchell (Moynihan and I had lobbied the Ford administration hard for Mitchell's appointment). Mitchell announced that Amin's remarks about Israel were "ridiculous" and that black Americans "do not need unsolicited advice on how to conduct their affairs."

Moynihan went to San Francisco to speak to a convention of the A.F.L.-C.I.O. In his speech he noted that the General Assembly had given a standing ovation to Amin, who was, in *The New York Times*'s words, a "racist murderer." It was "no accident," he told the A.F.L.-C.I.O., that Idi Amin was both a spewer of anti-Israel bile and the president of the Organization of African Unity.

There ensued an all-points storm. Unattributed State Department sources began making remarks to the press such as "What is Moynihan running for?" (At that point, he wasn't running for anything. It was the leakers and needlers who planted the seed of the idea, then had to watch it grow like Jack's fabled beanstalk.) The *New York Times* columnists William Safire and Anthony Lewis, in a moment of rare agreement, wrote that Moynihan was saying things that had to be said. He had struck a nerve.

During our early days at the Mission, Moynihan held a staff meeting every morning in the large conference room. It was invariably packed when Moynihan walked in, threw his worn briefcase on the table, and asked after the condition of "our battered planet." He went around the table asking for reports from the dozen or so representatives to the various U.N. committees, mostly Foreign Service officers, in order to get a feel for the day's business. Then he would launch into a sort of sunrise seminar on foreign policy. Pat asked questions and graded answers. Sometimes crisp, sometimes sloppy, funny or sour, he was always painfully well informed. When an answer was precise, he was brief, polite, flattering. When an unprepared officer recited State Department cant or tried to bluff, he was rude. His half-glasses would slip to the end of his nose. His eyebrows would arch into circumflexes. His mouth would form a surprised, disapproving circle, a perfect O like the smoke rings from the old Times Square billboard.

Just as Amin's visit was starting to agitate racial tempers, a cable arrived at the Mission from Mexico City, where the U.N.'s International Women's Year conference was taking place. One of the several ambassadors who inhabited our Mission, an earnest career diplomat named Barbara White, was representing the United States there. From the conference, Ambassador White sent us an exultant telegram about the meeting's final resolution and the great victory that had been won for women. The resolution included a condemnation of Zionism.

I sensed trouble and said so to Moynihan. He didn't need my help in identifying most issues, but on subjects Semitic he paid attention to my vestigial sense of smell.

The morning after Ambassador White's telegram arrived, Moynihan opened his staff meeting looking as benign as a well-fed golden retriever. Clasping his hands behind his head, he leaned back and said of the wire from Mexico City, "Well, that's certainly good news for the women's movement, and nicely detailed. But I see Len Garment squirming over there, which means he *thinks* he has something to say." So I told the State Department people, most of whom were just thrilled with the resolution out of Mexico City, what I had earlier told Pat: The Soviets would have liked to expel Israel from the U.N., but the United States had threatened to withdraw from the organization if they tried to place such a measure on the General Assembly agenda. So the Soviets, in a fallback strategy, were attacking "Zionism" and thus trying to declare Israel an illegitimate state. Something nasty was headed our way; what had been adopted in Mexico City would now be introduced during the General Assembly in New York. "Okay," Moynihan said. "Meeting adjourned. Garment, Weaver, Reis, Rosenstock"—the last two were the Mission's staff lawyers —"let's caucus in my office."

Chaim Herzog, the Israeli ambassador to the United Nations, had been born in Belfast, son of the Grand Rabbi of Ireland. He had led the defense of Jerusalem during the 1948 War of Independence. He was also a writer of military history and a former intelligence officer. Like many sophisticated people, he was surprised by the Zionism resolution. But unlike many American Jews and members of the Israeli government, Herzog grasped the importance of what was happening. In the enterprise that followed, he was a perfect political match for Moynihan, and the two of them quickly developed an excellent working relationship.

Moynihan, Herzog, and I met and talked almost continuously until we agreed on an approach: Though we would fight to defeat the resolution, we knew we were likely to lose. Therefore our aim would be to establish certain principles: that the resolution was a lie, that small nations voting for it would soon find it turned against them, and that if they passed the resolution as planned, as part of the U.N.'s "Decade for Action Against Racism and Racial Discrimination," it would make the antiracism program a dead letter and erode the legitimacy of the U.N. itself.

The Zionism resolution consumed most of the energy of the thirtieth General Assembly. We worked to line up our European allies, who had been drowsing when the condemnation of Zionism was passed in Mexico City. But we were not hearing any supportive words from the American Jewish community. Herzog called Rabbi Israel Miller, the president of the Conference of Presidents of Major Jewish Organizations. Why the silence? Miller said he had raised the matter with the Israeli embassy in Washington and had been told, "Forget it, it's a lot of nonsense."

The next weekend Israel's foreign minister, Yigal Allon, came through New York. Herzog gave a dinner for him in a kosher Chinese restaurant named something like Pins and Noodles. We told Allon about our dismay at the obtuseness of the Israeli personnel in Washington. What was the matter? Were they spending all their time talking to the "realists" at the State Department? I had spent considerable time with Allon in my White House days. He knew I was not a full-time hysteric. Allon said he would wake up the Israeli embassy in Washington.

The resolution was first submitted to the Third Committee of the U.N., where the lobbying was intense. The projected vote margin narrowed each day. The resolution's sponsor nations, mostly Arab and Soviet client states, delayed the vote, then introduced a new resolution that would have decoupled the Zionism issue from the Decade Against Racism and Racial Discrimination. I was the designated U.S. representative to the Third Committee and announced the U.S. position on this ploy: The resolutions were "inseparably linked." If Zionism was officially anathematized by the U.N., the Decade would go down with it.

We succeeded in our lobbying of our allies: Italy's ambassador, speaking on behalf of the European Community, declared support for the U.S. position against the resolution. But the Arabs proved willing to "buy themselves a majority," as Moynihan put it. And the Latin American countries, which we had assumed would be with us because of their large Jewish populations and lack of a direct stake in the issue, were not. The reason was a combination of internal leftist politics, covert Soviet pressure, "gringophobia," and anti-Semitism among some of their leadership.

The United States persuaded Sierra Leone and Zambia to propose tabling the Zionism measure for a year; the proposed delay would break the momentum of the resolution. On October 17, I was in the U.S. chair when the two countries introduced their proposal. We lost, and it was now clear that we would lose the vote on the resolution itself.

Before the vote, I spoke to the Third Committee on behalf of the United States. Moynihan sat in back of me and staffers Suzi Weaver and Cameron Hume and my friend Norman Podhoretz, all of them collaborators in the speech, were close by. The delegates were quiet as they listened to the words:

> This committee is preparing itself, with deliberation and foreknowledge, to perform a supreme act of deceit, to make a massive attack on the moral realities of the world. Under the guise of a program to eliminate racism the United Nations is at the point of officially endorsing anti-Semitism, one of the oldest and most virulent forms of racism known to human history. . . .
>
> Let us make no mistake: At risk today is the moral authority which is the United Nations' only ultimate claim on the support of our peoples.

Then Chaim Herzog spoke:

> How dare these people talk of racism to us—we, who have suffered more than any other nation in the world from racist theories and practices. . . .
>
> The Jewish people . . . shall survive this shameless exhibition. But we . . . shall not forget those who spoke up for decency and civilization. . . . We shall not forget those who voted to attack our religion and our faith.

Herzog shouted his last words: "We shall never forget."

The vote sped across the computer screen: 70 in favor, 20 against, 27 abstentions. The winners applauded. Moynihan walked over to Herzog and embraced him. "Fuck 'em," he said.

We knew that when the resolution reached the General Assembly, we would lose. All that remained was to make the moment clear. On November 10, the inevitable vote finally took place. Afterward, Herzog, noting that the resolution had been adopted on the anniversary of Kristallnacht, tore the paper to pieces and flung the fragments into the air.

For the U.S. speech to the General Assembly after the vote, Moynihan and Weaver had drawn on a memorandum by a Yale political theorist, Charles Fairbanks. Moynihan, almost the last speaker, began with a sentence chiseled as if in stone: "The United States declares that it does not acknowledge, it will not abide by, it will never acquiesce in this infamous act." He elaborated on Fairbanks's theme:

> Today we have drained the word "racism" of its meaning. Tomorrow, terms like "national self-determination" will be perverted in the same way to serve the purposes of conquest and exploitation. . . . [I]f we destroy the words given us by past centuries we will not have the words to replace them, for philosophy today has no such words.

Moynihan and I went off to a wind-up television interview. But the battle had just begun.

Moynihan was exactly right. The word "racism" has been largely vitiated through indiscriminate application, and the Zionism resolution contributed to the debasement of the language of human rights in just the way he said it would.

Moynihan sometimes used an old French saying to explain his posture at the United Nations: "This animal is very wicked. When attacked, it defends itself." The public, Congress, and many in the media welcomed the change in atmosphere that Pat had brought. But the U.N. community and the State Department deplored his strategy. Among the principal deplorers was Henry Kissinger; therefore the ritual procedure for a high-level bureaucratic defenestration was set in motion. It began just after the Zionism vote. Following a White House dinner, Kissinger invited Moynihan to his office for some collegial schmoozing. But an "authoritative" source close to Kissinger leaked something different to *Newsweek*, which reported that Kissinger had "raked [Moynihan] over the coals" for losing the Zionism vote by his hyperaggressive behavior.

Then Sir Ivor Richard, the U.K. ambassador to the United Nations, attacked Moynihan's supposed belligerence, saying, "Whatever the U.N. is, it is not the O.K. Corral and I am hardly Wyatt Earp." A Safire column in *The New York Times* suggested that Richard's speech had been personally cooked up by Kissinger and the British foreign secretary, James Callaghan. All parties roundly denied any conspiracy.

Moynihan decided he could not let all this pass and stay alive and functioning in his job. So the next morning, a Friday, he notified the White House that he was resigning and scheduled a press conference for midafternoon. This produced an immediate phone call from Kissinger, saying Pat must not resign, followed by a call from Dick Cheney, the White House chief of staff, saying Moynihan could not act without first speaking to President Ford. A date was set for a meeting between the two on Monday morning.

Kissinger called me later that Friday in great distress. How could Moynihan possibly think that he, Kissinger, had anything to do with Richard's speech? It was just troublemaking by Safire. I must do everything in my power to calm Pat down. Losing him at this point would be a tragedy for the country.

The country aside, losing Moynihan at that point would certainly have made trouble for Kissinger; there was no general sentiment for dumping the increasingly popular U.N. ambassador. I said that I would do what I could but that no one but the author of the continuing mischief could stop it. James Q. Wilson, a mutual and trusted colleague of Moynihan's and Kissinger's at Harvard, advised Moynihan to concede nothing: Otherwise a hopeful departure in U.S. foreign policy would be pointlessly sacrificed. Suzi Weaver prepared a bill of particulars detailing the ways in which the State Department had obstructed U.S. human rights initiatives at the U.N. Monday morning, Moynihan and I flew to Washington to see the president.

At the White House, Moynihan met alone with President Ford. Kissinger had to wait outside. When he was finally asked in, Moynihan saw that he was biting his upper lip in the trademark Kissinger reaction to acute disasters and situations requiring maximum self-restraint. There ensued a round of solemn banalities, in which the parties exchanged declarations of mutual esteem and support. When

Moynihan and I left the White House West Wing and headed for our car past a crowd of newsmen and photographers, I said, "Smile as if your life depended on it." The morning papers showed Moynihan smiling diplomatically and me laughing my head off. "Moynihan wins" was the photograph's message. It became the theme of the national news coverage.

All we had really won was a brief reprieve from Kissinger's ax. Kissinger's heart may have warmed to Moynihan's intelligence and passion, but the Kissingerian head warned that Moynihan was too unpredictable for Henry's magisterial sense of diplomatic authority. Worse, it seemed as if Moynihan and I really believed in the efficacy of formal human rights initiatives, whereas Kissinger mistrusted the whole business. Three days later, James Reston of *The New York Times* wrote knowledgeably that Moynihan had been given "a phony vote of confidence by Ford and Kissinger," who "didn't think the issue was worth another political flap."

As the Security Council began its Mideast debate, Kissinger came to New York to meet with Yigal Allon, by then Israel's deputy prime minister. The two of them lunched with Moynihan and me in Kissinger's suite at the Waldorf, and Kissinger and Moynihan laid out their respective views about the possibilities for American foreign policy. Kissinger spoke pessimistically. America's fundamental problem, he said, was the diminished authority of the American presidency. Syria's Assad had once said to Kissinger, "You sold out Vietnam and Cambodia. Why should we doubt that you will also sell out Israel?" Never again would a president be able to act the way Nixon had in the Yom Kippur War.

Moynihan was not so gloomy about long-term trends. The corruption and consequent economic weakness of Soviet communism were becoming apparent; eventually they would kill the regime. Vigorous Western human rights policies would add to the stress on the Soviet system.

This debate between Moynihan and Kissinger continued through January. On January 9, Moynihan went to Washington for another discussion with Kissinger, who thought the United States must give the Arabs hope that if the P.L.O. accepted Resolution 242, the blueprint developed at Camp David for a comprehensive peace and the return of lands won by Israel in the 1967 war, we would recognize the P.L.O. Kissinger told Moynihan that the threat to recognize the P.L.O. was the only incentive that would make Israel confront the need to deal with the West Bank.

This was Kissinger at the outset of what was to be his final year in office: exasperated with everyone, catching hold of himself just in time to avoid permanent self-injury and serious damage to others. One moment he raged against Israeli obstructionism; the next, he declared it unthinkable to force Israel back to its 1967 borders. "This," he said, to Moynihan, to me, to Israelis, and doubtless to others, "would leave them in the condition of Czechoslovakia after Munich."

On January 27, Moynihan saw President Ford and confirmed his intention to stay through the 1976 primaries and campaign, so as not to give ammunition to the Republican challenger, Ronald Reagan, who was now invoking Moynihan's name in his speeches. As he left Ford's office, he was given a note asking him to call Les Gelb at *The New York Times*'s Washington bureau. Gelb had a leaked copy of a year-end internal cable that Moynihan had sent to his State Department superiors four days earlier. Titled "The Blocs Are Breaking Up," it argued that the logic of history was now with the West. It also said that a large faction in the State Department had an interest in Moynihan's tenure being judged a failure. "This faction," Moynihan said,

> has not hesitated to pass the assessment on to the press and to Congress, and to parts of the Department that would otherwise have no view one way or the other. This is bad for the President's policy.

Nothing in the cable was particularly controversial in a substantive sense, though the special edge in Moynihan's writing would have lent electricity to a weather report. But along with the usual overheated reaction from State, there was a column in the *Times* by James Reston. It was a not unfriendly review by Reston of Moynihan's U.N. stewardship: "Pat's idea of confronting the U.N. was not only defensible but long overdue." But it also carried a private message for Moynihan: that Ford and Kissinger "support him in public and deplore him in private" and that, "[h]aving put him in the job, they can neither tame nor repudiate him." Moynihan concluded that he must resign. If he had not known, there was friend and author Theodore H. White to tell him: White saw the Reston column, phoned Moynihan, and said, "You know you have to go, don't you?"

Moynihan called Henry Rosovsky, dean of Harvard College, to say he had sent his letter of resignation to the president and that this would be announced at noon. Rosovsky said he was deeply disappointed. Moynihan said he was, too, but it had become impossible to stay at the U.N. "Oh," Rosovsky said, "You mean *that* president."

Of all the experiences I had at the U.N., the most important was to see anti-Semitism clearly for the first time. If it is possible to have a gradual epiphany, mine began the morning of the staff meeting in which, at Moynihan's prompting, I warned the State Department staffers at the U.S. Mission to the United Nations about the pernicious nature of the Zionism resolution. The reaction of most of the Mission staff to my warning was quiet hostility. Here were the permanent representative and his principal adviser, a belligerent Irishman and an outspoken Jew, both of them self-declared friends of Israel, outsiders with unrestricted access to the heavy weapons of political warfare, about to start a diplomatic brawl over some ritual language in a resolution. Amateur night on First Avenue had begun. Most of the Jewish career officers shared these sentiments, in thoroughly assimilated good faith.

When I went to the U.N., anti-Semitism was still an abstraction to me. I had been protected from the dust-ups and name-calling of the Brooklyn streets by my brothers, neighborhood solidarity, and the survival instructions of an anxious mother. The public schools I attended were almost entirely Jewish. The musicians I knew in the 1940s wanted you to play in tune and swing; they didn't care about anything else. There was that unpleasant blip at Camp Joseph

T. Robinson, but it was brief and expressed all kinds of mixed-up cultural hostilities. When I migrated to Wall Street, the sounds and smells of the anti-Semitic underground were more palpable but still muted. By the time I arrived, the country was deep into post-Holocaust sensitivity, and Jews and Christians were for the time being on their best behavior in each other's known presence. The Nixon White House had its well-publicized share of all-American anti-Semitism. But its expression was muffled by the presence of senior staffers who were known to be Zionists, and the same White House was consistently faithful to its pledge of support for Israel's military security. Behind closed doors, Nixon-Haldeman-Dean conversations were spiked with versions of Harry Truman's "kikes," Lyndon Johnson's "niggers," and the intra-ethnic slurs heard around the dinner tables of liberal Washington. The condescension of some Nixon staffers toward Jewish supporters of Nixon was transparently clear, but when Nixonites said nasty things about Jews, the explicit modifier or tacit context was usually "left-wing" or "anti-Nixon."

In the State Department and the United Nations, I did not observe this kind of redeeming complexity. With honorable exceptions, both these organizations were considerably more anti-Semitic in the operational sense than Richard Nixon's White House. In 1975 and 1976, among State Department professionals, American support for Zionism and the ties between American Jews and Israel were a bone in the strategic throat, an irrational distortion of the cultural map of the Middle East. The department's traditions ranged from the classic anti-Semitism of Breckenridge Long in the forties and fifties to the "Realpolitik" resentments of George Ball in the sixties and beyond. By the seventies, the attitude of department professionals was more intellectual than visceral—more Ball than Long—but deeply ingrained in the institutional soul: It held that the political power of American Jews tilts U.S. Middle East policy against U.S. national interests. The longtimers in the department's Near East Bureau who hold this view are, objectively, far more dangerous to Israel than locker-room blowhards who bluster about the goddamn kikes running the goddamn world but who have no power to influence anything.

As for the United Nations, when we were there it was a veritable arboretum of anti-Semitism. As Moynihan's deputy spokesman on the Zionism issue, I was on the receiving end of major league anti-Semitism for the first time: the snubs, glares, turned backs, homicidal notes from anonymous nut cases, and awkward coolness of even my State Department colleagues, all reflected my general unpopularity. It was a viscerally unpleasant experience for someone who likes to be liked. But I was acutely aware that I, unlike most Jews who have experienced anti-Semitism, was in a protected official position. I went home at night. Nobody was going to harm me physically or make me wear a yellow star or consign me to a wooden bunk in a barracks packed with dying men.

This was because after World War II, open anti-Semitism had become markedly less respectable. Therefore postwar anti-Semitism aimed at Jews indirectly, by attacking the State of Israel. Many attributes historically assigned to world Jewry were transferred to Zionism and its alleged worldwide conspiracy. The Soviets, heirs to their own anti-Semitic tradition and happy to use anti-Semitism to manipulate Third World nations, consistently fomented the issue. More than two decades before the Zionism debate they were circulating political pornography such as photos of David Ben Gurion entwined in a swastika and cartoons of hook-nosed Jews performing ritual religious crimes.

The Soviets were successful at the United Nations, which devoted an extraordinary amount of time to condemning Israel. The fabrications and fantasies of two thousand years made this image plausible to a great part of the modern world. When the Zionism resolution arose at the U.N. many Americans and even Israelis could not quite believe the continuing power of the old hate. Some even resented our reminding them of what they so wanted to forget.

I went on to Geneva to represent the United States at the annual meeting of the U.N. Human Rights Commission, where for six weeks I cheerfully, aggressively attacked the anti-American majority. Washington let my Geneva colleagues and me alone, and journalists, nostalgic for the newsy Moynihan days, gave us friendly coverage. For the first time in anyone's memory, the mischief at the mislabeled Human Rights Commission was regularly reported by the U.S. and European press. It became clear that the human rights issue had staying power; this fact furnished a potential answer to the standard Realpolitik question, "Why are we doing this?"

Moynihan resigned and returned to Cambridge. He worked for Senator Henry Jackson in the presidential primaries and began hearing from the Democratic party leadership in the Senate: "Run. You can beat Bella Abzug." Abzug, a New York City Democratic congresswoman, was seeking the party's nomination for the Senate seat held by Republican senator James Buckley.

Running against Abzug was an appealing idea, since Moynihan disliked her politics. He also knew that the fight would be a Pier 3 brawl, and Bella and her supporters would try to beat his brains in with selected passages from his hundreds of thousands of public words. And, of course, it would be the final good-bye to tenure at Harvard. This one was a real gamble, a nighttime dive into a shallow swimming pool.

Throughout the spring of 1976 Moynihan weighed the possibilities. I was back at Mudge Rose (inevitably), and made periodic trips to Cambridge to play the neutral counselor and offset the impassioned acolytes who argued, with the familiar passion of political jockeys searching for a horse to ride, that it was Moynihan's patriotic duty to run. At the last minute, Moynihan decided to enter the race. Suzi Weaver went up to Cambridge to help grade his final finals, and he and his wife, Liz, packed. They leased an apartment on the Upper East Side and we all went to work under forced draft.

The skeleton campaign staff was mostly volunteers, plus a few professionals like Joe Crangle, Buffalo's Democratic boss. Crangle supplied us with a young Buffalonian with a law degree, one Timothy J. Russert, a gusher of jokes, gossip, ideas, and word-perfect impersonations of candidate Moynihan. Russert was from the beginning an obviously major talent. In later years he became Moynihan's administrative assistant, a counselor to Governor Mario Cuomo of New York, the Washington bureau chief for NBC News, and the host of Meet the Press. Richard Eaton was another young upstate New York lawyer; he, like Russert, later did a substantial tour of duty as Moynihan's administrative assistant in Washington. When he joined the campaign, Eaton quickly distinguished himself by his hard-headed grasp of the political game and his wit, dry as Russert's was wet.

Judy Bardacke became our labor liaison, a job that was to prove crucial. Suzi Weaver headed the issues group; her principal assistant was William Kristol, later to gain national prominence as a Republican strategist. They got much help from Chester "Checker" Finn, then as now a keen student of education policy in particular and domestic issues in general. Our kibitzers were of the highest caliber —Norman Podhoretz and his wife, Midge Decter. Sandy Frucher, our campaign manager, spent a lot of time trying to bridge the cultural gap between his own pragmatic politics and the more ideological views of Moynihan's old-timers. He did not have much success.

The campaign would never have gotten out of the starting gate without Richard Ravitch, our jump-start fund-raiser and political consultant. At the beginning we had no money. We needed a lot, quickly. So I sat in Ravitch's office at his HRH Construction Company and watched him do it. My job was to twirl his mammoth Rolodex and dial numbers. His job was to deliver the pitch. In a few days he made a couple of hundred calls—needling, wheedling, calling in due bills, and eventually accumulating enough money to start the campaign and keep it in motion until the creation of a conventional fund-raising operation under Moynihan's friend John Westergard.

The campaign was agonizing. We had the problem, surprisingly, of low name recognition: Rank-and-file voters, it turned out, paid virtually no attention to the United Nations. Just as serious, despite all the political intellectuals on hand, the campaign was floundering on a long, rocky, summertime stretch of incoherence. Abzug's lead in the polls held firm. We had finally discovered the truth: If you can't describe the theory of a candidate's case in one sentence, you're in trouble.

The fever broke on the night Liz Moynihan—superrealist, chief campaign roustabout, Madame Defarge gone to finishing school— assembled a bunch of us (Pat, Norman, Suzi, Judy, campaign aide Penn Kemble, me, others beyond recall) around a large round table in a Manhattan fish restaurant. We were running out of time, she said; we were still going in circles. Long analyses were offered to explain why we were stuck. Suzi Weaver was, as usual, silent; she never tried to elbow past her voluble coworkers, and I knew that if you wanted her to speak you had to shut the others up and ask her a direct question. I did: "So what's the sum of it? What's the theme?" She said, "Well, there's only one theme. It's that we have a society worth defending." "Indeed," Moynihan said. We had a theme, a slogan, a way of distinguishing Pat from Bella—who, as we soon discovered, had never voted a dollar for American defense. For better or worse, we had our campaign.

This was not the end of the bad moments. My personal worst had to do with a wonderful man named Bruce Llewellyn—huge and handsome, smart and funny, a cousin of General Colin Powell and himself a field marshal of free enterprise. In 1976 he was head of an organization of Harlem businessmen called One Hundred Black Men. At Llewellyn's request I arranged for Moynihan to talk to the group. The distorted hullabaloo over "benign neglect" still hung in the air; this appearance would be important. "Make sure your tiger's in good shape and on time," Llewellyn reminded me cheerfully twice a day as the crucial meeting approached. It was scheduled to take place at ten P.M. in the Harlem Office Building on 125th Street. I was there early, pacing the lobby, watching the large audience pour in. By ten I was very nervous. By eleven, after five or six visits from Llewellyn ("Any word, pal?"), I was ill. I called all the numbers on Moynihan's schedule for the evening; no luck. At about midnight, surrounded by Llewellyn and several of his unhappy cohosts and in a barely suppressed fury, I finally got Moynihan on the phone. "Well, Len," he said, "I'm really a bit tuckered out. Why don't we just reschedule Harlem?" I shouted at him (for the first time), cursed him (first time), said I was getting out of the campaign, threw the phone against the wall and smashed it to pieces, took a cab home, drank several scotches, and went to bed. The phone rang about three A.M. It was Moynihan, purring like a cat and inquiring gently why in the world I was in such high dudgeon, leaving an event that turned out to be so successful and so much fun.

The Sunday before the primary, Grace and I ate dinner at the Gloucester House with Moynihan's friends Lane Kirkland, the president of the A.F.L.-C.I.O., and his wife, Irena, along with a couple of other campaign comrades. The contest was still a toss-up. But we knew we would learn the identity of the future victor at eleven P.M., when the next day's *New York Times* hit the street with its endorsement. Traditionally, the editor of the editorial page made the call. The incumbent, John Oakes, favored Bella; an endorsement for Abzug might well mean the end for Moynihan. But Moynihan's volunteer driver came rushing into the restaurant, waving a *New York Times* over his head like a flag. He brought a pack of papers to our table so we could see the editorial, which endorsed Pat unequivocally.

Later we learned that John Oakes had, as expected, decided to endorse Bella. He got the editorial ready for publication, then went on vacation. At the last minute, Arthur "Punch" Sulzberger, the publisher of the *Times*, intervened and overruled Oakes. A wonderfully written substitute editorial was produced. Oakes registered his dissent in a letter to the editor, which the *Times* duly printed.

Pat's victory in the primary was narrow. Twenty years later, at dinner on Fire Island, Max Frankel, who had been the editorial-page heir apparent at the time, told me he had written the endorsement editorial on condition that the authorship be kept secret to avoid adding to the already heated intramural controversy. I think the statute of limitations has finally run out on this particular piece of information.

Moynihan was easily elected in November. He went to the Senate, became a forceful voice on the Foreign Relations Committee, and was chairman of the Senate Finance Committee until the Revolution of 1994. Even in a Republican Congress he retains the power that comes with his intellect and experience.

One of the issues he pursued most persistently—with congressional colleagues, executive branch officials, and presidents—was nullification of the Zionism-is-racism resolution. Moynihan grew more powerful; opposition to his nullification campaign weakened and, finally, with the demise of the Soviet Union, ended. On December 16, 1991, by an overwhelming vote, the United Nations rescinded the Zionism resolution.

In many ways the summer of 1976 was a happy time for our family. Thanks to Bryce Harlow, who had returned to his job as head of government affairs at Procter & Gamble, Grace wangled a writing audition for the popular network soap *The Edge of Night*, which she passed with soap opera clichés flying. She was now writing regularly for the program. The children were enrolled at nearby St. Anne's Episcopal Day School, the asphalt equivalent of Burgundy Farm, and summering at the Interlochen Music Camp in Michigan; they seemed to be sailing equally into their teens.

I was busy with the Moynihan campaign and getting used to practicing law—slowly beginning to like it, like a stroke victim learning to walk again. Grace worked until late at night, so when I left for work in the morning I mostly saw her sleeping. She and I would talk briefly during the day about the kids, household things, script problems, campaign craziness. When I returned at night, whatever the hour, I would find her preoccupied, scribbling dialogue notes or typing her next script in a little study off our bedroom. We would talk about this and that until she said she had to get back to her soap opera family. I often fell asleep to the sound of her typewriting. She would dash off cheery notes to the kids at camp on the back of mimeographed copies of *Edge of Night* scripts, usually weaving in plot details from her shows as in this note to Sara:

It surprised me to hear Dad tell you to meditate—(I never see him meditate)—but perhaps it's not a bad idea. After all, Geraldine had been meditating quite a lot, and now she can get up out of her wheelchair. (But she fell over.) Today the show, which was written by yours truly, was quite good. It was about Nicole—after she ran into the woods and had the concussion. She was in the hospital in this episode—with a bandage on her head—her hair all neatly groomed above it, as if she'd just come from the beauty parlor. . . . Oh Lord, where will it all end.

Grace's involvement with her soap opera stories and characters was, I now realize, one of the few satisfying and continuous relationships in her life. She entered the fictional world and lived happily among her animated, talking dolls. There she had control and could work creatively, eavesdropping on her characters, shaping them to her will, imposing the order, continuity, and intimacy that were missing from her own existence. She emerged from her work only reluctantly to tend to the needs of her fragmented life, in which she saw herself exercising less and less power. Friends occasionally tried to drag her away to dinner, but she apologized that she was too pressed by deadlines. Soon everyone left her alone. But at least she did not look depressed. In fact, she seemed absolutely loaded with energy.

During that summer, I later learned, Grace was overdosing on speed-type drugs like Dexedrine and Dexamyl. For twenty years she had been using these drugs in more or less controlled amounts. When she began writing for *Edge of Night*, she would go up with speed to churn out her work, then go down with tranquilizers and barbiturates to get a few hours' sleep. It was a complicated calculus, but she did it for over a year of heavy lifting on *Edge of Night*, and it seemed to work. Over time, though, Henry Slesar, the show's chief writer, grew so pleased with her work that he increased her assignment from two to three weekly scripts. Her pharmacological management scheme was disrupted. She went into drug overdrive, ingesting amphetamines in larger quantities. She was now working weekends, so she had little time to recover. Her tolerance grew, and the quantities of speed increased still more.

In August, acute insomnia set in. Grace couldn't focus, write, manage the house, or look after herself. She dressed in nondescript clothes that she could put on in a minute, abandoned her elaborate makeup ritual, ate standing at the kitchen counter, and rarely left the house except to do minimal shopping. As her need for amphetamines grew and it became harder for her to get the drugs, the whole package of drug-addict horrors—panic states, withdrawal symptoms—descended on her. She reached the bottom on the day she tried to grab and run with a physician's prescription pad after he had declined to give her amphetamines. That hair-raising night, she went screaming through the halls of the house. The kids came home from camp to this chaos.

In early September, a consulting psychiatrist recommended that Grace enter Payne Whitney Clinic for drug detoxification. The clinic, one of the flagship psychiatric institutions of the country, was located in Manhattan, close to the family; we would be able to visit her regularly and have therapeutic sessions with Grace and her doctors. Desperate for a night's sleep, Grace agreed to go.

Members of the *Edge of Night* team sent cakes and cards and, in the dreamy spirit of soap opera solidarity, urged her to "take her time getting well." Slesar promised to hold her job open until she was ready to return. Grace told me that "Brandy," her favorite *Edge of Night* character, had called and said, "You'll be better than new in no time." Grace always used the actors' soap opera names. I don't think she knew the real ones.

In spite of its large reputation and mammoth endowment, Payne Whitney was an unmitigated disaster for Grace. The hospital was home to many of the great names of psychiatry, but they were presumably busy raising funds, writing papers, attending seminars, and being psychoanalyzed (then de rigueur for Payne Whitney doctors), and thus unable to spend much time with actual patients. So Grace was assigned to a humorless, colossally insecure young resident. He pumped her full of antipsychotic drugs like Thorazine and Mellaril, in quantities that turned her into a blank-eyed zombie. The drugs may have been the state of the psychiatric art in 1976, but the lack of compassion was unforgivable.

The resident and his assistant, in our family sessions, conveyed their thinly veiled distaste for the Garments. When Sara disagreed with the doctor, his carefully composed face would ripple with suppressed indignation at the nerve of this kid disputing his judgments. Grace, stuffed with drugs, would sit quietly as her doctor and family circled each other like a matador and three dehorned bulls. The experience was unredeemed by words of wisdom, humor, hope, or anything else that might have made Grace's "treatment" something more than an expensive incarceration.

Her eight weeks in Payne Whitney dealt Grace a series of psychic blows. There were locked doors, shabby rooms, smelly corridors (even the food smelled of Clorox), and a mixed community of dazed human beings—safe schizophrenics, mostly depressed manic depressives, anorexics, bulimics. One young lady habitually stole Grace's food, gobbled it down, then threw it up. The whole unhappy gang was always dozing or pacing or slouched before the TV or wandering around in the informal Payne Whitney uniform of polyester tights, a loose sweater, and moccasins or sneakers, waiting for access to the single, always busy, public phone. When Grace left Payne Whitney, her last shreds of self-esteem had been dissolved by the hospital's antipsychotic chemicals and cold condescension. She was passive and quiet. She had no plans, no thought of returning to *Edge of Night*.

Recently I got some evidence that my impression of Payne Whitney was not just a resentful invention. In 1994, the place was demolished to make space for a new hospital building. To mark the occasion, the psychiatrist David Hellerstein, who had trained at Payne Whitney, wrote a piece for *The New York Times* about the institution. During the mid-1970s, he said, the hospital was led by a doctor named Robert Michels, under whom "residency training was also psychic boot camp." After four years of his Queeg-like behavior, according to Hellerstein, "we emerged inculcated with the Payne Whitney attitude, a combination of arrogance, empathy, and the deep conviction that we alone knew what was best for the patient." This was the Payne Whitney I saw—except for the empathy, which was nowhere in evidence, doubtless because, contrary to Hellerstein's formulation, it is not often found in the company of arrogance. When I learned that Payne Whitney was about to be leveled, I felt primordial satisfaction.

Marilyn Monroe spent time at Payne Whitney until her husband, Joe DiMaggio, insisted on transferring her to Columbia Presbyterian. So why wasn't I as aggressive? Why did I assume that Payne Whitney knew what was best? Perhaps it was the years I had spent submitting to the shamanism of psychoanalysis. I knew a psychiatrist named Nathan V. Kline, an aggressively antibureaucratic innovator in the then new field of antidepressant medication. I wanted him to see Grace. Payne Whitney authorities said he could not see her while she was under their care; it would interfere with their treatment protocol. I now see that the reason was not really the "treatment protocol" but the tendency of elite institutions to erect barriers to entry by others. But I accepted their verdict without question. I would not do so today, nor should anyone else in such a situation.

During the months Grace was at Payne Whitney, catty-corner across the street at Memorial Sloan-Kettering hospital, suffering from a fast-moving lymphoma, was Gloria Hellman, the largely unrequited love of my long-ago law school years who had introduced me to Grace. Gloria was separated from her husband, an English movie producer, but the two of them lovingly shared a gorgeous four-year-old daughter, Amanda. The previous July 4, already in chemotherapy, Gloria had come to our house for a Bicentennial party, where we watched the tall ships and fireworks from our roof. She pumped Grace for funny *Edge of Night* stories and gossiped nostalgically about the days when she and Grace had collaborated on another soap opera, *Search for Tomorrow*.

In the fall of 1976, Gloria's lymphoma was reaching the terminal stage; she was in Sloan-Kettering for another round of chemotherapy. I would travel across the street from one hospital to the other, carrying stories and regards. Gloria repeatedly tried to phone Grace, but when the public phone on the ward wasn't busy, which was seldom, Grace herself couldn't be located. When Gloria was ready to go home, she asked me to take her across the street to see Grace. From Gloria's hospital room I called Grace—who said no. Nothing personal; she just wasn't up to it. "But wish her well for me," Grace said. "It must be a really rotten time."

There was a short burst of tears from Gloria, a long Kleenex blow, and a shrug. Another chapter finished. She began fussing with her wig and grinning into a hand mirror at the sight of her naked head; with or without hair, she was strikingly attractive. Assembling her kit of makeup tools, she held out her cheek for a good-bye kiss. "Don't forget," she said, "you promised to buy me a huge Italian dinner. Ciao for now."

What a collection of sadness. Gloria, yearning to live but doomed to death. Grace, in robust physical health, obliged to live even if she did not want to. Yet I suppose Grace was right about not seeing Gloria: What could the two of them say to each other?

On Wednesday, November 24, the day before Thanksgiving, Grace was released from Payne Whitney. It was a little bit like coming home from the hospital with a new baby, a mixture of hope and eggshell anxiety. Grace had been away from the hospital with me for a couple of short trips—once to a restaurant, once to a movie. Now she was quietly taking in the shimmering New York river and harbor from the F.D.R. Drive and the Brooklyn Bridge on our taxi ride home in the bright autumn sunlight.

Thanksgiving dinner was, well, Thanksgiving dinner. Grace

shopped and cooked. Sara helped. Paul and I watched football. The day was peaceful, but there was a sense of land mines all around. After we ate and cleaned up, the kids went off with their neighborhood chums; Grace and I bundled up and went for a walk and talk, the longest and calmest I could remember. We walked arm in arm through the holiday-emptied Brooklyn streets, up State Street to Flatbush Avenue Extension, down past Prospect Park, and out a good distance along Ocean Avenue, window-shopping stores and houses along the way, almost to the point where the ocean smells begin. There were no cruising cabs, so we walked home.

We covered a lot of our life together, mostly the good and funny times with friends. We talked about the way the kids were coming along. Grace said she was going to rest up and maybe go back to writing, but she wasn't going to rush; she wasn't sure she should or could do it. Then she said something I found strange: The doctors at Payne Whitney had told her she needed long-term institutional care, maybe two to three years away from the city—away, that is, from her family, which they thought was locked into a hopeless tangle of destructive behavior that Grace couldn't handle. I think this is the first time I heard about this dismal prognosis; if I had been told before, I'd simply closed my mind and memory to it. In any event, Grace said she wasn't going to go. She would continue seeing the psychiatrist, take her medication regularly, and try family therapy. But no more psychiatric hospitals, no more lockups. I don't remember thinking about the "what if"s. What if Grace had a serious relapse? Well, then the decision would be out of her hands and ours. But what if there wasn't enough time?

Over the rest of the holiday weekend, the routine was synthetically comforting. There was no more talk about family or illness, just visits to neighborhood friends, family meals, a movie. I read. Grace did a lot of sleeping. Nothing, it seemed, had changed.

Monday it was back to work and school. Grace returned to her household chores and exercise routine. I went back to preparing the defense of a corporate manslaughter case involving an explosion, a fire, and many deaths. The weather turned miserable—gray, wet, edge-of-snow cold. By midweek Grace was visibly slipping into depression. The kids were getting on her nerves with their fights. I made things worse by my nightly exhortations to her: "You've simply got to fight it. . . . It takes an act of will. . . . Give the antidepressants time to act. . . ." She had no intimate friends, no work, no *Edge of Night* family, and no Dexedrine for relief. It was crisis time again, sooner than anyone had anticipated.

I quickly scheduled our first family therapy session with the psychiatrist who had arranged Grace's Payne Whitney admission. The appointment was for Friday, December 3, at four P.M. Wednesday and Thursday nights, I came home to a familiar sight: Grace stretched out on her bed, wearing the faded jeans, pink tattersall shirt, and sneakers that had been her *Edge of Night* working uniform, staring at the ceiling the way she had for uncountable hours.

In the past, she had tearfully expressed her despair in more or less the same words: "I wish I were dead." But now she was dry-eyed and silent. I gave another cheerleading speech: We had that family therapy session coming on Friday afternoon. We could take time off, go south for a while. We could even sell the house and lead a different, simpler life. She told me not to worry. She was fine, just tired, not yet used to all the freedom. "Give me a few minutes," she said, "and I'll get dinner started."

Friday morning was truly miserable—darker, colder. Grace drove Paul to school and me to the subway stop. Our old Volkswagen always took a long time to heat up, and its interior that morning was like a refrigerator. During the short ride I caught a glimpse of Grace's face in the rearview mirror. It was fixed in a grimace, as if she were in physical pain from the cold; but so was I, so I didn't think anything of it. I said, "Remember, four o'clock at the doctor's office." I hesitated. "Do you want me to pick you up?" "No," she said, "I'll get there by myself. I've got some errands uptown." Quick and clear.

Sara was still at home; her first class wasn't until midmorning. She remembers that Grace came back, unloaded the clothes dryer, folded sheets and towels, made the beds, and straightened up. From Sara's room she removed some sweaters that Sara had borrowed, neatly returning them to their place in our bureau. Everything was in order. As Sara was leaving for school, Grace called from the second-floor landing, "Don't forget to wear a muffler, Sara, it's bitter cold outside." Sara called back that she didn't need one. She remembers slamming out of the house. Around lunchtime I happened to be in Brooklyn, at the fire department offices, getting information related to my manslaughter case. I fleetingly thought I might knock off for the day, go home, and drive with Grace to the doctor. Then I remembered that she was probably out shopping and I had an appointment at my office. I went back to Wall Street. Later I learned that Grace had told Sara and Paul a couple of times not to come home but to meet her at the doctor's office.

Paul, Sara, and I assembled at the therapist's office at four o'clock, but no Grace. Four-thirty. Five. Still no Grace. We called the house repeatedly, talked about traffic delays, then pretty much fell silent. We knew something had happened. I called our neighbor Joe Merz, who had a key to the house. Accompanied by Charlie Miller, another neighborhood friend, Joe searched the house from top to bottom and called back: Nothing. Dusk was settling as the kids and I crossed the Brooklyn Bridge on our way home. The few words we nervously exchanged in the taxi assumed the worst; we were getting one another ready. Joe was there when we arrived. A brief search turned up Grace's set of house and car keys and a bunch of credit cards. Nothing else. No note. The place was bare and neat as a pin.

Then it started. We called the police, who arrived quickly and went to work. We phoned friends who might be helpful. One of them, Richard Clurman—former chief of correspondents for *Time-Life*, author, and man of unrivaled competence and kindness—was first to arrive and stayed all night, helping with phone calls. Pat Moynihan was out to the house quickly, organizing the search and exercising his new authority as senator-elect to call the top brass of the police department and the F.B.I. for help. And so it went. There were no relevant reports of unidentified deaths in Manhattan or the region.

Bits of information began to accumulate. A Brooklyn Heights car service had logged a call from our house about noon. The driver remembered a well-dressed woman wearing a mink coat. She asked him to take her to Penn Station, chatted calmly and amiably, gave him a big tip, and disappeared into the Penn Station crowds. And that was it. Grace, alive or dead, had vanished. The state and local police and other investigators came up empty-handed.

Days, then weeks, went by. I returned to work, the kids to

school. I gave interviews to sympathetic journalists like Judith Michaelson of the *New York Post*, asking Grace to come home or simply let us know she was alive. Henry Slesar told the press that Grace was a professional perfectionist, the best associate writer *Edge of Night* ever had. Knowing how tight deadlines were and not trusting the mail or messenger services, she hand-delivered her scripts to his Manhattan office. Slesar said he was now writing the whole week's scripts himself, hoping Grace would return soon. The *Edge of Night* show was interrupted one day to broadcast a plea to Grace from the cast—one of the purest soap sequences in television history.

Over time, the kids and I began to half believe that Grace might have decided to change her life and identity, like one of her soap opera characters. Perhaps she had taken a train to a small southern town where she was working, say, as a librarian, writing seriously in her off hours, and kicking her hated lifetime habits. We raced one another for the day's mail. The police installed a tracer phone. With each call, we half expected to hear her voice.

Gradually this passed. We were not in mourning, because there was no confirmation of death. Everything, grief included, was in suspension. Paul disappeared into the basement and practiced clarinet endlessly. Sara resumed her school routine, defiantly cheerful. It was a small, seven-week taste of the psychological limbo in which survivors of the missing in action are trapped, desperate to know what happened so that they can celebrate survival or bury their dead.

During Christmas week I took Paul to Grand Cayman Island, where the family had spent a couple of happy weeks years before. Sara insisted on staying behind. Paul and I visited the old haunts—somehow expecting, though not saying so, that Grace might turn up as a waitress or hotel cashier or singer in one of the nightclubs.

Finally, back in New York, the seven weeks of suspense came to an end at the Metropolitan Club. I was meeting in a private conference room with Frank Markoe, a client and friend, and John Alexander, one of my partners. There was a phone call; Frank answered, then asked to be excused for a moment. The phone rang again; John answered. It was Frank, calling from the lobby. John told me two New York detectives were there, with news that Grace's body had been found. The detectives were on their way up to give me the details. John and Frank said what friends say at such moments and excused themselves.

The detectives traced the events of Grace's last few hours. After Grace left the taxi at Penn Station, she bought a pint bottle of vodka, a pack of double-edged razor blades, and a copy of *The New Yorker*. She took the train to Boston and checked into the semi-shabby Hotel Sussex, across the street from the train station. She registered under an invented name, Hilda Miller of Brooklyn, and paid for a night in advance. Then she went to her room, hung out the DO NOT DISTURB sign, and proceeded, apparently without much delay, to end her life, using sleeping pills and codeine to deaden pain, a razor blade, and a bathtub filled with warm water.

She died on Friday evening, December 3, about the time the search for her began. On December 7, the Sussex called the police to open Grace's room. They found *The New Yorker* open on the bed, as if Grace had spent her final moments distracting herself by reading the magazine until she was ready.

Her body and possessions were taken to the Boston morgue. But the Boston police somehow failed to connect this unidentified upper-middle-class woman with the detailed physical information about a missing Grace Garment that was then being circulated by the New York police to police departments in thirteen northeastern states, including Massachusetts.

After the initial sweep for Grace had failed, I asked the New York police to try again, with photographs and a circular targeted to specific cities in the Northeast. This time, Boston detectives made the connection. Because the mink coat had a Bonwit Teller label, the detectives now called Bonwit Teller's furrier, Gunther Jaeckel, who told them that to aid the police in recovering stolen coats, the owner's name was written on the back of the label. The Boston police removed the label and, after weeks of bureaucratic bumbling, finally had their woman. If just a little more time had passed, days or hours, Grace would have been buried in Boston's potter's field, and any hope of knowing whether she was dead or alive would have been lost forever. My life and my children's lives would have been altered in ways that defy speculation.

Boston authorities told the press they had sent a description of

Grace—clothing, photograph, her fingerprints—to the New York police, but it was somehow overlooked. A New York police spokesman told the press, "Apparently there was some missing of communications." Translation: Nobody worked very hard to identify this woman. After all, why get worked up about another anonymous stiff? And a suicide, at that.

My brother Marty and I flew to Boston the next morning to make a formal identification. The cold Boston morgue was dominated by a floor-to-ceiling refrigerator with individual sliding gurneys, like ice trays, each bearing a body wrapped in sheets except for the head. Marty went in first and came out to confirm wordlessly that it was Grace. Then I took my last look. She wore something like the grimace I had seen that final frigid morning when I caught a glimpse of her face in the rearview mirror of the Volkswagen. It was the determination of a novice rider on a roller coaster holding tight as the car starts its first sickening drop into space.

Among the letters sent to me on the day the news of Grace's death appeared in the papers was one from Nixon. I suppose it should have been no surprise that he, a world-class expert in suffering, would know what to say. "As I read the news about Grace in the morning paper I thought of the agony you must have been suffering. But now the long ordeal is over, and it is time to look ahead."

The funeral was small, a handful of relatives and close friends, quiet, uncomfortable, dry-eyed. No remarks by loved ones. The rabbi furnished by the funeral parlor, a total stranger, gave a brief eulogy, based on conversations with family and friends, that was surprisingly appropriate. He ended with some lines that he said were among Elizabeth Barrett Browning's favorites when she was dying of tuberculosis: "Not a tear must o'er her fall. He giveth his beloved sleep." This produced the day's only touch of open emotion.

Gloria Hellman, though not present at the funeral, was among those hardest hit by these events. After Grace's disappearance, when we knew she was probably dead, I called Gloria to tell her. She reacted with a short, choked cry and hung up without a word. A few months later Gloria flew to a Mexican clinic for last-ditch Laetrile treatment. Alan Pakula took time off from his film assignments to make the complicated transit arrangements that enabled Gloria to have a last look at her beloved Pacific. She spent her first day in

Mexico basking in the warm coastal sun and died in her sleep that night.

Grace needed a true room of her own in order to develop her expressive gifts, but she was never able to find or build one. The closest she came was her soap opera world—whose exhausting demands, ironically, precipitated the cutting of the ropes and safety devices from which she had hung suspended over her dark chasm. Her life embodied the elements of Camus's Sisyphean enterprise, except that the heavy stone she pushed uphill every day gave her no satisfaction. Her father was emotionally vacant and her mother coldly incapable of maternal care, valuing only religious devotion and intellectual achievement in her children. A cyclical depressive from childhood, an unhappy student who wearily achieved the highest average in the history of Julia Richman High School, Grace tried every kind of distraction, starting with her existential fling at show business. Nothing worked. Her depression made her incapable of sustained mothering, so she—with me as an unindicted co-conspirator—turned the kids over to housekeepers to feed and psychiatrists to nurture.

Though Grace abandoned the teachings and devotional routines of Mary Baker Eddy as soon as she left home, it was too late: Her adult life was a comprehensive system of denials and reversals of Christian Science precepts. She was obsessively anxious about her weight, appearance, physical health, mental health, hours of sleep, aging, death—everything related to the body that Mrs. Eddy said did not exist.

After Grace's death, Marty's wife, Sylvia, the family member closest to her, came to help me clean out her closets. Sylvia was startled by the drugstore-size collection, much of which I had never seen, of pills, potions, reducing equipment (such as a toe-to-neck plastic sweat suit), makeup kits, brushes, and pencils by the dozens, scissors and clippers of every size, false eyelashes, a huge collection of reading and sun glasses, wrinkle removers, and many other standard and obscure cosmetic devices. These items were not so strange in themselves; it was the quantity that was striking. Then there was Grace's cache of disguises—maybe a dozen wigs, all kinds of padding, boxes of costume jewelry, a large collection of dresses, suits, sports clothes, bathing suits, and formal wear, and a whole shoe store. Sylvia, a psychologist, paused in her cleanup work. "I've never seen anything like it in my life," she said. "The strange thing is that Grace hardly ever used any of it. She must have been satisfied just by buying the stuff." Sylvia had it right. The fantastic collection, I think, was Grace's ritual of rejection, an attempt to rid herself in every possible way of her Christian Science handcuffs.

There are almost always multiple factors in a suicide, and Grace's adult life—her career, me, the children—certainly provided some. But specialists in manic-depressive illness say that along with genetic vulnerability, an ingredient of most suicides is the grief, guilt, and anger that remain, unexpressed, after a great loss, such as the death of a loved one. This is particularly likely if the loss occurs at an early age, say twelve or thirteen. My guess is that Grace had formed an early belief that her life was over before it really began. Her depression was a kind of mourning for the death of her hopes.

But why no suicide note? One reason is obvious: If she had written a note declaring her intentions, she would not have simply and totally "disappeared." She must have been angry enough to prefer a complete vanishing, with its punishing consequences for her family and friends. I'm sure she forgot about the telltale Bonwit Teller label, if she ever knew about it; otherwise, she would have removed it.

Then again, what could she say in a note that would not have sounded false or hypocritical? That she was sorry for the hurt she was causing? She wasn't. That she loved us and knew we loved her? I'm not sure she thought either was true; otherwise she might have wanted to live. Grace had no more to say. She was finished with the pain of writing, acting, posturing.

And where was I during the years of Grace's downward spiral? Working, of course, frequently seven days and nights a week, like my father—and, like him, happy to leave the scut work of child rearing to Grace and her cadre of Caribbean helpers, doing occasional sandbox or Coney Island duty and feeling noble about it. At night, Grace and I would talk about our aspirations and the relative state of our depressions, which seemed to be the essence of our marriage. Grace tended the house, the kids, and her emotional troubles; I listened sympathetically, paid the bills, and fled to work. My guess is that Grace let me get away with it because I was her ticket of admission to a social scene in which there were funny, intelligent, attractive people who intermittently distracted her from the despair that was her only companion when she was alone.

The final blow to Grace was the way her family—mostly me— behaved when she came home from Payne Whitney. Within a few days, she knew nothing was going to change. "Home is so sad," Phillip Larkin wrote. "It stays as it was left." The people at Payne Whitney, for all their shortcomings, were probably right that Grace should have been hospitalized and treated away from home. When she told me about their recommendation, she said she had rejected it; but she might have said so expecting that I would press her to take the doctors' advice, or even take the decision out of her hands. If so, I missed the signal, because it was too subtle or because I didn't want to hear it. By then I had already had a taste, for a couple of months, of what it would be like without her. I missed her stories and jokes, her presence, even her lamentations. The house was big and lonely, and the kids were hard to handle. I did not even think about the possibility of Grace's going away. I now know what my father must have felt when my mother—his whole life, except for work and pinochle—was hospitalized for over two years.

Until recently I thought of my father as a stranger who rarely talked to me, or I to him. Yet for my whole life, his likes and dis-likes, habits of work, attitudes toward women, angers, frustrations, and secret passions have been imprinted on me. Now I hear his voice in my voice, and in the morning mirror I see his face emerging in mine. In my long postmortem conversation with him, I've come to know him better and even become his friend. I've come to realize that when the doctors wanted to send Grace away, I behaved not so differently from the way my father did when he wanted to bring my mother home from the sanitarium. When he tried to take her out of the hospital before the psychiatrists thought she should go, I liter-ally went to the mat for my mother against her husband. But there was no one around to do the same for Grace.

In the years after Grace's death, getting used to her permanent absence was the kind of ache that felt like it would last a lifetime. I found myself playing and replaying Stephen Sondheim's *Follies* until the record was worn thin; the brittle, sentimental songs about love, foolishness, and loss unearthed memories that brought tears. I had a full-time job, a large house to manage, and two understandably rattled teenagers. Then came another kind of trial, the "Let's get a girlfriend and/or wife for Lenny" phase. Nice people, nice girls, an embarrassing ritual.

After about a year of this, I began suffering Olympic-sized panics. For no discernible reason, on no notice, I started to feel I was smothering to death. My pulse would race, my heart would pound, and I would be drenched in sweat. I would wake in the middle of the night, throw on some clothes, and run into the street. I felt I was being buried alive. I'm sure many impulse suicides occur during these ghastly episodes.

During those years I withdrew from the law firm's management committee and cut back my practice to part-time work and pay, trying cases that other partners didn't want to handle. I passed a lot of time sitting on a bench on Fifth Avenue alongside Central Park, near my doctor's office, waiting for something or someone to come along; who or what I never could figure out. I spent hours driving around the city with Sara and Paul, taking in the late-night scenes, mostly in Coney Island or Harlem, to the accompaniment of jazz tapes. It was an improvised film that looped endlessly as we watched it, waiting for time to go by and hurts to heal.

After a couple of years the kids and I were rescued by Suzi Weaver. She and I had been professional friends and coworkers at the United Nations. She was separated, then divorced from her husband. She had left Yale and had begun working for Robert Bartley, the editor of the *Wall Street Journal* editorial page. After Grace's death, Suzi and I moved gradually through the stages of a more intimate friendship. In the spring of 1980 we were married at 40 Willow Place with the blessings of scores of friends and family members, particularly Sara and Paul, who had come to love Suzi almost as much as I did.

Also in 1980, a Brooklyn Law School friend of mine, David Shapiro, now a trial lawyer and senior partner in a Washington law firm, Dickstein Shapiro & Morin, joined me in sponsoring merger discussions between his firm and Mudge Rose. Don Zoeller and I presented our Mudge Rose colleagues with a strong case for proceeding with negotiations. Senior partner Bob Guthrie, now aging but still indomitable, hated the idea. He defeated us in less than a minute, tersely telling the assembled Mudge Rose partners about Dickstein Shapiro: "This is a smart, tough crowd. If you merge, in three to five years half of you will be gone. Face it, boys, you're just not good enough." No merger. Next case.

Shapiro urged me to make the move alone. More or less coincidentally, *The Washington Post* offered Suzi the job of editing the paper's Outlook section. She accepted tentatively but was dissuaded by Bartley, who gave her an associate editorship at *The Wall Street Journal* and a weekly column on Washington politics (she wrote the column, "Capital Chronicle," for seven years). By now Sara was at Wesleyan University, majoring in classics, and Paul had won a full scholarship to the Curtis Institute of Music in Philadelphia. Suzi and I were happy to pack our bags and begin a new life in an old place.

⟡ 11 ⟡

WORKS IN PROGRESS

I began work at Dickstein Shapiro & Morin. Shapiro moved me into quarters next door to the amphitheater that was his office. He applied his usual steamroller force to making sure that I would succeed and vindicate his decision to bring me into the firm over the doubts of several partners. They had argued that I was a chronic drifter, absent from the practice of law for a long time—and on the wrong side of Washington politics, since President Jimmy Carter would surely be reelected. This was a little unfair: Up until my departure for Washington, I had been trying cases. But they had a point. I was on foreign legal terrain and had to prove myself.

It was good to get back to litigating, but I also began advising and representing politicians in trouble. It was an activity that synthesized all my prior experience and that I came to describe as "political litigation." I found a ready market: After the surprising election of Reagan and Bush in 1980, many people who knew me once again moved into positions of power.

First I got to watch them reorganize themselves for governing. In the summer of 1980 Suzi and I went to the Republican presidential convention in Detroit, where we hung out with Frank Shakespeare, our accidental next-door hotel neighbor Jack Kemp, and some old White House and press friends. Everyone was speculating on the identity of nominee Ronald Reagan's vice president, and the evening the choice was to be made, word was that it was going to be Gerald Ford.

I dropped by George Bush's suite to commiserate at his loss of the vice presidential nomination. Bush was there shooting the breeze with his friend Vic Gold and a few staffers. I offered my friendly regrets. "Well, shit, Len," he said, "that's the way it goes. Give it your best shot. On to the next damn thing, whatever." There wasn't the hint of a whimper. So I went back to my room, just in time to turn on the television and hear that Reagan had chosen Bush after all. The call from Reagan to Bush signaling the reversal of fortune had come in the time it took me to ride the elevator from Bush's floor to mine.

A few minutes later, we had just stepped out onto the street when Bush's limo pulled out of the hotel garage, headed for the convention hall. I gave him a thumbs-up sign. Bush threw up both his hands in a gesture that said, "Go figure." Style had been rewarded. It was one of those promising Washington beginnings that always seem to end in disappointment.

Just after the 1980 election, everyone assumed that the next secretary of state would be George Shultz. The Council on Foreign Relations gave a private dinner in his honor to sample his views. I was there; so was Helmut Sonnenfeldt, a longtime Kissinger aide. At some point during the evening Shultz asked me to join him for a drink after dinner at the Regency Hotel. "Bring Sonnenfeldt along," he said. When we were settled in at the bar, Shultz drew from his breast pocket a copy of a speech on the Mideast that President-elect Ronald Reagan had delivered at a B'nai B'rith meeting in September.

Shultz had spent a great deal of time in the Middle East as president of Bechtel, a huge construction company with extensive commercial ties to Saudi Arabia. He took issue with most of Reagan's speech; he had underlined, as if in desperation, the few sentences in the speech that he thought injected touches of balance into the pro-Israel document. He asked us, "How can I in good conscience take the job at State if I disagree with the president on something as basic as his Middle East policy?"

Shultz listened somberly as we offered him our comforting cynicism. The speech was just traditional campaign stuff, we said. No, Shultz answered: You fellows don't know Reagan. If he says it, he means it. Sonnenfeldt and I tried again: You can take the job and try to change his mind; maybe you will change yours. But Shultz shook his head.

A week or so later, Shultz sent me his copy of the speech, complete with the underlinings. He asked me to take another look, talk to Suzi—whose views he held in high regard—and tell him how to reconcile his conflict. We wrote him a letter in which we did our best, saying the Saudis could be made to see that their safety and stability were in fact tied to Israel's.

After all that to-ing and fro-ing, the State Department job went to Al Haig, a man without an ambivalent bone in his body. Haig had fought for the appointment like a battlefield commander, courting and enlisting the support of the hard-liners in Reagan's West Coast kitchen cabinet and getting Richard Nixon to campaign, among Reagan insiders and with Reagan himself, for Haig and against Shultz (Watergate tape buffs will remember that Nixon had unkindly called Shultz a "candy ass").

After the Reagan inaugural, at a lunch Shultz's daughter gave for her parents and a few of their old friends, Shultz drew me aside: "Len, do you have any idea why I wasn't given State?" I gave the frankest answer I could: You were too diffident, you didn't fight hard enough, and you didn't do what politics demands, which is to grovel and manipulate so the president and his men know you're desperate for the job. And Nixon had a big hand in the choice: The appointment of Haig opens a pipeline for his foreign policy ideas.

Haig was not as distinguished a man as Shultz, but he was in some ways better qualified to run the State Department: For example, if Haig had opposed Iran-*contra*, he would have resigned with bells and whistles unless Reagan had stopped it, instead of just criticizing, then avoiding the issue. But Haig could not control his compulsion to take the hook every time the White House threw it in his general direction. His hopeless effort to outpower the White House staff, his press leaks, his tantrums over petty perks, and his unhappy relations with both Mr. and Mrs. Reagan definitively cooked his goose.

On June 25, 1982, Woody Goldberg, Haig's longtime assistant, called to tell me gloomily that Al was at that very moment over at the White House tendering his resignation to force Reagan to give him more authority. Haig had tried to do this before, and I had played therapist more than once: I had even stooped to reminding him that if he got himself fired, he would be using taxis and commercial airlines. This time, Woody asked me to come over at maximum speed, so I was sitting in Haig's office when he returned, ashen-faced, from the White House. I told Haig that this time the White House had been waiting for him to offer his resignation. Unless he could miraculously snatch it back, he was going to be dumped. By then, though, the decision had already been made. That afternoon Reagan called Shultz, who was in London. Shultz, not just a good teacher but an excellent student, did not make the same mistake twice; he accepted instantly.

There is always comedy. At one point when Haig's final crisis was boiling up, Suzi interviewed him in his office for her *Wall Street Journal* column. Undersecretary of State Lawrence Eagleburger was there as well; he announced to her, and later to me, that if they fired Haig, he—Eagleburger—would be the first one out the door after him. It took Larry a long time to pack. He didn't actually exit the building until after Bill Clinton was elected president in 1992. Given Eagleburger's skills, we should be thankful for his procrastination.

Cap Weinberger, another colleague from Nixon days, was now secretary of defense. But—again, the problem was the Mideast—our long acqaintanceship did not prevent complications. Weinberger soon became known as having a very low tolerance for Israel and its military actions, especially preemptive ones. Many American Jews attributed his attitudes to his long association with Bechtel or to anti-Semitism.

I don't think so. Weinberger was a friend of mine and of Safire's, Stein's, and Burns's, a lively, witty companion evincing no racial or religious hangups. Instead, I think Cap took on, as not a few people do, the coloration of the job he worked at—because the central strength he brought to each of his assignments was that of a gifted lawyer, loyal to his client and his "case," a passionate advocate and psychological devotee. Thus "Cap the Knife" at OMB became "Cap the Profligate" at Defense. He also wound up treating adversaries as enemies; lawyers often do.

Whatever the source, the animus was real enough. I first saw it in his office in 1981. I forget what the original reason for my visit was; I never got around to stating it, because Weinberger had learned earlier in the day that the Israelis had bombed the Iraqi nuclear reactor at Osirak. He was in a fury. I argued that I thought it was a hell of a good idea. He certainly didn't throw me out of his office; instead he made a terse, polite case for the proposition that the Israelis had flagrantly violated international law.

He left the office briefly to view post-bombing satellite photographs with the Joint Chiefs. When he returned, he was considerably calmer. He reported everyone's aesthetic appreciation for the accuracy of the bombing: "It was like the extraction of a tooth. The fence around the reactor was untouched—an absolutely splendid show. Why can't we perform like that?" Not enough practice, I offered; American lives are not at risk every day.

Sometimes our interests converged. In 1983 there appeared in the press a fabricated transcript giving a false version of a meeting that had taken place between Weinberger and Saudi Arabia's defense minister. In the document, Weinberger was depicted as promising the Saudis the latest in U.S. weaponry. The document was passed to the Israeli consul general in New York, who in turn gave it to New York's mayor, Ed Koch. The purpose was to put heat on Weinberger, and Koch cooperated by denouncing him. Weinberger was outraged and asked me to help. The bureaucracy was reluctant to release the genuine transcript. It was a standoff.

I went to work on the matter with the person I usually turned to for Defense Department help, Weinberger's aide, a young colonel named Colin Powell. Powell was clearly Weinberger's favorite; but the young man seemed too relaxed, too pleasant, and—most damning of all—too funny to go far in political life. Still, he had a knack for getting things done quickly in the face of bureaucratic resistance.

On this occasion, Powell and Defense spokesman Henry Catto wangled the real transcript out of the State Department. Then Powell and I proposed to the mayor a scenario for ending the nasty little controversy. Acting reluctantly but, in the clutch, as a patriot and fair-minded man, Koch gave in. My contemporaneous notes of the crisis contain a record of Powell's last phone message to me: "Powell for Weinberger. New York worked."

Weinberger was also right sometimes in larger Mideast matters. The next year, in June 1982, my friend Shlomo Argov, who had become Israel's ambassador to Great Britain, was leaving the Hilton Hotel in London after making one of his passionate speeches. Terrorists shot him in the head. Afterward, on June 5, 1982, the Israelis invaded Lebanon. At the time, President and Mrs. Reagan, Al Haig, Jim Baker, Treasury Secretary Donald Regan, and National Security Adviser William Clark were in Versailles for an economic conference, isolated from their staffs and already in a state of tense irritation with one another. The invasion caused convulsions among them, and the U.S. delegation spewed denunciations of Israel into the European air. Haig was talking about flying to the Mideast.

Back in Washington, the only cabinet officer with real authority in the area was Weinberger, whose antagonism toward Israel was by now no secret. But for the moment he was all the Israeli embassy in Washington had. And, in this chaotic state, all they had as a means of communication with him was me.

The Israeli ambassador, Moshe Arens, and the deputy chief of mission, Benjamin "Bibi" Netanyahu, had become my friends. Young Netanyahu was a political comer (to understate the case): He was M.I.T.-educated, handsome, charismatic, and the best Israeli polemicist since Abba Eban. His father, Benzion, was an eminent Israeli historian; his brother Jonathan had led the brilliant July 4, 1976, rescue of the hostages at Uganda's Entebbe airport and was the only Israeli commando killed in the operation.

Netanyahu and I developed the easy relationship of college friends. He would exercise to relieve his paratrooper's back problems on the floor of my living room and, his tongue loosened by painkillers and vodka, tell me hair-raising military tales. And I trusted his boss, Moshe Arens—a man of granitic character, formerly a successful aircraft designer and businessman, single-mindedly devoted to safeguarding Israel's security. Like their predecessors, Arens and Netanyahu occasionally used me to establish communication when there was a serious problem and direct access was blocked. When the Lebanon invasion sent U.S. leaders into a fury, Arens asked me to his office and took me into the embassy's electronically secure room. He told me that the Israelis had moved into Lebanon only to clean out nests of P.L.O. who were harassing northern Israel. U.S. interference would be catastrophic. It was urgent, he said, that I go immediately to Weinberger and ask him to convey to the presidential party in Europe Israel's categorical assurance, and Arens's personal warrant, that the operation was strictly limited and that Israel would go no farther than forty kilometers—twenty-five miles—into Lebanon. Storybook-style he looked me in the eye and said, "Len, I represent to you on my personal honor that this is the limit of Israel's program in Lebanon. You must help me persuade Weinberger that I am telling the truth."

I went directly to Weinberger and reported the conversation. He said he liked and believed Arens. But he wasn't sure Arens could speak with certainty for all Israeli officials, Defense Minister Ariel Sharon in particular. He would convey Arens's message to the president. He would also include his own personal reservations.

Weinberger had this one right. When Sharon reached the twenty-five-mile limit he just kept going, with the acquiescence of Prime Minister Begin (and a widely reported earlier wink from Al Haig). Among the consequences: the massacre at Sabra and Shatilla, heavy Israeli casualties, and hundreds of U.S. deaths at the marine barracks in Beirut from a terrorist's car bomb.

I started doing well at "political litigation" not just because I knew people in office but because they were more vulnerable than ever. I had helped create the market for my own speciality: Watergate was the proximate cause of developments like the Ethics in Government Act, with its cat's cradle of conflict and disclosure rules. Watergate bred the hair-trigger independent counsel system for investigating government officials. The modern age of scandal was upon us, and I was to be one of its principal professional beneficiaries.

I was introduced to this phenomenon by e. robert ("bob") wallach—this was the way he insisted on spelling it. One day in 1981 he did not so much walk into my office as materialize there. He was deeply tanned and thin to the point of disappearance, sporting a set of dark eyebrows that seemed to weigh more than the rest of him. His voice was a deep, hoarse, warm whisper, his words as orderly as a formal text.

Wallach described himself as a West Coast plaintiffs' personal injury lawyer. He had founded an advocacy program at Hastings Law School and been president of the San Francisco Bar Association. He was a liberal Democrat, he explained, interested in Jewish affairs and Israel and in human rights. Yet Wallach's closest friend since law school days was President Reagan's White House counselor Edwin C. Meese. Wallach thought that Meese's single-view staff was giving him inadequate advice, thus making him seem like the political equivalent of Attila the Hun. Wallach's aim in Washington, he said, was to introduce Meese to more diverse and balanced political views.

So what did he want from me? Just some advice about the Washington culture, the names of people to talk to, opportunities for public service. He had free access to Meese, but wanted to know the best Washington base from which to offer his views.

I suggested possibilities. Wallach liked the idea of being appointed to the advisory board of the United States Information Agency—which happened to be one of the most fought-over patronage prizes in Washington, since it consisted of influential Washingtonians and its agenda involved much international travel and regular access to foreign leaders. A part-time assignment, it placed no restrictions on private law practice. I thought to myself, if Wallach can carry off this appointment, he will decisively confirm his allegedly close relationship with Meese. He did.

Wallach called me from California on New Year's Day, 1983, and introduced me to my first political scandal case: "Can you have breakfast tomorrow morning with Charlie Wick at his home?" I had first met Charlie and Mary Jane Wick in 1981 at a welcoming dinner given for them by Bill and Helene Safire just after Charlie was named head of the United States Information Agency. He was not exactly your typical political appointee. He had worked hard for the Reagan-Bush ticket, but more important was the long, affectionate relationship between the Wick and Reagan families, begun when Mary Jane Wick and Nancy Reagan carpooled their kiddies. The two families always spent Christmas together; on top of the Wick piano was a photograph of grown-up Charlie sitting on Santa Reagan's lap.

Charlie had been a dance-band pianist and an arranger with Tommy Dorsey's orchestra. He still had his near-perfect pitch and a way with the piano. He delighted Reagan with his inexhaustible stock of old and new jokes and his ability to invent high-quality puns with lightning speed. But Charlie's idiosyncratic style boded trouble. At the Safires' dinner party, after Bill's graceful and witty toast, Charlie responded—with a long, substantive, deadly serious, and nearly incomprehensible speech. I thought, my God, this guy is disaster-bound.

At U.S.I.A., Charlie further marked himself for grief. One day, for instance, the leader of a small African state, with entourage, came to visit Wick. Charlie called for coffee. A long line of U.S.I.A. staffers soon appeared, each bearing part of the necessary supplies—coffee, tea, cream, cups, cookies. As the parade snaked through the room, Wick, neurons humming, leaped to his feet and burst into song: "Oh, when the saints go marching in. . . ." The visitors were mystified, the U.S.I.A. bureaucrats mortified. Before the day was over, Wick had told the story to five hundred friends.

Charlie had a penchant for putting everything on tape. I learned about this habit early. Just before the inauguration, which Charlie co-chaired, Suzi interviewed Wick for a *Wall Street Journal* column. He asked if he could record his answers. "It's not that I don't trust you," he said. "It's just that if I don't get these things down immediately, they're gone forever." So I wasn't surprised to learn what kind of trouble Charlie had finally gotten himself into. Somebody at U.S.I.A. who did not like Wick had leaked to Bill Safire the news that Wick had been taping telephone calls without the knowledge and consent of the other parties to the conversation. Safire and Jane Perlez, a *New York Times* reporter, called on Wick at his home, deposited their own tape recorder on the coffee table, and proceeded to grill the startled Wick on his taping practices.

Wick admitted the tapings, explaining them as benign aids to a frenetically busy, memory-deficient mind. But it turned out that Wick's habit violated a Federal Communications Commission regulation, albeit one with no real penal consequences (I think they can take away your telephone). In some states where Wick had originated phone calls, the practice constituted the crime of eavesdropping, though such statutes were rarely enforced. The interview with Charlie resulted in a twofer: a news story by Jane Perlez and a column by Safire that ran on the same day, full of sulfurous outrage about Wick's villainous invasion of others' privacy. A big Washington commotion had been started. Charlie was worried; he knew it could threaten his job and reputation.

At our first breakfast, I told Wick that he should personally apologize to everyone he had taped without notice, return the original tapes, and issue a public apology for the invasion of privacy. I would draft the statement. Wick fiercely resisted the public mortification (almost everyone does), but with the aid of Mary Jane Wick and Bob Wallach, I finally got Charlie to acquiesce.

The multiple apologies took a while and covered a lot of terrain. For instance, in a private club in New York, I asked Charlie to go to a telephone booth, phone former president Jimmy Carter, and apologize for taping a phone call Charlie had made to congratulate Carter on an anti-nuclear-proliferation speech. After about ten minutes, Charlie still hadn't returned. I went to the phone booth to see what was happening and found Charlie on his knees in the booth: Carter wanted the two of them to pray together telephonically, and Charlie was obliging him.

But such apologies were not the end of the story, which went on for about a year and a half. Bill Safire was not buying contrition or prayer; he wanted Wick's head. Bulldog Safire communicated directly with district attorneys in jurisdictions like Florida and California that had eavesdropping laws; he pressed them to investigate Wick's alleged violations. So Charlie and I hit the road to make peace with one state law enforcement official after another. Meanwhile, we responded to Safire's hectoring columns with invective of our own in letters to The New York Times. (Bill and I had agreed to "suspend" our friendship until the struggle was finished.)

Safire was able to keep up his attacks only because he had cooperation from high inside the White House staff, where someone was leaking word that Wick was in deep trouble. I was puzzled: Why would any of them want to help Safire push Charlie out the window? His power was confined to a minor area of foreign policy; he was a personally generous man, and great fun. I finally concluded that the main target was not Charlie but Mary Jane Wick. She was the one with unrestricted access to President Reagan through her best friend, Nancy Reagan, and others could get derivative access through Mary Jane. Someone in the White House, probably one of Jim Baker's staff leakers, did not like seeing Baker's control subject to this random disruption.

I told Mary Jane to make one of her Jockey Club lunch dates with Mrs. Reagan, tell her what was happening to Charlie, and ask that the prime White House suspect or suspects be told to knock it off. My suspicions must have been sound: After the lunch, the anti-Wick leaks ended with the suddenness of a guillotine drop. Charlie stayed. More than that, he gradually gained strength and support and was eventually lauded by previous U.S.I.A. directors, Democrats and Republicans, as one of the most creative, hands-on best in the agency's history.

Did this mean that the Wicks lived happily, politically speaking, ever after? Of course not; this was Washington, where the trauma of scandal breeds near-psychotic anxieties. After the public brouhaha subsided, Wick still had a continuing paranoid nightmare. He had been taping phone conversations for years. In storage, at U.S.I.A. and at home in Los Angeles, were hundreds, maybe thousands, of conversations—with persons living and dead, nonentities and celebrities like Frank Sinatra, song-pluggers, actors, agents, producers, tailors, Roto-Rooter salesmen, and supplicants of every description. Charlie had it indelibly in his mind that some investigating committee might want to trace the origins of his government taping, or that some private litigation might stir the matter up. He gathered the tapes together, and soon they were piled high in shopping bags in the Wick study.

I never met a man more inventive in imagining catastrophes, but Charlie did have a point: A subpoena of pre-government tapes could be used to embarrass him. So we took the next step: Was it legal to destroy the tapes?

Nixon redux. We met for a couple of evenings to discuss the issue, calmed by drafts of chilled vodka. Three of the four Wick daughters—lively, independent young women—joined in the family tape festival. I finally persuaded Charlie and Mary Jane that they had an absolute legal right to destroy the tapes: There was no proceeding pending, nobody had subpoenaed them or had reason to, and they were Charlie's personal property. I wrote a case-law-laden opinion letter to the Wicks, detailing the authoritative basis for their right to destroy the materials and categorically recommending that they do so.

Now the next question: how to destroy them. More conferences. We discussed a backyard bonfire, flying them out to sea by chartered plane and dumping them, depositing them in Capitol Hill trash baskets, electronic measures—but somehow, in these scenarios, some of the tapes always wound up back in the Wick living room. In the middle of one of these séances, Charlie and I were startled by the sound of Mary Jane screaming angrily in the nearby study. We ran in and saw her snatching a smoldering tape out of the fireplace. The Wick daughters, weary of the endless discussions, had taken the initiative and begun burning the stuff. Smoke filled the room. The stench was awful. Worse, the tapes were only slightly singed.

I ordered Charlie to take the damned things to U.S.I.A. in the morning and have one of the junior technicians electronically erase them. Done. But the technician, instead of throwing out the now-blank tapes, conscientiously delivered them back to Charlie. We still had them, along with Charlie's anxieties: Now he was concerned that there might be surviving snatches of talk on the tapes. I finally took the bagged blanks home and put them in the garbage.

So Wick came perilously close to the lifelong stain of expulsion from government for no good reason. Yet he was able to cling to the cliff's edge by his nails only because he and his wife had a special relationship with the Reagans. Anyone else would have been long gone. There have been not a few cases of this type since Watergate, and the ending has rarely been so benign as Charlie's was.

The following year, 1984, I found myself being interviewed in a borrowed Georgetown house by Ed Meese and his wife, Ursula. Meese was then attorney general–designate. He was also in trouble. His nomination had become the occasion for a flood of charges, in Congress and the press, about conflicts of interest, improper gifts, job awards to cronies, cover-ups of interest-free loans, and much more. The objective, of course, was to bar Meese's confirmation; but the momentum of the campaign against him had surged past the politically embarrassing into the realm of potential criminal liability.

When things reached this pass, Meese, portrayed in the press as an affable dummy, did something quite smart: He performed a type of scandal judo, turning the post-Watergate independent counsel statute against his tormentors by demanding an independent counsel investigation of himself. As a result, procedural whistles blew, the congressional and press barrage stopped, and Meese averted the sudden death of his candidacy. Now he had a due-process forum and some breathing space to organize a defense. The charges would be examined by a court-appointed counsel and professional staff, not by a school of congressional piranhas determined to eat him alive, whatever the facts.

Before meeting Meese, I shared the general Washington view of him as an apple-cheeked, right-wing, perpetually cheerful Orange County farmhand with a law degree. But my first conversation with Meese, while it confirmed his affability, also revealed a shrewd, calculating legal and political intelligence. I asked him whether there was any merit to the criminal charges against him. No, he said, flatly. Was he prepared to go the distance? Yes, he said, just as flatly. Meese asked me to represent him. I said yes.

We chose a strategy of full disclosure—or, rather, overwhelming disclosure. My alter-brains—Wallach, Peter Morgan, John Kotelly, Paul Stevens, and some young associates—divided into teams to answer the various allegations. Through the spring, summer, and fall of 1984, we assembled the evidentiary pieces into briefs and presented them separately to Stein and his staff. They questioned us like an appellate court en banc and gave no hint of their views. We could see that the suspicious aura surrounding each charge was dissipating.

But new allegations, thin as gruel, emerged periodically from Senators Edward Kennedy and Howard Metzenbaum via the press and threatened to preempt the independent counsel's investigation. I drafted a strongly worded letter to the Judiciary Committee on which Kennedy and Metzenbaum sat, demanding that the leaks and press events be stopped. We were, the letter reminded them, in the middle of a criminal investigation.

After Meese reviewed the draft, he asked me to come to his White House office. There a large crowd of people, including Meese, Wallach, and most of Meese's staff, was assembled. Many were scratching away at copies of my draft: "Line 3, paragraph 2, page 2, should read 'the outrageously political motives of . . .' "

"No, Tom, I think that's too heavy-handed. Let's try . . ."

I could feel my blood pressure rising with each off-the-mark comment, every one an uninformed suck-up to Meese. I also saw before me a reprise of the collective editing process that had helped destroy Nixon.

I asked Meese and Wallach into an adjoining office, where I announced that I intended to withdraw unless the collective editing stopped and never started again. Watergate, I said, taught me there is a client and a lawyer. You are the client and I am the lawyer. Otherwise, let's start looking for a replacement right away.

We went back to Meese's office. He told his staff he was satisfied with my draft. The group disbanded.

The independent counsel's report, when it finally appeared, did not find sufficient basis for an indictment of Meese on any charge. It had gone through seven back-breaking drafts, supervised by Stein, to achieve what he thought was a fair tone. Senator Kennedy announced publicly and, I thought, decently, "We've had our shot. Let's move on."

Nevertheless, the final vote on Meese's confirmation as attorney general was a cliffhanger, and his victory made possible mainly by the former senator and liberal Republican Jacob Javits. We learned early in the case that Javits was interested in helping us with it. The former giant of liberal politics was facing a slow, unpleasant death from amyotrophic lateral sclerosis, Lou Gehrig's disease. He needed grist for his churning, unimpaired intelligence, something to distract him from his twilight existence in a wheelchair surrounded by a web of tubes. Javits was a friend of mine from White House days. When I invited him to take part, he asked me to send Meese to see him. He would judge whether Meese had the competence to be attorney general; if so, he would help. They met in New York. Meese, as usual, benefited from the abysmally low expectations created by his press portraits. The two men, for a complex of personal and professional reasons, anything but political, liked each other. Occasionally, despite the harrowing physical difficulties, Javits came down to Washington to meet with Morgan and me to discuss the case.

Senator Charles "Mac" Mathias, a liberal Republican from Maryland, was a key vote against Meese, because he would carry others with him. After a long, private talk with his best congressional friend, Jack Javits, Mathias went off on an ocean cruise in late 1984. The Senate confirmed Meese in a squeaker, what can be described as the last of Javits's numberless acts of superb political management. It was no doubt done for the sheer survivor's hell of it. Javits died in Palm Beach not long after the confirmation.

When Richard Nixon was first elected president in 1968, he wanted me to be a Washington lawyer; the Meese proceeding made me one. I received a lot of publicity; as a result, I had interesting cases and got to see, as Mel Brooks would put it, the great and the near great.

During those years, through my old firm, Mudge Rose, I worked for Toshiba in an antitrust matter. An American company, Zenith, had charged Toshiba, Panasonic, and others with pricing their products artificially low in order to drive American companies out of the market. A district court had dismissed Zenith's claim, an appeals court had reversed, and now Toshiba wanted the Supreme Court to accept the case for review. The Court had asked the U.S. government for its position, which could be very influential. We wanted the government to support Toshiba's petition.

My colleagues, mostly New York antitrust lawyers, wanted to concentrate their persuasive efforts in familiar territory, the special trade representative's office and the Antitrust Division of the Justice Department. But I thought that in a matter involving U.S.-Japan diplomatic relations, the key person in our quest would be the undersecretary of state for economic affairs, Allen Wallis. Wallis, a former chancellor of the University of Rochester, was a strong supporter of free international markets, so he would be on our side on the merits. Moreover, his "boss," Secretary of State George Shultz, deferred to Wallis on international economic matters, out of both intellectual respect and historical gratitude: Wallis had recommended Shultz to be dean of the Business School at the University of Chicago, whence Shultz entered public life. So we went to visit Wallis. Acting as master of ceremonies, I introduced the case and called on the other lawyers to deliver assigned pieces of the argument. They poured it on. Wallis listened quietly, asked a few pointed questions.

I knew Wallis as a gentle man with a lively sense of humor. So in winding up the proceedings I started in the customary fashion ("Mr. Secretary, we appreciate your time and attention, blah, blah . . .") and then shifted to a more serious tone: "Remember, sir, you can Panasonic, but you shouldn't Nakasone." There was an isolated chuckle in the room. It was from Wallis, who had a broad smile on his face. "I'll keep that in mind, Mr. Garment," he said. The pun actually came from Charles Horner, a veteran Washingtonian and truly accomplished punster, who had made it up when I told him about the case. As we lawyers left Wallis's office, the fine young attorney for Panasonic was furious at me for taking his client's name in vain and trivializing a serious matter.

But Wallis recommended support for certiorari, Shultz concurred, and word was conveyed to the White House, which then instructed the Justice Department to support that position. The case was finally argued in the Supreme Court by my former assistant at Mudge Rose, Donald Zoeller, who had brought me into the matter. It resulted in a 5–4 decision that reduced predatory pricing doctrine to a shadow of its former self and saved our clients literally billions of dollars.

Not all my adventures in the Japan trade were so straightforward. My Mudge Rose colleagues soon called on me for another project: counseling Toshiba on a fast-breaking political and commercial catastrophe. The company had been accused by the U.S. government of unlawfully selling the Soviets a highly classified automated milling machine that produced ultra quiet submarine propellers, thus making Soviet nuclear subs harder to detect. In the wake of the charge, Senator Jake Garn of Utah had quickly gotten legislation moving to ban all of Toshiba's multibillion-dollar export sales to the United States. Congresswoman Helen Bently of Maryland had been nationally televised hammering a Toshiba radio to pieces on the steps of the Capitol. Disaster! Ruin! Hara-kiri!

The first meeting I attended on the Toshiba crisis was a mob scene in a vast conference room in New York, which was needed to accommodate what looked like 50 lawyers, 100 public relations persons, and 150 smiling Japanese vacationers on a tour of midtown Manhattan. The situation, it emerged, was not what the charges made it seem. The Toshiba subsidiary that delivered the forbidden goods was in fact not managed or controlled by the parent company. Moreover, the classified machinery involved was no longer secret: A French company had already breached the secrecy with sales of milling machinery to the Soviets.

Armed with these justifications, the teeming team of advisers around the conference-room table was Churchillian in its advice: Fight them on land, on sea, in the air, fight them on the beaches . . . I offered a contrary view: It was too late for an aggressive strategy. Yes, the company was not guilty as charged. But blaming things on the French was unlikely to deflect Jake Garn or neutralize the general protectionist, anti-Japanese sentiment in Congress. The momentum was already too powerful.

Instead, the company must accept responsibility for wrongdoing and apologize to America in full-page advertisements. They should set out all the exculpatory facts, but forget about pointing fingers at the French. The aim should be to slow down the rush to legislative judgment so a deal could be worked out with Congress and the Defense Department that would spare Toshiba and the thousands of U.S. companies and workers who would suffer from a flat trade ban.

I suspected going into the meeting that I could not count on my persuasive powers alone. So I brought along former National Security adviser Bud McFarlane. McFarlane met privately with the Japanese president of the company's American subsidiary and seconded the argument that it was not feasible to fight. The Toshiba executive respected Bud and had the imagination and courage to accept our recommendation. Within days the full-page ads were running across America. The aged, respected president of the company in Japan committed symbolic seppuku, resigning with abject apologies. Negotiating lines were opened to Congress and the Defense Department. From Cap Weinberger I solicited U.S. requests for Japanese defense-sharing commitments and for assistance by the government of Japan in furthering the co-production of Japanese aircraft. Toshiba moved the requests along with the Japanese government, and these acts of cooperation were fed into the discussions with congressional leaders. In the end, after three years of negotiations, Toshiba received a *de minimis* punishment amounting to a three-year ban on sales of its products at military PX's.

By taking this course, the president of the U.S. subsidiary, the son of a former Toshiba C.E.O. and a man who was slated for a leadership role in Japan, saved Toshiba vast sums. But he was dismissed from his post because of the loss of face his action was thought to have caused. With his firing, I stopped worrying that the Japanese would achieve economic dominance of the world.

Sometimes the cast of characters was more glamorous. One problem involved Fiat, the giant automobile company and conglomerate. In mid-May of 1986 Henry Kissinger phoned me and rumbled affably, "I have a small client for you. I know you'll forget this act of friendship when you're recommending advisers and writing your memoirs, so just do a decent job. It's Agnelli. A Fiat problem. You'll hear from a man named Furio Columbo today. He's Agnelli's man in America."

Columbo called in about an hour and came to Washington a day or two later. He was the president of Fiat America, not only as handsome as Marcello Mastroianni but a serious man, a commentator on American politics and culture for the Turin newspaper *La Stampa*. His mission was to look me over and explain the case. I and my partner, Michael Horowitz, apparently passed Furio's preliminary muster, because at the end of the meeting he asked me to visit Turin to meet Signor Agnelli, who insisted on personally approving outside attorneys retained to handle significant Fiat legal problems. And this one, like the Japanese propellers, was significant.

A U.S. boycott was in force against Libya, which President Muammar Qaddafi, the Strange One, had made a source of and sanctuary for the worst terrorist elements. But Libya owned a large block of Fiat stock. The U.S. government was unhappy about this, and proposals were afoot to prohibit Fiat's U.S. subsidiary from bidding on any U.S. defense business. Qaddafi, for his part, had no desire to sell his profitable interest in Fiat. I was supposed to come up with a solution.

Suzi and I, with our five-year-old daughter, Annie, had been planning a spring vacation, and we decided to use a couple of days of it to visit Gianni Agnelli in Turin. We found him more than imposing. His face was pure Roman, his close-cropped white hair and deep tan accentuating the classic features. He looked like a man who could order a coffee or a death sentence and get equally speedy performance. So I prepared for a difficult hour. I was seated next to him, with Suzi on his other side. Agnelli exchanged greetings with me and said that Kissinger had spoken generously of my work. Then he turned to Suzi—with whom he conversed for the rest of the lunch. Agnelli, no doubt the beneficiary of Furio's good staff work, had read the obituary Suzi had written in *The Wall Street Journal* of our friend Theodore White. Agnelli had also known White well, but —as I would discover, was usual with him—he wanted to know more, more, digging for every insight he could extract.

I tried discussing worker-management relations with my other luncheon partner, Fiat's C.E.O., Cesare Romiti, known for his muscular labor policy; but he politely offered information on the best out-of-the-way museums in southern France. At the end of the lunch Agnelli rose, shook my hand, and wished me well on the Libya matter. Maybe he figured that if I had enough brains to marry well I couldn't be too much of a risk.

From Turin, we were to travel via Fiat jet to Rome for dinner with the U.S. ambassador, Max Rabb, whose son Bruce and daughter-in-law Harriet had worked for me in the White House. Agnelli's wife, Marella, was going to hitch a ride with us. But first we had to get to the airport. We were belted into a superheated Lancia. Preceded and followed by police cars, sirens screaming, we zigged and zagged through traffic and red lights to the Italian autostrada like the drivers in *The French Connection*. Then the driver gunned it. At speeds exceeding 120 miles an hour, we quickly reached the police-guarded airport gates—then, slowing to about 80 (pulse 140), rolled through them. More police, with Uzi-type rapid-fire weapons, swarmed around the Fiat hangar. What, I finally asked, was going on? Someone explained there was great fear that Agnelli or his family or senior executives would be kidnapped. So everything was done in a rush, at high speeds, without notice, and accompanied by lots of police, guns, and noise. "You're lucky," he said. "If Agnelli himself was going to Rome with you, he would be driving, only faster, with one hand on the back of his seat, occasionally glancing at the highway while chatting with you and your wife."

There was something wrong with the air-conditioning on the jet we were going to use, so another jet was wheeled up. Annie fell asleep, covered by Mrs. Agnelli's leather-and-mink Hermès blanket. Hoo hah.

After all that, I actually had to do some work on the Fiat matter. Weinberger handed me the key to the solution. He was in Lisbon, at dinner with Frank Shakespeare, who had become the U.S. ambassador to Portugal, when I called to tell him I was on the case and asked for a general road map. Weinberger remembered a structure he had once assembled when he was in private practice that segregated profits from a particular subsidiary and spun them off to a separate corporation. Why don't you work with that? he said. We did, creating a corporate structure to collect and freeze all funds that might result in dividend distributions to Libya while allowing distributions to other shareholders.

Qaddafi may be crazy, but he knows when he's been had. After a decent interval and a short negotiation, Libya sold its Fiat shares to Fiat.

In the late 1980s I was involved in my most publicly important cases. I also came close to professional and physical obliteration.

Bud McFarlane came to my home on a Sunday in November 1986, shortly after his mission to Tehran had been disclosed in the Lebanese newspaper *Al Shiraa*. That morning, Bud had been notified by phone that the investigating committee chaired by Senator David Durenberger of Minnesota had served a subpoena on him at his office. The subpoena ordered him to appear and testify about the Iran matter—the next day, Monday.

The first thing I did was to call Durenberger and ask what the rush was about. "Well, you know, Len," he said affably, "we're in a race for the roses"—i.e., the cameras—"with the House." Then I called Peter Morgan. He came over, and we began a review of McFarlane's Iran tale. McFarlane was absolutely confident that he had no criminal exposure. So, he said, "I have no problem going up tomorrow." I consulted with criminal lawyers in my firm, who said that under no circumstance should I permit McFarlane to testify before we had made a preliminary review of the documents involved and considered possible pleas under the Fifth Amendment (self-incrimination) and Sixth Amendment (right to consult with counsel). But Bud was having none of this. He said he would not assert any constitutional privilege under any circumstances. He wanted no motions made to delay his appearance. He said, "I have a duty as a public official to explain promptly what happened. I don't have the slightest problem with the facts." The three of us went back and forth for a while, then returned to going over Bud's Iran story, which was crisp, straightforward, and exculpatory.

At one point Peter Wallison, counsel to the president, called. He assumed, he said, that McFarlane was not going to testify on Monday. Wrong, I replied. Wallison was astonished. From that point on, he later told me, White House strategy in the Iran affair, soon to become Iran-*contra*, was shaped by the need to respond to McFarlane's testimony. For some members of the White House staff—particularly Don Regan, who had already used defamation as a tactic to force Bud out of office—the strategy was simply to blame everything in Iran-*contra* on McFarlane.

While Shultz, Weinberger, Regan, and the president distanced themselves from the proceedings, Oliver North and John Poindexter proceeded to take the Fifth, and Bill Casey died. So Bud was the only newsworthy figure available to the congressional committees and press for months. He became the all-purpose witness—and, with Don Regan's energetic sponsorship, the White House's designated scapegoat. He wound up being ferried back and forth between the Senate and the House and eventually the independent counsel and the Tower Commission. All these bodies worked overtime to produce piles of documents that refreshed McFarlane's recollection of some detail or other of the story, none crucial but each one enough to raise questions and produce headlines for editors who were utterly indifferent to the fairness of the coverage.

Thus McFarlane bore the brunt of the scandal publicity and unfairly came to epitomize the whole Iran-*contra* mess. He was already exhausted and wound tight as a watch spring from his efforts to move U.S. foreign policy forward in the critical U.S.-Soviet sphere, his attempts to mediate the constant feuding between

Shultz and Weinberger, and, finally, the stress of his resignation. McFarlane came to feel personally responsible for the consequences of the Iran initiative and the lost opportunities in other areas of foreign policy. He fell into a severe clinical depression, whose power was such that he thought he could make amends and force national attention back to his basic foreign-policy goals—such as gaining the decisive strategic advantage over the Soviets, which he had done much to achieve—by committing suicide. His February 1987 suicide note to me included other notes, laying out his foreign-policy views, to be delivered to congressional leaders and a journalist friend.

I was in McFarlane's office when I learned about his suicide attempt from a press call; Vice President Bush, extremely upset, called me minutes later. He and McFarlane were good friends, and he asked me to keep him advised of McFarlane's condition. Ross Perot also made an early call. He asked permission to come and see McFarlane and offered him all kinds of quiet help over the next months.

Nixon phoned McFarlane's wife, Jonny, the day after the suicide attempt and said he wanted to see McFarlane as soon as the doctors gave permission. He was McFarlane's first visitor. He arrived from New York alone and quietly, saw McFarlane for an hour or so, and went back home just as quietly. McFarlane later said that Nixon's opening was unforgettable: "Bud, I've been just where you were. You've accomplished great things on nuclear weapons—not Kissinger, not Reagan, but you. You coordinated two talented misfits, Cap and Shultz, and got something done. You're not the first or last to go through this kind of thing. Just rest up—and get rid of the shrinks."

The most memorable thing about Nixon's visit, McFarlane said, was that "for the first time, he looked me straight in the eyes." This, I know, took some effort. My guess is that Doctor Nixon wanted to do whatever was necessary to drive his message home. Perhaps he also felt a sense of kinship with McFarlane, who was now a member of the society of the shipwrecked.

Bud made a gradual recovery, the reward for which was that he was soon back testifying before the various investigating committees. The independent counsel appointed to investigate Iran-*contra*,

Lawrence Walsh, eventually made known that he would require McFarlane to plead guilty to a felony; otherwise, he would indict him, charging him with multiple felonies. McFarlane, Morgan, and I were astounded. McFarlane had testified quickly and fully. The mistakes in his testimony were minor, attributable to his testifying promptly and continuously, before documents were available to aid his recollection. The charges that were contemplated against him, which involved lying to Congress, were based on earlier testimony before Congress, which had not been given under oath; charging him would be unprecedented and legally dubious. We knew Walsh's hard-line stance was the result of pressure from his senior staff.

Weeks of briefs and contentious arguments followed. Then two fortunate things happened. First, Walsh brought in a new staff assistant named Chris Todd to make an independent evaluation of the case. Todd was a Texan, with excellent prosecutor's credentials from his service in the Southern District of New York. He also had a sense of humor and human proportion. Second, I left for Hawaii to attend a bar conference and get my temper out of everybody's hair. I had taken to screaming obscenities at Walsh, which was not good for McFarlane or me. I left Morgan in charge. When I got back, Walsh had come down to misdemeanors—which, though not perfect, was 179 degrees better than felonies. McFarlane was still unhappy, tossing the issue of pleading or not pleading from one hand to the other. He finally agreed to accept misdemeanor charges, hating every bit of the decision. A date was set for Walsh and McFarlane to sign the plea agreement and close the case.

Suddenly McFarlane disappeared from my radar screen. Then I got a message from his assistant, Caroline Scullin: "Bud wants you to cancel the meeting with Walsh. All bets are off." I couldn't get McFarlane on the phone, but it was worse than that. Suzi and I were remodeling a house we had just bought. In the interim, we—Suzi, Annie, Lola the ninety-pound golden retriever, and I—were living in the basement of the McFarlanes' Georgetown house. We thought it would be a few weeks; it stretched into months. So not only couldn't I get McFarlane on the phone; I could hear the phone ringing, unanswered, upstairs, along with his feet thumping back and forth as he paced off his rage at having to plead to crimes he knew he hadn't committed.

Then I picked up a crucial piece of information: The day before the signals were switched, McFarlane had gone to New York on some mission. On a hunch, I called Henry Kissinger in New York and Richard Nixon in New Jersey: Did McFarlane happen to visit them to get advice about his plea? Yes. Both men had met with him and told him to fight the charges. Kissinger said he did so because it was outrageous to yield another inch of ground to those congressional bastards and add still more to the paralysis of U.S. foreign policy. I laid out the potentially grave consequences for McFarlane. Kissinger said, "Look, that's your department. I told Bud what I thought he should do. For him to let himself be made into a criminal by Congress and Walsh is insane." Kissinger thought Iran-*contra* another infuriating episode in the American retreat from responsibility. He refused to play sentimental games or discuss lawyers' concerns.

With Nixon it was different. He was restrained, even sheepish, when we spoke, saying, "I thought Bud wanted to be told to fight." I explained the legal nightmare McFarlane faced if he was charged with multiple felonies. Nixon said the analysis made sense, and he hadn't known enough to give a prudent opinion. The best thing, I said, would be for Nixon to speak to McFarlane again. Nixon said he would do it first thing the next morning: "I'll call him about some Chinese stuff we left hanging, and then I'll tell him I had second thoughts about his plea." Then, just as the words were forming in my mouth, Nixon added, "And don't worry, Len. I won't tell him you called me."

My telephone line to McFarlane opened the next day. The canceled meeting with Walsh was rescheduled, and the plea agreement was worked out.

Around this time, I became sick with something more serious than back trouble or big-case exhaustion. I had been having a lot of stubborn colds and flus, then fainting spells. I went through various blood tests, bone marrow studies, and CAT-scans, and was told that I had chronic lymphocytic leukemia. I probably had five years.

At first I wasn't as alarmed or depressed as I thought I would be. This is one of the blessings of lifelong hypochondria: The disease itself is nowhere as bad as the anticipation of it. I also began experiencing good things more vividly, trying to disregard trivial annoyances, and focusing more on the family, especially Annie, our beautiful, bright, five-year-old.

But over time, the anxieties of the disease began to generate increasingly splenetic behavior. I experienced an angry mania, with all the attendant symptoms: excitement, irritability, sleeplessness, tremendous bursts of energy. I couldn't find enough things to do. My energy produced successes at work, but when I took on a case, it quickly became a cause, then an obsession. I not only felt I had to win but was sure I would.

The summer and fall of 1987 were among the busiest of my life. They included the "silent submarine" case, a potential criminal antitrust proceeding against a large American corporation, Iran-contra, Agnelli and Fiat, the defense of Woody Herman against eviction proceedings, meeting with South African businessmen on a deal for Nelson Mandela's release, and more. Particularly satisfying were the meetings that Suzi and I had with Avital Sharansky, as part of the effort to get her husband, Natan Sharansky, released from a Soviet prison.

This continuous collection of cases, hearings, social occasions, and such came to a halt in early October. From then until October 28, my calendar entries say, almost exclusively, "Bork." In our family and in my old law firm, that period is known as the time I went crazy.

On July 1, President Reagan nominated Robert Bork, then a judge on the U.S. Court of Appeals for the District of Columbia, to the Supreme Court. Twice before, Bork had been passed over for tactical reasons. Now it was his turn, and the liberal interest groups prepared for total war.

Right after Justice Lewis Powell's resignation, toward the end of June, Jeffrey Blattner, a Judiciary Committee staff aide to Senator Edward Kennedy and a student of law professor Lawrence Tribe, prepared a statement that Kennedy could use if and when Bork was named to the Court. One hour after Reagan made his announcement, Kennedy delivered the statement, accusing Bork of favoring back-alley abortions for women, segregated lunch counters for blacks, and police without warrants making nighttime raids on private citizens. Thus was launched the dirtiest opposition campaign in Supreme Court history.

I first met Bork when I was in the Nixon White House. While there, I often called the Yale law professor Alex Bickel for advice. Bickel, a Democrat, suggested that the Republicans start harvesting their own academic advisers, of which there were many of high quality. He offered as examples Professors Robert Bork and Ralph Winter of Yale. I discussed this with Ehrlichman. Before long, Bork was solicitor general, and Winter was named to the Second Circuit Court of Appeals.

Bork and his wife, Claire, and Grace and I became friends. Bork and I enjoyed the essentials of a comfortable relationship: We smoked, talked, and laughed a lot, and drank very dry martinis, straight up. We did not often discuss constitutional issues. For one thing, I didn't know much. For another, my range of legal responsibilities in the White House was limited, comprising mainly civil rights and civil liberties. On these, Bork was my ally. When he was nominated to the Supreme Court, I assumed his confirmation would be a breeze. I was amazed, then alarmed, as his well-organized enemies slandered him to a pulp and the White House put up a lousy defense. The "practical" conservatives in the Reagan administration started pushing Bork to withdraw and putting out word to the press that he was preparing to quit, which undermined whatever chance he had.

I asked Bork for permission to deny that he was planning to withdraw. He said I could do this, but he did not want to conduct a campaign. I entered the shadowland of being Bork's authorized-unauthorized advocate. Suzi was as angry as I was. A day or two before the Judiciary Committee was to vote, she wrote a full-page substantive advertisement detailing the falsities in the campaign against Bork.

On October 6, the Judiciary Committee, in an orgy of sanctimony, voted against the nomination, 9–5. Now it would go to the full Senate—unless Bork withdrew. He was inclined to do so.

All the life-and-death uncertainties of my frenetic year, plus the abysmally unfair course of the Bork proceedings, produced in me the largest manic explosion of my recurrently manic life. I was determined to drop everything else and take up his fight. The first step, obviously, was to persuade him not to withdraw.

The evening of October 7, I called Bork. On the pretext that my son, Paul, home on holiday from orchestra work in South Africa, wanted to say hello, I said we'd like to come over. Bork was depleted and depressed but said okay. When we got there, the Bork family was sitting around, grimly winding up the debate on the issue of withdrawal. Bork was rumpled, haggard, hoarse, and less than happy to see me. I accepted a drink, persuaded him to join me, and launched into my spiel. Ethan Bronner's fine account of the Bork fight, *Battle for Justice*, pretty accurately summarizes the way I "harangued" Bork to stay in. Principles were at stake. Pulling out would legitimize the distortions and let the liars off the hook. I finally got up to leave, and Bork said he would think about it.

The next day, between breakfast and dinner, Bork decided to stand and fight. His family, it turned out, was not composed of quitters. They thought he should take his case to the full Senate, make a record, and force them to vote. Senator Alan Simpson called to say he now shared the view of the conservative senators who wanted Bork to stay the course. Simpson promised that he and his colleagues would offer history an honest picture of Bork and of his opponents.

Bork announced his decision. "A crucial principle is at stake," he said. "The principle is the way in which we select the men and women who guard the liberties of all the American people." With this, I began my unbecoming public struggle to reverse what my rational self knew was irreversible. I went on all the available TV and radio shows, gave interviews to everyone who asked, called those who didn't ask, buttonholed senators, and generally carried on like a man possessed. One day at ABC-TV I was waiting to do an interview about Bork; my companion was the Washington lawyer Robert Strauss, one of the wisest and most decent political men in modern Washington history, who was being interviewed on another subject. Strauss said, "Nice try, Len, but I hope you know it's hopeless." I harrumphed my disagreement. Strauss harrumphed back. "I wish you luck, son, but I'll buy you the biggest steak in Washington if you shift one vote. Those guys have made all their arrangements, and every vote is set in concrete."

The best part of the struggle was what I found when I started assembling a collection of pro-Bork volunteers. Michigan's Republican party chairman, Spencer Abraham, now a U.S. senator, became our political strategist, fund-raiser, and advertising coordinator. Judge Griffin Bell, Jimmy Carter's attorney general, and Carla Hills, who had been an assistant attorney general, H.U.D. secretary, and special trade representative, joined me in creating the Committee to Safeguard the Supreme Court Confirmation Process.

A day or two after Bork's announcement, I got a call from Mike Armstrong, a leading New York trial lawyer. I knew him only by reputation: He had been an assistant U.S. attorney and counsel to the Knapp Commission, which investigated and prosecuted New York police corruption. Armstrong "asked in" on the Bork campaign, as he put it, and did so memorably (here in a sanitized version): "This is the goddamdest thing I ever saw. I don't know Bork and I don't know that I agree with his decisions, but he's obviously qualified. What burns me most is that cheesy Irish fraud Kennedy, and the way he slandered Bork to start the campaign against him. If those charges were true, Bork should be in the slammer, not on the Supreme Court. And Kennedy, that bum, still gets away with it. Okay. What can I do to help?"

"Come to Washington right away," I said. He did. Armstrong was massively large, Irish, an intellectual street fighter, who looked just the way he sounded on the phone. We agreed that he would enlist a group of qualified New York appellate lawyers to rebut the negative report on Bork's decisions that had just been issued by the Senate Judiciary Committee's majority. I would get these "white papers" into the hands of every senator.

Mike lined up an extraordinarily high-quality bunch of New York lawyers who gave nights and weekends to analyzing and meticulously shredding the majority report. I attended a meeting on October 17 of the Second Circuit Judicial Conference, in Hershey, Pennsylvania, where I made a speech and circulated a petition drafted by Suzi denouncing the politicization of the Supreme Court nominating process. Twenty-three federal district court judges signed it; more would have but for Chief Judge Wilfred Fineberg's order to court of appeals judges not to take part.

It was, as Strauss predicted, a losing battle. By the time the Senate debate began, most senators saw it as pro forma. We were trying to extend it through the end of the week, so that we would have the time we needed to complete and distribute the white papers to the senators and persuade any who were open to documented persuasion. But, the story goes, Bork and his family threw in the towel on Thursday, Senator Simpson told me the news Thursday evening, I cried on his shoulder in weary frustration, the vote took place Friday, and that was that.

Except that neither Bork nor his family really tossed in the towel on Thursday.

After Simpson told me Thursday night that Bork had quit, and I recovered from my crying jag, I was rather peeved that Bork had failed to do me and a dozen distinguished volunteer lawyers the courtesy of telling us what he had planned to do. And I was puzzled: That was not the way Bork behaved, no matter how tired or depressed he was. I called his house repeatedly from a Senate phone. No answer. Finally, around nine or ten o'clock, the Borks got home from dinner and Bob answered the phone.

He said, "What's up?" I said, "Why didn't you warn me you were packing it in, so I wouldn't be up here making a goddamn fool of myself?"

"What are you talking about?" he said.

"The Republicans just announced they wanted a vote tomorrow because that's what you and the family wanted."

"That's absolutely untrue," he said. "Simpson called me to say Byrd was threatening to pull the nomination off this year's calendar if the debate dragged on. I said I wanted to get my full case on the record but not hang up the whole process. It's within the power of the leadership to call it quits, but I didn't tell anyone I wanted a vote tomorrow. This is the first I've heard of it."

Bork said that if the press called, he would confirm this account.

Now I had to figure out whom to call with the story. I phoned Marty Tolchin of *The New York Times*, who outlined the drill: "Call the Washington bureau. They'll put you in touch with Craig Whitney, who's bureau chief. There's time to catch the next deadline." By now, the police had politely escorted me out of the Senate, and I found myself in the middle of a very cold night on Capitol Hill. The first two phones I tried were broken. I finally found one that worked, reached Whitney at home, and told him the long story. He listened patiently, asked for my phone number, and said he would check with the reporter on the story.

That would be Linda Greenhouse. She had been annoyed, justifiably so, by the way I was pounding around the Senate pressroom in my efforts to rouse interest in the moribund Bork nomination. She had also been pronouncedly anti-Bork in her coverage. But I thought this was a matter on which her professionalism had to win out. Whitney called back and told me what Greenhouse said: Her story accurately reported what she had heard from the Republican leadership before she filed. She would stay with the story as she had filed it.

Didn't she want to talk to Bork? Apparently not.

Long after midnight, I reached home. I called *The Washington Post*, but they couldn't find my pal Bradlee—or he wisely refused to wake up. I woke Meg Greenfield, the *Post*'s editorial page editor, and started, like the Ancient Mariner, to tell my story again. Meg wearily interrupted. "It's three A.M. and I have to write my *Newsweek* piece tomorrow, so please, for the love of God, just go away." Now that I am cold sober and certifiably sane, I am still appalled by the corruption of the legislative process that denied Bork his seat on the Court. But there were costs to this campaign.

The Monday after the vote, my friend and partner, David Shapiro, came into my office. "Mind if I say something you're not going to want to hear?"

"Sure," I sighed. "You'll tell me anyway."

"You've hurt yourself badly with this Bork business," he said. "I was with Bork and with you. I don't think you were crazy, the way a lot of people have been saying. But you looked unreliable—a zealot, not a prudent Washington lawyer. It was as if you forgot everything you ever knew. It's going to take a lot to get it back."

Shapiro was right. After Bork, new business stopped calling. Some old clients faded away. I became a shopping center for human-rights cases. Yet somehow I can't bring myself to feel much regret. Besides, as I calmed down, clients returned. Business picked up again. (Washington, despite what people say, can be a forgiving place —or do they simply forget?) And there was a happy medical ending to the leukemia story. In late 1987, after a second evaluation, a doctor at the National Institutes of Health concluded that what I had was not chronic lymphocytic leukemia but a rare, treatable condition unpleasantly named "hairy cell leukemia." My data and I were shipped to Chicago to see Harvey Golomb, the nation's hairy cell maven, who recommended treatment with Interferon. After a year, the disease went into remission.

In and among the cases and crises, events kept returning me to the issue of the Mideast. One day in late 1985 I was at lunch at the restaurant downstairs in my office building when my secretary called me to the phone. "A bunch of Israeli officials are here," she said, "and they want to see you right away."

Had I forgotten to return the rented car in Tel Aviv? I went upstairs and found what looked like half the Israeli foreign-affairs apparatus pacing the firm's reception area. When they stopped circling, I made out Meir Rosenne, Israel's ambassador to the United States; Eliakim Rubinstein, Rosenne's deputy chief of mission; former ambassador and cabinet minister without portfolio (i.e., chief troubleshooter) Moshe Arens; Hanan Bar-On, a senior official in the Israeli foreign ministry, and two strangers. One was small and dumpy—probably a bureaucrat. The other was natty and self-important—undoubtedly a lawyer.

In my office I learned that the subject of this visit was the spy Jonathan Pollard, whose case had erupted a couple of weeks before. What I knew of the story came from media accounts: Pollard, an employee of U.S. Naval Intelligence and a Jew, had been charged with supplying large amounts of classified information to Israel.

Arens started bluntly, "We need some off-the-record advice." The Jerusalem-based members of my group of visitors had just arrived in Washington, and the whole contingent was headed for an emergency meeting with Secretary of State George Shultz. What guidance would I give? How bad was the U.S. government atmosphere? The American Jewish atmosphere? What tack should they take with Shultz?

Arens asserted that Pollard's operation had not been authorized by senior Israeli authorities. I got a similar assurance from Ram Caspi, the man who looked like a lawyer and turned out to be one. I trusted Arens but not Caspi, who was clearly the Jerusalem version of a Washington insider. I learned later that he was reputed to be Prime Minister Shimon Peres's closest political adviser; I could see that he was a tricky blusterer, wrong on most of the technical issues we discussed.

The other stranger, when I asked his name, said smilingly, "Call me Avraham." He turned out to be Avraham Shalom, chief of Shin Bet, Israel's hard-fisted domestic counterpart to the Mossad. Shalom was later relieved of duty for his role in the beating to death of two Palestinian terrorists in Israeli custody.

Since I had no facts, I gave general advice: The reaction was bad, especially among Jews. More facts had to be known. More detailed expressions of regret and acts of repair were needed. Most important, I said: No cover-up. Don't try to bamboozle Shultz. He'll find out, and he will be unforgiving.

But surely, I thought, experienced diplomats could figure this out without my help. So I made a more practical offer: "Why don't I call Abe Sofaer and ask if he'll see you before your meeting with Shultz? That way you'll get guidance from someone who knows something." Sofaer was a former federal judge whom I had recommended to Shultz for the post of legal adviser to the State Department; he had come to function as the secretary's trusted private counsel.

Sofaer came right over. Should I stay? I asked. No, he said. And that, I thought, was that.

Soon a communiqué from the two countries suggested that all would be well.

Then, in May 1986, the Justice Department disclosed that Pollard had revealed the name of his Israeli contact in the U.S.—who had apparently played, contrary to Israeli representations, a major role in the affair. The *Los Angeles Times* quoted the comment of one U.S. official: "The Israelis lied to us." The Israeli that Pollard had named was an Air Force colonel named Aviam Sella.

In a country filled with exceptional soldiers, Sella was particularly exceptional. He had planned and led the Israeli bombing raid that destroyed the Iraqi nuclear reactor at Osirak. He did the same in the air battle that took place after Syria emplaced surface-to-air missile sites in Lebanon. Sella was now scheduled to take command of a major air base in the Negev and was among the handful of officers thought to be on track for eventual command of the Israeli Air Force, the spine of the country's defense.

Sella, it turned out, had been in the United States taking an advanced computer course at New York University when a mutual friend had introduced him to Pollard. Pollard said he wanted to supply classified information to Israel. Sella passed Pollard's proposal to Rafi Eitan, head of Israel's scientific intelligence unit, who authorized the transfer of documents.

It later became clear why the Israelis had tried to keep Sella's name out of the investigation: U.S. intelligence experts would have known that if an officer of his importance was involved in the operation, it would never have taken place without high-level approval.

The United States threatened to indict Sella but offered to await a formal proffer of evidence from him. The Israelis decided that Sella needed American counsel. His Israeli counsel, Chaim Zadok, a former minister of justice who was also Sella's father-in-law, retained me. I flew to Tel Aviv.

Zadok met me at Ben-Gurion Airport and took me to his comfortable home in Tel Aviv for lunch. Aviam Sella was there; so was his brother Menachem, a law partner of Zadok's and a co-counsel in Sella's case. As I'd somehow expected, Aviam was a Central Casting Sabra: dark, slender, and handsome, with the lines and shadows of intense combat concentration visibly etched under his tan. He seemed helpful, friendly, modest, crisply responsive, and more or less at ease, except for his acute annoyance that the tensions of the pending legal hassle had sent him back to smoking. We chatted about Israeli security, U.S. politics, mutual friends, and my earlier experiences in Israel. By the time we were finished, we were comfortable with each other.

After lunch, when we began to discuss the case, the atmosphere stiffened perceptibly. Zadok conceded Pollard's initial contacts with Sella and Sella's transmitting Pollard's offer to Eitan, but insisted that all of Sella's other contacts with Pollard were casual, social, and coincidental. The legal task, Zadok thought, was to work this version of events into a formal proffer to the Justice Department, one convincing enough to persuade Justice to drop the probe of Sella or grant him immunity.

At the Tel Aviv Hilton, I was summoned to a large meeting—composed mostly of security officials and presided over by one of Peres's political advisers—to discuss the case. They spoke Hebrew. I pointed out that I did not speak Hebrew. They continued speaking

Hebrew. I left. Back in my room, I read a John le Carré novel, *A Perfect Spy*. I realized that I had problems with my own spy dilemma. The Justice Department's version of events was detailed, logical, and accompanied by corroboration. The conflicts between it and the Zadok version were stark. I could play it safe and assume a messenger's role. I could wade in to learn what had happened; but if I then concealed what I knew, I risked committing an obstruction of justice. So I settled on a course that made sense to me as an American, a friend of Israel, and—as the reader knows by now—a fairly nervous person. I had worked closely with most of the people who would play roles in disposing of the case—Meese; Shultz; the State Department legal adviser, Abraham Sofaer; the U.S. ambassador to Israel, Tom Pickering; and almost all the Israeli political leadership. So I would learn what I could, then try to use the political process, rather than legal means, to achieve a comprehensive solution. Zadok agreed.

The next afternoon, Aviam and Menachem Sella spent most of the day in my room. Later, halfway through dinner, Menachem excused himself to go home, saying, "He's all yours." This was the first time I had been left alone with Sella, who then told me most of what had actually happened. After dinner I returned to my room and wrote out, in red ink on yellow paper, everything I remembered of Aviam's account.

I pursued my political grail. Each day I conferred with Abe Sofaer by phone and with Ambassador Pickering in person. Sofaer and Pickering told me what they thought was needed to work out a political settlement. One potential formula would be an admission, even an oblique one, without naming names, that there had been high-level Israeli knowledge of the goings-on.

I spent a couple of hours with Defense Minister Rabin in his Tel Aviv apartment. We had coffee and nostalgia; then I delivered my spiel. Rabin, his voice a familiar, hoarsely impatient grumble, acknowledged that the conflicting versions were a problem. Then he offered me one of his shrugs. He knew nothing about any high-level Israeli authorization to Sella to deal with Pollard. How about some more coffee? The same scene, with the same dialogue, took place at Moshe Arens's home. More coffee.

At least with Prime Minister Peres, late that night, I got some food. Mrs. Peres, in a housecoat, greeted me at the door and put out a huge cream cake, coffee, and brandy before she left the room. Peres followed my narration with professional attentiveness but could not help. Halfway through the brandy, he began a learned monologue comparing Russian, Israeli, and American literature; the name Isaac Babel stands out in my alcohol-blurred memory. As for my proposed settlement, he thought it was not realistic, but there was no harm in my trying. I said I would send him a memo expanding on the idea and a draft statement he might issue.

I didn't try to see General Ariel Sharon, which was a big mistake: Rafi Eitan was Sharon's protégé.

When I got home to Washington, I conferred with Attorney General Meese, then sent Peres the draft statement I had promised. The note dropped into a deep well, and I never even heard a splash.

In June 1986, Zadok and company arrived in Washington with a new proffer for Justice and State. I met with Zadok in the bar of the Mayflower Hotel to take a look at the current model. It was identical to the draft I had read and rejected in Israel. I protested once more, but Zadok remained adamant; he was almost certainly bound by official instructions. "Enough," he said. "We'll be in touch with you over the weekend."

The meeting with State and Justice would take place Monday, and by then we had to come up with an explanation for the inexplicable. Working alone, I modified Zadok's proffer. Little was untouched.

We finally had our meeting on Sunday at my home. The Israeli contingent that grimly trooped in consisted mostly of friends: Ambassador Rosenne, Elie Rubinstein, Hanoch Bar-On. Zadok was there and Ram Caspi may also have been; if he was, he stayed in the background this time. I handed around my suggested draft of the proffer. I was overruled; the Zadok draft would stand. I said I wouldn't present it: It was demonstrably false, and the U.S. prosecutors could prove it.

The argument grew more heated. How, said the Israelis, did I know the "facts" in my version of the proffer? What made me so sure? I took out the handwritten memorandum of my dinner conversation with Sella in Tel Aviv and read it aloud. They reacted memorably:

THEM: Give us that paper.
ME: You must be kidding.
THEM: You have no right to it.
ME: These are my personal notes.

Zadok asked me to leave the room for a few minutes. When he brought me back in, they announced a solution:

THEM: You are discharged as Aviam's counsel. Now give us
       the paper.
ME: I have a lawyer's lien on it. I also have photocopies in my
    office. If you don't stop this, you're getting out of here.

After a while, peace was restored. Zadok said he would go to work on a new draft. Suzi brought in the second meal of the day for the group. At the beginning of the meeting, they stopped talking when Suzi came in. They knew she was a journalist. But stereotypes die hard; after all, she was wearing an apron. By the end of the day she was typing and fiddling with Zadok's rewrite in our study upstairs.

The "new" draft, though, was just a transparent gloss on the old one. I arranged to postpone the proffer meeting with Justice and State, saying that we just weren't ready. At a pro forma meeting, the Israelis said they had to go back to Israel to consult on specific issues of fact and get wider authority to proffer security-sensitive details. We then celebrated the absence of catastrophe with a lavish lunch. The Israelis, manifestly relieved, went home.

In due course, Zadok and I made up. But the settlement never materialized. I withdrew from the case, waiving any fees. Actually, "withdrew" is not an accurate term; throughout the proceedings, I realized, I had never functioned as Sella's attorney. I was hired to be a prop in a political contest entirely directed by political players. A proffer was eventually made. Sella was indicted. Under U.S. pressure, Israel canceled his base command. He remained in Israel; his indictment is still outstanding.

There was a time when I worked for Pollard's release; there is little doubt that his life sentence was excessive and obtained by dubious prosecutorial tactics. Then, in 1994, at Pollard's request, I

CRAZY RHYTHM / 375

visited him at Buttner Penitentiary in North Carolina. It was the first time we had met. I saw a dazed, disturbed, prison-stunted man, enfolded in his spy case like a conspiracy fanatic, largely unable to give a straightforward account, fully capable of contradicting himself on critical issues a dozen times during an hour of soliloquies. I thought what I had seen must have been the result of personality disintegration brought about by his imprisonment. But when I reported what I had seen to people who had known him—classmates, colleagues at work, friends—they said he had been basically the same personality before he went to jail.

This discovery did not change my view of the Pollard sentence. But Pollard is not a martyr; he was and is a fantasist. He used the rhetoric of Jewish righteousness as a mask for the adolescent excitement of spying. He violated his obligations under American law and his responsibilities to other Jews. He received and spent spy pay. He divulged names and acts almost as soon as he was caught.

Were Israeli leaders right to use Pollard despite the risks of harm to American Jews and U.S.-Israel relations? The answer simply depends on the value of the purloined information to a nation always at war. I don't know enough even to guess whether it was worth it; only a few Israelis do. But if Israeli leaders showed a lack of enthusiasm for sending a soldier like Sella to drag Pollard off the battlefield, it is hard to fault them.

Sometimes dealing with U.S.-Israel relations was more satisfying, as it was when I represented a young girl named Tali Griffel. It began in tragedy. On October 3, 1985, after the return of the Sinai peninsula to Egypt, a group of Israeli tourists arrived after dark at Ras Burqa in the Sinai for a four-day camping trip. One afternoon, as the tourists climbed a dune to watch the sunset, an Egyptian policeman named Mohammed Abdel Khater suddenly, without provocation or warning, started shooting at them. One of the children shot was Tali Griffel, six years old, who was on the camping trip with her mother, Anita. Tali sustained a flesh wound in her back from ricocheting shrapnel. Anita Griffel was shot twice in the back, one bullet exiting her stomach. She covered Tali with her body, holding her on the ground and instructing her not to talk or move. The Egyptian military police, in a panic, would not allow medical personnel to administer to the wounded. Anita shielded and reassured Tali for about two hours, until she lost consciousness and died.

The political aftermath was strangely muted. It was a jittery time for Israel and Egypt. They were engaged in a long-running dispute over the ownership of Taba, near Eilat; there were allegations that General Ariel Sharon had moved border markers in order to give Israel possession of a strategic ridge. The disagreement had so chilled relations between the two countries that the peace agreement was threatened. Doubtless neither Mubarak nor Peres wanted to incite extremist fever at such a time.

But there remained the matter of damages to the injured and the families of the deceased. The unhappy state of relations between Israel and Egypt had frozen all claims—with one exception. At the time of the shooting, Tali Griffel's parents were divorced, and her father, Andy Griffel, was living in America. He was an American-Israeli, which made Tali an American citizen. Our State Department could diplomatically "espouse" her case—that is, take it up directly with the Egyptian government and try to achieve a negotiated solution.

In 1986, Tali was living with her father in the Washington area, severely traumatized by her experience. Andy met State's legal adviser, Abe Sofaer, through the school that both men's children attended. Abe arranged for me to meet Andy, and Tali became my client.

The State Department was vigorous and prompt in espousing Tali's claim. The reaction of Egyptian diplomats was equal and opposite: resistance and delay. But at length the clumsy process started moving into gear. The lawyers for the Israeli Ras Burqa claimants agreed to defer to Sofaer and me. Egypt eventually created a special tribunal to assess the Ras Burqa claims.

Then it got more interesting. If the award to the claimants was too high, the Egyptian public would be offended. If it was too low, it would insult the Israelis. So the settlement would have to be part public and part secret. At the time, together with a young partner of mine, Lewis Libby, I was representing the financier Marc Rich, who was living in Switzerland, a fugitive from a tax evasion indictment obtained against him by then U.S. attorney Rudy Giuliani. Rich gave me discretionary authority to commit up to $500,000 of his funds if I needed it.

Finally, as with most political deals, we had to find an alchemist, a micromanager who could blend all the ingredients into the final potion. In 1988, on my way to Cairo to pursue the search, I stopped briefly in Jerusalem. While there, I had lunch with an Israeli journalist, Hirsh Goodman, who wrote on Mideast issues for *Newsweek* and now edits the *Jerusalem Report*. I told Hirsh my problem, and he said, "Well, that's easy. Your man is Osama-el-Baz." To which I replied, "I never heard of him." To which Goodman said, "Ah, but that's the beauty of the man. He keeps a nicely delphic distance from the press, which is sound policy in the Middle East if you want to keep your job and your head. No one in Egypt is closer to Mubarak than Osama-el-Baz."

In Cairo, Ambassador Frank Wisner arranged for me to meet Osama, the Deputy of Everything. I found him to be a small, thin, dark man with a large voice and an even larger sense of humor. I knew we would get along. His office, bigger than Cap Weinberger's, was undoubtedly the hottest and most humid in the world. During my first, sweaty presentation to him, he stood up, removed my glasses, and gently wiped the perspiration from my face with his pocket handkerchief. "Why in the world did you order hot coffee?" he asked with an avuncular smile. "An iced Coke now?" I wanted to kiss him in gratitude. Afterward, Wisner, who had been at the meeting, said that wouldn't have been a bad move. The leisurely pace of events ended; we were now in gear.

I made my next trip to Cairo with Abe Sofaer. We were now talking about money and camouflage arrangements. Osama—a sophisticated jazz enthusiast, as luck would have it—opened our meeting with another stunt: He slipped a tape into a cassette player (the tune was "Mean to Me") and challenged me to identify the singer and the saxophonist. He said, "If you get it right, Garment, you've got a settlement. If you don't, you'll have to sweat a lot more." It was a snap—one of the records I had been raised on. "The saxophonist is Lester Young," I said. "The singer is Billie Holiday." Then I couldn't resist being a smart-ass: "Benny Goodman is also on that date. It was a 1935 or 1936 recording, originally on the

Decca label." Osama the Joker was delighted: "Wonderful. Now all we have to do is agree on terms."

We eventually did. I had to commit $400,000 of my "European sponsor's" contingent authorization, and my last trip to Cairo was for the purpose of delivering the funds. This time, my arrival at the airport was not attended by the usual State Department air-conditioned limo. Everything was sub rosa, at least as far as the U.S. government was concerned—for a number of reasons, but most of them spelled out the name of my Swiss client, M-A-R-C R-I-C-H.

Well, Egyptian taxis are no worse than New York taxis, and in Cairo there's not much chance you'll have to talk to the driver. At the hotel, a message at the desk said Osama was waiting for me. He gave me my personal sightseeing schedule for the next few days.

First he took me to the palace for a visit with President Mu-barak, who talked for half an hour about all the fierce and nasty things he had said to "that idiot" Qaddafi at the last Arab League meeting. Then Mubarak asked for my help in repairing the decrepit Cairo Museum and fixing the nose on the Sphinx (or did I imagine that last one?). A nice man, not stuffy at all. Osama ran in and out of the room like H. R. Haldeman at an obligatory meeting Nixon was having with someone hugely unimportant. Next came a plane ride to see highlights of the Nile—the Valley of the Kings, the Aswan Dam, the whole relic-rich neighborhood. That evening I was taken to see the minister of culture, a handsome charmer who spoke French. Internal communications in the Egyptian government must have been quite good, because he raised the same subjects as Mu-barak: the Cairo Museum, the Sphinx, and American assistance for Egyptian cultural restoration projects.

In midmeeting I heard the distant swirl of sound and air that signals the approach of a Very Important Person. Osama burst in: "Well, Leonard, enough culture. How about dinner?" "A splendid idea," I said. He asked, "Do you mind eating with Yasser Arafat?"

Great. Sure. Who else could I possibly want to break pita with?

Our dinner that night was given for Arafat by an organization of Cairo attorneys. We were rushed onto the crowded terrace of the Cairo Hilton, an elegant place nicely perched over the famously busy Nile River, with its feluccas and other colorful traffic floating beneath us. Arafat was accompanied by a number of aides, and a small army of bodyguards surrounded the flame-lit dining area. Old Arab women were baking bread. The huge table was loaded with an endless procession of Arab dipping foods, yogurts, vegetables, meats. Naturally Osama the Whimsical made sure I was seated next to Arafat. I ate large, nervous quantities of food while trying to conduct a conversation that wouldn't get me killed. It wasn't easy. The only thing I could think of was the name "Rita Hauser." She was (a) a lawyer, (b) a friend of mine, (c) a friend of Arafat's. Arafat waxed lyrical about "Rita," but after half an hour of our inanities, he gave up and began talking Arabic mama-loshen to the lawyers and diplomats assembled around the table. Could he be discussing the rule in Shelly's case? Doubtful.

That night, my last in Egypt, turned into a digestive nightmare. We had all eaten the same food from the same dishes, so I was fairly sure I hadn't been poisoned. Instead, my pain came from ingesting a lot of exotic stuff while my viscera were squeezed into a fist by modern anxiety and primordial guilt. And not a drop of alcohol to ease the cross-cultural pain.

In the end, decent regrets were expressed and decent payments made to the Israeli families of the Ras Burqa victims. This closure, in turn, proved to be the key to unlocking the Taba issue and bringing about a reconciliation between Israel and Egypt, a precondition for more progress in the peace process. The bone was out of both countries' throats.

The result for Tali Griffel was a trust fund to pay the costs of her prolonged medical and educational needs. What gives the Ras Burqa story a redemptive quality is that as I write this, Tali is sixteen, a five-foot-seven-inch, strong, attractive young woman, a soccer star and general jock. She made it all the way back.

Of course, where governments are concerned there is usually a sour postscript as well, and there was one in this case. As our dealings were concluding in Cairo, I asked Osama to write me a letter confirming Marc Rich's role in the settlement. He did, saying straightforwardly enough, "The assistance provided by your associate in Europe was as crucial a factor as any in resolving the Ras Burqa controversy last year. We are grateful to him and to you, of course, especially if we bear in mind that the constructive and friendly resolution of the Ras Burqa matter helped create the atmosphere in which the stubborn 'Taba' controversy was finally settled a few weeks later. I want you to know that President Mubarak is most appreciative." I asked Ambassador Wisner, on the eve of his departure for a new post in India, to "certify" the authenticity of the letter—whose authenticity was in fact not in dispute. I did not ask the State Department to *do* anything; I just wanted a confirmation of fact for purposes of talks we were hoping to conduct with the U.S. attorney's office in New York. Wisner said, "Of course." Then, a few days later, he said he couldn't do it. An astounded Wisner had been told by the legal adviser's office, then under the direction of Abe Sofaer's successor and presumably after consultation with the Justice Department, that he could not even confirm the letter's authenticity. I began to understand why so many sane, sober people become agitated by the words "federal government," and some snap completely when you say "State Department."

During those years, I dealt with more than one fugitive. Once in 1989, not long after the Berlin Wall fell and the two Germanies were reunited, I was in Munich exploring the possibility of a plea agreement with U.S. authorities for a German client in a fraud case who was offering national security information to the United States in return for a break from the authorities. His local counsel—a lively fellow, once a Communist, but now, since the fall of East Germany, a Socialist, who originally hailed from East Berlin—said my partner John Kotelly and I must see the sights. First we should visit a typical Munich beer hall. Then we must see the Alte Pinakothek Museum. "They'll give you the real flavor of the city," he said. I think he knew what he was doing.

That evening, our chosen beer hall was jammed to its quaint wooden rafters with sausage, beer, and overweight men consuming huge quantities of both. It was not a pretty sight, but much worse was the nightmare of noise that enveloped everything. It came from an oompah band, which produced the most assaultive music I have ever heard. The combination of the decibels and the strident beat made it worse than the heaviest of heavy metal. We didn't stay long.

The next morning, I looked forward to the quiet of the Alte Pinakothek. But what I found inside, in the silence, was worse than the previous night's noise. The first floor was largely filled with immense religious canvases by the seventeenth-century painter Peter Paul Rubens. I had known Rubens mainly for his dumpling-like cherubs and luscious pink-fleshed women. But the paintings in the Alte Pinakothek were pornographically detailed scenes of hell, graphic depictions of torture, mainly by fire, surrounded by towering flames. It struck me with unarguable force that here was a prefiguring of the Holocaust.

I did not know how much those paintings disturbed me until the next day, on a plane to Madrid, when I fell asleep into a strange dream. It was made up of the noise of the beer hall, the flames of Rubens's paintings, and a well-known Hebrew-Yiddish song, "Eli, Eli," that I used to sing in junior high school. I woke up in a sweat and remembered the words of the song clearly, even after fifty years: "God, why have you forsaken me? Day and night, God, I live in fear and reverence of your law. Why am I condemned to fire and flame?"

So, finally, after an assimilated youth, an increasing involvement with Israel, and personal experience with anti-Semitism, I became engrossed in the mystery of the Holocaust. We know that mass killings, barbaric cruelties, and ethnic hatreds are all too ordinary. But such butchery and primitive passion, combined with ideological justification, technological thoroughness, and bureaucratic implacability, was historically unique.

During World War II, when my mother heard about the slaughter of our family in Europe, she retreated to a sanitarium. I tried to understand the systematic German exterminations by reading much of the literature—including the works of Raoul Hilberg, Lucy Dawidowicz, Martin Gilbert, and Gavin Langmuir, as well as a number of specialized studies. Though no scholar, I thought I saw some patterns of causation.

Simon Schama, in *Landscape and Memory*, suggests a starting point: By Roman times, he writes, the warriors of Germania were known to be extraordinarily strong, capable, fierce, and, as Tacitus put it, "never without a weapon in their hands." Germanic armies triumphed over Roman legions, and Germanic military tradition continued unbroken into the 1940s.

Germany was also the nation whose warrior-peasants, in 1096, during the opening Crusade, undertook the first mass slaughter of European Jews. In the sixteenth century, Martin Luther, founder of German Protestantism, wrote his religious missive "Jews and Their

Lies." In it he called Jews "children of the devil." He urged his followers to burn synagogues and Jewish homes, arguing, "It is our own fault that we . . . do not slay them." Luther continued in this vein for forty horrifying pages. His demonic view of Jews informed the religious instruction in Germany and proximate areas of Europe during the next five hundred years. In the nineteenth century, German thinkers transformed their German-ness and that of their countrymen into an explicit ideology. Johann Fichte offered a rationale for radical contempt of all things non-German. He argued that everything "original" was German, everything else, "foreign"; that German was the "only genuine language"; that Germans alone were "truly a people"; that to have a true character and to be a German were the same. These ideas permeated the operas of the German genius Richard Wagner. They were given their most brilliant exposition by Friedrich Nietzsche, whose distinction between the superman and inferior individuals was so sharp as to be almost a description of two different species. On a less sophisticated level, occult beliefs in the Aryan superman, a conspiracy of racial inferiors, and an approaching triumphal apocalypse were rife in Germany and surrounding territory. One such set of deranged doctrines, something called "Ariosophy," the creation of a group of influential pan-Germans operating under the symbol of the swastika in Vienna before World War I, attracted the attention of young Heinrich Himmler and Adolf Hitler.

What happened to Germany in the early twentieth century—the defeat in World War I, the harsh peace of Versailles, hyperinflation, unemployment, the impotence of the Weimar Republic—was the cocking of a loaded pistol. Germany was ready for Hitler and his Himmlers.

Rarely has a piece of history been so powerfully overdetermined. Rarely has a culture been so vulnerable to a phenomenon like Hitler. Yet Germany's Jews thought that conscientious assimilation was enough to solve their problem. Most could not conceive that the cultured, civilized, thoroughly modern German nation was capable of planning their extermination as if they were subhuman, or carrying out the assembly-line killing of millions of men, women, and children as if it were no more morally problematic than a highway project.

The vulnerabilities of the world to genocidal maniacs, and the deeply embedded anti-Semitic history that Germany has had to struggle against since World War II—these are the second-largest lessons I have taken from the Holocaust. The most chilling lesson of all lies in the disproportion between the reality that surrounded the Jews of Germany, and of Europe, and what they saw of the murderous trap being fashioned for them.

Recent years give some reason for hope. Mainline Christian churches have renounced theological doctrines that demonized the Jews for their alleged culpability in the death of Christ. The Catholic church formally recognized the state of Israel, while the Lutheran church explicitly disavowed Martin Luther's incitements to violence against Jews. Germany itself is making strenuous efforts at change. In November 1994, Pope John Paul II announced that he planned to mark the third millennium of Christianity by urging repentance for the reign of silence during the years of totalitarian oppression and genocide and for centuries of official church hostility toward Jews. But the Pope also recognized that this would be a monumental effort. He knows how long it takes to uproot cultural propensities like the ones that bred the Holocaust.

I last saw Richard Nixon at his wife's funeral in 1993. The ceremony was held on the grounds of the Nixon Library in Yorba Linda, and everyone from his past who could walk was there. At the funeral's end, Nixon lost control, the first time I ever saw this happen, shuddering in convulsive sobs as he was helped away from the crowd and into the library building. As the rest of us gathered in the library rotunda for coffee, Nixon reappeared, thoroughly recovered. He climbed onto a chair and delivered a lively summation of the travails that Pat Nixon had been forced to overcome during her years with him. He remembered the time after Watergate when he was critically ill, at death's door, and she had told him that he mustn't quit; his mother would have said just that. He ended his speech with a reprise of the Nixon theme: Never look back with regret. Always look ahead with anticipation. These were the same words he had written to me when Grace died.

Suzi and I stuck ourselves at the end of the receiving line so that

Nixon might have a chance to chat with us, which he did. Mostly he talked to Suzi about her work. She had written a book about political scandal. Nixon said he also had a volume under way.

His hair had finally gone gray. Up close, his features seemed larger, rounder, softened by age. I never saw him quite so loose and at ease. He seemed to have passed some finish line of his own, taking a slow cooling-off trot around the track after the race was run.

We said what turned out to be our final good-byes. I forget who said to me that with Pat gone, Nixon would be dead within the year; whoever it was turned out to be right.

On a spring day a couple of years ago, I finished breakfast at New York's Westbury Hotel—a mnemonic plate of Richard Nixon's corned beef hash with a poached egg—and hailed a cab for La Guardia. On impulse I asked the driver, a large Haitian woman, to take me to the airport via the Brooklyn Bridge and Atlantic Avenue. I explained that I had some time and thought I might like to see my old neighborhood, Brownsville, and the house where I was born, 277 Pennsylvania Avenue.

Nothing remained. The area looked like Dresden: firebombed, abandoned, then only partly rebuilt. It was a bleak assemblage of public housing, dilapidated and walled-up tenements, threadbare stores, piles of bricks, junk, garbage, and empty space. Where the house I was born in had once stood, there was now a paved-over lot with a grim little gas station and a grimmer manager. I wanted to use his phone to call my brother, with a credit card, and check our old address; he said curtly, "Use the public phone." In front of the station there were six public phones; but every one was broken, the receivers hanging down like the elongated tongues of New Guinea statues. I learned this year that 277 Pennsylvania Avenue no longer legally exists. It has been, as they say in the urban development trade, "demapped." When Thomas Wolfe said "You can't go home again," he couldn't have imagined anything as drastic as this.

In another sense, though, I made it home.

I have a woodcut by Leonard Maurer titled *Old Man Mad About Drawing*. In it a Japanese artist tells us that everything he produced before the age of seventy was "not worth taking into account." By the time he was seventy-three, he "had learned a little about the real structure of nature." And, he says, "when I am a hundred and ten, everything I draw, be it a dot or a line, will be alive. I beg those who live as long as I do to see if I do not keep my word." So I continued working on cases and causes through the early 1990s without any thought of stopping. The variety remained abundant. I represented Ed Gray, former chairman of the Federal Home Loan Bank Board; he casually blew the whistle on the senators who, through their intervention with the Board on behalf of the financier Charles Keating, came to be known as the Keating Five. The most memorable character in the televised investigation that followed was Bob Bennett, counsel to the Senate investigating committee, a first-rate Columbo-style criminal trial lawyer ("Look, fella, help me understand this stuff, I'm kinda lost . . ."). Bennett went on to represent President Clinton in some of his Arkansas legal troubles. More important, he became a member of my monthly poker group, which also included the Supreme Court justices Bill Rehnquist and Nino Scalia.

Mike Armstrong and I, encouraged by the State and Justice departments, spent a few days in Honolulu with Imelda Marcos at a hilltop home borrowed from her friend Doris Duke. We were supposed to act as middlemen, to see whether Imelda could be persuaded to make financial disclosure and restitution to the Philippine government and thus free herself from her criminal troubles in New York. Mrs. M. talked nonstop, sang Broadway songs, and played ninety-minute videos of political speeches by her son Bongo—yes, Bongo—and of Marcos family visits to the Reagan White House. She took us on a spooky motorcade to the above-ground shrine where Ferdinand Marcos was temporarily encased pending his return home for burial. But Imelda was smart. Instead of negotiating with us she hired a "backwoods" trial lawyer, Gerry Spence, who beat the pants off a crowd of condescending Justice Department prosecutors and won Mrs. Marcos an acquittal. She drank champagne and sang show tunes all the way home.

In 1993 I turned seventy, and my colleagues at Dickstein Shapiro assumed I was drifting off into semiretirement, with its calm and financial perquisites, but that wasn't for me. Far better, I decided, to stay with what I knew: the challenge of hard, interesting work, as long as there was light. For instance, during the past five years, and counting, I've struggled with a State Department–Saudi Arabia partnership determined to beat back legislation that would provide access to U.S. courts, or arbitration, for Americans tortured by governments that have no independent judiciary. The parade of worthy puzzles, thank God, never ends. A group of us—cheer-led by David Levy, head of Washington's Corcoran Gallery of Art—are working to create an international jazz museum in New York City.

The law of coincidence saw to it that on the morning of Richard Nixon's funeral I was in London, having participated in a panel discussion of a new British documentary film on Watergate. A fellow panelist was the former Watergate special prosecutor Archibald Cox, still courtly and elegant. The two of us appeared on an early morning BBC radio show, all fires banked. Cox praised the former president's abilities and puzzled over why Nixon had so mistrusted him and his investigation: "I don't really know why President Nixon thought I was out to 'get' him. I was simply interested in discharging my duties under the law, nothing more, nothing less." I'm sure that as Cox spoke those words, he meant them. Suzi and I left the studio and boarded a plane for Los Angeles, en route to Whittier and Nixon's interment.

The funeral was more stunning than sad, with its attendance by foreign chiefs of state and ambassadors, a huge delegation from Congress, and every living president. Eulogists Bob Dole and Henry Kissinger were in tears. President Clinton, child of antiwar, anti-Nixon political activity, delivered a fine, admiring speech. Sometimes America's politics are more poetry than prose and more music than poetry: Here were the members of the country's political leadership, gathered en masse, ritually marking their acceptance of the great fact of modern American political life—the fact that the flawed, furiously human Richard Nixon, a man of dark nightmares and optimistic dreams, was part of each of them, as mysterious to them as he was to himself.

The mystery only deepened in the spring of 1996, when there appeared a book by Monica Crowley, who had been Nixon's young foreign policy assistant in the last few years of his life. After each of her many conversations with him, she made a written record. After his death, she—with Nixon's unspoken but implicit consent, she tells us—chose excerpts and assembled them into a book.

Whether or not Nixon consented, he committed a large blunder: The whole book is a large vertical finger for not just his enemies but his friends as well, and not even an entertaining finger, at that. Here is Nixon at his worst—by turns craven, pompous, vain, vindictive, and, most unforgivably, silly. After years of struggle to redeem his posterity, after the impressive state funeral, once again we see Nixon wallowing in the mud, and courtesy of whom? Why, Richard Nixon himself, of course.

When in the course of writing this book I spoke with Henry Kissinger about Nixon, Kissinger made the shrewd observation that Nixon always expected to lose—that he believed it his destiny to lose, and his life was an exercise in fulfilling this prophecy. Indeed, he sometimes seemed determined to win a lot so as to have more to lose; Nixon made his worst mistakes, Kissinger said, after a victory, like Dostoyevsky's gambler.

So Nixon put most of his late-life winnings on the line in an imprudent gamble that Crowley would either perform a miraculous act of literary abstention or produce a brilliant record of his final years out of his idle chatter. Of course the wheel came up double zero, an embarrassment, a final uncontrolled act of self-revelation: Richard Nixon's self-activated last tape.

But, as Nixon would have said, "The game's the thing, and the public arena is the only stadium." Maybe it was this, not posterity, that kept him pushing the rock up the mountain; maybe he didn't really care what Monica Crowley wrote after he was gone. If he had a hope for a decent place in history, he might have thought only a distant generation of scholars would provide it.

Sometimes prose seems inadequate to deal with such complexities. Not long after the funeral I read, in a book of Gore Vidal's essays, an unexpectedly friendly piece on Nixon. I asked my daughter Sara what she thought of it, and she answered with a poem:

Standing in a bookstore browsing
Gore Vidal's brief essay
which marvels at the paradox of Richard Nixon,

he whom so many
(perhaps himself included)
damned, but also made.
The contradiction of character
does battle in itself
as well as with the world,
and deeds are finally character revealed;
for all the skirmishes he lost along the way
Vidal claims that Nixon staged
a winning strategy for his own private war,
the stature of his greatness to be measured
not by his lies or cowardice or fraud
but by uniting enemies at bay
on the highest plane of power
to which they all aspired.
The craft of being devious
made Nixon apprentice to insight,
knowing that his adversaries' minds
had every chance of being just as rife
with all the wiles and bile
which he was driven by,
outsmarting those who wanted more
by giving it to them
before they took it for themselves.
Nixon's mixed travails in this way
embody the greatest hope for human nature,
that the most profound self-interest
will, by necessity,
cause us to be wise.

About a year after Tali Griffel's Bat Mitzvah, in January 1995, came my daughter Annie's turn. She was blessed with a mind like a sponge and a fearless temperament, so preparing for the ceremony was straightforward. A couple of months before the great day, Annie said she wanted me to read from the Torah at the services. "How much do I have to read?" I asked. "Oh, not much. About three sentences," the treacherous child replied. I was happy to say yes.

But the sentences were long ones, in ancient Hebrew. The synagogue's cantor, Arnold Saltzman, was young, full-throated, and cheerfully rule-bound. No phonetic cards. I was going to have to do it right. Saltzman gave me a tape recording of the three sentences. I started memorizing the melody—and found I couldn't do it. I had spent a lifetime playing jazz, but these tropes were put together in what was to my ear a musically counterintuitive way. Each phrase slid instantly in and out of my brain. I spent—this is no exaggeration —a couple of hundred hours practicing, at home alone, in the office, in the car, and under Suzi's severe tutelage (she had learned this stuff when she was young and malleable). Sometimes, toward the end of the ordeal, she would say, "Stop. That's wrong," and if I didn't stop she looked like she was going to hit me on the head with a ruler the way Rabbi Cohen had sixty years before.

So the day arrived. I had my little passage mastered one minute, then blew it the next.

Annie was better than letter-perfect. Her lyrical voice, beauty, and confidence brought tears to lots of eyes, preeminently my own. She sang as if she were singing for the millions of Jewish children who had not survived to sing. Then it was my turn. I looked out at the audience—Suzi, Paul, Sara. My brother Charlie was there, with my sister-in-law Alice. Marty was also there, but without his beloved Sylvia, who had recently died of cancer, leaving a large, empty space in our lives where she should have been. There were assorted aunts, uncles, cousins, nieces, nephews, in-laws, and friends—and they were all waiting expectantly, smiling. Why were they smiling? What were they expecting?

I silently offered a highly personal prayer: Adrenaline, do your stuff. A deep breath and I was off, assertively but only vaguely in the right direction. Cantor Saltzman, ready for trouble, stood close by. Once I came especially close to blowing it. "Back up, you skipped a line," the hovering Saltzman whispered at the speed of light without moving his lips. I managed to finish, as I had started, loud and strong, satisfying the primary requirements for a successful show-business performance. I finally had the Bar Mitzvah ceremony that circumstances had withheld when I was thirteen.

People were ecstatic about Annie, even strangers who were in the synagogue simply for the Shabbat service. I got marks for sheer nerve. Jerry Leitner spoke the truth: "Close enough for jazz, Pops." Norman Podhoretz, when he first heard I was going to read Torah, thought I had come unhinged. After the ceremony he said, "Now for some bungee jumping?"

The Israeli ambassador, Itamar Rabinovitch, was there. Shlomo Argov was not. The terrorists who shot him in the head in May 1982 left him with his mind virtually gone, except for a cruel capacity to feel endless anxiety. He lives and is cared for in Hadassah Hospital in Jerusalem. Instead of having a big hotel bash, Annie chose to hold her party at home and give Shlomo's hospital a contribution for medical equipment. (If everyone gets one miracle, the one I choose is that Shlomo should recover sufficiently to meet her.)

So there were not as many people at the party as we would have been happy to see. But those who were there were an ecumenical congregation, disparate types accumulated by Suzi and me over the years and around the country through marriage, friendship, work, accident—and, for a few hours, everyone seemed to love everyone else.

I looked at Sara and Paul and realized how bravely they had pulled themselves out of the debris of their mother's death. Sara had graduated from college as a prize-winning classics major and was attending the Harvard Divinity School when a particularly virulent form of diabetes cut her schooling short, but the disease did not manage to stop her writing or cloud her talent. Paul, after Grace's death, had won prominent orchestra chairs in the United States and abroad and become an exceptionally versatile and successful freelance musician.

Paul played alto sax at Annie's party, and the rest of the jazz trio was also first-rate. Our friend, Washington jazz star Steve Novosel, played bass, and, as fate would have it, the guitarist, unexpectedly in town from New York, was Joe Cohn, son of the late Al Cohn, my world-class band mate whose nightly improvisations had persuaded me that my future was not in music. The kid, like his father, was terrific.

All of us were aging; but all of us were made happy, for a moment immortal, by the sense of completeness and love in the house.

Philip Larkin had something to say about this:

They say eyes clear with age,
As dew clarifies air
To sharpen evenings,
As if time put an edge

Round the last shape of things
To show them there;
The many-levelled trees,
The long soft tides of grass
Wrinkling away the gold
Wind-ridden waves—all these,
They say, come back to focus
As we grow old.

In the middle of the journey, as Larkin knew more than most, we find ourselves in dark woods where the right path seems lost. But even so melancholy a poet saw for a prophetic moment that at the end of the confusion there is sometimes a clearing in whose sunlight things appear more distinct and precious than ever before.

FOUR YEARS LATER . . .

As I LOOK BACK ON THE ENDING I WROTE four years ago for *Crazy Rhythm*, complete with lines from a Philip Larkin poem and a paean to an old age filled with peace and sunlight, I do not know what I could have been thinking. True, Larkin wrote the words I quoted; but in that same poem he reflected ironically on the sentiments they expressed. Besides, as Larkin could have told me, after a certain age your life does not acquire new moods or themes; it just repeats the old ones in new configurations. My life was not serene before *Crazy Rhythm* and has become no more serene since. The stories that populated the book have simply sprouted new chapters; the characters have merely taken on extended roles.

Here is one example: In the late 1970s, after Richard Nixon had resigned, I was once again practicing law at Mudge Rose in New York. I had also begun serving as chairman of the bipartisan committee appointed by Senator Pat Moynihan to recommend candidates for nomination as federal judges and United States Attorneys. One of the would-be nominees to come before the committee was a smart, experienced, aggressively confident young Democratic lawyer named Rudolph Giuliani. He said he wanted to be a federal judge or, failing that, a U.S. Attorney. Even when judged against the self-assured group of lawyers who had selected themselves to appear before the committee, Giuliani was awe-inspiring in his open ambition. We thought he was a bit young and turned him down, confident he would return.

Which he did, but not quite in the way any of us had foreseen. Giuliani changed his party registration to Republican and, after Ronald Reagan took office as president in 1981, went to Washington to become Associate Attorney General. As such, he supervised the appointment of U.S. Attorneys throughout the country. In time Giuliani got the opportunity to become Attorney General—but, to the surprise of most observers, passed up the chance. Instead, he chose to make what was seen as a lateral move, becoming U.S. Attorney for the Southern District of New York. The Southern District was the most prestigious and powerful prosecutor's office in the nation. It was also a prime staging area for a political career if you wanted to become, for instance, Mayor of New York City.

When Giuliani arrived at the Southern District, two able prosecutors in the office, Martin Auerbach and Morris—known as Sandy—Weinberg, had already developed what Giuliani recognized as a blockbuster case against the persons and companies of Marc Rich and Pincus Green. These were two immensely wealthy commodities brokers who were U.S. citizens but who also lived in Switzerland and maintained their business headquarters there. The investigation had begun as a search for possible violations of the regulations governing price controls on oil but had turned into a massive tax fraud case.

Both before and after the indictments in the case, Rich and Green were defended by a crowd of lawyers, led by Edward Bennett Williams and former federal judge Marvin Frankel. The lawyers competed with one another in devising strategies hostile to the government. Such tactics succeeded only in rendering the prosecutors even more inflamed than they were by nature and in goading the judge in the case, Leonard Sand, into imposing $50,000-a-day contempt fines.

The companies owned by Messrs. Rich and Green finally pled guilty in 1984 and agreed to pay the federal government some $150 million, the largest collection of taxes, penalties, and fines in the history of the criminal tax laws. When U.S. Attorney Giuliani received the money he called a press conference, where he waved the check above his head for the benefit of the awed media. Indictments remained outstanding against Messrs. Rich and Green, who chose not to return to the U.S. and stand trial. They remained in Switzerland, a country from which they could not be extradited on tax charges, and became fugitives from American justice.

I had not paid much attention to Giuliani's career after he appeared before our committee, and I knew almost nothing about the early stages of the Marc Rich case except what I read in the newspapers. In 1985, however, when I had once again moved to Washington and was practicing with the firm of Dickstein Shapiro and Morin, I got a phone call from Robert Thomajan, who had worked for me at Mudge Rose in the days before Nixon's election as president in 1968. Thomajan, now the principal attorney for Marc Rich, wanted to know whether I would be interested in traveling to Switzerland to meet Rich and to see whether there was anything more that could be done about the case.

My first impression was that not a lot could be done. The corporate guilty pleas were entered, the indictments of the individuals handed up. But before I turned down Thomajan's offer, I thought to phone my guide in all things international, Henry Kissinger, now head of his own successful consulting firm in New York. Kissinger did not purport to know anything about the case. But he did know, he said, that Rich was a very interesting man. Meeting him would be worth the trip.

I asked Steve Kaufman, a friend and an experienced New York criminal lawyer, to come with me. With this bit of prudence, I began my representation of Marc Rich, which continued spasmodically from 1985 through 1992. Constraints of confidentiality made it impossible to tell much of the story when I wrote *Crazy Rhythm*; but now, as everyone knows, things have changed.

I found Rich to be approximately the opposite of what you would expect in an indicted commodities trader. He was the soul of understatement. His face was usually impassive. His voice was almost always quiet. He spoke English very precisely but with a slight accent, a reminder of his refugee childhood. His clothes were invariably conservative. His guarded watchfulness was no surprise in a man who had seen so many lawyers take so much money to do so little. His brilliance at his chosen trade was obvious even to someone who knew very little about it.

Rich's home in Zug was understated in the same way its owner was. True, there was the elaborate security apparatus, complete with bodyguards; but the house itself was medium-sized and the furniture called no attention to itself. The one special feature of the house—no small one—was the art, both painting and sculpture, totally without flash and utterly first-rate.

During the years when I visited Rich, I saw him depart from his disciplined quiet in only three respects. First, he smoked large cigars. Second, he was devoted without reservation to his three daughters. Third, this quiet man had a bubbly wife, Denise, who wrote music—not just any music, but popular songs. And this was not just a rich lady's hobby: By the time I met Denise, she was a published songwriter of some note. She was, as the rest of America would one day discover, irrepressible.

At our first meeting with Marc, Steve Kaufman and I told him that even before we could make a judgment as to whether we could represent him, we would have to assess the merits of the dispute. At first we thought we could make such an assessment on the basis of documents that were already organized and legal memoranda that already existed. Such was not the case. For all the complex, labor-intensive legal maneuvering in which Rich's team had engaged in the years before the corporate guilty pleas and Rich's fugitivity, it turned out that no one had really investigated the question of whether or not he was guilty of anything. I am sure most of his lawyers felt from the start that he was guilty as sin.

When Steve and I embarked on our inquiry in 1985, Scooter Libby, whom I mentioned briefly in *Crazy Rhythm*, had recently joined my law firm—or, more properly, had been dragged into it, by me. I had already seen how some of the tax lawyers purportedly defending Marc Rich had simply assumed his guilt. So I wanted a lawyer who was not a tax specialist to analyze every piece of paper we could get our hands on, re-interview the whole cast of characters, and come to an independent view of the legal merits of the case. It was a huge project. Unfortunately for Scooter, he had the endurance and intellectual capacity to undertake it. So Scooter sat in his office for months with the documents and the results of his interviews, assisted sometimes by a young tax associate, Mike Green. At length Scooter began to emerge and, from time to time, explain to me (insofar as I could understand the stuff) one piece or another of the puzzle that he was progressively untangling.

The first thing I understood from these briefings was that the particular type of trouble Rich and Green had fallen into was, in a sense, my fault. Their complex oil trades, which had so aroused the suspicion of the prosecutors, were the product of the oil price controls imposed by the Nixon administration in 1973. At that time I was Counsel to the President. The Arab oil-producing countries had imposed an embargo on production during the Yom Kippur War, and the resulting shortages were wreaking domestic political havoc in the United States. Innocent of economic knowledge, I sent Nixon an impassioned memo urging him to take the dramatic action necessary to maintain his posture of leadership. (There was also the small matter of Watergate, which was, to use John Dean's imagery, beginning to metastasize.) I and my ilk helped persuade Nixon to undertake the price control program.

One day during my representation of Marc Rich, I cheerfully mentioned to him and Pinky the wry coincidence between my actions then and my role now. Pinky, characteristically, laughed. Marc stared at me with narrowed eyes through a cloud of cigar smoke.

But Scooter's investigations established more important things than my policy guilt. One day he walked into my office and said, disbelieving it himself, "There was no tax liability." He had concluded, unavoidably, that Rich and Green were not only free of criminal tax liability; they were free of civil liability as well. They did not owe the government any money, let alone evade taxes in a criminal manner.

Shortly after we came to this opinion, the Department of Energy issued a decision, in a case involving Atlantic Richfield, a trading partner of Rich and Green, that performed essentially the same analysis and reached the same conclusions. We took the facts of our case to two of the country's leading and most independent tax experts, Martin Ginsberg of Georgetown University Law Center and Bernard Wolfman of Harvard Law School. If the facts were as we represented, both of them agreed, there was no tax liability.

The opinion of these authorities was cheering but raised a deeper question. If Marc and Pinky were so clearly not guilty, why had they been so reluctant to return to the United States to face trial? Just as Scooter had gone back over the oil trades to determine what taxes Marc and Pinky actually owed, we now reviewed the history of the investigation to try to determine how it had become such a juridical mess.

Here is what emerged. In 1970, Congress passed the Racketeering Influenced and Corrupt Organizations Act; the ungainly name of the legislation was devised so that its acronym would be RICO, after the gangster played by Edward G. Robinson in the film *Little Caesar*. RICO was a response to a very real problem: When pursuing organized crime, prosecutors would often convict a mobster only to see his criminal enterprise continue without him.

Under the new RICO statute, prosecutors could seize the assets that constituted such an enterprise. If a defendant was charged with having committed two racketeering-type crimes within ten years, his assets could be frozen even before a trial took place. If other people had received funds from the defendant, even through honest transactions, the government could seize those funds. At the trial itself, the prosecution could introduce evidence of other misdeeds by the defendant in a way that was not normally permitted.

One problem with RICO was that the long list of "racketeering" offenses included crimes that involve common types of transactions and are extremely easy to charge. For this reason and others, RICO caused a huge outcry among lawyers, judges, journalists, and private organizations like the American Civil Liberties Union. The Department of Justice finally adopted guidelines to prevent federal prosecutors from using RICO in tax cases such as the Rich prosecution.

In the early 1980s, however, these guidelines were not yet in force. Thus Rich, Green, and all their businesses were charged not just with tax and energy offenses but with racketeering, the first such use of RICO in the statute's history. This meant that all of their assets in the United States were subject to seizure even before any court made a determination of guilt. More important, it meant that third parties, such as creditors and trading partners indispensable to a commodities trading business, could reasonably fear that they would be forced to forfeit any funds received from transactions with Rich and Green. Because of this fear, third parties began refusing to deal with the two men. The refusals threatened the swift and total collapse of Rich and Green's business.

The only rational thing to do, from a business point of view, was for the companies to plead guilty, end the RICO prosecutions, and survive. This is what they did—reciting in open court, through company counsel, an allocution drafted by the prosecutors that admitted the companies' commission of the various and sundry acts alleged in the kitchen-sink indictment. But for Rich and Green as individuals, those business-preserving guilty pleas were fatal; one way or another, the pleas would become evidence against the two men in their individual trials. Thus the trap sprang shut.

I knew better than to think that if the authorities were simply presented with the underlying tax case and an explanation of the widely decried perversities of RICO, they would undo what had been done and invite Marc and Pinky home. Prosecutors do not let go of historic cases so easily. But I hoped that as personnel turned over in the U.S. Attorney's Office, leaving fewer people there who were personally wedded to the Rich case, more attorneys would be willing to listen.

That did not happen. We spent several years trying to get meetings, preparing for meetings, holding meetings, attempting to follow up on meetings. The prosecutors would not talk about the merits of the underlying case. Some of their positions, like their vehement feelings about fugitivity, were understandable. Some were not. The low point at one of our meetings came when a young prosecutor said that it didn't matter whether Marc and Pinky actually owed taxes or not; what mattered was that they *thought* they owed taxes and nevertheless did not pay them. The two men, in other words, had stolen their own car.

Such a doctrine is not exactly a foundation of the tax laws. Perhaps more to the point, however, was a later comment by one of the prosecutors: "There's just too much history." Indeed there was.

Meanwhile, Marc and Pinky continued to engage in the kind of traditional, large-scale philanthropy—most prominently, Jewish philanthropy—that would arouse so much suspicion and hostility some fifteen or so years later. Once, as recounted in *Crazy Rhythm*, Marc contributed a sizable amount to help resolve the stalemate between Israel and Egypt over the massacre at Ras Burqa.

The resolution of Ras Burqa, in turn, enabled the two countries to come to an agreement over the fate of the Sinai Peninsula, an achievement that the U.S. government considered important to its Mideast policy. I thought the settlement was very much in the national interest; I asked Marc to contribute to it on the theory that cooperation with the government might weigh in the balance if we ever reached the stage of discussing a settlement. Of course, things never got that far. I suspect but do not know that Marc performed other services for the government; I doubt that his prosecutors were ever influenced by such actions.

In 1992, I left off representing Marc and Pinky. First of all, I thought that now there really was nothing more to be done. Second, I knew how my habit of joking must have grated on Marc, sounding like a dismissal of his problems (shades of my father in his sickroom). I thought Marc was owed a fresh start for that reason as well. Scooter continued to do some work on the merits of the case, but he had no further role in seeking to persuade the government.

And that was that, until Bill Clinton threw me together with Marc Rich again in the Great Pardon Controversy. On January 21, 2001, the *New York Times* and the *Washington Post* reported that President Clinton, during his very last hours in office, had granted pardons to 176 people, including Marc Rich and Pincus Green. Marc and Pinky, it turned out, had not just settled into Zug and given up after the presentations to the U.S. Attorney's Office were over and I was gone. They had, among other things, hired a new lawyer, Jack Quinn, who was President Clinton's friend and former White House counsel. Denise Rich, now divorced from Marc and living in New York, had become a Democratic Party fundraiser and a friend of President Clinton. Quinn had persuaded her to aid the pardon effort. He had persuaded others to take similar actions. The pardon had been granted with virtually no opportunity for the Department of Justice to make its position known (not that this position was in much doubt).

The cast of characters was, media-wise, irresistible. There was the fugitive financier, perpetually enveloped (in the photographs) by cigar smoke. There was the expensive ex-wife. There was the political crony. There was President Clinton, taking actions that were, in the view of his critics, quintessentially Clintonesque. There was a circus.

I almost escaped the uproar. But one Saturday afternoon, when my wife and I were sitting around our daughter's room at college on parents' weekend, about to go out to a movie, the phone rang. It was Scooter. "I hate to bother you on a weekend," he said with characteristic calm, "but there's a torpedo heading our way." The torpedo in question was the false claim by ex-President Clinton, in an article he had written for the *New York Times* defending his pardon of Marc Rich, that Scooter and I had "reviewed and advocated" the case for the Rich-Green pardons. We of course had done no such thing. I still know very little about the process by which the pardon decision was made; I am afraid I do not want to know more. Clinton's article had already been printed in some editions of the *Times*.

Scooter was somewhat constrained in responding: He was back in government, this time as chief of staff and national security adviser to Vice President Dick Cheney and assistant to President George W. Bush. But I was not similarly limited. Chaos ensued for the next several hours, as I phoned every media person I knew who was within shouting distance of the story to try to prevent it from getting lodged in the media mind and following me around for what now looked to be my short remaining life.

I did the job; but, naturally, it occurred to me to try to do something more. Press people writing about the pardon wanted to know what the Marc Rich case was about. After a short refresher course, I was happy to tell them. Every chance I got, I explained that I hadn't represented Marc Rich for a decade; I wasn't carrying a brief for him; but they had to understand why the case developed as it did— the multiple counts, the corporate guilty pleas, the fugitivity. There was this statute, RICO . . . .

They always professed to be very interested but almost never wrote about it. RICO wasn't the scandal; therefore it wasn't the story. Indeed, admitting any ambiguity into the account of Rich's crime would confuse the portrait of Bill Clinton as a despoiler of the Presidential office. Thus I found that when it comes to scandal journalism, matters have certainly not improved and may even have gotten worse.

But there are compensations. Rudy Giuliani went on to become Mayor of New York, a job at which he was very good and in which he learned a thing or two about enduring personal scandal. Along the way, Giuliani got himself into some trouble with the arts community of New York. In 1999 and 2001, the publicly supported Brooklyn Museum of Art mounted exhibitions that were, let us say, adventurous. The one that got the most media attention was a painting of the Virgin Mary adorned with patches of elephant excrement. Another exhibition featured a photograph of the Last Supper with Christ portrayed by the artist, a woman, in full frontal nudity. Many citizens of New York were outraged. One of them was the Mayor, who publicly asked why New York's tax dollars should be used to support this sort of thing.

The Mayor appointed a Citizens' Commission, instantly dubbed the Decency Commission, to investigate what the city could do about offensive art in publicly supported institutions. A Deputy Mayor called to say that because of my experience—recounted in *Crazy Rhythm*—in chairing, with John Brademas, the independent commission on the National Endowment for the Arts, the Mayor would like me to chair the drafting committee of the city's commission. As a New Yorker looking to build a jazz museum in Harlem, I saw that this was an offer I couldn't refuse.

Once again I was in the business of managing arts and riots. But it was easier this time around—or so it seemed at the start. The draft report of the Mayor's commission laid out the same principles as its national counterpart: (1) No, you can't discriminate in funding works of art on the basis of their points of view, as expressed by their content. (2) Yes, in allocating public funding for the arts you can take into account the sensibilities of the community as a whole and the role of the arts in meeting community needs.

During the drafting process, I heard that the Mayor thought the report's recommendations were not punitive enough. But I could not have predicted what the Mayor would do about his displeasure. I was on family vacation in Provincetown when I got another one of those alarming phone calls, this one directing my attention to a front page article in that morning's *New York Times*. A member of the commission who was also a friend of the Mayor's had drafted an alternative set of recommendations and thoughtfully supplied them to the *Times*, which of course printed them. His recommendations, not surprisingly, had the punitive tone that the draft report deliberatively avoided.

What was particularly offensive was the allegation by this commission member that I was the one who assigned him the job of drafting his recommendations. I had not.

I spent hours on the phone getting the recommendations disavowed by all parties and making clear that I had not given this guy any assignment. During the process, he carelessly allowed to the *Times* that people in the Mayor's office had encouraged him in his work. At a subsequent press conference, the Mayor said he had an open mind about the report and looked forward to its official release. He was back to square one.

It was a strangely familiar episode. Giuliani is a man of large talent and acknowledged accomplishment. Yet he encouraged aides and friends to commit acts that served no purpose other than to express his private angers, inviting political embarrassment and even disaster. Like a lot of politicians. Like Richard Nixon.

Meanwhile, Clinton's pardon of Marc Rich spurred a new round of investigations, some focusing on the pardon process and some on Rich himself. As I write, the investigations are continuing, their life support system pumping strongly. Today it seems even less likely than before the pardon that Marc Rich will ever be able to walk down a New York street without looking over his shoulder. His story is not over.

Neither are the other stories and cases. Some are as old and endless as a river. Others are both new and not new, tied to the past by personal history, memory, and coincidence. The connections are thick, crowding the crossroads of a long life. Osama Al-Baz, principal adviser to Egypt's president Hosni Mubarak and prime architect of the settlement of the Ras Burqa massacre, worked his wizardry again years later, when I asked him to help curtail the international piracy of intellectual property. Judith Terra, whom I briefly represented upon the death of her husband Dan, the arts philanthropist, became my client in her fight to preserve the Terra Foundation's independence from political raiders in Chicago (never a very happy place for friends of Richard Nixon).

I also returned to Watergate. In 2000, I published a second book, *In Search of Deep Throat*. In it I sifted through the evidence on the great political mystery and offered my conclusion. More important, I examined the role played by the symbolism and legend of Deep Throat in post-Watergate American politics. The most satisfying result of the book's publication was an invitation to write the essay on Watergate for the *Oxford Companion to American Law*. After 77 years, I was finally an authority on something.

More ominously, one of the ugliest experiences of my public life—the "Zionism is racism" resolution passed by the United Nations in 1975, when I was serving there with Pat Moynihan—rose from its crypt. The first time around, the Soviet Union was behind the idea, using it to transform the UN's Conference Against Racism, which should have been focused on issues such as African economic development, into a platform for anti-Semitism and anti-Americanism. U.S. State Department officials, to their credit, steadily pressed the UN to repeal the resolution; in 1991, in the wake of the Gulf War, they finally succeeded.

In 2001, the UN was preparing for another conference on racism. The issues were now even graver, including the AIDS calamity in Africa and the question of reparations for the deep wrong of slavery. Suddenly, on the agenda of a pre-conference meeting, it appeared again—a resolution condemning "the increase of racist practices of Zionism." This time it was not the Soviets exploiting the issue of race. It was certain Arab nations, who saw the coming conference as an opportunity not to address their own role in the perpetration of slavery but to extract still more profit from Africa. The stakes were newly grave for Israel, where renewed terrorist attacks had exposed the insubstantiality of the peace process which had aroused such fervent hopes. What had not changed was the Western response: In 2001 as in 1976, it reflected ambivalence, internal division, and a profound lack of confidence.

In contrast, perhaps the most satisfying reappearance since the publication of *Crazy Rhythm* has been the coda to the unfinished story about the birthday party, jazz concert, and glorious jam session that President Nixon threw in the White House for Duke Ellington. Because of the bitterness of Vietnam, I wrote, no recording of that concert had ever been made available to the public in the United States. But, not long ago, search parties were organized to hunt for the original United States Information Service film of the evening; in the end, parts of it were located. More important, primarily through the efforts of jazz musician and historian Bill Kirchner, a usable audio recording of the concert was found at the National Archives. With Kirchner's editing, the recording will finally be released to the world by Blue Note in the coming months, some 32 years after the evening the music was made.

As if to commemorate the event, Random House has just published Ralph Ellison's collected writings on jazz. Among them is Ellison's "Homage to Duke Ellington on His Birthday," originally published in 1969 in the Washington *Star*, which noted that after years of neglect by America's musical establishment, Ellington was about to be honored at the White House. "That which our institutions dedicated to the recognition of artistic achievement have been too prejudiced, negligent, or concerned with European models and styles to do," Ellison wrote, "is finally being done by presidents." An unambiguously happy ending.

Crazy Rhythm, when it was published in 1997, was received generously, clung to life for a while, then faded out of print, though copies could be found in rare book shops and on the Internet. At the beginning of this year, John Radziewicz of Da Capo Press called with a stay of extinction. Da Capo, a prominent publisher of books about the jazz scene, planned to issue *Crazy Rhythm* in paperback.

A jazz publisher? Well, of course. After I had staggered through 77 years trying to shape a workable identity for myself in law, politics, government service, and the like, and after spending sizable chunks of the past decade scribbling hundreds of pages trying to describe and define that identity, the mystery was suddenly cleared up with the clarity of a C major chord. In the eyes of the people who know about these things, *Crazy Rhythm* was the biography of a jazz musician, if a failed one. All those journeys to here, there, and elsewhere were simply a lifelong effort to recover the early and irreplaceable excitement of making music.

Because of jazz, I was able to continue looking at the world—usually—through the eyes of a kid. The consequences of this perspective were not all good, but it's been a lot better than being old too soon. Understanding this does not change what happened on those journeys, which were, indeed, spent mostly in law, politics, and government service. But it does explain the distance that always seemed to separate me from those professions. And it explains my pattern of behavior: I would start at the edge of the action and vamp until ready—until, that is, an opportunity came along that provided a little of the old improvisatory pleasure. Then I was off and running again.

In being thus formed by jazz I am not in such bad company. Two of my literary heroes, Ralph Ellison and Philip Larkin, were—or considered themselves—failed jazz musicians. Ellison played trumpet, Larkin drums. "Few things," Larkin wrote, "have given me more pleasure in life than listening to jazz." The rhythms and mood of jazz shaped the words and colored the memories of both men. I sometimes wish I had been able to transmute jazz into another art the way they did. But I like to think that jazz also plays a formative role in lives like mine. For me, jazz has beautified what was otherwise painful, incoherent, or unintelligible, working the kind of transformation of reality that I once associated with religion. Which is, after all, what art is supposed to do.

This reminds me of a story about John Coltrane, who used to explain his endless saxophone solos by telling people, "I just can't stop playing." He said this once to Miles Davis, who responded, "Just take the fucking horn out of your mouth." Which I will now do, after one last, as-yet-unfinished story: I am still working, with others, to establish the jazz museum in Harlem that I wrote about at the end of *Crazy Rhythm*. So far I have learned this: The museum will come into being and succeed only if it can find a way to perform a supreme act of storytelling. It must make a narrative, literary and musical, about an art form that has flowed through virtually every capillary of American culture and set the mood for almost everything we think and feel about ourselves.

This may not be as hard as it sounds. It will come about naturally if the museum consistently celebrates this country's ability to assimilate the discordant pieces of its reality through the irrepressible will to improvise—to live with music, as Ellison put it, rather than die with noise.

It may well work. After all, Harlem is in the midst of what may be its second Renaissance. It has even become the official head-quarters of that eminent failed jazz musician, William Jefferson Clinton.

And after that? The answer is obvious: four more years.

August 15, 2001
Washington, D.C.

THANKS

"ACKNOWLEDGMENTS" HAS ALWAYS SEEMED to me a somewhat grudging word; hence the above. Since I am one of those people who have to talk in order to know what they think, you can imagine how much talking I did in the course of assembling this mega-*meiseh*. I am grateful to those who listened and talked back. First and foremost were my wife, Suzanne, and my children, Paul and Sara. My brothers, Charlie and Marty, proved to be supreme sources of Garment family facts and insights. My law partner, Lewis (Scooter) Libby, let me chew his ear off while he was in the process of editing his own first, splendid novel, *The Apprentice*. My former partner, the patient Peter Morgan, told, as he always does, legal and literary truths.

Three friends of mine read the first draft of this manuscript: Ronald Berman, Norman Podhoretz, and Ray Price. Given their quality as writers, it is no surprise that each of them offered wise, experienced advice. I tried to follow it, though I hereby offer them the ritual absolution from the book's failings and its idiosyncratic point of view, which are mine.

My Random House keepers were led by publisher-editor Peter Osnos, the devil who made me do it. I did not set out to write a book. In 1989 I wrote a *New Yorker* piece in which I told the story of my law partner Richard Nixon's Supreme Court argument in the

Hill case and his extraordinary midnight memorandum to me about his performance. Osnos said I should write a book about Nixon and me. He made the process sound, if not easy, civilized. Seven years later the manuscript and I staggered to completion. Now that it's done, of course, I'm happy I did it. It taught me a lot about the improvised, sometimes loony life I have led; on written reflection, I look crazy like a fox.

During the writing, Osnos periodically dosed me with encouragement and guidance. So did senior editor Jon Karp, Osnos's gifted henchman, who set the editorial course and steered me away from many of writing's Bermuda Triangles. Sean Abbott, Karp's skillful associate, was always there when Jon wasn't. I thank my copy editor, Kate Scott, and applaud the decision she made to live and work in Falmouth, Mass., amid the thundering silence of Cape Cod culture, so that she could concentrate on locating syntactical errors in the manuscript. Production editor Benjamin Dreyer managed my first-time-author's confusion with craft and discipline, humor and patience. Naomi Osnos, Robbin Schiff, and Gabrielle Bordwin supervised the book's physical shape expertly and sympathetically and generously permitted my daughter Annie to make a contribution— a substantial one—to the design of the book's jacket.

Tom Evans—my friend, Nixon Mudge law partner, and 1968 campaign colleague—gave me access to his manuscript "Nixon Mudge," a treasure trove of the firm's history. The section of my book dealing with the law firm is based on Tom's careful research.

Without Suzanne Naylor and Theresa Bartos Eckert, I would still be chiseling the book's first chapter onto a stone tablet. They were not only intelligent and indefatigable editorial assistants but models of tolerance. Bless them both.

My law firm, Dechert Price & Rhoads, lived up to its strong *pro bono* reputation by offering forbearance and support while I finished this book.

The book's title, *Crazy Rhythm*, is a joint creation of Leon Wieseltier and me. Leon said the title had to be the name of a jazz tune; I looked up one day and there it was.

INDEX

/ 411

Black September, 193
Blattner, Jeffrey, 363
"Blocs Are Breaking Up, The"
 (Moynihan), 315
Bloustein, Edward, 84
Bobst, Elmer, 58, 69, 85–86, 125,
 299
"Body and Soul" (Green), 28
Bonnett, Sara, 34, 35–36, 40, 43,
 47
Bork, Claire, 364
Bork, Robert, 90, 221, 286–87,
 363–68
Borodino, Battle of, 195
Boys Clubs of America, 112
Brademas, John, 170
Bradlee, Ben, 368
Brady, Matthew, 194
Brando, Marlon, 242
Brennan, William J., 90
Brezhnev, Leonid, 175, 194, 247,
 285, 286, 287
Brink, Jimmy, 27
Bronner, Ethan, 365
Brookings Institution, 297
Brooklyn, 3–6, 8–14, 16, 30–35,
 40–46, 69–75, 222
 Bedford-Stuyvesant section of, 24
 Brownsville section of, 4–6, 384
 Crown Heights section of, 14,
 22–23, 33
 in election of 1972, 75
 legal community of, 70–72
 LG's apartments and houses in, 5,
 45, 46, 53–54, 69–73, 112, 148,
 158–60, 327–28
 LG's attachment to, 46
 Park Slope section of, 51–52
Brooklyn Academy of Music
 (BAM), 304
Brooklyn College, 25, 26, 40–42
Brooklyn Heights, 49, 140
 LG's homes in, 53–54, 159–60
 Nixon's tour of, 73
Brooklyn Law Review, 43
Brooklyn Law School, 42–45, 47, 71
Brooks, Mel, 48, 49, 353
Brown, Bill, 220
Brown, Edmund G. (Pat), 58, 115
Brown, H. Rap, 121
Brown, John, 218
Brown, Les, 27
Browning, Elizabeth Barrett, 333
Brownsville, 4–6, 385

Brown v. Board of Education, 203,
 210, 217
Brubeck, Dave, 172
Buchalter, Louis (Lepke), 19
Buchanan, Pat, 113, 114
 in Nixon campaign, 100, 106,
 107, 122, 125–26, 129, 141
 school desegregation and, 205–7,
 210–13
 Watergate and, 270, 271, 292
Buchen, Philip, 301–2
Buckley, James, 319
Buckley, William F., Jr., 129
Bull, Steve, 196, 273
Bunker, Ellsworth, 248
Bureau of Indian Affairs, U.S.
 (B.I.A.), 225, 229–36, 238
 occupation of, 230–35
Burgundy Farm Country Day
 School, 295, 303
Burns, Arthur, 107, 155, 174–75,
 200
 Office of Economic Opportunity
 appointment and, 147–48, 156
Bush, George, 131, 339, 340, 360
busing, 220
Butterfield, Alex, 246, 273, 276–77,
 282
Buzhardt, Fred, 195
 Watergate and, 264–65, 268,
 270–71, 272, 274–79, 281, 285,
 287, 288, 290–93, 295–96, 298

Caceres, Ernie, 27
Caesar, Sid, 48
Café Pechora, 173
Caldwell Mitchell & Trimble, 62,
 117
Califano, Joseph, 267
California:
 LG's visits to, 101–6
 politics in, 57, 58, 115
Callaghan, James, 313
Cambodia, 251, 252, 262, 314
Cambridge University, 163, 165
Camp David, 196
Camp Joseph T. Robinson, 29–30,
 33, 316–17
Camp Kee-Wah, 14–16, 38
Camp Unity, 15
Carlucci, Frank, 148, 155, 232–34
Carman, Harry, 42–44
Carmichael, Stokely, 121, 231
Carnegie Hall, 20

ABOUT THE AUTHOR

LEONARD GARMENT served on the White House staff from 1969 to 1974 as special consultant, then as counsel to President Richard Nixon. In 1975, President Ford named him U.S. representative to the United Nations Commission on Human Rights. He is currently counsel to the law firm of Dechert Price & Rhoads. He lives in Washington, D.C., with his wife, Suzanne Garment, and their daughter.

CPSIA information can be obtained at www.ICGtesting.com
Printed in the USA
BVOW04s0320160114

342028BV00003B/261/A